A POISONOUS THORN IN OUR HEARTS

JAMES COPNALL

A Poisonous Thorn in Our Hearts

Sudan and South Sudan's Bitter and Incomplete Divorce

HURST & COMPANY, LONDON

First published in the United Kingdom in paperback in 2014 by
C. Hurst & Co. (Publishers) Ltd.,
41 Great Russell Street, London, WC1B 3PL
© James Copnall, 2014
All rights reserved.
Printed in India

Distributed in the United States, Canada and Latin America by
Oxford University Press, 198 Madison Avenue, New York, NY 10016,
United States of America

The right of James Copnall to be identified as the author of
this publication is asserted by him in accordance with the
Copyright, Designs and Patents Act, 1988.

A Cataloguing-in-Publication data record for this book
is available from the British Library.

ISBN: 978-1-84904-330-4

www.hurstpublishers.com

This book is printed on paper from registered sustainable
and managed sources.

CONTENTS

Acknowledgements	vii
Author's Note	ix
Non-Exhaustive List of Interviewees	xi
Maps	xvii
Abbreviations	xxi
Introduction	1
1. People and Identity	9
2. Politics	41
3. The Economy	77
4. Development	109
5. Insecurity	141
6. The Sudans and the World	179
7. The Sudans	215
Conclusion	245
Afterword	253
Notes	261
Index	299

ACKNOWLEDGEMENTS

A place is only as interesting as its people, and the Sudans are two of the most fascinating countries in the world. This book would not exist without the many conversations I had with Sudanese and South Sudanese people over the three years I lived in their country—or, as it became, their countries. Sometimes the setting was a formal interview. More often than not, I learnt the most about the two Sudans in conversations with friends, acquaintances, and people I never saw again, in Khartoum, Juba and elsewhere. It is impossible to name everyone here, but I am deeply grateful to all my interlocutors.

Some of them deserve a special word of thanks. Alsanosi Ahmed was a great fixer, and a better friend. Opheera McDoom and Guillaume Lavallée were hospitable colleagues when I first arrived in Khartoum, became firm friends, and then bailed me out of trouble when I needed it most. Mohamed Abd al Ati gave invaluable advice, and was a fearsome defender on the football pitch. Mohamed Osman took me to the best little Turkish restaurant in town, for regular informative lunches. Ahmed explained everything over coffee and cakes, and, true to Sudanese tradition, almost always paid for us both. Harriet Martin helped me think about how a book like this could be written. Mading Ngor welcomed me to Juba, and was always ready to set me straight on South Sudanese history. Mayen Chop was a wonderful guide to Leer. Hez Holland was always around when the bombs fell.

Alsanosi, Opheera, Mading, Mohamed Osman, Isma'il KushKush, Brian Adeba, Laura Bromwich, Apeksha Kumar, Sohrab Farid, Fergus Nicoll, Jonas Horner, Edward Eremogo Luka and James Sharrock all read parts of the book, and made invaluable comments. Any errors are mine alone. *Shukran jazilan.*

ACKNOWLEDGEMENTS

I would like to thank the various BBC bosses who sent me to Sudan, and then around the country on reporting trips.

Michael Dwyer at Hurst believed in the idea from the beginning, a great reassurance to this first time author.

This was also a family affair: Jules Littlefair transcribed faint recordings of hour-long interviews. Caroline Murray-Browne made useful comments on every chapter.

Above all, none of this would have been possible without Bilqees: my in-house editor, best friend, and now my wife.

AUTHOR'S NOTE

This book is built from conversations with hundreds of Sudanese and South Sudanese, from all walks of life, and many parts of the two countries. From 2009 to 2012 I was the BBC Sudan correspondent, based in Khartoum, but travelling extensively in the rest of Sudan, and in what became South Sudan. In addition to the people I spoke to for the BBC, I conducted dozens of extra interviews for *A Poisonous Thorn in Our Hearts*. Many of the most significant interviews are listed on the next page.

I have only recorded the source of a quote in a footnote when I did not conduct the interview myself. In all other cases, I interviewed the person quoted.

There are several different ways to transcribe Arabic names, of people and places, into English. You say al Bashir, I say el Beshir, and so on. I have chosen to spell names as they were given to me by the people concerned, and follow what has become convention in Sudan and South Sudan, even when this leads to inconsistency.

Throughout the book I have referred to people as they are widely known in the two Sudans. So Sudan's President Omar Hassan Ahmed al Bashir is shortened to Bashir from the second reference, while his South Sudanese counterpart, Salva Kiir Mayardit, becomes Salva.

NON-EXHAUSTIVE LIST OF INTERVIEWEES

Note: the majority of the names on the list were interviewed for the book. On some occasions I have included people I spoke to for the BBC, if the interview was particularly significant. Many people I interviewed did not want to be named.

SUDAN

NCP

Ghazi Salaheddin Atabani
Amin Hassan Omar
Ibrahim Ghandour
Ahmed Haroun
Sabir Mohamed al Hassan
Said al Khatib

SAF and NISS

Salah Abdallah 'Gosh'
Khalid Sawarmi

Officials

Awad al Fateh (Under-secretary at the Ministry of Petroleum)

Just Peace Forum

Tayyeb Mustafa

Opposition politicians

Hassan al Turabi
Sadig al Mahdi

Mariam al Sadig al Mahdi
Mubarak al Fadil al Mahdi
Hassan Satti
Siddig Yousif

Economists, businessmen and farmers

Abda Yahia al Mahdi
Haj Hamed
Osama Daoud
Mustafa Khogali
Mohamed Said
Mohamed Babikir Alamin

Rebels

Tigani Seisi
Malik Agar
Abdel Aziz al Hilu (phone)
Yassir Arman
Gibril Ibrahim
Ahmed Tugud (phone)
Ahmad Hussein (phone)
Minni Minawi
Ali Trayo
Abu Gassim Imam

Religious leaders

Sheikh Yagout Sheikh Mohamed Sheikh Malik Sheikh al Imam
Sheikh Qaribullah
Abu Zaid Mohamed Hamza

Activists and human rights defenders

Hafiz Mohamed
Mohamed Hassan Alim 'Boushi'
Albaqir Alafif Mukhtar

Journalists

Mahjoub Mohamed Salih
Al Tahir Satti

NON-EXHAUSTIVE LIST OF INTERVIEWEES

Artists

Rashid Diab

Misseriya

Sadig Babo Nimr
Ahmed Dirdiry

Nuba Mountains

Nagwa Musa Konda (development worker)
Mahmoud Badawi (aid worker and businessman)
Younan Al Baroud (SPLM-North)
Kamal al Nour (Heiban commissioner)
Yassir Ajour (teacher)
Al Nour Burtail (historian and politician)
Chatinga (*Kujour*)
Angelo Adam Juju Baba (SPLA soldier)

Others

Hawa Ibrahim (Darfuri tea lady)
Abdelaziz Hussain (half-Dinka, half-Misseriya cow owner)

SOUTH SUDAN

SPLM

Salva Kiir
Riek Machar
Pa'gan Amum
Lual Deng

SPLA, including military intelligence

Mac Paul
Philip Aguer
Mangar Buong

Ministers

Nhial Deng
Peter Adwok Nyaba
Alfred Ladu Gore

Barnaba Marial
Majak D'Agoot
Elizabeth Bol
'The Minister'

State governors, ministers, MPs, county commissioners

Paul Malong
Taban Deng
Simon Kun Pouch
Rizik Zacharia Hassan
Kuol Manyang (phone)
Sapana Abuyi
Ayii Bol
Gabriel Duop Lam
Joseph Konyi
Goi Jooyul
Peter Lam Both
Garang Majak

Ambassadors

Akec Khoc
Mayen Dut

Officials

Steven Wondu

Oppostion politicians

Lam Akol
Onyoti Adigo
Manyang Parek Von Chief Parek

Rebels

Bapiny Monytuil
Carlo Kuol
Peter Gadet
Bol Gatkouth

David Yau Yau (phone)
George Athor (phone)
Jacob Nyier

Religious leaders

Archbishop Daniel Deng Bul
Bishop Emeritus Paride Taban

Academics

Alfred Lokuji
Jok Madut Jok

Cultural figures

Emmanuel Jal
Daniel Danis (Woyee Film and Theatre)
Victor Lugala
Mary Boyoi
Joseph Abuk
Derek Alfred

Leer

Gatgong Jiech (cow owner)
Mayen Chop (works at MSF)
Peter Nyok (Leer senior administrator)
Chief David Kor Gok
Chief Peter Gatjeng
Colonel David Gatluak
Dol Mading (elder)
Gatluke (trade unionist)
Reverend James Kai

Miscellaneous

Mary Padar (Atuot bead worker)
Garang Thomas Dhel (head of Aweil hospital)
Robert Napoleon (hospital administrator)
John Penn de Ngong (journalist, activist)

Peter Biar Ajak (economist)

OTHER COUNTRIES

Johnnie Carson
Jendayi Frazer
Princeton Lyman
Cameron Hudson
John Prendergast
Alex de Waal
Xiao Yuhua
Hu Shaocong (Chinese embassy, Juba)
Western diplomat, Khartoum
Wang Jianchao (Chinese businessman, Juba)

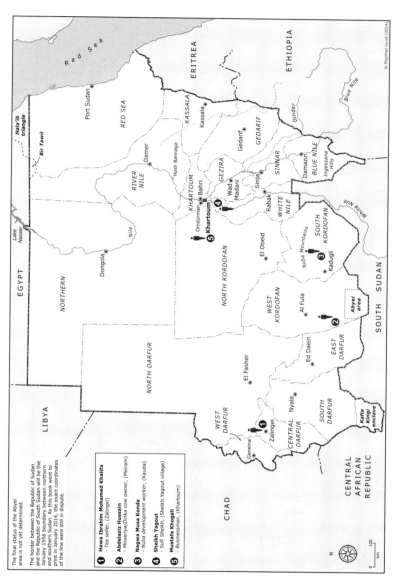

The final status of the Abyei area is not yet determined.

The border between the Republic of Sudan and the Republic of South Sudan will be the January 1956 boundary between northern and southern Sudan. As this book went to print in January 2014, the exact coordinates of the line were still in dispute.

1. **Hawa Ibrahim Mohamed Khalifa**
   - *Tea seller, (Zalingei)*

2. **Abdelaziz Hussain**
   - *Misseriya/Dinka cow owner, (Meiram)*

3. **Nagwa Musa Konda**
   - *Nuba development worker, (Kauda)*

4. **Sheikh Yagout**
   - *Sufi Sheikh, (Sheikh Yagout village)*

5. **Mustafa Khogali**
   - *Businessman, (Khartoum)*

Map 1: Sudan

© Mapman.co.uk (2014)

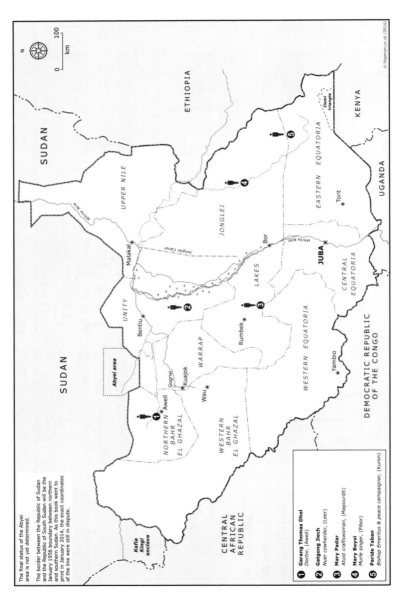

The final status of the Abyei area is not yet determined.

The border between the Republic of Sudan and the Republic of South Sudan will be the January 1956 boundary between northern and southern Sudan. As this book went to print in January 2014, the exact coordinates of the line were still in dispute.

SUDAN

SUDAN

Kafia Kingi enclave

Abyei area

UPPER NILE

WHITE NILE

UNITY

NORTHERN BAHR EL GHAZAL

Awell

Gogrial

Kuajok

Wau

WESTERN BAHR EL GHAZAL

CENTRAL AFRICAN REPUBLIC

Bentiu

WARRAP

LAKES

Rumbek

Malakal

Jonglei Canal

JONGLEI

Bor

White Nile

WESTERN EQUATORIA

Yambio

DEMOCRATIC REPUBLIC OF THE CONGO

CENTRAL EQUATORIA

JUBA

EASTERN EQUATORIA

Torit

Ilemi triangle

ETHIOPIA

KENYA

UGANDA

N

0   100
km

1 **Garang Thomas Dhel**
   Doctor, (Aweil)

2 **Gatgong Jiech**
   Nuer cowherder, (Leer)

3 **Mary Padar**
   Atuot craftswoman, (Mapourdit)

4 **Mary Boyoi**
   Murle singer, (Pibor)

5 **Paride Taban**
   Bishop Emeritus & peace campaigner, (Kuron)

© Mapman.co.uk (2014)

Map 2: South Sudan

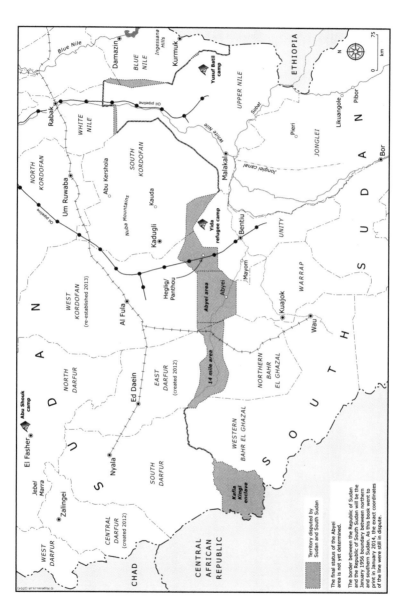

Map 3: The disputed border and conflict areas

ABBREVIATIONS

ABC	Abyei Border Commission
AU	African Union
AUHIP	African Union High Level Implementation Panel
CAR	Central African Republic
CBC	Congressional Black Caucus
CNPC	China National Petroleum Corporation
CPA	Comprehensive Peace Agreement
DDPD	Doha Document for Peace in Darfur
DPA	Darfur Peace Agreement
DRA	Darfur Regional Authority
DRC	Democratic Republic of Congo
DUP	Democratic Unionist Party
EF	Eastern Front
ESPA	Eastern Sudan Peace Agreement
EU	European Union
GNPOC	Greater Nile Petroleum Operating Company
GoNU	Government of National Unity
HAC	Humanitarian Affairs Commision
ICC	International Criminal Court
IDP	Internally Displaced Person
IGAD	Intergovernmental Authority on Development
IMF	International Monetary Fund
JEM	Justice and Equality Movement
JEM-Bashar	Justice and Equality Movement—Bashar
JIU	Joint Integrated Units
LJM	Liberation and Justice Movement
LRA	Lord's Resistance Army

MSF	Médecins Sans Frontières
NBI	Nile Basin Initiative
NCP	National Congress Party
NGO	Non-Governmental Organisation
NISS	National Intelligence and Security Service
NRRDO	Nuba Relief, Rehabilitation and Development Organisation
NUP	National Umma Party
PCA	Permanent Court of Arbitration
PCP	Popular Congress Party
PDF	Popular Defence Force
SAF	Sudanese Armed Forces
SDG	Sudanese Pound
SLA-AW	Sudan Liberation Army—Abdul Wahid
SLA-MM	Sudan Liberation Army—Minni Minawi
SPLA	Sudan People's Liberation Army
SPLA/M	Sudan People's Liberation Army/Movement
SPLM	Sudan People's Liberation Movement
SPLM-DC	Sudan People's Liberation Movement—Democratic Change
SPLM-North	Sudan People's Liberation Movement—North
SRF	Sudan Revolutionary Front
SSDA	South Sudan Democratic Army
SSDF	South Sudan Defence Force
SSLA	South Sudan Liberation Army
SSP	South Sudanese Pound
TFA	Transitional Financial Assistance
UN	United Nations
UNAMID	African Union/United Nations Hybrid Operation in Darfur
UNMIS	United Nations Mission in Sudan
UNMISS	United Nations Mission in South Sudan

INTRODUCTION

On 9 July 2011, the flag of the independent country of South Sudan was raised in an emotional ceremony in its new capital, Juba, attended by heads of state from around the world. Thousands of onlookers sang, cheered and waved their own small flags, producing abstract swirls of South Sudan's colours: a yellow star on a blue triangle, and thick bands of black, red, and green interspersed with white borders. The South Sudanese were united in their joy, although each arm waving a flag cut its own individual shape in the sky. Independence came after decades of divisive civil war in which an estimated two and a half million people had died. Grown men cried—for joy and for the memory of those whom they had lost.

In the Sudanese capital 1200 kilometres to the north, on the other side of a new international border, the descendants of Ismail al Azhari slowly wrapped a black shroud along the white outer wall of the family home. Al Azhari had been one of the founding fathers of Sudan's independence from joint Egyptian and British rule in 1956. Now his children and grandchildren were covering the house in black to mourn the loss of the southern part of their country. The dream of a united Sudan, a diverse nation linking the Arab world to sub-Saharan Africa, had evaporated like a slick of water under the Sudanese sun. Across town in the centre of Khartoum, hundreds of extremists,[1] who had long detested the southern Sudanese because of the cultural, religious and ethnic differences that distinguished them from the northerners, celebrated together. 'This is our real independence day!' one said.

South Sudan's secession was not the conclusion of a long and frequently tragic story; it was merely the end of a chapter. Sudan and South Sudan are joined by more than a name and their people will have no choice but to write a joint narrative for many years to come.

1

Nine months after she celebrated the birth of her new country, Fatna Khamis Bilal was living rough on the streets of Omdurman, one of the three cities that make up the Sudanese capital. Like millions of other South Sudanese she had been stripped of her Sudanese nationality, although she had lived in what was northern Sudan for almost all her life. Fatna had left her house as she prepared to move to South Sudan after separation, but she lacked the small sum of money she needed for the journey. Home was now a makeshift shelter made from a faded cloth adorned with floral patterns. The burgundy and ivory fabric suggested that she had once known better days. 'I'm living outside, I'm hungry, and I want to go to South Sudan', Fatna said. She frowned, and her face rumpled into deep creases. A few days later, Sudan and South Sudan were at war, making Fatna's situation even more precarious.

But can Sudan and South Sudan move on from decades of conflict, and learn to trust each other? This will not be easy, as a cursory glance through the history of the united Sudan makes clear. In 1820, an Egyptian army moved south into a land known to medieval Muslim geographers as *Bilad al-Sudan*, the 'land of the blacks'. The soldiers created what became known as the *Turkiyya*, a colony named after the Egyptians' own Ottoman overlords, the primary purpose of which was to provide slaves and gold to Cairo. The slaves largely came from the black African groups to the south. Under the *Turkiyya*, the beginnings of central administrative control were extended into what is now South Sudan, although the motivation was economic plunder, rather than building a state.

Disgust at high taxes and heavy-handed officials later bolstered the resistance movement of Mohamed Ahmed 'al Mahdi', a northern religious leader who forced out the foreigners and killed their mercenary commander, General Charles Gordon, in 1885. The Mahdi is celebrated as Sudan's first national hero. Thirteen years later, the British exacted a belated revenge on Gordon's killers, paving the way for a curious mix of British and Egyptian governance known as the Anglo-Egyptian Condominium which ruled Sudan from 1898 to 1956.[2] Despite the apparent sharing of responsibilities, the British took the lead on most matters. The colonialists incorporated the Sultanate of Darfur in 1916 and gradually overcame the remaining groups in southern Sudan that had resisted the imposition of this new state.

The colonialists perceived northern Sudan as Arab and Muslim, in contrast to the south, where African peoples followed traditional religions, and Christianity. This rather simplistic view of Sudan's complicated ethnic mosaic persists to this day. The two areas were governed very differently, adding to the divisions that already existed. Northern Sudan, or at least the heartland around Khartoum, benefited from the colonialists' attention and resources. Southern Sudan, as well as large parts of the northern periphery, remained terribly under-developed. Sudan became independent on 1 January 1956. This was one of the consequences of the 1952 Egyptian revolution;[3] it was also the first sighting of the great decolonising wave that proceeded to sweep over sub-Saharan Africa.

Sudan was a difficult country to govern. It was Africa's largest state, with dozens of very different ethnic and language groups within its borders. The geography of the place, including the deserts of the north and a cloying swamp in the south, made it hard to maintain control, or develop the areas far from the centre. For all these reasons and more, governments in Sudan have often been weak. In the first third of a century after independence, three different military officers overthrew elected governments. The last of the trio, Omar al Bashir, took over in 1989 and has been in power ever since. The periods either side of military rule, the 'democratic interludes' as they are sometimes known, were characterised by fragile coalitions that left the country's many problems unresolved.

The tensions between northern and southern Sudan, which had been exacerbated by colonial rule, increased after Sudan's independence in 1956. Southern Sudanese soldiers had mutinied even before the British and Egyptians left, and things did not improve much subsequently. The leaders in Khartoum were unable or unwilling to bridge the gap between north and south. As a result, Sudan suffered two long-running north-south civil wars. In the first, from 1955 to 1972,[4] southern Sudanese fought to secede but ended up with a degree of regional autonomy. In the second, from 1983 to 2005, John Garang de Mabior's Sudan People's Liberation Army/Movement (SPLA/M) struggled for a reformed 'New Sudan'. Garang wanted to change the whole country, making it a fairer place economically, politically and socially; but many of his soldiers and commanders hoped for independence for southern Sudan.

In January 2005, the Comprehensive Peace Agreement (CPA) was signed, ending the war. In July of that year, Garang died in a helicopter crash, just three weeks after being sworn in as vice president. He was replaced by his deputy, Salva Kiir Mayardit, a secessionist. Over the next six years, known as the 'interim period', the SPLM governed Sudan alongside President Bashir's National Congress Party (NCP). The CPA also granted the southern Sudanese a referendum to choose whether to remain part of Sudan. Both the SPLM and the NCP had committed themselves to 'make unity attractive', but Garang's death ended any hope of this happening. In January 2011, the southern Sudanese voted almost unanimously to secede. Garang's fight for a reformed Sudan had ended with the country splitting in two.[5] The internal contradictions of the state left by the British, coupled with the disastrous rule of successive Khartoum governments, were simply too much to overcome. South Sudan broke away, becoming Africa's fifty-fourth state.

The creation of the new country is the starting point for this book. The period after separation was every bit as dramatic, and almost as bloody, as the decades that preceded it. By the time of the split, a new Sudanese civil war had broken out in South Kordofan. Shortly afterwards Blue Nile was at war too. In both areas the rebels had once fought Khartoum as part of the SPLA/M. South Sudan's secession left them north of the border, with their grievances intact, and fresh battles to fight. In these new conflicts in old war zones, Khartoum's troops have been accused of serious abuses, including ethnic cleansing and indiscriminate bombing of civilian areas. The pattern was depressingly similar to Darfur, where the civil war that broke out in 2003 showed no sign of coming to an end. South Sudan also struggled to overcome rebellions, in Unity, Upper Nile and Jonglei states, as well as inter-ethnic clashes in which thousands of people were killed. All these conflicts were, in part, created by the unresolved tensions of the united Sudan. Khartoum and Juba blamed each other for intensifying and even provoking the wars on their soil. Sometimes this angry rhetoric was superseded by direct military action. In April 2012, Sudan and South Sudan fought on their disputed border, and the Sudanese air force frequently bombed the border areas of the new country. The two states are still joined by conflict.

Their economies are intertwined too. In January 2012, South Sudan took the extraordinary decision to shut down its own oil production as part of a row with Sudan over how much it should pay to export its oil through Sudan's pipelines. Oil had provided 98 per cent of the South Sudanese government's revenues. Suddenly South Sudan was in danger of collapse, and Sudan could scarcely keep its head above water either. Sudan had already lost the South Sudanese oil and would now find itself without oil transit fees, as well as billions of dollars of compensation for its lost oil reserves. Economic salvation could only come through a successful conclusion to the acrimonious ongoing negotiations between the two countries.

The period after separation also saw heightened tensions within the NCP and the SPLM. The power struggle at the heart of Sudan's ruling party, both for control of the country's direction and to replace Bashir one day, dragged in soldiers and Islamists, security officers and pragmatists. These competing forces seemed united only in their desire for prominence, and their ruthlessness in maintaining their uneasy coalition in power. In South Sudan, the SPLM has no real rivals. The 'liberation heroes' controlled parliament and cabinet, but were bitterly divided. The disagreements between the president and the vice president led to a damaging split two years after independence, with the potential to divide the army and the country on ethnic lines. In both Sudans, politicians attempted to strike a nationalist tone by denigrating the old enemies across the border; in both, the difficult business of governing was often neglected in favour of the cross-border rivalry and domestic squabbling.

Above all the people of the two Sudans, who had co-existed for so long, were still bound together, by marriage, trade, and pastoral migration with the seasons. The new borderlines on the map (which are disputed by both sides) are further blurred by the movements and relationships of the people of the two countries. Separation was not a total rupture; it was, and is, a bitter, incomplete divorce.

The struggles of the two Sudans matter, for the people of the two countries, but also for the region and for the wider world. In 1975, Jafaar Nimeiri, Sudan's president, made the case for the importance of his troubled state:

The Sudan is the biggest country in Africa. It lies in its heart and at its crossroads. Its extensive territory borders [nine] African countries.[6] Common frontiers mean common ethnical origins, common cultures and shared ways of life and environmental conditions. Trouble in the Sudan would, by necessity, spill over its frontiers.[7]

It did exactly that on many occasions over the next three decades. Millions of refugees created a burden for the Democratic Republic of Congo (DRC), Kenya, Uganda, Egypt, Ethiopia, Eritrea and Chad, among others; and the united Sudan's internal conflicts drew in many neighbouring states, and, at times, flooded back over their borders.

A Poisonous Thorn in Our Hearts is an account of Sudan and South Sudan in the period immediately after separation, and an introduction to the two Sudans' people, politics and prospects. Each chapter starts with Sudan before addressing the new country, because South Sudan's political, economic and security dynamics are so often framed by its history in the united Sudan. At a time when there is a tendency to analyse the two Sudans separately, this book focuses on their common past, interwoven present and mutually dependent future—a hard knot that will take many years to unpick. The South Sudanese were 'a poisonous thorn in our heart', according to a leading Sudanese politician,[8] and separation did not change his view. Many South Sudanese feel the same way about their former compatriots, the Sudanese—or at least about the Sudanese political class. Yet this mistrust cannot completely hide some more fraternal bonds between the people. This confusing mix, of love, hate and continued interaction is at the core of this book.

The first chapter examines the peoples of the two Sudans, moving beyond the often stated but fundamentally flawed dichotomy of Arab and Muslim Sudanese and African and Christian South Sudanese. It describes the incomplete but vital struggle to find a unifying national identity in both Sudans. The subject of chapter two is the politics of the two countries. Sudan has, in theory, been governed by Islamists since 1989, yet real power is actually held by a complicated coalition of ideologues, opportunists and uniformed officers. In South Sudan, the SPLM's dominance is unchallenged, but the party and its leaders must make the difficult transition from rebels to politicians, and smooth over dangerous internal tensions.

The chapter on the economy shows how Sudan is struggling to cope with the loss of the oil reserves that disappeared with South Sudan's secession. The new country, on the other hand, must diversify before its oil runs out. South Sudan had a terrifying preview of a future without oil when it shut down its own oil production. The following chapter shows why many ordinary people in the two Sudans have hardly benefited at all from the wealth flowing in to the two capitals. At independence, South Sudan was one of the most underdeveloped countries in the world. Some areas of 'rump Sudan', as post-separation Sudan is sometimes known, are every bit as neglected.

Chapter five examines how the stability of both Sudans is threatened by rebellions and inter-ethnic conflict. The racism, religious discrimination, bad governance and under-development highlighted in the preceding chapters are some of the reasons for the fighting. The next chapter describes Sudan and South Sudan's differing relations with countries around the world, including America, China, African neighbours, Arab states, Iran, and Israel. The final chapter addresses the most important relationship of all: that between the two Sudans. In the period immediately after separation, this included negotiations and interrupted love affairs, proxy wars and direct conflict, and even tentative signs that both sides recognised the path towards a more harmonious future.

A Poisonous Thorn in Our Hearts explores these issues through the experiences, opinions and hopes of all sorts of Sudanese and South Sudanese, from politicians in three-piece suits to barefoot cow-herders, along with superstar singers and Darfuri tea ladies. As the title of the book suggests, separation has not ended the capacity of the two countries, or more precisely those who lead them, to do each other irreparable damage. If the right choices are made, however, the Sudans' mutual dependence, which will endure for decades, could be a force for good in both countries. During the turbulence, economic conflict and outright war that followed separation, that seemed an unlikely prospect.

1

PEOPLE AND IDENTITY

The first chants surprised the street, a west to east thoroughfare not far from the Khartoum International Airport. *'Al fuul ghali, ya wali'* the six brave protesters chanted: *fuul* (the Sudanese staple dish of fava beans) is expensive, governor! A momentary hush swelled around the chanting circle, and then people began to join in. Within a few minutes, a crowd of fifty were marching and singing; next someone dragged a tyre into the middle of a crossroads, and set it on fire. The spiralling black smoke signalled trouble. Soon, inevitably, the riot police arrived, sirens whining, truncheons whirling, to chase the protesters and the passers-by away. Having grabbed some sounds of the demonstration for a BBC radio report on this latest outburst of anti-government feeling, I too had to leave quickly.

Ducking into a side street, I stumbled upon a woman heading back from the market, seemingly unaware of the ruckus to her right. Another quick turn, and here was a group of men sitting in the late-afternoon sun, discussing last night's wedding or the painfully hot weather. It was as if the demonstration, the fear, fury and violence of those few minutes had not existed; yet that evening's news item on Sudan would talk of nothing else.

Too much of the international coverage of Sudan, and now South Sudan, is concentrated on those pockets of mayhem, outside which millions of people live, some luxuriously and some in the most degrading poverty, but most just trying to feed their children and earn enough for the odd treat. The negative image of both Sudans is something that understandably infuriates the people of both countries. This book will not entirely escape that trap: after all, the wars inside and between the two nations, as well as the often brutal behaviour of their rulers and the crushing lack of development, still mould the lives of so many. A sense of who the Sudanese and South Sudanese are, and how they live, far from the TV cameras and gunshots of the latest crisis, is what this chapter seeks to convey. It also introduces some of the key debates over identity that shape both Sudan and South Sudan.

SUDAN

'Sudan is not really a country at all, but many. A composite of layers, like a genetic fingerprint of memories that were once fluid, but have since crystallized out from the crucible of possibility.' [1]

Jamal Mahjoub, Sudanese novelist.

'Sudan, largely Muslim and Arab, and South Sudan, populated by black Africans who follow Christianity and traditional religions…'

Explanatory sentence in thousands of news reports.

The question 'Who are you?' might seem straightforward. Nevertheless all over Sudan and South Sudan, in government offices, refugee camps, places of worship, simple huts and imposing villas, I have met people who have struggled to answer it simply—or who came up with a conclusion very different from the one even a family member might arrive at. For some the question directed them first of all to an ethnic identity, or their religion; others opted for their gender, home town, profession or nationality. Of course, people have complicated, sometimes shifting identities, made up of all the above ingredients and many more. 'Sudanese people differentiate themselves—or have been differentiated by others—using a range of overlapping criteria: lines of descent, common language, place of origin, mode of livelihood, physical characteristics, and political or religious affiliation,' the anthropologist John Ryle has written.[2]

Colonial divisions

Just as each individual is, to adapt Mahjoub's phrase, a composite of many layers, so the countries known today as Sudan and South Sudan are made up of many groups, often forced together by circumstance and outside intervention. The people of the two Sudans are exceptionally diverse. The conflicts between what are now Sudan and South Sudan have often been presented as the Arab, Muslim north against the black African Christians and followers of traditional religions from the south.[3] This apparent division is not new: the British ruled what they perceived as the Arab north and the African south of Sudan very differently, at times restricting travel from one part of the united Sudan to the other: in 1922 the Passports and Permits Ordinances defined much of the South as 'Closed Districts' which northerners required special permission to travel to.[4] Legal systems were often based on traditional or customary law, entrenching divisions between different parts of the country.

Some colonial officers were devoted to the south and its peoples, but in general the British looked more favourably on the north than the south. In the 1920s, one minor colonial functionary in southern Sudan described the people he ruled as 'black-skinned savages, these being of as primitive a mentality as any known'.[5] (The obvious racism reveals much more about the writer than it does about the subjects of the phrase.) The colonial administration worked to keep the two halves of the country separate. Christian missionaries were encouraged in southern Sudan, and forbidden from operating in the north, in order not to antagonise the sentiments of Muslims living there.

This different treatment is often used by Sudanese leaders to account for their subsequent inability to incorporate southern Sudan into a harmonious nation-state, though their own failures of leadership are at least as much to blame. Notwithstanding its durability, the shorthand of black African south versus Arab Muslim north is oversimplified and often misleading. In fact, the various nation-building projects of the late nineteenth and twentieth centuries roped together an array of ethnic groups and political entities under one flag.

Following South Sudan's secession, even the Sudanese 'rump state' remains an uneasy coalition of multitudes, rather than a homogeneous nation. Nevertheless, it is possible to tease out certain key themes that will start to compose a picture of the people of what is left of Sudan. Over the next few pages I will introduce you to some Sudanese from different parts of the country and differing social spheres. Later on it will be the turn of the South Sudanese. It is difficult for any individual to represent much more than her or his own self, but their lives are a starting point to talk about some of the many ways the people of the Sudans live.

FAITH

Since separation, Sudan's people are overwhelmingly Muslim: almost 97% according to the government,[6] although the Sudanese churches dispute this figure.[7] It hasn't always been this way. The people of the great Nubian civilisation worshipped ancient Egyptian gods, and at one point conquered Egypt itself. The pyramids and temples at Jebel Barkal and Meroe, along the Nile to the north of Khartoum, attest to the sophistication and power of this period. From the 6th century onwards, Christian kingdoms dominated the territory now known as Sudan, or at least its riverain heartland. Startlingly beautiful murals of the nativity, complete with what tour guides describe as 'African' faces, are preserved in the National Museum in Khartoum.

In time, Islam supplanted Christianity, though it never truly set down roots further south. South Sudan's secession took away a large non-Muslim minority; but even after separation Sudan has many Christians and followers of traditional religions in the Nuba Mountains of South Kordofan, and in Blue Nile state. Islam, too, has often been subtly altered by its contact with pre-Islamic traditions. According to the anthropologist Wendy James, studies of modern Muslim communities in the Nile Valley 'reveal a layering of religious belief and practice that owes more to the continual recreation of vernacular ideas than to the formalities of the mosque, or the profession of faith, prayer, fasting, alms-giving and pilgrimage that constitute the five pillars of Islam.'[8] Whatever form Islam takes, in most areas of Sudan the mosque and the imam make up the cornerstone of each community.

> Sheikh Yagout Sheikh Mohamed Sheikh Malik Sheikh al Imam.
> Sufi holy man, White Nile state

The *Sheikh* or religious leader has made his mark. The village where he lives is now named after him: Sheikh Yagout. It's a small settlement just to the east of the sluggish flow of the White Nile, no more than a few huts and low brick buildings clustered around the tarmac road that runs north to Khartoum. A conical silver roof, with a crescent on top, indicates the tomb of Sheikh Yagout's father. This and the mosque are by far the tallest buildings in the village. As the sun sinks to the horizon, turning the light to a soft peach colour, and sending the shadows of the minarets ever further into the courtyard, Sheikh Yagout sits on an *angharaib*, a wood and rope day bed, to meet the dozens of his followers who have come to seek his divine blessings.

People travel from all parts of Sudan, elsewhere in Africa, and even further abroad, to pray with the Sheikh, and overcome their health, financial and family problems. Men in white *jallabiya* (a traditional Sudanese robe) kneel at his feet. One by one they kiss his right hand. Sheikh Yagout is wearing brown leather shoes, and his white robe is hoisted over one shoulder. His skullcap is white, as is his bushy goatee. His grey hair is receding under the cap, and there are black spots on the mahogany of his face. The only splashes of primary colour in this scene are provided by the women, sitting with their children off to the Sheikh's right, in their bright *tobes* (a long piece of cloth wrapped round the body and over the head). After each supplicant has seen the Sheikh, he hands him a small amount of money, the equivalent of a few dollars. The notes are then discretely placed under a pillow on the *angharaib*.

Sheikh Yagout took over when his father died in 1962. He has built up the mosque, and an Islamic study centre that sometimes has as many as 600 students. Sheikh Yagout sees his role as a simple one: 'I teach people about Islam, and how to practise it. It comes from the heart, how to know Allah. Everything comes from the Koran, and his Prophet Mohamed, peace be upon him.' Sheikh Yagout also gives medicines to the sick, which often include a special extract from the Koran. If someone dies in a far away village, the Sheikh will give his blessings by telephone.

Sheikh Yagout is a prominent figure in the Sammaniya *tariqa* or Sufi brotherhood, one of many such groups in Sudan.[9] There is a growing tension between the Sufis and the Salafists. The latter want a society regulated entirely by the words and deeds of the Prophet Mohamed, with the strict implementation of *sharia* or Islamic law. They have been inspired by Wahhabi teachers from Saudi Arabia. Sufis like Sheikh Yagout say they are more concerned with the essence of religion rather than appearances; they seek a more personal path to God. Sheikh Yagout says that 85 per cent of Sudanese are Sufis, and there are villages and towns named after Sufi holy men all over the country. The Salafists admit they are a minority. They disapprove of the veneration of people like Sheikh Yagout, one of many Sufi practices they believe are un-Islamic. The tension between the two groups has even resulted in fights in the capital.[10] Following South Sudan's secession there is a debate about which course Sudan should take, and the Salafists and the Sufis wish to have their say.

ETHNICITY

Even after South Sudan's secession, dozens of ethnic groups live in Sudan.[11] One of the biggest divides is between those who speak Arabic as a mother tongue and those who don't. Arabic-speakers, who are probably the majority, dominate a sphere that radiates out from the capital and takes in most of the country. Many Sudanese claim they can trace their origins back to the Arabian Peninsula, and for the lucky few, to the Prophet Mohamed. Arabs came to what is now Sudan even before the coming of Islam, albeit in small numbers. In the 7th century, a *baqt* or treaty was signed which regulated the relationship between the Nubians and their Arab neighbours for centuries.

It was only in the late 13th century that the Christian Nubian kingdoms began to crumble, and the Arabs arrived in large numbers. The Arabs intermarried with local African groups and Muslim pilgrims from West Africa, and gradually spread Islam throughout what is now Sudan. The Sudanese historian Yusuf Fadl Hassan has described this process as 'peaceful infiltration'.[12] After centuries of intermarriage these groups could be best described as Afro-Arab; Fadl Hassan talks about 'Arabized Nubians', to give one example.[13] Nevertheless, not all Sudanese choose to highlight both parts of this heritage. According to the human rights activist Albaqir Alafif Mukhtar, 'Sudanese live in a split world. While they believe that they descended from an Arab "father" and an African "mother", they identify with the father and suppress the mother.'[14]

Other groups see themselves as entirely Arab, such as the Rashaida in the East. The Rashaida are relatively recent arrivals from the Arabian Peninsula, and many live as far removed from the constrictions of the state as possible. In fact, 'Arab' has a curious dual valency in Sudan. It can be a badge of pride, denoting origins among those peoples who were the first Muslims, in the Arabian Peninsula; and it is sometimes used as an insult against the 'uncivilised' Arabs living on the periphery. The economist Hassan Satti, who has North African and Arab origins, is very much part of the northern elite. He sees himself as part of 'Arabic civilisation', but bristles at the idea that he is Arab:

If you call me an Arab I will not accept it. I will call it an insult: in my village it is an insult. We think we are more civilised than the Arabs. They are savage, they are backwards, their traditions are very different. The Rashaida are still living the same way as they have been in Saudi Arabia, in tents, the way they treat the women is the same as in Yemen.

Satti's words hint at the ethnic tensions that have contributed to the marginalisation of so many Sudanese.

The Arabic-speakers of the Nile Valley, north of Khartoum, dominated the Sudanese state from the outset. During the Anglo-Egyptian period, they had the closest contacts with the colonisers. The big families benefited economically from the opportunities this presented, and their children got the best education. This pattern continued after Sudan's independence in 1956. Since then the ruling class has largely come from what some call the Three Tribes: the Jaaliyin, the Shaigiya and the Danagla. These are the *awlad al bahr*, the children of the river, the northern riverain elite. In 2000, a pamphlet appeared on the streets of Khartoum called 'The Black Book: Imbalance of Power and Wealth in Sudan'. The Black Book laid out in shocking detail the historical and contemporary domination of the people of the northern region, including the wildly disproportionate number of northern ministers in successive governments.[15] Being born into one of the Three Tribes is not a guarantee of success or prosperity, but it does make both considerably more likely.[16]

Mustafa Khogali
Khartoum businessman

Mustafa, a businessman, musician and cultural entrepreneur in his late 30s, is a well-known figure in the Sudanese capital. He describes himself as a 'Khartoumie'. He organises concerts and spoken word poetry evenings, and runs a free magazine, *In the City*, which promotes Sudanese culture and Khartoum events alongside adverts for the latest mobile phones. When he speaks English the occasional word hints at the decade he spent in the US. Mustafa made his money in the oil industry, but subsequently moved into mobile phone infrastructure, and then various media and cultural projects. His two-tone Mercedes, predominantly in dull silver, is one demonstration of the success he has made of his life. His two sons now live in Dubai, where he feels they will get a better education. Mustafa is happiest when pounding a frenetic, controlled rhythm on the West African *djembé* drums he imported from Guinea.

Mustafa's family tree is sprinkled with glamour. An area of Omdurman was named after an ancestor; a great uncle was the first head of the Sovereignty Council, the governing body at Sudan's independence in 1956. Mustafa was born in Abidjan, Ivory Coast, where his father was stationed at the African Development Bank. 'I wouldn't say we were rich, but it was a very educated background,' he says. 'At that time the educated were the people who were governing the state, which eventually, of course, gave their offspring the ability to be well-educated and have good jobs.'

If pressed, Mustafa says that he is from the Jaaliyin, one of the Three Tribes. But Mustafa does not identify strongly with his ethnic group. 'I am a Sudanese and I try to leave it at that.' His insistence on a predominantly Sudanese identity is not unusual among those from the Nile valley heartland. As Ryle has written about kinship in Sudan, 'the greater the distance from the centres of power and the reach of central government, the greater the importance likely to be accorded to it, and the less compunction in invoking it.'[17]

The Non-Arabs

There are others in Sudan who reject any Arab origins. By and large they can be found on the periphery of the country, like the Beja in the East, the Zaghawa, Fur, Masalit and many others in Darfur to the West, small groups like the Ingessana and the Uduk from Blue Nile, in the South-East, as well as the Nuba in the South-West.[18] Most, but not all, of these groups are predominantly or entirely Muslim. Most define themselves as African. Each ethnicity has its own history, of course. Some migrated from other parts of the African continent: for instance Fellata refers (sometimes dismissively) to those of West African origin. Often they have been in Sudan for several generations, after their ancestors stayed on following an overland pilgrimage to Mecca. In recent times, the Fellata have begun 'to assert an Arab identity, illustrating the flexibility in ethnic affiliation that is a persistent theme in Sudanese history.'[19] However, for those who do not see themselves as Arabs, a key difference is that they will usually speak their mother tongue first, and then Arabic as a *lingua franca* or language of education.[20] One of Sudan's tragedies is that Sudan's non-Arab groups have been politically and economically marginalised, because of racism, religion, or simply their distance from the capital. Many Arabs feel marginalised too, an indication that race is not the only factor here.

For Mustafa Khogali, Sudan's many ethnic groups, its African and Arab components, are—or should be—a source of strength: 'We identify with a Sudan that is made up of so many tribes and we see the benefit of that diversity.' Many do not. Mustafa regrets that the South Sudanese are mocked for their skin colour. Zaghawa has become a jokey insult, too, he says, and the Fellata are teased about their supposedly foreign accents when they speak Arabic. Such jokes have taken on a harsher tone over the years, he feels. In Darfur, in particular, the civil war has been presented as pitting Africans against Arabs, although there are often blurred lines between these categories. Ethnic identities have been consolidated, and sometimes militarised, by the fighting. Yet in Darfur there are also frequent deadly clashes between different Arab groups.

Mustafa is a Sufi, who says that Islam is the guiding principle that he relies on for every major decision. However he believes that faith has caused Sudan to over-emphasise part of its nature. 'Our religion has pushed us to identify with the Arabs more so than the Africans, which I think is a negative approach,' he says. 'It alienates us from all of our neighbours and puts us with a group that is nowhere near us geographically.' The National Question of who the Sudanese are—Arabs? Africans? Muslims? People of many faiths?—has preoccupied Sudan since its birth. Generations of politicians in Khartoum tried, to a greater or lesser degree, to Arabise and Islamise the rest of Sudan. This, along with economic and political marginalisation, ultimately led to South Sudan's secession. In its current incarnation it threatens the harmony of what remains of Sudan.

Hawa Ibrahim Mohamed Khalifa
Fur tea seller

Hawa Ibrahim thinks of herself first and foremost as a Fur, and only then as a Sudanese. The Fur are an African group from Darfur. They have been among the most disadvantaged people in the country, and many Fur took up arms against the state when the Darfur civil war broke out in 2003. 'I feel it is my identity, and I am proud to be Fur,' Hawa says. 'I feel proud of it when you say Darfur. We are respected, and we should be, because Darfur is named after us and we were the first people there.' Darfur means 'homeland of the Fur', an indication of the historical power of an ethnic group that still largely inhabits the Jebel Marra highlands, and the surrounding plains.

Hawa is pleased to be asked about her identity. 'We are African,' she states proudly, differentiating the Fur from people like Mustafa whose first language is Arabic. She believes that Sudan is an African country.

Hawa has put on her best clothes for the interview, an orange *tobe* with gold edges. She has a round face, and laughs a lot. Her earrings catch the eye, a trio of gold circles cascading from each ear. She claims a distant family connection to the Fur Sultans, but she is far from rich, partly because she was never educated.

Hawa grew up in Zalingei, a small town in West Darfur, at the foot of the Jebel Marra mountain range. Her family had three *tukuls*, or huts, inside the town. Every day she would get up early in the morning, and walk for a quarter of an hour to the fields. 'Our basic work was to farm the land,' she says. 'We grew onions, *dura* (sorghum) and okra. We just ate what we farmed in our house, we didn't send anything to the market.' Her childhood, regulated by the seasons and hard work on the farm, has left Hawa with a great longing: 'I would have loved to go to school, but I didn't go. I started in the fields at the age of nine or ten. It was really difficult work. Farming is hard. But life is tough isn't it?' At this point Hawa laughs.

Hawa might have had things easier if she had been male. When she was growing up in the 1970s, girls were much less likely than boys to get an education. Since then the gap has narrowed, but it has not closed completely. Women find it harder to get a job too: in 2012, 20 per cent of women were unemployed, according to figures quoted by the UN, while for men the figure was 13 per cent.[21] Women like Hawa are more likely to have low-paying jobs.

Sudanese society, and in particular the form of Islamism used to govern the country, also imposes strict restrictions. Wearing 'inappropriate clothing' in public is an offence, and many women have been flogged for wearing trousers.[22] In the most high profile case, in July 2009, the journalist Lubna Hussein sent out an email to diplomats, human rights defenders and journalists, inviting them to witness her court case and 'flogging'. Under the glare of international publicity, she eventually received a fine, rather than lashes, for the 'crime' of wearing trousers. Hawa's experience has been less extreme, but her gender has added to the difficulties imposed by her ethnicity and lack of education.

Hawa was born in 1968, though she doesn't know the exact date.[23] In the early 1980s, shortly after she got married, she came to Khartoum for the first time. She was fourteen or fifteen. For Hawa, farm work has been replaced by long days as a *sitt al shai*, a Khartoum tea lady who sits under a mango tree and serves hibiscus tea and spiced coffee; it is a common job for women from Sudan's peripheries. 'I don't know if you can consider it work, really,' she says. On a good day she will earn two dollars. Hawa can only afford to keep three of her six children in school. If pushed about what she does to relax, Hawa seems at a loss. 'I contemplate about how hard life is, and I remember things and I say *Alhamdulilah* (praise be to God) for what God has given me.'

Identity benefits

Despite the multi-faceted nature of almost any individual identity, in Sudan who you are, or at least who you are perceived to be, matters a lot. The Sudanese often class themselves as 'Arab' or 'African', even if these categories have substantial overlaps. From a purely physical perspective, many of the 'Arabs' would be described as black in Western countries, and the foreigner often struggles to differentiate between those who see themselves as African and those who describe themselves as Arab. The writer Leila Aboulela describes living as a Sudanese as 'To be among Arabs too African and among Africans too Arab.'[24]

In spite of these confused boundaries, Sudan is a society in which coming from the right group can confer substantial advantages. Mustafa was always more likely to do well than Hawa.[25] An Arab identity, however much effort has gone into its construction, can position one closer to the centre of power. This dates back several hundred years:

Since the 16th century, when the Funj king, Badi III, issued a royal decree announcing that he and his folk 'descended from the Arabs, and indeed from the Ummayyads', all ethnic groups in this part of the world, knew that claims to Arabic and Islamic identity helps in bringing them closer to the power circles and the privileges that come with it.[26]

For many Sudanese, an Islamic identity is most fully expressed as part of an Arab one; but millions of Sudanese Muslims, like Hawa, are not Arab at all.

RACIAL AND RELIGIOUS DISCRIMINATION

In a powerful essay on race and conflict in pre-separation Sudan, the human rights activist Alafif points out that many Sudanese call black people *abeed* or slaves.[27] This is a poisonous legacy of the time when southern Sudan and other areas were a source of slaves for the north. It is not an exaggeration. I have heard people in Khartoum refer to South Sudanese as *abeed*. On one occasion a young man told me no Sudanese could ever marry a South Sudanese woman, and anyway, he said, they would not want to as 'they are all ugly and they all smell.' It is worth underlining that not all Sudanese have such racist attitudes. The man's friends told him off, and there are of course marriages between Sudanese and South Sudanese.[28]

Alafif identified a distinct pecking order among the united Sudan's diverse groups, based on both race and religion.

At the bottom of the hierarchy is the black African component of the country, namely the Southerners, the Nuba, and the Angessana, especially the non-Muslims among them. A step higher come those among the first category who professed Islam. A step higher come the black African tribes of Darfur, who are 100% Muslims. A step up the ladder come the Baggara tribes of Kordofan and Darfur who extensively intermarried with their neighbouring Southerners and Nuba, until they become very dark, nick-named *al-Gharaba* (westerners). A step above come the other Arab tribes of northern Kordofan, mainly the Kababish, (some of them in northern Darfur). With this category or close to it come the Beja of Eastern Sudan, as well as the Rashayda. Although this category is not considered racially inferior to the ruling class, they are considered inferior in terms of culture and modernity. At the top of the racial hierarchy sit the people from the riverain North from whom the ruling class is drawn.[29]

This is not a rigid caste system, as Sudanese society and attitudes are much more flexible than this; but it does highlight a real and damaging issue. Some accounts of Sudan's troubles identify racism as the fundamental cause. In fact it is one of several, as this book will show. All the same, understanding the role racial and religious discrimination plays is vital to understanding all the political and social problems that have held Sudan back for so long.

Nagwa Musa Konda
Nuba development worker, Kauda

As a Christian Nuba woman, Nagwa Konda comes near the very bottom of Sudan's loose racial and religious hierarchy. Her life certainly hasn't been easy, but thanks to her father's obsession with education, and her own strong will, it has been a very successful one. Nagwa was born in 1976, in the village of Kambara, not far from the small town of Kauda.

She is an Otoro Nuba; the Otoro are one of the many language groups that form the Nuba. The Nuba Mountains, which are probably more accurately described as hills, make up one of the most linguistically diverse areas of Africa.[30]

When she was three, Nagwa's father landed a job as a security guard in Kadugli, the capital of South Kordofan. Nagwa is full of admiration for her father, Musa Konda Kuku, who passed away during the war in the Nuba Mountains in the 1990s. He was a tolerant man, she says, who was propelled by his Christian faith. He kept prayer mats and a clean pitcher of water in case Muslim friends or colleagues visited. There are Christians and Muslims among the Nuba, as well as many followers of traditional religions, and they pride themselves on their religious tolerance.

Like most Nuba of his time, Nagwa's father had not received much education, although he had taken literacy classes at a late age. Unusually he made sure all his nine children attended school, even the girls. School wasn't always easy. Classmates mocked Nagwa's dark skin.[31] Teachers, fellow students and even school cleaners criticised her Christian faith, calling her 'infidel' or 'firewood'—someone destined to burn in the fires of Hell. 'They tell you if you are Christian you are very primitive.' Nagwa's tone shows no sign of rancour, but the vivid memory pushes her into the present tense. This verbal abuse goes against the Koran's stated respect for the People of the Book. Nevertheless, such experiences are not at all unusual for the Nuba.

In response to just these attitudes, Yusif Kuwa Mekki, the Nuba leader who joined the SPLA/M in the 1980s, wrote a poem in praise of his African identity, called *My African-ness:*

Despite all the talk,
About my Arabism
My religion,
My culture…
I am a Nuba,
I am black,
I am African.

African-ness is my identity
It is entrenched
In my appearance
Engraved in lips
And manifested by my skin.[32]

In the British colonial period, the Nuba Mountains were a Closed District, cut off from the rest of Sudan. Subsequently there were attempts to convert the Nuba to Islam. Leni Riefenstahl's famous photo books of naked, proud Nuba, published in the 1970s, gave the region a certain international fame. Many Sudanese felt the images revealed the 'primitive' nature of the Nuba, and successive governments in Khartoum tried to change their ways.

In the hills above Nagwa's hometown, I met a man who personifies much of what the Sudanese elite hate about the Nuba. Chatinga, as he is known to everyone, is a *kujour*, a 'popular sacred spiritual person who conducts many spiritual deeds'.[33] An old man who moves stiffly, he introduces himself as Abdrahman Kujour. He has adopted the forename under pressure from the authorities, he says, but he isn't a Muslim. The Christians call him Noah, he adds in his deep voice, but his true faith is clearly almost as old as the mountains he lives in. The spirits speak to him, and like Sheikh Yagout, people travel from far away to be blessed or healed. The faith of the *kujour*, which pre-dates Islam, infuriates the Islamists in Khartoum. For people like Chatinga and Nagwa, the state's attempts to Arabise them has led instead to a renewed pride in being Nuba.

After successful studies, Nagwa got a scholarship to Ahfad University in Omdurman. Only girls are admitted to this admirable establishment, and the man who runs it, Gassim Badri, has made a point of giving scholarships to young women from the marginalised peripheries of Sudan.[34] Racial and religious discrimination may be a dominant political paradigm in Sudan, but a considerable number of Sudanese make sure they do not fit into it. Nagwa's education, which was completed by a Master's degree at Swansea University in Wales, allowed her to get a job at the Nuba Relief, Rehabilitation and Development Organisation (NRRDO). She eventually became NRRDO's director.

A HARD LAND

All Sudanese, wherever they are from, are hampered by one of the most challenging geographical settings imaginable. The majority of the country is inhospitable desert, sandy plains which blend into seemingly never-ending swathes of beige scrub-land. If you fly over the country, mile after mile appears to be entirely empty, before you catch sight of a small settlement of huts or brick buildings, sometimes not even connected to the rest of the world by much of a road. The hilly areas are concentrated near the borders, most notably Jebel Marra in Darfur, in the west; the Nuba Mountains in South Kordofan, near the border with South Sudan; and a stretch of hills in the east, near the Red Sea. Sudan is extremely hot, regularly pushing 50°C in places.

Two great rivers flow into the country: the White Nile, moving powerfully from its Ugandan origin, through South Sudan, and up through the south of Sudan; and the Blue Nile, which descends rapidly from the Ethiopian highlands. The Blue and White Niles meet in Khartoum, the Sudanese capital. Once the Niles merge there, they flow together to Egypt, and the sea. Sudan's main agricultural areas are concentrated either side of the banks of these rivers, and in the fertile, irrigated lands in between the Blue and White Niles. In general the further south you travel, the more it rains, although some of the hilly areas in the north are an exception to this.[35] The desert has been creeping further south, and the dwindling rainfall is one of the many causes of the civil war in Darfur. The savanna near the new border with South Sudan is prized, but semi-nomadic groups like the Misseriya and the Rizeigat still travel every year to South Sudan to seek better grazing.

LIFE ON THE SUDAN-SOUTH SUDAN BORDER

The difficult geographical conditions are one of the reasons for the continued interdependence of those living either side of the new international border. A shared history, of conflict, trading and inter-marriage, has also joined the people together, even if the state they once all lived in has split in two.[36] For the more than 13 million people who live in the border states,[37] their relations with the people on the other side of the frontier are every bit as important as their relationship with the capital, if not more so.

Abdelaziz Hussain
Misseriya/Dinka cow owner, South Kordofan.

Abdelaziz Hussain feels he has been split in two alongside his country. His father was Sudanese; his mother is from South Sudan. Now his life is parcelled out between two nations, his heart divided by an international border. 'For me it is too hard because it is dividing families,' he says. 'These two peoples have been together for so long, and now the link has been broken. My family has been broken.' Abdelaziz, a short, stocky man, was born in 1964. His father was from the Misseriya, an Arab group based in Kordofan and Darfur, near the border with South Sudan.

Traditionally Misseriya own cows. They are part of a larger grouping, the *Baggara*, which loosely means cattle owners, as distinct from the *Abbala* or camel herders further north. Cows are the most important thing for the Misseriya, Abdelaziz explains, and often looking after them is the only thing they know how to do. Their area is under-developed; but their ties with the Khartoum government have enabled many Misseriya to obtain weapons, and an unspoken licence to raid South Sudanese areas and take what they find there. Sometimes this has involved taking slaves, including female ones; this is perhaps the major source of mixed Misseriya-South Sudanese children.

Abdelaziz now lives in Meiram, a frontier town. He owns fifty cows, making him relatively prosperous, though the colour on the crease of his shirt collar has faded with years of wear and sun; it looks like a line of white spray on a pale blue sea. If Abdelaziz needs money, he sells a cow, for 500 Sudanese pounds (a bit less than one hundred dollars) in Sudan, or 600 South Sudanese pounds on the other side of the border. Abdelaziz cannot imagine how else he could earn any cash. The Misseriya are often described as nomads. In fact, they usually have fixed homes, but spend several months every year travelling with their cattle to find pasture. These great treks push deep into South Sudan, and now have to cross an international border.

Abdelaziz takes a special pleasure from travelling to South Sudan as his mother is from the Dinka, the largest South Sudanese ethnic group. He speaks Dinka, as well as Arabic. Most people don't pick up on this dual heritage, but when they do, Abdelaziz's loyalties are sometimes called into question. 'This is a problem for me,' he sighs. 'They ask me "do you belong to the Dinka or the Misseriya?" because my skin is more black than some. I say I am Dinka or Misseriya, it is all the same for me.' In the immediate aftermath of separation the tensions between the two Sudans made the Misseriya's annual trek south particularly difficult. For Abdelaziz, it underlined how his life depends on both Sudans, like so many people on either side of the border.

DANCING LIKE AFRICANS TO ARAB MUSIC

The lives led by Sheikh Yagout, Mustafa, Hawa, Nagwa and Abdelaziz, a Sufi sheikh, a prosperous businessman, a tea lady, a development worker and a dual-heritage cow owner, could not be more different. This diversity of experiences and origins could have been an advantage few other states could boast. 'I believe Sudan is like a bouquet of flowers: each flower has its own beauty, but when you bring all these flowers together as a bunch there is symmetry, harmony and splendour',[38] is how the artist Rashid Diab puts it. More prosaically, he says that the Sudanese 'dance like Africans to Arabic music'.

All these varied peoples and cultures could have produced a confident nation that would bridge the gap between the Arab and African world more than just geographically. So far, that hasn't been the case.[39] Ethnic and religious discrimination have torn the nation apart. The secession of the southern provinces, and with it the end of the Southern Question, has not ended the need for an answer to Sudan's National Question: who exactly are the Sudanese, and how should Sudan define itself? It is argued over by Islamist politicians and their religious critics, secularists and ethnic nationalists, and dismissed as a matter they will have no say in by far too many of the Sudanese people.

SOUTH SUDAN

'If we split like groundnuts, the chicken will collect us all'.

Clement Wani, Governor of Central Equatoria

South Sudan is a state in search of a nation: a new country on the map, populated by people without a particularly strong common identity. Every year, inter-ethnic clashes kill hundreds or even thousands of people, the most visible sign of the tensions between different groups.[40] For decades the southern Sudanese were united in nothing so much as their hatred for the Sudanese. Now, as an independent country, they have to build a common identity on a much broader base than mere antipathy for the *Jallaba* (a pejorative term for northerners from the time of the united Sudan). This is no easy task. As Francis Deng wrote, years before South Sudan seceded, 'without the confrontation with the North, the still vivid history of rapacious invasions by northern slave raiders, and the more recent attempts by the post-independence governments to dominate the southern peoples, there would be no South as a viable political entity.'[41]

South Sudan's leaders are well aware of the difficulties facing them. 'We need to build a nation' is how one minister puts it.[42] The ethnic identities so many fall back on hamper the creation of a strong sense of a common South Sudanese purpose and destiny.[43] Others use more colourful language than the minister: 'Everyone is talking about unity, because unity is the backbone of the country,' the governor of Central Equatoria state, Clement Wani, told a local radio station.[44] 'If we split like groundnuts, the chicken will collect us all. Let us all get united. We are the children of South Sudan, and we are South Sudanese. If we get united, our martyrs will be happy, and they will help us in building a strong nation.'

Building blocks of remembered pain

The South Sudanese writer Victor Lugala says that the new nation will grow from a singular starting point: 'A South Sudanese is someone from an African identity, who has African roots.' Lugala, like many others, pushes back at what he feels was a systematic denigration of the southern Sudanese when the Sudans were one. 'In Khartoum, they used to tell us we had no culture,' he rails. 'We have a culture, we have dances, the oral tradition, we give our children names according to our ancestors.' Pride in a sense of being African, and a range of cultural practices often frowned upon by the northern elites in Khartoum, are components of the new national identity. This strong identification with an African culture is perhaps, in itself, a reaction, as Francis Deng has written: 'In the Sudanese context, the more the North asserts its Arabness, the more the South asserts Africanness as a counter-identity.'[45]

The academic Jok Madut Jok says that South Sudanese can refer to a succession of historical events, dating back to 1821, that served as symbols around which people rallied: 'Many were a reaction to negative things, like the slave trade, Turco-Egyptian occupation, against government or what used to pass as government, against the British.' In more recent times, Jok points to the (admittedly slow) integration of southern Sudanese into the civil service, which brought people from different regions and backgrounds together, as well as the unifying effects of two north-south civil wars. It is estimated half a million people died in the first conflict, and over two million in the second.[46] The vast bulk of the casualties were in southern Sudan, though many northern families suffered the pain of losing loved ones too.

By some estimates, the majority of the deaths in combat came in clashes between different southern Sudanese forces, rather than in fighting between the southern rebels and the Sudanese army.[47] This was largely due to Khartoum's policy of providing weapons to some groups in a deadly game of divide and rule. However, as in many wars, more people died from hunger, disease and other side-effects of the fighting than in battle itself. It is difficult to find a South Sudanese family that did not cry for a lost relative.

As well as the astonishing death toll, millions were displaced to northern Sudan, principally Khartoum. Here they picked up 'northern' cultural practices. Others fled the fighting to become refugees in neighbouring states. Overall at least 4.5 million southern Sudanese were displaced, inside and outside the country.[48] In the recent literature of South Sudan, there is a large sub-genre of 'Lost Boy' books. These are autobiographies, ghost-written or not, of young men who walked for months to flee the fighting, or to join the SPLA rebels and their battalions of child soldiers, facing unthinkable dangers and hardships along the way.[49] In South Sudan, the decades of war had a disastrous impact on education, the economy and the health services, as well as on the lives of those who survived the fighting.

No accurate description of the South Sudanese and their country can discount the effects of such trauma; yet the South Sudanese identity is also being built from this tragic history. The atrocities committed by the Khartoum government convinced southerners they had more in common than not, according to Jok. Yet many South Sudanese groups have bitter memories of fighting their southern neighbours. The wars brought groups together, and tore them apart; they changed the life of every single South Sudanese.

Mary Padar

Atuot mother and craftswoman, from Mapourdit, Lakes state

Mary Padar's life was transformed by marriage, and then swept in unimaginable directions by many years of war. She finally found stability in the freedom brought by peace. Mary was born in '1960-something'— she is not sure of the exact date—near Yirol, in the centre of what was then the southern part of Sudan. She is an Atuot, a small ethnic group with links to both the Nuer and the Dinka, South Sudan's biggest groups. The three groups are Nilotics, and traditionally cattle-herders.

Mary's early life was rural, like four out of five South Sudanese. Her family grew sorghum, sesame, groundnuts, green peas and beans. If there was a surplus it was sold, but the main focus was getting enough to eat. Life was generally peaceful, except when local conflicts over cattle broke out. Even after independence, cattle raiding is a serious concern in Lakes state. In January 2013, for example, at least twenty-five people were killed in clashes between rival cow-herders.[50] The situation in Jonglei state has been much worse: hundreds have died in a single day's fighting.[51]

In her village, Mary's home was a grass-thatched hut of mud walls and wooden poles. Like most girls at the time—and like Hawa in Darfur—Mary did not go to school. She did learn the art of bead-making from her mother: coloured beads are aligned on thread to make necklaces, corsets or other types of jewellery. Different colours are used depending on the age and sex of those who will wear them. Young men are given some before they get married. Women wear them too: 'during the time for celebrations, the young ladies put the beads on when they go to dance, so that the men admire them,' Mary explains. Her face is broad, and four scar lines depart from a point just above her eyes, and extend to each side of her face. There are similar patterns on her arms, legs and stomach.

Mary doesn't smile that often, but when she does it usually turns into a light, rhythmic laugh that conveys youthful energy. She put all that force into a dangerous activity: making food for the SPLA rebels who had begun to fight Khartoum. She might well have been killed if she had been caught. Mary says that it wasn't a difficult decision to take. 'People were fighting on my behalf, so I had to help. They were fighting for our liberation.' Mary's brush with the war became a full-time engagement. The soldiers had no money to pay her, but they promised training and some cash once the war came to an end.

When peace eventually arrived, in 2005, Mary was enrolled in a programme to reintegrate members of the rebel groups into society. Initially she struggled to get by on a stipend of one hundred Sudanese pounds a month, around thirty-five dollars. Salvation came in the big city, Juba, through a village skill Mary had abandoned many years previously. A centre called Roots was set up to promote South Sudanese cultures. Mary found she could make money through bead-work. In particular, she was able to piece together a traditional corset, an ability many had lost during the war years. She proved to be so skilful that she was invited to an international craft festival in Santa Fe. 'My trip to America was wonderful,' Mary says, smiling again. 'I saw different things. America was very developed, and my place is not like that.'

Mary has given birth to eleven children, though three have since died. The bead money enables her to send them to school, some in Juba and some in Mapourdit, her home village. She now lives in a house on the outskirts of Juba, near the *Jebel* or mountain whose jagged outline looms over the city. A neem tree provides shade in the courtyard, and here she can afford a tin roof, and meat in the supper stew. It's quite a change from her childhood. This recent and relative prosperity has come through the 2005 CPA, a peace deal between the governing NCP and the SPLM. It eventually led to South Sudan's independence. Mary is aware what she and her country have obtained is still as vulnerable as a grass roof in a storm: 'My fear is that we have a fragile peace with the Khartoum government. I fear we could go back to war. We as South Sudanese, we need peace, but we do not know what our neighbours think.'

RELIGION

While there are competing claims about whether more South Sudanese follow Christianity or traditional religions (with Muslims certainly a minority, but very much present), there can be no debating the importance of faith in South Sudanese life. Studies of the religious thought of the Nuer, Dinka and Azande from the Anglo-Egyptian period are among some of the most well known in the anthropology of religion. The folds in South Sudan's religious tissue are too numerous to examine here, but traditional beliefs have survived the arrival of Christianity and Islam. This is despite many efforts at conversion. In the late 19th and early 20th centuries, the British colonial officers allocated different parts of southern Sudan to different strands of the Christian faith.[52] The missionaries provided basic education, often to serve the perceived greater goal of learning the scriptures. Gradually they won over many of the southern Sudanese to their faith. Following Sudan's independence in 1956, there was a continuing effort, which fluctuated in intensity, to convert the southern Sudanese to Islam. Some did. More still flocked to the Christian churches to mark their opposition.

Paride Taban
Bishop Emeritus of Torit, living in Kuron, Eastern Equatoria.

For a man who has devoted his life to God and reconciling his fellow men, Paride Taban's entry into the Church owed a lot more to the sartorial than the spiritual. On his way to sit an exam, he caught sight of several young priests in training, and their striking cassocks and sashes gripped his attention. 'I asked them "From where did you boys come?" "The seminary," they said. "Give me the spelling of that seminary!" I said.' Once he passed his exam, his lobbying for a sash of his own succeeded. It was only after joining the seminary that his 'true vocation' to become a priest emerged. Initially Paride's family wasn't happy, particularly his Muslim father. In the end his parents relented, and converted to Christianity before his ordination in 1964, just as the Sudanese President Ibrahim Abboud was expelling all the Christian missionaries from southern Sudan.

Over the next 40 years, Paride served the Catholic Church and the southern Sudanese people in some of the most difficult conditions imaginable. During the first civil war, he and other priests were arrested and accused of transporting weapons to the southern rebels. Only the brilliance of the southern lawyer Abel Alier, who was later to become the united Sudan's vice president, proved that the weapons had been planted on the priests by the Sudanese army. During the second civil war, Paride lost count of the number of times the area he was in was bombed by the Sudanese air force. When the SPLA captured Torit, Paride, by then the bishop of the diocese, was held captive for more than three months; securing his freedom became an international *cause célèbre*. He is not a bitter man, but he believes that Khartoum created huge suffering: 'the government wanted to turn the whole south Islamic. It caused two decades of civil war'.

Everywhere Paride went, he worked to educate those around him, driven by his belief that the church should 'develop the whole human being, body and soul'. The church offered services the central government and the rebels could not or would not provide. Paride set up open-air classrooms for people who had been displaced. When he visited the US he returned with tents, and his own saved him from rain, snakes and scorpions. His fame, as a man of principle and one prepared to criticise both the government and the SPLA, grew.

Paride travelled all over the world to lobby for peace in South Sudan. With a jewelled cross hanging from a silver chain around his neck, and a white and grey beard partly masking an exceptionally strong jaw, he certainly looks like the campaigning man of religion he has become. When the CPA was signed in 2005, Bishop Taban said the first prayer. He realised that even the Sudanese President, Omar al Bashir, knew who he was. 'Omar was also there, and he asked: "Is that the very stubborn Bishop Taban? But today he prayed for me, he prayed well!"' Paride remembers, laughing.

A religious nation scared of religious nationalism

The writer Victor Lugala is one of those who thinks that Christianity has lost a little of its hold following the end of the northern Sudanese 'occupation'. Go to any market, he says, and 'people are drinking beer, people are dancing—churches are shrinking in the markets. The music has swallowed the preaching!' But Christianity, apart from its spiritual importance, is linked in the eyes of many to 'civilisation'. It is seen as intrinsically tied to education and the economic and social opportunities it brought and continues to bring. The South Sudanese elite are more likely to be Christian than the rural poor, and President Salva Kiir often preaches in the church he attends in Juba.

For many South Sudanese, Christianity also benefited from a very particular selling point: they believe that the Bible mentions their ancestors. Verse 18:2 of Isaiah speaks of 'a people tall and smooth-skinned, a people feared far and wide, an aggressive nation of strange speech, whose land is divided by rivers.'[53] The South Sudanese say that this is a reference to the dark-skinned (and famously tall) Nilotics living around the White Nile river. The description of an aggressive nation is held to refer to South Sudan's long and tragic history of conflict.[54] For many believers, the Bible even foretold the running up of the new country's flag: the following verse of Isaiah, 18:3, says that the 'people of the world' will see when a 'banner' is raised.

Christianity is sometimes held up as a source of unity for the new nation. At hearings on the interim constitution, church groups argued against the separation of state and religion.[55] Manyang Parek von Chief Parek, a minor opposition politician from a well-known family, is rarely seen without his hat draped in a brightly coloured cloth, which is adorned with a cross. He believes that Christianity can provide a common ethical framework for South Sudan. 'Don't forget we are a tribal society. We need an ideology to bring us together, a Christian ideology. You get John in Wau, you get John in Juba, and so on. It is the only ideology that can bring us together.' However, Muslims said the same before the country split in two, and the scars of Sudan's attempt to unify a divided nation through a single faith make many South Sudanese wary of anything other than a secular state.

ETHNIC DIVISIONS

Von Chief Parek's diagnosis of a society divided on ethnic lines is, though, an accurate one. There is some debate over just how many ethnic and linguistic groups live within South Sudan's borders. The Gurtong Project, a website set up to blunt the sharp edges between communities, identifies sixty-four South Sudanese peoples.[56] The government of South Sudan talks of at least sixty-six,[57] divided into three larger groupings: the Nilotics, the Nilo-Hamitics, and the South-Western Sudanics. Others think the figure is even higher.[58] The picture is muddied by the sub-divisions among many of the ethnic groups, some of which speak sufficiently different dialects as to make mutual comprehension difficult. Competition with the neighbours over land, cattle and scarce resources has led to conflict as long as memory goes back, fluctuating with the seasons and according to very local dynamics. Of course, in many areas differences do not create hostilities.

In 2004 Bishop Paride Taban decided to set up a peace village, a place to encourage some of South Sudan's different ethnic groups to live in harmony. 'The worst idea we have in South Sudan is tribalism,' he says. He believes that too many South Sudanese grow up separated from their neighbour 'on little islands', by which he means in their isolated cattle camps. His project eventually flowered from the seeds of his own childhood. Paride was born in Opare, not far from Nimule in Eastern Equatoria. If pushed, he will say he is from the Madi ethnic group, and trot out a well-worn joke: 'Madi, not the Mahdi.'

Paride grew up in a town called Katire, enveloped in the rolling beauty of the Imatong mountains. The British colonisers had set up a sawmill, and brought people from all over Sudan to work there. In Katire, all the different groups and faiths got on well, and that experience became Paride's inspiration. 'It was very difficult for the Holy Father,' Paride remembers. 'He thought I was being crazy. I had eight years left as a priest. They sent me to a psychiatrist to see if I was sound!' The psychiatrist confirmed he was sane, and so Paride was released from his duties. He felt there could be no greater mission in South Sudan than reconciling feuding communities and helping them live prosperously together.[59]

Nilotic pastoralists

South Sudan's two largest ethnic groups are the Dinka and the Nuer. These Nilotics are traditionally pastoralists for whom cattle are a vital resource.[60] At one point southern Sudan was divided into three provinces: Equatoria, in the south, Bahr el Ghazal, in the north-west, and Upper Nile in the north-east.[61] The Nilotics are predominant in what were Bahr el Ghazal and Upper Nile. Traditionally they spend the rainy season in their villages, where they grow crops, before they head out to cattle camps near rivers during the dry season. Decades of conflict and the lure of various economic opportunities mean that many Dinka and Nuer now live in towns all over South Sudan, and abroad. Although they have 'closely-related languages and similar ways of life',[62] clashes between different subsections of the Nuer and the Dinka have been common for centuries, as has fighting within each ethnic group. These deadly divisions highlight the great nation-building challenge South Sudan faces.

The Shilluk are a similar but smaller group, who mainly live on the west bank of the White Nile, between Malakal and Renk. Unlike the Dinka and the Nuer, the Shilluk have sometimes been described not so much as an ethnic group but as a political kingdom, a group of peoples under the rule of a *Reth* or king.[63] All these identities, at least linguistically, are a foreign construct: the Dinka actually refer to themselves as Jieng or Muonyjang, the Nuer call themselves Naath, and the Shilluk's name for themselves is Chollo. These three ethnic groups have tended to dominate the many smaller groups living around and alongside them.

Gatgong Jiech
Nuer cowherder, Leer, Unity state

Gatgong Jiech still dreams of getting an education, but at fifty he accepts it probably will never happen. With his skinny legs protruding from yellow swimming shorts, and his shiny blue sleeveless sports shirt, there is something of the schoolboy to him. But this is belied by the grey hairs on his head, and the six horizontal scar lines running across his forehead, one of the traditional ways to show a Nuer has become a man. He started looking after his father's cows as a youngster, and he has done little else since.

Several of his ten children head out every morning to escort the cows to water. They run after each other through the long grass, practising throwing a spear, and imagining how they will ward off cattle-rustlers.

Gatgong did exactly the same, through the very same fields, forty and more years ago. However, his older kids are at school. This is one of the benefits that came when the CPA was signed. 'They must all go, boys and girls. One of them can become a doctor, or a priest, or an engineer,' Gatgong says. His eighteen-year-old son, Kueh Teny, interjects 'I'll be President!' and then chuckles at the idea. Perhaps it is not too far-fetched: South Sudan's first Vice President Riek Machar Teny was from Leer.

Education is not the only benefit the CPA brought: the whole family celebrated when South Sudan declared its independence. To mark the happy event Gatgong called his baby girl Nya-Juba, after South Sudan's capital.[64]

The life Gatgong envisions for his children is very different from his own. When he was a teenager his front teeth were removed, with a fish spear, as one of the rites marking the end of childhood. When he was around twenty it was time for the *gaar* or facial markings, which identify Gatgong as a member of the Dok Nuer. 'I was placed on the floor, lying down, between a man's legs. I was cut with a *ngom* (a small and very sharp blade). It was very painful!' he says, then laughs, three decades having soothed the ache. 'I was very happy, because now I was a *wut*, a man. I didn't care about the pain. I was respected.' For the first time girls noticed him. Four years later, he married his first wife. Since Gatgong was marked, it has fallen out of fashion. Nuer intellectuals and government officials argued that the ritual scars were out of place in the modern world. Gatgong says that he came to realise the practice was wrong: the marks don't make the man. 'My children have no *gaar*.'

Gatgong hopes some of his children will grow up wealthier than him, but it's not in his nature to complain. 'I have ten cows, I am not rich, but I'm alive!' he says. Gatgong will obtain many more cows when his daughters become old enough to get married. 'Cows are important to us for so many things,' he explains. 'If you have no food, then you can sell them. It is also very important if you are getting married.' He paid for both his wives with cows. These days the dowry can cost fifty or sixty cows, so young men need contributions from relatives and even friends if they are to get married. It is also one of the reasons for South Sudan's debilitating cattle-raiding problem.

Gatgong, like many Nuer and Dinka men, sings songs to praise his most beautiful cows. Cows are more than just walking wealth: great efforts are made to present them at their best. Gatgong is an expert at shaving the horns of young bulls. Using a sharp spear or knife he shaves one horn to encourage it to grow straight up, and another to make it curve down. One day he will teach his sons the trick. Early anthropological work on the Nuer crystallised an image of men obsessed with cows at the expense of almost everything else.[65] They still provide an alternate source of wealth: a man can live in the poorest of huts, but is considered rich if he owns many cows. However the Nuer, like other groups, make up a dynamic, changing society. As Gatgong remarks, 'We have seen that if we sell our cows we can even buy cars!'[66]

Like many people in South Sudan, Gatgong no longer follows the religion of his father. 'I am a Christian now,' he explains. 'My father followed our traditional religion, but after the Christians came we all went to church. The Gods we worshipped were banned.' Gatgong's father believed in Biel, who protects cows, and the female prophet Nyakulang. 'But we found out there was only one God in heaven,' Gatgong says, 'so we left our gods and shifted to the one God.' All the same, Nuer prophets still carry great weight, particularly in rural areas, and traditional beliefs often coexist with Christianity. While Christians believe the Bible predicted South Sudan's independence, many Nuer make similar claims for the prophet Ngungdeng Bong.[67]

The Equatorians

In the south and south west, a number of groups including the Azande and the Bari-speaking peoples have traditionally been sedentary farmers.[68] It is no surprise that the symbol of Western Equatoria, the Azande heartland in South Sudan,[69] is the pineapple. The Azande are considered to be the third largest ethnic group in the country.[70] In the 18th century an Azande 'conquering aristocracy', the Avongura, created an empire that incorporated people from other groups[71]—yet another sign of the fluidity of some ethnic boundaries.

The Bari-speakers, which include the Bari themselves, as well as the Mundari, the Kuku, the Madi and the Pujulu, form the biggest group in Central Equatoria, and South Sudan's capital Juba is on Bari land. In Eastern Equatoria, groups like the Lotuko, Didinga and Acholi tend to practice a mix of agriculture and livestock rearing.[72] Although the Azande are part of the South-Western Sudanic groups, and the Bari, for example, are from the Nilo-Hamitic peoples, to use the government's classification, a regional identity exists too. People sometimes describe themselves as 'Equatorian', in contrast to the Nilotics from the Greater Upper Nile and Greater Bahr el Ghazal regions to the north.

WOMEN

South Sudanese society is male-dominated, just like Sudan's. Women are expected to marry, not least because this brings wealth to the family. In many communities, particularly among Nilotics like Gatgong Jiech's Nuer, dowries for girls are paid in cattle, and can be extremely expensive. Families tend to decide who their girls marry, and the wedding may happen when the girl has only just reached puberty. The SPLM has promised to improve the status of women in society. A quarter of all seats in parliament are reserved for women, as is the case in Sudan, but President Salva has publicly committed to raising this to 35 per cent. In a speech marking International Women's Day in 2013, he also said girls must go to school, and spoke out against early marriage. The SPLM's determination to give women the same opportunities as men seems genuine, but it runs up against deeply ingrained traditions.

Mary Boyoi
Singer and human rights activist, Pibor, Jonglei state.

Mary Boyoi certainly looks like a star. Wearing tight blue jeans and a sparkly purple top, which matches her open shoes, she fiddles with a smart phone as she talks. When she becomes animated, the tight curls framing her head shake in unison. Her prominent cheekbones and wide smile are familiar from the posters all over Juba advertising her latest album. The launch was sponsored by a mobile phone company, a bank and an insurance company. Italian producers are keen to make her a star in Europe too, blending her voice with Eurohouse beats. In South Sudan she is better known for R&B-tinged songs calling for peace, or talking about love. Her 'Single Ladies' number, a South Sudanese version of Beyonce's worldwide smash, is so popular people that shout out 'Single Lady' at Mary when they spot her across the street.

That's a very bitter-sweet compliment. Mary was forced into marriage when she was still a young girl. It is an experience she refers to as rape. Under-aged marriage is relatively common among the Murle, the small ethnic group in Jonglei state which Mary comes from. 'He was very much older than me,' Mary says. She begins to cry, tears forming along her eye-lashes and then rushing down her cheeks. After a short pause, she con-tinues. 'I was only fourteen when he took me. I think he was thirty-five. It's very common, you can even give young girls to a man who is fifty.' Her husband took her to Nairobi, the Kenyan capital. According to Mary, he locked her in the house, and beat her until she almost died. Eventu-ally a friendly neighbour alerted the police, who broke into the house and saved her. It's not the only tragedy she has overcome, either. Years earlier, Mary's father had been killed as he tried to rescue his sister from cattle rustlers. Mary was only nine.

Mary has not let this litany of pain hold her back. She found work with Non-Governmental Organisations (NGOs), who were impressed with the English she had learnt in Kenya. One took her to Pibor, the main town in Murleland, where she was reunited with her mother. How-ever, her years in exile had changed her, as they have so many South Suda-nese. 'Everything was different. Even my own family started to look different to me,' she says. Nevertheless, Mary is proud of her identity as a Murle. She campaigns for better treatment for her people. Many Murle fought on the side of Khartoum during the civil war and the Murle have often clashed with the Nuer and Dinka in Jonglei. Both are groups with far greater influence in South Sudanese politics, and so the Murle often feel marginalised.

The Murle are divided into age groups, which play a very important role in society. Mary's age group, which extends roughly from 20 to 35, is called *Botot nya*, a wild bird. 'It's for men only,' Mary says. 'Women, we don't have a group, we go in the group of the men. Among my people women do not have voices.' Mary is an exception to that, or at any rate she is able to make her voice heard outside her community. It started with music. She began singing as a ten-year-old in church, and soon found she was able to compose songs.

She had never thought of it as a career, until her song about social problems in South Sudan began to get heavy play on local radio stations. Mary begins to sing some of the lyrics, about avoiding cattle-rustling: 'It is because of cows to get married, but there is a solution, it is education.' The song gifted her not one but two new careers. 'The United Nations (UN) invited me to so many events. They called me a peace activist.' Soon she became one. She accompanied ministers and even the vice president on tours to promote peace, and then for the 2011 referendum which resulted in South Sudan's independence. After that, Mary decided to sing more about love than politics.

GEOGRAPHY

The geography of the country has shaped occupations and identity. The pastoralists care for their herds in the ironstone plain of Bahr el Ghazal in the north-west, and in the grasslands of Upper Nile in the north-east. When it rains, the latter area turns into a clogging mud, the defining characteristic of what is known as black cotton soil.[73] Further south, people are more likely to be sedentary farmers. In Western Equatoria, the home of the Azande, for example, the soil is less treacherous. Plants, trees and crops grow quickly in the forested areas.

The White Nile, which arrives from Uganda in a broad surge, meanders through the capital Juba, and loses energy in one of the world's most impenetrable swamps, the Sudd. The Sudanese leaders in Khartoum tended simply to ignore this region, even though it was home to a large proportion of the southern Sudanese. The land surrounding the White Nile and its tributaries in the north of the country is also the site of South Sudan's greatest resource, oil.

The mountains of the south-east, and the forests of the south-west, as well as the swampland running through the heart of the country, have kept communities isolated from their neighbours. Before the creation of the united Sudan, this geographical setting favoured the creation of small self-contained polities rather than vast empires, and made it very difficult to develop the area. The impact of this was still apparent decades later, after South Sudan's independence.

BRINGING THE GROUNDNUTS BACK TOGETHER

Every South Sudanese life is different, of course. But here, more than in many countries, communities have been set against each other by geography and history. So what must the South Sudanese do to create a common identity? Joseph Abuk is a good man to ask. In the run-up to independence in July 2011, this cultural activist, poet and theatre director was on the committee charged with creating the new country's national anthem.

When I met him slightly over a year later, Abuk was wearing a jacket over a green polo shirt and a gold bracelet glittered on his arm. He was still glowing from the success of the Shakespeare play *Cymbeline*, which he translated into Juba Arabic, and then directed at a world Shakespeare festival in the UK. The play, which revolves around the tensions between a small nation which fought a bigger rival, was picked because of its strong resonance for the South Sudanese. For many years to come, the wars with Khartoum will form an inescapably large part of the new nation's identity.

Abuk believes that the national anthem, which was chosen from numerous poems[74] and then set to music, is a fitting representation of South Sudanese life, as well as the aspirations of the newly-independent nation. It had to be agreed on by Abuk's committee, and then defended with some 'noisy talking' in front of the 'military hierarchy' who run the country. The anthem is short—just eighty words—and the tune sounds both mournful and impossibly jaunty at the same time. As the independence celebrations approached, people all over the country practised the lyrics, including the millions of South Sudanese who do not speak English well or at all.

The anthem starts by praising and glorifying God: something all South Sudanese can agree on, it seems. South Sudan is described as a 'Land of great abundance'. A sense of both celebration and aspiration, following the decades of war and misery, is conveyed by the lines:

> And sing songs of freedom with joy
> For justice, liberty and prosperity
> Shall forever more reign.

The anthem's fourth theme remembers the sacrifices of the nation's martyrs, before the hymn to the new country ends, simply:

> We vow to protect our nation
> Oh God bless South Sudan.

It will take a many years and much work to construct a common identity in South Sudan, but the South Sudanese shouldn't be afraid of the challenge. As the national anthem points out, South Sudan wouldn't even exist without a sustained struggle against all the odds.

* * *

It is common to describe the Sudanese as Arab Muslims, and the South Sudanese as African Christians. In fact, this is a misleading shorthand.

Getting to grips with the many forms of ethnic and religious identity in both countries is necessary in order to understand the two Sudans. Racial and religious discrimination has contributed to Sudanese civil wars in Darfur, South Kordofan and Blue Nile. It was one of the main reasons for South Sudan's secession. The new country is fragmented: inter-ethnic clashes kill hundreds or even thousands each year, and building a cohesive nation is proving difficult. Both nations must find a way to see their staggering diversity as an asset, not a hurdle. This is not the only similarity. Religion plays a central part in life in the two Sudans. Women are poorer and less powerful than men in both countries. Last but not least, a shared past, inter-marriage, and the yearly descent of Sudanese cow-herders seeking grazing in South Sudan have created ties that separation could not break.

2

POLITICS

SUDAN

On 11 July 2012 Sudan's President, Omar al Bashir, opened a new sugar factory in White Nile state, several hours' drive south of Khartoum. The complex is in a remote spot, so to make sure the president had a good audience, more than thirty buses brought in people from other parts of the state; afterwards they would be given a good meal and cold cans of soda. All the same, more than half the crowd was made up of men in uniform, some from the Sudanese Armed Forces (SAF), and some from the state-sponsored militia known as the Popular Defence Forces (PDF). One of the PDF, almost certainly a new recruit, seemed to be no older than fourteen or fifteen; the sleeves of his camouflage uniform were rolled up to near the shoulder, scarcely touching his skinny arms. Men in drab safari suits prowled around, eyes flitting in every direction: these were members of the National Intelligence and Security Service (NISS), a feared body.

A marquee the size of an Olympic swimming pool kept the sun off the heads of the dignitaries, who competed to sit as near as possible to the president and one of his right hand men, Bakri Hassan Salih. The two were part of the small group which seized power in a coup in 1989, and had exercised it ever since. They had presided over a failed Islamist project, wars in southern, eastern and western Sudan, and the splitting up of the country, after the 2011 referendum in which southern Sudanese voted almost unanimously to secede. This speech, which came almost a year to the day after South Sudan's independence, saw Bashir and his regime at one of their lowest points. The president's prestige had been dented by the dismemberment of his country, and the 'rump state', as Sudan is sometimes called, had a failing economy, which was pushing growing numbers of people on to the streets to protest.

As Bashir approached the podium, a portly figure in a dark suit, the noise of the crowd swelled: '*Allahu akbar*'—God is greatest—they shouted. The president and his party are Islamists, which means that they believe society should be governed by laws derived from the Koran. Bashir began his speech, as he usually does, with religious exhortations; as he talked, printed posters of his own face stared back at him. The president made hardly any reference to the sugar factory, or the deteriorating state of the economy; instead he fulminated against 'foreign powers' and warned the protesters hoping for an extension of the Arab Spring that they would burn in the heat of the Sudanese summer. As always, he used the colloquial language of everyday Sudanese conversations. At every rhetorical highpoint, the crowd marked its approval: *Allahu akbar! Allahu akbar!*

The scene contained many of the components of Bashir's regime: the military; the security forces; a reliance on religion as something that appeals to almost every Sudanese, and is difficult to criticise; and the co-option of parts of the population, through coercion or patronage, to keep the regime in power. At one point during his speech, Bashir began to dance, waving his swagger stick in the air. The crowd went crazy, illustrating another, often ignored dimension: Bashir is more popular in Sudan than many in the West would like to believe. Yet for all the cheers, Bashir must have been aware that many of the ideologues, politicians and uniformed officers who made up his regime were also pushing for greater influence within it, and even, in some cases, thinking about how to replace him.

Losing the south

On 9 July 2011, South Sudan declared its independence, to scenes of jubilation in hastily named Freedom Squares and Independence Stadiums all over the new nation. Two north-south civil wars had cost an estimated 2.5 million lives,[1] and devastated many more. During the two-decade-long second conflict the SPLA had won control over most of the southern Sudanese countryside, with the government remaining in charge of garrison towns and some of the surrounding areas. In January 2005, the CPA was signed in Naivasha, Kenya.[2] The accord gave the SPLA's political wing, the SPLM, de facto control over all of southern Sudan, almost 50 per cent of the oil revenue generated on its territory, and the promise of a referendum on southern Sudan's future in 2011.

Both parties were meant to make unity attractive to the people; both signally failed to do so. The SPLA/M's leader John Garang de Mabior died in a plane crash six months after the CPA was signed. His vision of a 'New Sudan', a democratic country benefiting all of its citizens regardless of their race or religion, and in which southern Sudan would remain a vital part of the republic, disappeared with him. The nearly 99 per cent vote for separation by southern Sudanese in January 2011 seems, with hindsight, like a confirmation of the inevitable.

While the South Sudanese danced and drank to commemorate the birth of their new country, one of Bashir's relatives held his own party. Tayyeb Mustafa, Bashir's maternal uncle, and a self-confessed hardliner,[3] organised celebrations for Sudan's own 'independence day' in Khartoum. Men in black waistcoats and white *jallabiya*s jumped over swirling swords to a frenetic drumbeat, while the onlookers clicked their fingers and praised Allah. Separation corrected a 'historical mistake' made by the British, Tayyeb said: southern and northern Sudan should never have been part of the same country. Now Sudan would be almost all Muslim, and Tayyeb was happy his country was rid of its troublesome southerners, who Tayyeb believed had been 'a poisonous thorn in our heart'.

Tayyeb's reaction might well have put him in a minority: many ordinary Sudanese were sad that their country had been split in two. They blamed Bashir and the NCP. The Sudanese often proudly reminded people they were 'Africa's biggest country, a million square miles'; neither point was true after 9 July 2011. South Sudan's secession also deprived Sudan of three-quarters of the daily oil production, sending the economy into free-fall, with disastrous consequences for many Sudanese.

Already Bashir was treated as a pariah by the West, in particular because of the International Criminal Court (ICC) indictments for alleged genocide, war crimes and crimes against humanity in another Sudanese civil war, in Darfur. This hadn't always dented his popularity in Africa or the Arab world, or even among the Sudanese. The ICC's charges were cleverly portrayed as an assault on Sudanese sovereignty and on Islam. Nevertheless, after more than two decades in power marked by continuous war and countless human rights abuses, Bashir's political capital was dangerously low. Separation diminished it even further. Sudanese opposition politicians and rebel commanders, and some of South Sudan's leaders, sensed that this was the moment when Bashir might fall. This chapter will show how Bashir relied on all of the elements of his regime, the military, security, Islamists and political pragmatists, to stay on his perch.[4] It will also explain how all these different factions were pushing for influence and even power, so that one of the greatest threats to Bashir came from within his own unwieldy coalition.

THE PRESIDENT

Over the years, Bashir became increasingly central to the regime, as perhaps the only person in every circle of the Venn diagram of Sudanese power.[5] Omar Hassan Ahmad al Bashir was born on 1 January 1945 to working class parents in the rural village of Hosh Bannaga, near Shendi, to the north of Khartoum. After moving to the capital, he joined the army in order to support his younger siblings, according to a source close to him.[6] His distinguished service fighting alongside the Egyptians in the 1973 Arab-Israeli War won him rapid promotion up the ranks.[7] Later, he took part in the war against the SPLA, like every Sudanese officer.[8] At the time the Sudanese military had the reputation of being hard-drinking womanisers, although Bashir's supporters insist he is a religious man, who never misses prayers and fasts twice a week.[9]

The bloodthirsty dictator, as he is often portrayed in the West, is known to his compatriots as an inveterate dancer. If he made a speech without jigging around, people would immediately assume he was sick. In one video, which was widely shared on Sudanese websites, Bashir can be seen dancing at a wedding, surrounded by gently gyrating women;[10] this is exactly the sort of scene many of the hardliners in his movement find abhorrent.[11] Bashir is seen as hospitable and sociable, in the best Sudanese tradition, often attending weddings and funerals, and even visiting sick opponents. The President is also, according to those who know him, a funny man. 'He tells a lot of dirty jokes, actually,' says the source who works with him.

In public, the president can be amusing too, and certainly knows how to excite a crowd. Bashir gives two types of speeches: in the first, he sticks to the script; in the second, he improvises, often to the delight of the listeners. In the run up to the 2010 elections, he warned international observers that 'if they interfere in our affairs, we will cut their fingers off, put them under our shoes, and throw them out.'[12] This sort of rhetoric, usually framed as defiance to Westerners who are determined to destroy Islam, is surprisingly popular, making it harder for internal opponents of the president to gain any traction.

It also reveals the harder edge to his character. Bashir is stubborn to a fault, and his fiery language is not restricted to his speeches. A visitor to the presidential palace told me that he saw Bashir fly into a rage and loudly denigrate some of his staff.[13] If he is pushed in one direction, by Sudanese public opinion or meddlesome Westerners, Bashir is more likely to choose the opposite course. Above all, his long period in charge has shown he is prepared to do anything to stay in the presidential palace. Under Bashir's watch, human rights have been routinely abused, dissent squashed, and brutal ethnic militias used to fight off rebellions. This ruthlessness, combined with a fair amount of political cunning, helps explain why Bashir has stayed in power longer than anyone else in Sudanese history.

The one area that truly exercises Bashir is regime security, and he gets briefings nearly every day from NISS.[14] To Hafiz Mohamed, the head of the rights group Justice Africa Sudan and a strong critic of Bashir, the president's 'only interest is staying in power'. Bashir's involvement in day-to-day affairs has fluctuated, but his presence at the very heart of the regime never has. This is because of his rare ability to appeal to the military, the security organs, and the NCP's Islamists and pragmatists. This sometimes goes to his head: even the source close to him, who is an admirer, admits that 'too many people tell him he is indispensable'.

A military-Islamist coup

Bashir was a relatively unknown army officer when he overthrew the democratically-elected prime minister, Sadig al Mahdi, on 30 June 1989. Bashir's long years in the presidential palace can be split into two periods. For the first decade, he was nominally in charge, but in reality the Islamist ideologue Hassan al Turabi, who masterminded the coup, was calling the shots; Bashir even swore an oath of allegiance to Turabi in December 1989.[15] In the second phase, from 1999, Bashir has been in full control.

Soon after the coup, Turabi imposed a more stringent form of *sharia* law, and the morality police oversaw every aspect of society.[16] Many people were flogged for making or consuming alcohol. The white-bearded Turabi, who has a disconcerting, high-pitched laugh, also invited Osama bin Laden and other radicals to live in Sudan.[17] The Islamists' stern vision of society often alienated the tolerant northern Sudanese. Sudan's most famous writer, Tayeb Salih, had vividly depicted the drinking and crude language used in a Sudanese village in his masterpiece, *Season of Migration to the North*.[18]

"We've heard," said my grandfather, "that Bint Majzoub's cries of delight had to be heard to be believed."

"May I divorce, Hajj Ahmed," said Bint Majzoub, lighting up a cigarette, "if when my husband was between my thighs I didn't let out a scream that used to scare the animals tied up at pasture."[19]

The novel was briefly banned in Sudan in the early 1990s, at the height of the government's moralising drive. Salih wrote a famous article about Turabi's hardliners, who seemed to him so different from the rest of Sudanese society: 'Where did these people come from?' he asked.[20]

Turabi's revolution had to be imposed, and so the internal security forces were beefed up. Opposition parties were banned, trade unions neutered,[21] and thousands of people 'disappeared' in the infamous Ghost Houses, which quickly acquired 'a fearsome reputation for bestial interrogation, torture of every conceivable means, and mock executions, as well as the use of drugs, electric shock, and death.'[22] Many of the most educated Sudanese fled the country. From the early 1990s onwards the security forces, along with the military and the Islamists, were the key components in Turabi's coalition.

Under Turabi and Bashir, Sudanese society was militarised too: the paramilitary PDF was set up, and the new recruits received religious indoctrination along with their military training. Young men flocked to carry out *jihad* or holy struggle in southern Sudan, prompted by TV shows extolling the war's martyrs and their celestial rewards. The 1990s are recalled with great horror by the South Sudanese, and many Sudanese too. The impact of this period persists to this day: even two decades later the school uniforms worn by Sudanese children are camouflage prints. Turabi sees himself as a moderate reformer, but he presided over the most hardline and brutally transformational period in post-independence Sudanese history.

In one key way, the *Ingaz* or Salvation regime did not bring about radical change at all: like every previous Sudanese government, it has been dominated by the northern elite, and in particular people originally from the Nile valley north of Khartoum. In essence, this meant the Three Tribes: the Danagla, the Jaaliyin and the Shaigiya. Bashir's mother is from the Jaaliyin,[23] and First Vice President Ali Osman Taha is Shaigi. The northern region accounted for barely 5 per cent of the population, but between 1954 and 1999 it was claimed that well over half of the ministers came from there.[24] Bashir's fifteen man National Salvation Revolutionary Command Council, which was set up when he seized power in 1989, was dominated by ten northerners, including Bashir himself.

In 1999, Bashir, to general surprise, won a power struggle with Turabi.[25] The Islamist movement's *éminence grise* would spend much of the next decade in prison; in or out of jail he was Bashir's strongest critic. The war in the south had stretched resources, and Turabi's grand dreams, undercut by the pervasive human rights abuses, had led only to international isolation, including US sanctions.[26] After Turabi's departure, the Islamists put aside any great ambitions of remaking society and providing a model for the rest of the Muslim world.

From this point on, although they framed every policy decision as an Islamist one, staying in power became the main goal for Bashir and his supporters, even if they included noted Islamists like Taha and Ghazi Saleheddin Atabani.[27] The pragmatists had joined the ideologues, the soldiers and the security agents. Disgruntled Islamists began to say that the government had lost its way.[28] However from 1999, an oil boom allowed Bashir's NCP to spread wealth around. Patronage bought off a lot of dissenters, even among those who had criticised the government's new direction. That became much harder in 2011, once the oil-rich south seceded.

THE MILITARY FLEX THEIR MUSCLES

If you drive through Khartoum, it's impossible to miss the new Ministry of Defence buildings just to the north of the airport. The multi-million dollar tower blocks are a mix of light grey concrete, and reflective dark blue windows; but the real distinctive feature is the design of the buildings themselves. The army headquarters is a fortress; the navy building looks like a ship, the walls curving to a prow; and the air force is housed, naturally enough, in a stocky plane, complete with wings. Outside this architect's joke, which spreads a martial shadow over the surrounding roads, is a statue recalling Sudan's triumphs. It is simple in concept: a hand with two fingers stretched upwards into a V-for-victory sign. However if you approach it from the other direction, along the new slip road, the statue looks very much like a British insult: two giant fingers up to the rest of the world.

The military have always been a key part of Bashir's ruling coalition.[29] Chief among the military stalwarts are Bakri Hassan Salih and Abdel Rahim Hussein, both of whom have served as interior minister and as defence minister, among other roles. Bashir even tells a joke about how close he is to Abdel Rahim:

Somebody came up to me and said he had had a wonderful dream last night, in which he saw me in paradise. I said 'Thank you, but let me ask you something: was Abdel Rahim with me?' The man said no, he wasn't. I told him it couldn't have been me then![30]

Like Bashir, Abdel Rahim is wanted by the ICC for alleged crimes committed in Darfur.

In the period just before and just after Sudan split in two, the military elbowed the other components of Bashir's coalition out of the way. Several sources say the military did not seek instructions from the politicians before sending their tanks into the disputed Abyei region in May 2011.[31] SAF's assault overcame the small South Sudanese contingent in the area, and forced more than 100,000 people to flee. Around this time the men in uniform also began to play a more prominent role in the negotiations with South Sudan, led by Defence Minister Abdel Rahim.

The Islamist Ghazi, who was a presidential adviser at the time, confirms the politicians' powerlessness in the period after separation: 'politicians and the political institutions within the country are moving backward, actually what's going to the fore now, leading the country through the decisions, priorities, budgets and so on is the military and the security,' he says.[32] According to Ghazi, who has himself been near the centre of power since 1989, questioning the priorities of the military or putting forward a reform agenda in the military-dominated post-separation period was seen as 'an act of treason'.

THE POWER OF THE ISLAMIST BRAND

The pendulum may swing back towards the politicians and the Islamists, but whoever is in charge within Bashir's uneasy coalition relies on an appeal to Islamic identity, repression, and the co-option of parts of the opposition and society as a whole to stay in power. The president and his supporters use Islamist rhetoric at every opportunity, hoping to give their political movement the force of their faith. Opponents are regularly called 'communists', implying that they are unbelievers.

At a speech in late 2010 in the eastern town of Gedarif, Bashir laid out a terrifying future for non-Muslims: 'If southern Sudan secedes, we will change the constitution and at that time there will be no time to speak of diversity of culture and ethnicity,' the president said. '*Sharia* and Islam will be the main source for the constitution, Islam the official religion and Arabic the official language.' Bashir also defended police who had been shown flogging a woman in a much-discussed video which had been posted on YouTube. 'If she is lashed according to *sharia* law there is no investigation. Why are some people ashamed? This is *sharia*,' he said.[33]

Bashir's statement against 'diversity of culture and ethnicity', and his promise to impose an even tougher form of *sharia*, went down extremely badly in the Nuba Mountains, one of the last parts of the country where there are lots of non-Muslims. When Nagwa Konda, the Nuba development worker, heard Bashir's speech, it made her scared and angry.

This has really changed the position of many Nuba people. Even if they are Muslim or NCP, they disagree completely with this statement. Many of them changed their direction from supporting the NCP. This has opened their eyes: he does not want anyone who is not Arab.

If Bashir did not accept Sudan's diversity, Nagwa warned, South Kordofan would become 'another Darfur'. Sure enough, by June of the following year the region was at war.[34]

The NCP felt Nagwa and the other Nuba were the least of its concerns. Bashir played the religious card in part because of a fear that many Sudanese Muslims no longer saw the NCP as all that religious. People may have their doubts about the politicians, but they are loyal to the faith, and for years the NCP's genius had been to conflate the two. Over the party's long period in power, however, the success of this approach had diminished. In the run-up to South Sudan's independence, there was considerable discontent about the pervasive corruption and human rights abuses, which are forbidden by Islam. In the aftermath of separation, the NCP was frequently criticised by Islamists, from both inside and outside the party.

Tayyeb Mustafa, the president's uncle, often spoke out against the way-wardness of his fellow Islamists. He told me that there was corruption in the government, and a lack of democracy: 'there are some practices which are against Islam,' he concluded.[35] Further criticism came in a series of memoranda written by disaffected Islamists, some of which Tayyeb published in his newspaper *Al Intibaha*.[36] Religious fundamentalists like Abu Zaid Mohamed Hamza, the leader of the Salafist[37] group Ansar al Sunna, felt that the more than two decades of Islamist governance had not met his expectations. 'The government hasn't done anything' to implement *sharia* properly, Abu Zeid said.

In mid-November 2012, the Islamist intellectual Ghazi, who is often portrayed as a moderate, seemed poised to take the leadership of the Islamic Movement, the ideological heart of the Islamists, at its eighth general conference in Khartoum. He had the support of the Saihoon, or God-fearing wanderers, a new group which had written at least one of the memos. In the end, Ghazi decided not to run when it became clear a less reform-minded NCP loyalist was primed to win. Once more the NCP pragmatists had overcome the idealists.[38] My source close to President Bashir is one of the Islamists who are distressed at how things have turned out: 'The Islamists have failed,' he told me. Ideological politics had been replaced by factional fighting. 'We spend far too much time and energy just trying to stay in power.'

REPRESSION

The NCP survives in part by intimidation, and the weaker it gets, the more repressive it has to be. If the army's building looks like a castle, and the air force officers go to work in a colossal concrete plane, forever grounded on the runway, the NISS headquarters a few blocks away should look like giant electrodes; or so the joke goes.[39] While the military plays an ever larger role in the decision-making process, and the party uses the language of faith to shore up its political strength, NISS is responsible for dealing with any dissent.

The press is tightly controlled, and NISS often confiscates newspapers when it doesn't like an article. Cameramen filming demonstrations regularly have their cameras seized, and I was hit on three separate occasions while I covered protests.[40] According to one press freedom index, Sudan is among the ten most repressive countries in the world for journalists.[41] The opposition parties are targeted too: they struggle to make their voices heard on the state radio, and they are not allowed to hold rallies in public places. Any sign of disobedience in the universities or in the streets is clamped down on hard.

Yet after separation, some Sudanese felt fear retreating, like the shadow of a palm tree as the sun nears its zenith. One day in December 2011, a crowd gathered in an outdoor courtyard at the University of Khartoum, next to colonial-era buildings with elegant curved arches, to listen to Nafie Ali Nafie speak. Nafie is the deputy head of the NCP and a former head of national security. He is one of the most feared men in Sudan.

After Nafie's speech, Mohamed Hassan Alim, who is known to his friends as 'Boushi', took the microphone. He unleashed a torrent of barbed criticism, calling the supremely powerful Nafie a 'coward'. Boushi said NCP thugs had been appointed to political office. 'You dare talk about morality and Islam, Islam is innocent of you,' Boushi said. He accused Nafie of getting a plum job for his son, while Boushi, who has better qualifications, had been unemployed since 2007. 'How could a country be respectable when you're in charge?' Boushi asked.

When a mobile phone recording of the speech was uploaded to the internet, it created a sensation.[42] More than 200,000 people watched the clip in just a few days. The astonishing outburst made it seem as if the fear barrier had been breached, if not swept away entirely.[43] A few days later I went to see Boushi. As he walked towards the car I was in, dressed in a long white *jallabiya*, I could see he was concealing a knife in the loose sleeve of the garment. When he realised it wasn't a trap, and I wasn't an NISS agent, he relaxed, and led me to his house.

Over sweet milky tea, Boushi claimed that as an opposition activist he had often been arrested and tortured, including by being electrocuted, and stripped naked.[44] 'When you have been bitten by a snake once, you are not afraid to be bitten a second time,' he said. A few days later Boushi was arrested again: his hidden knife wasn't enough when several NISS agents arrived at his house. He was released, after more torture, following twenty-two days in detention. Reports by the US government and many others have made it clear Boushi's case was part of a pattern of massive human rights abuses.[45]

NCP officials, from Bashir down, always stress they won democratic elections in April 2010. In fact the polls were far from free and fair. Most of the main opposition parties boycotted the elections, giving the NCP an almost uncontested victory in northern Sudan. The opposition alleged there had been substantial gerrymandering, and then, on the day of the vote itself, electoral fraud, including members of the military being transported around in buses to vote in several locations. In one case, an election official secretly videoed his colleagues stuffing a ballot box with NCP votes.[46] After the clip went online, YouTube was blocked in Sudan for some time. The elections' flaws were obvious, but the international observer missions gave only muted criticism at best, out of a desire not to put the upcoming referendum at risk.[47]

Ironically, the NCP might well have won a real contest, given the diminished nature of the competition. The opposition, which largely comes from the same northern elite as the NCP, has already tried its hand at governing, with only limited success.[48] The main opposition parties can be divided into three categories: sectarians, Islamists and secularists. Sadiq al Mahdi's National Umma Party and the Democratic Unionist Party (DUP) fall into the first grouping. Both draw their strength from religious sects, the Umma from the Ansar or followers of the Mahdi, who now profess fealty to his descendant, Sadig; and the DUP from the Khatmiyya, who owe their political and religious loyalty to Mohamed Osman al Mirghani. I once saw a man from the Ansar drop to his knees and kiss the ground Sadig had just walked over.[49] Turabi's Popular Congress Party (PCP) is the main Islamist opposition party. The government feels particularly threatened by it, because many NCP members are suspected of secretly supporting Turabi, and because of the NCP's fear that Turabi best expresses the Islamist ideology that underpins the government's legitimacy.[50]

The final category, the secularists, contains a fading force and a banned one. The Communist party once possessed a powerful voice in Sudanese society, but is now only really popular among a few urban intellectuals.[51] SPLM-North, the northern wing of the rebels who won independence for South Sudan, only to find themselves on the other side of the new border, is much stronger. John Garang's New Sudan vision appealed to many northern Sudanese, as well as his fellow southern Sudanese. In 2005, Garang, the SPLM's leader, came to Khartoum for the first time after launching his rebellion, to celebrate the CPA. The reaction was overwhelming: hundreds of thousands of people, perhaps even more than a million depending on who you believe, came out to welcome him, and not just southerners.

Garang's death just three weeks later robbed his New Sudan vision of some of its potency, but by no means all of its supporters. SPLM-North also controlled territory in the Nuba Mountains and southern Blue Nile state that it never relinquished to Khartoum. However, SPLM-North has been tarred by the NCP as a party of the geographical margins, closely tied to the old enemy in South Sudan. As a result it has found it difficult to attract new supporters, particularly in the northern heartland. SPLM-North was banned in September 2011, with its armed wing already fighting the government in the two areas partly under its control, South Kordofan and Blue Nile. Hundreds of its supporters were locked up.

With SPLM-North removed as a political force,[52] the NCP turned its attention to neutralising the other parties politically. Turabi's unconditional hostility to Bashir ruled him out, but feelers were put out to the other major political leaders in an attempt to create a coalition government that would soften the blow of secession.[53] In the end, the Umma party refused to participate in government, but one of Sadig's sons was named as a presidential adviser, alongside one of Mirghani's. In November 2011, Mirghani announced that the DUP would join the government, to the fury of many of the party's members, in particular the youth wing.[54] The DUP's participation allowed the NCP to hail a broad-based government uniting to face Sudan's many problems. In practice, however, the DUP did not obtain any key ministries, and simply served to deflect some of the pressure from the NCP.

INTERNAL SPLITS

Over more than two decades, some of the regime's pragmatists have developed useful economic strategies; some Islamists have contributed to what is seen as a more moral society; and there are many military officers who have strong nationalist pride. Overall, though, Bashir's period in power has been a disaster for Sudan. The president, who holds all the different factions in check, will not be around forever. Bashir, who is just as weighed down as his country by the ICC indictment, has visibly aged.

At one ceremony in Darfur in February 2012, Bashir used his swagger stick, which he usually employs to enliven his dancing, to help him walk past the troop line-up at the airport. Ever the soldier, he shuffled in perfect time to the military band.

Bashir's health has been a concern. In October 2012, he had throat surgery in Qatar.[55] Officially this was to remove benign lumps called polyps, but the opposition was quick to speculate it was cancer. Bashir first talked about stepping aside at the 2008 NCP convention,[56] only for the ICC indictment to persuade him to stay on. He has since said on several occasions that he will not run in the 2015 elections. Whether Bashir respects this commitment or not, the battle to succeed him has been raging for some time.

The NCP headquarters, on a side street near Khartoum International Airport, gives a good idea of the main contenders. The aquamarine minaret of the complex's mosque towers above the office buildings. Outside, a ten metre long banner, put up around the time of secession, shows the NCP's best image of itself. There are photos of modern agriculture, a dam, and the impressive Khartoum skyline, pointing to the economic progress the party says it has brought. Over to the right are pictures of Sudan's ruling triumvirate: President Bashir, Ali Osman Taha, and Nafie Ali Nafie.

Taha is the First Vice President, a veteran Islamist politician who served Turabi for many years before breaking with his mentor. Nafie is a security officer, and a presidential aide, the man Boushi criticised so strongly in the famous YouTube video. Nafie and Taha are deputy chairmen of the NCP. Bashir, Nafie and Taha make up the main components of the regime: a soldier, a security officer and an Islamist politician. In August 2012, the NCP's Amin Hassan Omar told me that either Taha or Nafie was likely to replace Bashir eventually.

Bashir and Taha have not always been the best of friends. 'Everyone is aware of the conflict' is how my source close to the president puts it.[57] Taha's stock dipped when he negotiated the CPA, as many hardliners felt that he gave away too much. In 2006, Taha spent some time in apparent exile in Turkey.[58] Nafie was criticised when he signed an agreement with SPLM-North in July 2011.[59] There are some, like the well-connected opposition politician Mubarak al Fadil al Mahdi, who believe that both Nafie's and Taha's chances may have passed. 'Nafie is part of the security apparatus, but is not as important as he used to be, because the military are calling the shots,' he says. The same logic would also sideline Taha. There is also a growing feeling within the rank and file of the NCP that a younger, less tainted generation is needed; however, the old guard is not keen to move on.

Dealing with too-powerful pretenders

Salah Abdallah 'Gosh', the former head of NISS, is one of the most frightening men in a country not short of frightening men. Under Gosh, the security forces expanded so much that their military branch, rather than SAF, apparently played the central role in fighting off the attack on Omdurman by the Darfuri rebels JEM in 2008. The following year Bashir sacked Gosh as head of NISS, almost certainly because he had got too powerful.[60] It was a move many thought could never happen, given Gosh's knowledge of the regime's secrets, and support within the security apparatus. 'I thought there would be a coup within the hour', the source close to Bashir admitted to me. Instead, the president had judged his move to perfection, although he almost certainly needed the backing of the military (and maybe others from his inner circle) to pull it off.

On 22 November 2012, Gosh was one of several security and army officers who were arrested, and accused of conspiring to 'sabotage' the regime.[61] As always in Sudan, there were numerous theories about the apparent plot. Some felt Islamist reformers like the Saihoon were involved, and Gosh had perhaps been added to the list to make sure the public didn't sympathise with the plotters; others thought that Gosh was the real mastermind; while another view was that the government was getting rid of presumed dissidents, who may not have been actively plotting at all.[62] Whatever the truth was, the incident highlighted the dissatisfaction felt by many in security, the military and the NCP. The biggest threat to Bashir's regime may well come from within. However even when Bashir leaves, whether in peaceful circumstances or not, there is no guarantee this will alter the fundamental characteristics of the regime in Khartoum at all.

Too many interest groups

One of the inevitable consequences of the components of Bashir's coalition jockeying for power is that those in charge rarely speak with one voice. Ghazi complains that leading figures in the NCP take very different positions on the same issue on the same day. Sometimes this cacophony of opinions serve a useful purpose, allowing hardliners to threaten, while Bashir can appear to be more moderate (or the reverse). Yet it also reflects a discomforting fact: the more the different groups pull in different directions, the less anyone is sure who is really calling the shots.

The Islamists, the military, the security and the pragmatists all want to take decisions, and it is not always clear who is able to do so. Sometimes the differences are ideological, based around, for example, the military's strong sense that it is the guardian of national sovereignty, or the Islamists' desire to regulate society according to their interpretation of Islamic morality. Most often, though, these different power bases simply want to be in control.

'There is no centre of power at the moment, there is a diffusion of power,' explains Mahjoub Mohamed Salih, Sudan's most distinguished journalist. Salih began reporting in 1949 and covered Sudan's independence, South Sudan's secession, and everything in between. 'Every one of these components has part of [power]—and that's why it becomes so confused.' Bashir is the hub, a military man who speaks the language of the Islamists, but thinks like a pragmatist. However he is influenced by whichever of his regime's components appears to have the upper hand, and this changes frequently. The result is a weak, inconsistent government, which relies on shows of strength to survive.

THE NCP AND THE PEOPLE

'Nafie was in a car with Taha and Bashir. He stuck his head out the window, and soon dozens of people had gathered round the vehicle to cheer him. He was delighted. "That's nothing", Taha said. "At my last rally there were five thousand people." Bashir snorted. "If I give the word, there will be tens of thousands outside the presidential palace, chanting my name", the president said. The driver laughed. "If I drive this car over a cliff," he said, "35 million Sudanese will applaud me!"'

—Sudanese joke

As the joke illustrates, the Sudanese have a healthy scepticism about their leaders. This is not a place where it is impossible to mock those in power. In late 2011, internet-savvy Sudanese rejoiced in a fake Twitter account called 'Bashir's diary', in which they made up increasingly unlikely or outrageous things the president had done that day. Several referenced the then ICC chief prosecutor, Luis Moreno Ocampo; one joke entry suggested Bashir's barber always mentions Ocampo, to get Bashir's hair to stand on end and make it easier to cut. The security forces stamp out any sort of protest on the streets, and do not allow articles on sensitive subjects in the press, but people are allowed some outlets for their frustration, as long as this does not threaten regime security.

So how popular are Bashir and his followers? It is not hard to find NCP supporters all over Sudan. The party has been in power for so long, disseminating its views over the state media, and distributing patronage, that this should be no surprise. Bashir's charisma and outrageous speeches give him a certain appeal too. However, this is a party that has never been tested in a credible election, and clearly would not care to be. Even the much-publicised new constitution, which was due to be put to the people soon after separation, had not materialised two years later.

Bashir, the great survivor, was at his most vulnerable in the period after South Sudan's secession. Mustafa Khogali, the foreign-educated businessman, had once been caught up in the Islamists' rhetoric. He joined up for *jihad* in 1991, before he turned eighteen, though he never actually went into battle.[63] Now, he says, young men like him would not make a similar decision to enlist in the military. The NCP is reviled by the traditional opposition, fighting off rebellions in the periphery, and has lost ground among its usual supporters. Even its military, security and Islamist components cannot agree on which direction it should take. Without the power and presence of the internal security forces, it would not last long.

SOUTH SUDAN

A short drive along a brand new road heading north from the national capital Juba is the sprawling headquarters of the SPLA, the rebels who have become South Sudan's national army.[64] It is 29 February 2012, and the 6th Division is about to be deployed. The soldiers have been gathered for a final briefing before they are sent to Jonglei state, the location of South Sudan's worst inter-ethnic fighting, to carry out a dangerous and unpopular civilian disarmament campaign. In the first year after independence, men from these barracks would also fight the old enemy in the north, Sudan. Despite the risks they will face, the troops are in good spirits. A sergeant shouts out a refrain, and the soldiers, arranged in three sides of a rectangle to face him and the senior officers, sing back: 'SPLA, Woyee!' This is the emblematic shout of praise to South Sudan's military, and to the almost indissociable political party, the SPLM, which governs the country.

A few kilometres away in the newly-refurbished National Assembly, South Sudan's politicians debate the numerous challenges that have to be overcome to build a country from scratch. Here the men all wear suits; but the majority are former rebel soldiers, who spent the greater part of their adult lives in military fatigues, fighting for their own country or just to carve out some local territory and wealth. After decades of conflict, this is a society where all, and not least the MPs, have seen the rewards the gun can bring.

Despite the apparent harmony of the scene, with rows of men and women all dressed in sober business attire, the ethnic tensions that divide the country persist even among the MPs—as well as within the camouflaged ranks of the armed forces. Creating institutions strong enough to overcome the ethnic fractures and a deeply militarised society is perhaps the biggest difficulty facing the young nation. In its first two years of existence, South Sudan would also have to face a power struggle between the two most important men in the land: rebel commanders and old enemies who at independence became South Sudan's president and vice president.

From rebels to politicians

When John Garang founded the SPLA/M in 1983, the political wing was subsumed into the military. He had learnt the lesson of the first Sudanese civil war, in which the proliferation of political parties and rebel groups hampered the war effort.[65] According to Peter Adwok Nyaba, a veteran of the struggle and until the 2013 reshuffle the Minister for Higher Education, the SPLA/M 'structure was partly political, partly military, and sometimes I used to think that it has evolved like Siamese twins conjoined in the head, and any operation to separate the two would result in the mutual death of both.'

Almost all of South Sudan's political leaders are former soldiers, who are deeply aware that their power base, and in fact their very position, depend on their military legitimacy. South Sudanese were surprised and pleased when President Salva Kiir Mayardit removed thirty-five generals from the active list in January 2013, and then more than one hundred the following month.[66] It was seen as a difficult but important step to take against under-performing potentates, whose credit for winning South Sudan's freedom was already fading away.

Having fought for more than two decades, the rebel army and the politicians who came to prominence in it now have real power. In many cases they are entirely unsuited to their new roles. Victor Lugala recognises the problem, even if he has not yet lost the optimism created by the birth of his new country:

Many of us do not know how to run a state, yet. Some of these people who are in government now, some of them were fighting in the bush, some of them went when they were young, some of them never worked before. Some of them were soldiers, in the barracks. And now they are in offices. They cannot manage the affairs of state. But I think the future is bright: we will struggle, and hopefully learn from our mistakes, and make this country what we want it to be.

Alfred Lokuji is the acting dean of Juba University, a complex of charming brick buildings with a prominent clock tower in the centre of the city. Only a small number of the SPLA soldiers studied at Juba or any university, and Lokuji says that the limited educational background of many of the liberation heroes is a real problem: 'Illiteracy usually means they have no other skills than operating an AK47.'

In February 2013, Luka Biong, a senior SPLM politician, published a revealing article on the problems which face many liberation movements—including his own.[67] Freedom fighters have legitimacy, but are not best placed to govern, which requires a different set of skills. In perhaps the most frank admission of the SPLM's failings since independence, Biong wrote that although it was too soon to judge fully, 'some early indicators strongly suggest that the SPLM is at the early stage of being affected by the "curse" of liberation. Various reports and internal evaluations indicate that the SPLM is depleting its political capital and losing its grass root support.'

Military heroes who need to change

Despite South Sudanese efforts, and millions of dollars of foreign aid for security sector reform, the armed forces do not behave in a professional way. As its members are largely uneducated former rebels who were responsible for many atrocities during the civil war, this is not surprising. In the years up to and after independence, the majority of the fighting in South Sudan was inter-ethnic, but some of 'the violence that has taken place is at the hands of the army,' according to the academic Jok Madut Jok.[68] He concludes that this 'subtracts from any gains of independence. This current generation cannot be made professional. They just have to phase them out.'

A new army with more qualified personnel would remove many of the problems, but simply isn't feasible, given the sacrifices made by the SPLA during the war years. Downsizing to a smaller, more tightly controlled army would make sense; but there is little chance of this happening either. There is a general belief that the threat posed by Sudan requires a large military; officials will not comment on how big the army actually is, but estimates go up to 200,000. Furthermore, the police, fire service and wildlife service are stuffed with 'former' soldiers, ready to be called on if necessary. 'We have colonels directing traffic, and generals running game parks', is how one senior SPLM figure puts it.[69]

Despite the large numbers of men (and women) in uniform, South Sudan still has a debilitating security problem. Clashes among civilians, and even between civilians and the SPLA, cause thousands of deaths every year, far more than the fighting with Sudan, or with the various South Sudanese rebel groups. In theory, the police are responsible for protecting civilians, but they are under-armed and lack training, so that the SPLA is often called on. The early evidence suggests the two bodies are not up to the task. The lack of good roads makes it very difficult for the SPLA or the police to get to trouble spots on time. They are sometimes out-gunned by the civilian population, which is heavily armed following decades of war and unrest.

The army is also frequently accused of human rights abuses, and violations of the peace. In one particularly bizarre case, policemen and soldiers were involved in a shoot-out at a meeting that had been called to restore peace following an inter-ethnic clash. The 'peace meeting' in the small town of Mayendit ended with dozens of deaths, including many civilians.[70] 'Each side thought they were attacked,' the then-Deputy Defence Minister Majak d'Agoot explained. 'It was a problem largely produced by lack of effective command and control.'

The large and sometimes unruly military is the most potent force in South Sudanese society, and its leaders feel that they are entitled to receive their due reward for their many years of suffering. Generals and politicians have built multi-storey houses in South Sudan and abroad, and drive cars the size of ordinary people's huts. Corruption has become a defining feature of the new country.[71] Entitlement, says Lokuji, is 'a nice general term for SPLA behaving like mercenaries: we fought for you, now its pay-up time.' He points out that not everybody behaves like this. Nevertheless, only the SPLA/M leaders appear to have full rights to the dividends of peace.

THE DOMINATION OF A SINGLE PARTY

South Sudan's militarised society is also not far off a one party state. The CPA reduced all the complexities of Sudanese political life into a simple relationship between the NCP, in what was then northern Sudan, and the SPLM in the south. Opposition parties in both parts of the country were shut out of the negotiations and of power itself.[72] Rebel movements other than the SPLA/M had no voice either, and the same goes for civil society, and the people in general.

This carve-up between two old enemies was formalised by the 2010 elections; indeed it looked to many people as if they had signed a secret pact to do just that, though this has been denied.[73] Overall the SPLM's victory in southern Sudan undeniably represented the will of the people, but the vote was no cleaner than the elections in the north. The SPLA was accused of intimidating voters, and impeding the campaign of the main opposition leader, Lam Akol.[74] Lam and his breakaway party, SPLM-Democratic Change (SPLM-DC), are particularly reviled by the SPLM leaders, who claim Lam is funded by Khartoum.

The SPLM was also accused of rigging as many as six of the ten gubernatorial races, mainly against SPLM members who had run as independents after not being chosen as the party's candidates.[75] One of the most controversial cases was Unity state, where the SPLM's Taban Deng was announced as the winner over the independent candidate Angelina Teny, the wife of South Sudan's then-Vice President Riek Machar. In Riek's home town, Leer, they still haven't got over the disappointment. 'It started as a democratic election, but they changed the results,' one Leer resident said in late 2012. 'That is why we don't like the government of South Sudan.' Across southern Sudan several of the losing candidates went into rebellion, including General George Athor in Jonglei state.

In the elections for the Southern Assembly, which became the National Assembly after separation, the SPLM won all but a handful of seats. In the opening session of parliament after the polls, each MP called out his name, and his party. 'SPLM—Woyee!' they congratulated themselves, time after time. When one of Lam Akol's opposition party members stood up, he let out a tentative cry of 'SPLM-DC—Woyee!' It was drowned out by the mocking laughter of the SPLM politicians.

Life outside the party

It is not easy being an opposition politician in South Sudan. State television is a propaganda tool for the SPLM, and regularly criticises anyone opposed to the governing party. The leader of the opposition in the National Assembly, SPLM-DC's Onyoti Adigo, was beaten up by security agents two days before South Sudan became independent. He lost two of his teeth. SPLM-DC's leader, Lam Akol, achieved a sort of temporary reconciliation with Salva, and lived for a while in a hotel in Juba. A bodyguard followed him wherever he went.

Soon enough, though, he was back in exile. I met him in his house in Khartoum. 'I fear for my life,' he said; though his detractors believe that the real reason was his alleged ties to the NCP. 'The SPLM sees itself and South Sudan as one and the same,' Lam shot back. 'If you are opposed to SPLA you are opposed to South Sudan. If you say things contrary to their opinion you are either a traitor or in the pay of Khartoum.'[76]

The SPLM has made life hard for journalists too. When one newspaper published a poorly-judged piece criticising the marriage of Salva's daughter to a foreigner, the writer and the paper's editor were both detained for a few days. One of South Sudan's most respected journalists, Mading Ngor, received threats for the regular questioning tone of his radio show 'Wake Up Juba'. Ngor was also knocked to the ground by security agents in the national parliament. MPs dithered for months over drafting a law that would protect the freedom of the press. Lugala, who has worked as an editor for a South Sudanese radio station, says criticising the liberation heroes is vital. 'We don't hate them but we want them to change their ways,' he explains. 'If freedom fighters went to liberate the country, I have the right to talk.'

At the heart of the SPLM, and the state

The South Sudanese flag that fluttered on independence day represented freedom. It also highlighted the conflation of the SPLM and the state:

the new nation is represented by the SPLM's flag. In addition, the supposedly national army is still known to one and all, including the president and the military spokesman, as the SPLA. The rebels have become the state. The party is now in a similar situation to liberation movements across Africa in the years after they took their countries to freedom, such as the Front de Libération Nationale in Algeria, the National Resistance Movement in Uganda, or the African National Congress in South Africa. For some time to come, the most important debates and political changes will occur within the confines of the governing party; the weak and divided opposition, which has next to no chance of getting into power, is almost an irrelevance.

The SPLM certainly does not speak with one voice, and it is the party's internal discussions, and arguments, which will have the greatest impact on the country's future. Lam is not alone in his belief that a large part of the SPLM leadership still desires regime change in Sudan, while others are more focused on developing the new country. South Sudanese talk about the 'Bahr el Ghazal group', which includes key figures from in and around Salva's home area, including Nhial Deng, the Minister of Foreign Affairs until July 2013.

Another senior member of the government, whom I will call The Minister as he does not wish to be named, is a regular source in this book. He admits that 'there is a struggle within the SPLM. There are different groupings, each trying to get the attention of the president.' Shortly after independence, he highlighted the tensions between Salva and his Vice President, Riek Machar. Riek led a breakaway movement in 1991 which almost destroyed the SPLM, before returning to the fold. The party does not fully trust him. Nevertheless, his role as vice president was seen as vital in keeping him on side, along with at least some of his large ethnic group, the Nuer.

In the founder's footsteps

The SPLM has been disproportionately shaped by its founder, John Garang. After a short stint with the Anyanya rebels during the first civil war, and higher education in both Tanzania and the US, Garang developed what he called his New Sudan vision. If this had been achieved, Sudan would have been reshaped to give equal priority to all its regions, religions and ethnic groups. He argued for unity, not separation, though perhaps above all he was a pragmatist.[77] (Salva, on the other hand, was a committed separatist, despite the public positions he sometimes had to take).[78] Garang spoke the language of human rights, and democratic participation. He inspired people from both Sudans, and his vision still does even after his death.

The SPLM was forged as a reaction to dictatorship and inequality, and as a result its 2008 constitution reflects the finest ideals: 'In its composition and functioning, the SPLM shall be non-racial, non-sexist, anti-racist and against any form of institutionalized tribalism, exclusivism, or ethnic chauvinism.'[79] The constitution explicitly calls for respect for all ethnic and cultural groups, and promises freedom of speech, and to work for the emancipation of women.[80]

However, Garang was far from democratic in the way he ran the SPLA. At the height of the war he told a TV crew that the SPLA was 'a tool to bring about democracy, we are not democratic in ourselves.'[81] The movement went many years without a meeting of the top leadership; dissenters were arrested, and sometimes killed without trial. When Riek and Lam broke away in 1991 they accused Garang of human rights abuses and dictatorial behaviour. The hollowness of their proclaimed moral superiority was revealed within three months. Riek's soldiers and armed civilians from his Nuer ethnic group devastated Garang's home area, killing at least 2,000 Dinka civilians in what became known as the Bor Massacre.[82] The point is that all the liberation movements committed crimes, and it was often ordinary people who suffered.

Garang's leadership style was decisive, but he kept his cards very close to his chest. 'He was a manipulator, a very smart man no doubt, but a lone worker, who didn't share,' the university professor Lokuji believes. 'The mess we are in now is because Garang didn't bother to set up a system.' In a tempestuous meeting of the senior SPLA/M leadership in Rumbek in 2004, Salva accused Garang of keeping the entire movement in his briefcase.[83]

Garang's supporters, like the former minister Lual Deng, say the real problem is that Garang's vision has not been implemented. Equally it was difficult for Garang to set up a real political system while fighting a war, and as he died three weeks after he was sworn in as Sudan's vice president there is no way of telling whether he would have changed his governing style in peacetime. Above all, the SPLM leaders have had years in which to come out from under Garang's shadow. They have failed to do so.

GOVERNANCE

Once the CPA was signed in 2005, making southern Sudan a semi-autonomous region, the SPLM rushed to build the foundations of a state. A central bank was set up, and the National Assembly, along with state assemblies throughout the regions. The government of southern Sudan was established, and the limited civil service already in place was expanded. However, the institutions are extremely weak and are often bypassed, which The Minister says is the biggest barrier to good governance.[84] In theory, the SPLM has a political programme, but there is little sign of it being followed. In cabinet 'people take their own decisions, they do their own thing, there is no direction,' The Minister says. 'The legacy of the SPLM during the liberation phase, the war, is the deliberate attempt to frustrate any type of organisation or building of institutions. What you see today is exactly that.' The result is a sort of personalised political chaos. According to The Minister, after independence President Salva, Vice President Riek, the speaker of the national assembly, James Wani Igga, and the SPLM Secretary General, Pa'gan Amum, each ran their own system, complete with their own power base.

In the run up to independence, Salva set up a committee to review the interim constitution, which was a creation of the CPA, to make it fit for an independent country. The committee was dominated by SPLM members, even after an outcry from the opposition and the small civil society. The predominance of the SPLM did not stop a serious struggle. Vice President Riek apparently tried to reduce the president's powers.[85] It didn't work. In the version of the constitution eventually approved by the national assembly, article 102 (2) states that in a power vacancy the vice president will only take over for a maximum of fourteen days before the governing party decides which of its own members should be in charge.[86] This seemed deliberately designed to make it clear to Riek, who is widely believed to want the top job, that there was no prospect of him ever obtaining it.

Despite some resistance from opposition parties and civil society, considerable power is also concentrated in the hands of the head of state. The transitional constitution passed just before independence, which should in time be replaced by a permanent document, even allows the president to dismiss elected state governors. All the same, there was considerable shock when Salva actually did this, sacking Chol Tong Mayay in Lakes state on 21 January 2013, with no official explanation.[87] Six months later he removed a former ally, Taban Deng, as governor of Unity state.

Speaking before those decisions, the Juba University Dean Lokuji expressed concern that his countrymen were following Sudan's model:

It is the same way Khartoum does business, the same high centralisation of authority. The ultimate discretionary power rests with the head of state and those around him. The generation that is doing something in the public arena is the generation that has come up under Khartoum, under the all-Sudan system.

After the CPA, the late leader of Sudan's Communist party, Mohamed Ibrahim Nugud, wondered whether Sudan and its southern region would end up as 'two states, one system'.[88] The remark annoyed the southern Sudanese at the time, but there was considerable concern in the period after independence that Nugud might have been right.

The President

The man with the ultimate responsibility for South Sudan probably never imagined himself running a country. Salva Kiir Mayardit, a Dinka from Gogrial in Warrap state, is reported to have been born on 13 September 1951.[89] He fought in the first civil war, and was one of the Anyanya rebels integrated into the Sudanese army, eventually rising to the rank of captain of military intelligence. He joined the SPLA at the start of the second civil war, and spent many years as the rebel movement's chief of staff. Salva's years as an intelligence officer are revealed by his watchful nature. In meetings Salva listens, and observes, and if he takes a decision it will be at the very last moment, according to several people who know him.

Malik Agar, the leader of SPLM-North who was once Salva's deputy, describes him as a 'professional soldier, with a cool temperament, he is clever and reasonable.' However, Malik thinks that South Sudan would be better served by the more decisive style Garang showed: 'South Sudan needs aggressive leadership like Garang'. My unnamed source, The Minister, has known Salva for many years, and is dismissive: 'Salva shares his sovereignty with his bodyguards and advisers! His spear masters and *kujour* [traditional holy men] tell him what to do.' At separation, others believed that Salva's usually cautious, consultative style was well suited to South Sudan's divided society.

The president gives halting, rather dry speeches, though he is much better when he makes unscripted remarks; he only rarely consents to be interviewed. At the African Union (AU) summit in Addis Ababa in January 2013, most presidents gave off the cuff interviews to journalists, or held press conferences. Salva strode through the hall in his trademark black cowboy hat, surrounded by his bodyguards and protocol men, most of whom were a head taller than anyone else in the room, refusing to speak to anyone.

The Sudanese are dismissive of Salva, pointing out his lack of education. However Emmanuel Jal, the well-known South Sudanese rapper, says that this should not be confused with a lack of intelligence. 'Our president does not have a degree, but a PhD does not make a leader!' The academic Jok Madut Jok, who is from Salva's area, is another who defends him:

He's just, he's a man of equity. He rewards loyalty but he remembers everyone. He doesn't need to meet you more than once to remember you the next time. He's a classic intelligence gatherer, speak little, listen more. He's an honest man. He's very dedicated to this cause of taking this boat to shore.

However, Salva is simply not that visible as a president. 'If he has a vision for this country, people need to see it,' Jok says. 'If he has an opinion, he needs to get on TV and say it.'

The Big Tent

Perhaps the one policy fully associated with President Salva is his 'Big Tent' strategy. The CPA was signed between the NCP and the SPLM, almost entirely ignoring other armed groups. The South Sudan Defence Force (SSDF), another rebel movement, though one with strong ties to Khartoum, was hostile to the SPLA. As a result, 'it was widely believed that the signing of the CPA would set the stage for a south-south war,' according to the Sudans expert John Young.[90] Garang had opposed integrating the SSDF into the SPLA, but after his death Salva proved much more accommodating. On 8 January 2006, Salva and the SSDF's Paulino Matip signed the Juba Declaration, which brought most of the SSDF into the SPLA.[91]

Matip was named deputy commander in chief, a largely ceremonial post that he held until his death six years later. At a stroke of a pen, the prospect of a war which might have engulfed the whole southern region disappeared, although remnants of the SSDF continued to fight Juba even after independence. Even fervent supporters of Garang admit that he simply would not have taken this vital decision.[92] Salva continued the Big Tent policy throughout the interim period, offering amnesties to rebel groups on two occasions. This largely kept the peace, but it did also encourage small-scale rebellions, as their leaders knew there would be a good chance they would be reinstated at a higher rank.

Politics on the periphery

More than two decades of war created numerous regional strongmen, who owe their success to ethnic solidarity, prowess in war, luck, or a combination of all these factors. Salva and the SPLM have no choice other than to rely on men like Paul Malong, the governor of Northern Bahr el Ghazal state, on the exposed and disputed border with Sudan. This is a man who was made by conflict. In the hour-long conversation I had with him, Malong was most animated when discussing his war heroics. He said he had been shot eleven times, and never received proper hospital treatment. Malong talked with real relish about a crushing victory against SAF north of Aweil on 22 January 2001, in which he destroyed the railway line. He agreed with my assessment that he is a 'natural fighter'. According to popular belief, Malong cannot read or write. When I asked him, Malong claimed to be literate in Dinka.

It is said that the governor owns huge herds of cattle, and has over eighty wives. Malong told me that he had only thirty-three wives. He added that it was better to have a hundred wives and be faithful to them, than to have only one wife but see a thousand women outside of marriage. The governor, an austere-looking man with gold-rimmed glasses, is known to give giant bottles of whisky as presents. One Saturday in February 2012, I was part of a group that had dinner at his residence in Aweil. We ate and drank, but received no gifts. Two magnificent pet ostriches patrolled the patio where we ate, observing the scene.

From one perspective, Malong could be seen to represent everything that is wrong about the South Sudanese governing class. Garang Majak, a member of the state assembly, would agree. On 19 December 2011, Majak accused the governor and his finance minister of misappropriating money from the Northern Bahr el Ghazal state budget. Malong flew into one of his well-known rages. 'When we were in the bush I was a general and you were a soldier', he stated, correctly, before allegedly threatening to kill Majak. The following day Majak was arrested, even though as an MP he should have had immunity. Eventually he fled to Juba.

Not surprisingly, Governor Malong's version is different. Majak was wanted for money laundering, the governor said. I asked Malong whether he had threatened to kill the MP. 'If I wanted to kill him, what would prevent me?' was his response. He also rejected the corruption allegations. Whatever the truth of the matter, the key point is that even in the height of his anger, Majak said he couldn't even contemplate leaving the SPLM. This sort of local tension takes place in different ways all over South Sudan, almost always within the framework of the SPLM.

Malong is far more than just a cartoon thug ruling through fear. He has worked hard to repair the relationship between the people of his state and Arab groups over the border in Sudan, who were responsible for some of the worst atrocities of the second north-south civil war.[93] Regular conferences are held in Aweil to smooth over any tensions, and set the parameters within which the Misseriya and the Rizeigat can bring their cows into Northern Bahr el Ghazal's rich pastures on their seasonal migrations. If nothing else, one of his critics admits, Malong 'has ignored all this hostile rhetoric from Juba regarding the Arab tribes', recognising this is not in the interest of his people.[94]

ETHNIC DIVISIONS

The rivalry between different ethnic groups is one of South Sudan's greatest problems. The ethnic fractures are also present in the SPLM. Many South Sudanese complain about 'Dinka domination', in reference to the group which makes up around a third of the population, and a large part of the SPLM leadership.[95] Garang was a Dinka, and so is Salva; however the phrase has long roots, going back before either was a prominent figure. In the first period of semi-autonomy for southern Sudan, in between the 1972 Addis Ababa agreement that ended the first civil war and the start of the second conflict in 1983, there were growing complaints about the numbers of jobs awarded to the Dinka.[96]

For years after it was founded in 1983, Garang's SPLA was routinely described as a Dinka army,[97] even if many Nuer and others joined at the beginning too. The make-up of the SPLA/M changed considerably with time; however, it has always been led by a Dinka. After independence the perception is that Dinkas have an advantage in business, and are more likely to receive jobs in the many ministries controlled by their kinsmen.

There are also tensions over what is perceived as 'land-grabbing' in Juba: the Equatorian locals object to the Nilotics, principally the Dinka and Nuer, coming to Juba and taking over their land. Robert Napoleon is an Equatorian doctor who sees echoes of the problems of the 1970s. 'If you get in a fight in the market, you will find a Dinka in the police station, and you will automatically be thrown in jail.' he says. Many Dinka are understandably frustrated about the criticisms they face. 'People shouldn't curse the Dinka for dying in large numbers for the country,' one former soldier told me.

It is not just the Dinka: any individual in a position of power is expected to help those who come from his ethnic group or region. Groups of unemployed people with the horizontal facial scars of the Nuer queue up outside the ministries run by men with the same markings. It is a similar story in departments controlled by other groups. 'If you want to know the tribe of the top man, you go to the messenger boy,' Lugala says.

Divisions, and what they could mean

If the politicising of ethnicity is a concern, so too are the ethnic divisions in the army. A large number of the soldiers are Nuer, particularly after Matip's SSDF were integrated in 2006. Although the SPLA has a Nuer chief of staff, James Hoth Mai, the Nuer are not believed to represent a similar proportion of the top commanders as of the rank and file. This sometimes causes resentment. The younger generation in the army is more likely to rely on the support of 'comrades' rather than those from the same ethnic group, but this does not hold true for their seniors.[98] The ethnic splits in the SPLA make it difficult to intervene in certain interethnic conflicts: Nuer troops are less likely to want to curb Nuer youth groups on the rampage, for example.

In this context of deep divisions, Salva made a conscious decision to appear to be as even-handed as possible when he named his first cabinet after independence.[99] Historically, South Sudan had been divided into three regions, and the cabinet posts were doled out between them: ten to Greater Equatoria, ten to Greater Bahr el Ghazal, and nine to Greater Upper Nile.[100] This was Salva's Big Tent strategy again. The finance and interior ministries both went to Equatorians, to relieve some of the fears of Dinka domination. In general Salva's choices were well received: the headline in the *Southern Eye* newspaper said the cabinet 'consolidates unity'.[101] However, the choice was clearly a deeply political one. Only one state, Unity, did not have a minister, perhaps to undermine Riek Machar, who comes from there. The opposition leader Lam Akol also said that many of the deputy ministers were Dinka, and he suspected that they would wield the real power.

There are growing ethnic splits within the SPLM, The Minister explained in early 2012: 'You can't avoid talking about ethnicities and the Nuer factor in the whole of this now,' he said, referring to the second largest ethnic group. 'The kind of feelings running up now among Nuers are that they should take the leadership of this country.' Salva and Riek are rivals, and they also represent a potential Dinka-Nuer split. However, The Minister and others believe that Riek does not have the full support of his Nuer kinsmen. The Minister said it was possible the Equatorians might ally with the Nuers and other Nilotics against the Bahr el Ghazal Dinkas who form Salva's most loyal supporters. This admission, from someone at the very top of the SPLM, shows just how divided the party was after separation.

THE (SECOND) SPLIT

In mid-2013, it seemed as if many of The Minister's predictions would come true. Salva's rivalry with Riek, a potent if undeclared force in South Sudanese politics for years, surged to the surface. Their differences were at least as much political as they were ethnic: both wanted to be in charge. However, given South Sudan's history, its militarised society and the country's ethnic tensions, any division ran the risk of compounding several fractures.

Riek has a broad face, and a distinctive gap in his upper front teeth. A mechanical engineer who studied in Khartoum and then in Bradford in England, Riek is idolised by Nuers from his home area, Leer in Unity state. He is often despised by Dinkas and Garang loyalists, because of his attempted coup against Garang's leadership of the SPLA/M in 1991. After independence, Riek was an extremely active vice president, dealing with much of the day-to-day business of running a government. This was not enough for him. Less than two years into South Sudan's independent history, Riek made another push for power—a peaceful one this time. Riek made it clear he intended to take on Salva for the chairmanship of the SPLM at the upcoming National Convention, a post which would almost certainly guarantee a victory in the 2015 presidential elections. One well-placed source says Pa'gan Amum and James Wani Igga expressed similar desires, as did Rebecca Nyandeng, John Garang's widow.[102] Riek, however, was the most open, telling the *Guardian* that 'When a president has been in power for a long time, it becomes inevitable that a new generation arises. It is a natural process,' Machar said. 'To avoid authoritarianism and dictatorship, it is better to change.'[103]

The National Convention was postponed, and Riek stripped of some supplementary powers. In June two ministers, Deng Alor and Kosti Manibe, were suspended to allow a corruption investigation to take place, an unusual step that was seen as a political move. On 7 July, Taban Deng was removed as governor of Unity state, perhaps because his support for Salva appeared to be slipping away. Then, on 23 July, Salva made the most decisive political move of his presidency, sacking Riek and the whole cabinet, and suspending Pa'gan, who had recently criticised the direction the SPLM and the country were moving in. After a long period of observation, the former intelligence officer had finally decided to act.

The sacking raised fears of a repeat of the 1991 split, which resulted in years of bloody clashes among antagonistic southern Sudanese factions, often arrayed along ethnic lines. When a Dinka man fought a Nuer in Konyo Konyo market in Juba shortly afterwards, panic rippled through the town. Nevertheless, the initial response to Salva's reshuffle was thoroughly democratic. The SPLA Chief of Staff Hoth Mai made it clear that the army supported the president. Riek acknowledged his rival had every constitutional right to sack him. Pa'gan contended his suspension was illegal, and took his complaint to the courts. The ministers went quietly into the night. In one further sign of institutions slowly developing, the parliament vetted Salva's new cabinet, and even rejected his nominee for justice minister, Telar Ring Deng. Telar had been portrayed by many as the covert force behind Salva's decisions, and blocking his appointment may well have seemed like good, democratic revenge for former ministers sitting on the National Assembly's plush seats.

On 25 August Wani Igga, the former speaker, was sworn in as vice president. The Equatorian rebel commander with a penchant for wide, bright ties and gleaming suits was now the second most senior figure in the administration. He will be expected to rally Equatorian support for Salva for the 2015 elections. Riek has made it clear he wants the presidency, and he is not the only one. Several of those removed in the reshuffle became more openly critical of the president. In response, Salva worked to consolidate his support within the party. South Sudan needs a powerful opposition, whether it comes from within the SPLM or not. But the country's militarised history and ethnic tensions, as well as the swelling ambitions of its leaders, make many South Sudanese nervous about the forms such political rivalry could one day take.

If there is one thing everyone seemed to agree on, it was that the political trajectory of the country in the period after independence was a harmful one. In his inauguration speech, Wani Igga criticised corruption and bad practices, saying that laziness had become 'prevalent and productivity reduced to zero level in our nation.' The new vice president called for a new start, to break away from the errors of the post-independence era: 'a phase where we drastically overhaul and move away from any past bad or unacceptable practice. Phase Two is a stage of deep-rooted corrections, objective reforms, and profound transformation of our governance and leadership styles.'

THE SPLM AND THE PEOPLE

The independence celebrations on 9 July 2011 marked the high point of the SPLM's popularity. The new nation was, for once, united in its support: 'SPLM–Woyee' they chanted in Juba and Aweil, Yambio and Malakal, Pibor and Tonj. A rebel movement that had been created to reform Sudan had, instead, split it in two. After decades of war, and even longer being treated as second class citizens, the South Sudanese were deeply grateful. That incredible, emotional day, one most South Sudanese never thought they would see, reduced old soldiers to tears. The long and bloody struggle had come to a joyous end.

It was inevitable that such unbridled euphoria could not last. Frustration at the ruling class grew after independence. One study, carried out in April and May 2013, found that a majority of participants believed that although life was better than it had been in the united Sudan, it was also true that their country was headed in the wrong direction.[104] Those polled complained about jobs and services being allocated according to ethnic ties, and about food shortages, poverty and insecurity. All of this is because, The Minister concludes, the 'energy of the elite is absorbed in the struggle for wealth and power' rather than helping the people.

Curtailing dissent

In the west of Juba there is a sight that is strangely familiar to anyone who has lived in Khartoum: a towering building of grey concrete and reflective blue windows. This imposing construction is an almost direct copy of the NISS building in Khartoum, and it serves the same purpose here.[105] The South Sudanese security officers do not just share a taste in architecture with their Sudanese former colleagues; they, too, have been accused of widespread human rights abuses. The most serious incidents included 'extrajudicial killings, torture, rape, and other inhumane treatment of civilians' according to the US government. Some were the work of rebel groups, but by no means all. Just like in Sudan, those who carry out abuses tend to get away with it.[106]

The information minister lashed out at the report, and other senior officials bridled at the accusations too. The SPLA/M have been portrayed for years, by the Western media, activists, politicians and church leaders, as heroic freedom fighters struggling against an evil regime in Khartoum. Now the party is seemingly unable to take any public criticism. Very often the liberation heroes find it difficult to see why anyone who did not fight in the struggle should be able to question their actions. However one veteran SPLM leader told me, with great sadness, that the ideals Garang fought for were being tarnished by so many human rights abuses.[107]

In the early hours of 5 December 2012, the blogger and government critic Diing Chan Awuol was gunned down outside his house in Gudele, in the west of Juba. He was shot in the face at close range. A couple of weeks previously he had published a piece, under his usual pen name Isaiah Abraham, calling on Salva to foster better relations with Sudan, and to stop supporting rebel groups fighting Khartoum. A week before his murder he received phone threats telling him to stop writing, according to his brother.[108] The brutal killing of Diing, a pastor and a former major in the SPLA, shocked South Sudan.

This sort of assassination of a dissident is exactly what the South Sudanese had fought against for so long.[109] Just over a month later, the journalist and peace activist John Penn de Ngong, a former child soldier who knew Isaiah Abraham well, found a plastic bag on his bed. It contained two animal jawbones, a bullet, and a misspelt note warning him to stop speaking out, or end up like his murdered friend. John Penn fled the country. 'If I can still be a refugee, when I fought for our liberation as a child soldier, it is a great, great disappointment to me,' he said.

Home truths

Of all the criticism the SPLM has started to receive, perhaps the most hurtful came from Captain Mabior Garang de Mabior, the son of the national hero John Garang. 'I am afraid the country has started on the wrong foot,' he said.[110] Mabior highlighted the particularly sharp feeling of disappointment experienced by people all over South Sudan who had believed in the SPLM: 'The armed struggle was waged because we wanted to end injustice. The fact that there is injustice today in the Republic is nothing short of a betrayal of the aspirations of the citizens of South Sudan.' Mabior's conclusion was stark: 'Either we have an honest and free dialogue on the future of our Republic, or we can descend into the abyss.' South Sudan is, after decades of war and underdevelopment, an extremely difficult country to run. The liberation heroes are still in credit with the people of South Sudan; but unless they can overcome their antidemocratic, authoritarian tendencies, this will not last long.

* * *

Omar al Bashir is one of the great survivors of Sudanese politics, staying in power for longer than any other politician in Sudan's history. To achieve this he has relied on his fellow soldiers, as well as Islamist ideologues, pragmatists, and an increasingly powerful security body. Patronage, and populist diatribes against the West and South Sudan, have helped too. Yet in the years after separation Bashir looked increasingly vulnerable, his prestige damaged by letting the south go, the race to succeed him accelerating, and the different parts of his governing coalition elbowing their way to prominence.

The South Sudanese politicians were created by their opposition to Khartoum, both before and after Bashir's coup in 1989. After independence, old soldiers wanted rewards for their war heroics, and their place in the new political hierarchy was often dictated by their military past. The rebels left the bush for Juba, the new capital, but in many cases they were poorly equipped to govern a country. The SPLM is riven by ethnic divisions and personal rivalry, and its internal tensions threaten the stability of South Sudan itself. The fall-out between Salva and Riek could have repercussions for many years.

Fighting broke out in Juba just as this book went to press. President Salva Kiir accused soldiers loyal to his former deputy, Riek Machar, of attempting a coup. These clashes are covered in the Afterword.

3

THE ECONOMY

SUDAN

At the confluence of the Blue and the White Niles, and so at the very heart of Khartoum and of Sudan, a new forest of skyscrapers pushed up in the first decade of the 21st century. Tinted windows reflect the full glory of the sun; cranes piece together the skeletons of high rises to come. It could be almost anywhere in the oil-rich Middle East—and it seems light years away from the image of Sudan as a deeply impoverished country. One building is shaped like a wizard's hat, its three metallic staves bending gracefully to meet at a high central point, the floors in between sheathed in a glass skin. This is the headquarters of the Greater Nile Petroleum Operating Company (GNPOC). The financial district, and Khartoum itself—though by no means the rest of the country—were visibly transformed by a decade-long oil boom.

Sudan began exporting oil in 1999, after many years when oil exploration had been interrupted by civil war. In the decade that followed, the economy soared: growth averaged 7 per cent, almost double that of the previous ten years.[1] The petro-dollars financed buildings, dams and roads, purchased patronage, and slipped into the pockets of those without full rights to them. The 2005 CPA granted southern Sudan almost half of the oil revenues produced under its soil, and a referendum on its future. However the billions of dollars the region received weren't enough to persuade the southern Sudanese to vote for unity. When South Sudan ran up its flag, Sudan's boom years were over: three quarters of the daily oil production was in the new country.

Sudan's economic prospects changed overnight. 'The economy is in a state of total collapse' is how Hassan Satti, an opposition politician and economist, put it a year after separation. Giving up South Sudan's oil meant Sudan had to cope with the loss of more than 70 per cent of its foreign exchange earnings, and half of the government's revenue, according to economists and officials.[2] After more than a decade of steady growth, the economy contracted at painful speed. The International Monetary Fund's (IMF) projected figures for 2012 showed Sudan's real GDP shrinking by 11.1 per cent.[3] Suddenly Sudan had one of the worst performing economies in the world.

Economic disaster and political consequences

It wasn't the country's first financial crisis. The Sudanese economy, over the years, has suffered from an over-dependence on a single sector. In the 19th century, the rapidly changing contours of the nascent Sudanese state were financed by gold and slaves, the latter mainly coming from what is now South Sudan. The British, once they took control, set up the vast Gezira Scheme, an irrigated project between the Blue and White Niles just to the south of Khartoum, to produce cotton for the factories of North West England. Sudan's fortunes fluctuated with world demand and prices, and the Gezira Scheme 'came to demonstrate the dangers of national dependence on a single commodity.'[4] Later on, in the 1970s, Arab-funded mechanised farming projects attempted to make good Sudan's apparent potential as the 'breadbasket' of the Middle East, to little avail. The controversial British businessman Tiny Rowland launched a joint-venture with the Sudanese government to develop the world's largest sugar plantation on the White Nile.[5]

Sudan's biggest businessman, Osama Daoud, points out that in Sudan economic crises have had political implications. A tall man, wearing an open-necked shirt when I met him, he has the easy charm so typical of the Sudanese. In his Khartoum town-house, surrounded by some glorious examples of his extensive collection of Rashid Diab's paintings, he explained how a series of economic failures contributed to Bashir seizing power in 1989. The rot set in, Daoud believes, under Jafaar Nimeiri, a coup-leader himself twenty years before Bashir, when he 'started with nationalisations and confiscations'. Then he adds, with the money-maker's rueful laugh, that nothing could be worse than having your business confiscated.

Nimeiri was deposed in a popular revolution in 1985, in part because of the disastrous economic situation. After that, a period of weak democratic rule was characterised by coalitions concerned more with petty politics than the interests of the country. The Prime Minister, Sadiq al Mahdi, was unable to restore much in the way of economic order, encouraging Bashir to seize power. 'The army were not happy, the people were not happy, everyone was unhappy. And the economic situation of the country was not good,' Daoud explains. The first communiqué of Bashir's National Salvation Revolutionary Command Council highlighted the 'terrible deterioration of the economy' and 'the social class of scoundrels getting richer by the day' as two of the justifications for the coup.[6]

OIL BOOM AND BUST

Ten years after Bashir came to power, the oil started flowing, propping up his regime, not least by allowing the purchase of more weapons for the war in southern Sudan.[7] It did great things for the economy too. The budget quintupled between 1998 and 2011, when South Sudan seceded.[8] This welcome influx of cash allowed the government to stabilise the economy, and bring what had been triple-digit inflation down to single figures. Oil revenue and the stability brought by the CPA led to increased investment, helping to fuel a real estate boom in Khartoum, including those glittering skyscrapers, and improved telecommunications throughout the country.[9]

Unsurprisingly, anyone who could tried to get in on the act. Mustafa Khogali, the well-connected and enterprising Khartoum businessman, was one of those who succeeded. 'I was in the oil and gas industry because at the time it was the only industry that was really making a lot of money,' he says. Khogali supplied drilling equipment for oil wells, before eventually moving out of the business when it became apparent that southern Sudan would secede, and he could no longer guarantee his work would continue in the new country.

Mustafa was more foresighted than Sudan's leaders. As a senior NCP official admitted,[10] too many of the ruling elite refused to believe the country would split in two, and so they didn't plan for the financial crash to come. In the run-up to separation, the Sudanese government said it had been receiving $4–4.5 billion a year in oil revenue.[11] Some international experts believe the real figure was higher than this. The battle to make up that loss would define the economic—and political—future of the NCP, and Sudan itself, in the aftermath of separation.

After the split

Sudan does have some oil left. GNPOC began producing oil in the Heglig basin in 1999, which eventually helped pay for that futuristic building in Khartoum. Following separation, most of the oil reserves in this area are now firmly on the South Sudanese side of the border, but Khartoum retains control over a number of oil wells near the town of Heglig, as well as some a little further north.[12] (South Sudanese know Heglig as Panthou, and claim it is part of South Sudan. The countries would even fight over the oilfields in April 2012).[13] Overall, according to several Sudanese officials, Sudan produces 115–120,000 barrels per day, a far cry from the half a million the united country churned out before separation.[14]

This should be enough to cover Sudan's domestic needs. However, the oil firms are entitled to a share of the production. Sudan has to buy these barrels back, to meet domestic consumption.[15] In December 2012, three new oilfields were opened, in Al Najma, Bursaya and Hadida. The hope is they will produce another 40,000 barrels per day.[16] In July 2012, Bashir attended the signing of exploration licences granted for nine blocks covering a reported 40 per cent of Sudan's area.[17] The licences were taken up by fairly small companies, suggesting a relatively low probability of finding large-scale commercially-exploitable oil reserves. In the short term, new oilfields can help Sudan to meet its own fuel requirements, but barring a dramatic discovery, the country's days as a major oil exporter have come to an end.

A prolonged crisis

How much does the loss of the oil matter? The impact on the government's budget was certainly substantial, sending it into crisis mode. However, athough the reduction in the oil revenue was a devastating blow to the government, the Sudanese people were not entirely dependent on it.[18] Despite the oil boom, most Sudanese actually work in agriculture, even if typically these are low-paying jobs or family subsistence farming.

So perhaps the economists' greatest concern after separation was the loss of foreign exchange. Put simply, without the oil exports, Sudan is unable to bring in many dollars, which are needed to import products. With the central bank unable or unwilling to furnish dollars to businesses, many were forced to use the black market. The widespread lack of faith in the economy, both at home and abroad, led to a dramatic fall in the value of the Sudanese pound (SDG). Soon after separation, the SDG was unofficially trading at above 5 to the US dollar, compared to an official rate of 2.7. Although the government let the official rate slide to 4.4, by the end of 2012 the black market rate was hovering around 7 SDG to the dollar.[19]

The exchange rate's slow-motion crash was particularly damaging because during the oil boom Sudan had become hooked on imported goods. In 1999 the total imports were about $1.3 billion. During the last three years before separation it went up to around $9 billion.[20] Even food was brought in from abroad, accounting for a fifth of the total imports, leaving Sudan in a dangerous position. When the Sudanese pound fell against the dollar, the cost of importing wheat and sugar spiked sharply.[21] The leading businessman Daoud, who produces pasteurised milk, is scandalised that Sudan imports $200 million worth of powdered milk every year.

At the same time, inflation soared to over 40 per cent in October 2012,[22] as the government was forced to print money to balance the budget. There were dramatic rises in the costs of many basic commodities, which hit ordinary people and not just the petro-elite. In Khartoum's markets, the prices of meat are broadcast through traders' loudspeakers, every announcement a crackly soundtrack to increasing desperation. The cost of meat almost doubled in 2012, and sugar and vegetables increased by over 40 per cent,[23] leaving urban families in particular struggling to cope. When I met her in Omdurman's main market in May 2012, Mariam, a housewife from a lower-middle class area, said that she had been forced to cut down her purchases. Sometimes she was not able to give her children more than one meal a day, she said.

The natural resource trap

To the great frustration of the Sudanese, this debilitating state of affairs could have been avoided. During the oil years, the government simply neglected the rest of the economy. The opposition politician Hassan Satti highlights the huge levels of income the government raked in over more than a decade: he estimates the total income from petroleum, loans and investments from 1999 to 2011 at $110 billion, an unprecedented sum in Sudanese history. If it had been spent in the right way, the Sudanese economy would have been in a very good shape, even without South Sudan and its oil. Instead, Satti says, the money was spent on unproductive infrastructure, patronage and consumer goods—as well as the military.[24] Sudanese society as a whole became a consumer society, Daoud believes, obsessed with the latest imported goods, rather than producing things for itself.

Sudan is certainly not the only country to have fallen into this trap. Economists speak of the 'resource curse' that tends to afflict countries that depend too heavily on a single natural resource. It can lead to 'Dutch disease',[25] which the Oxford University professor Paul Collier summarises as follows: 'The resource exports cause the country's currency to rise in value against other currencies. This makes the country's other export activities uncompetitive. Yet these other activities might have been the best vehicles for technological progress.'[26] In 2007, oil made up about 96 per cent of Sudan's total export revenue. The next biggest export-earner, sesame, accounted for less than 1 per cent.[27] Apart from the oil, Sudan's industrial sector was relatively under-developed, at only 10 per cent of GDP, meaning Sudan did not have much industry to fall back on once the oil production was reduced.

Dutch disease, and a lack of foresight to invest in the rest of the economy, had combined to place the Sudanese economy in what Collier calls 'the natural resource trap'.[28] This hasn't escaped some Sudanese officials. 'We should have used the oil revenue to restructure the economy, diversify our economic base, and avoid the oil disease,' the NCP's Sabir al Hassan admits. Those sort of much-needed reforms didn't happen during the oil years; but they became a key part of the government's approach, when it had no choice, after separation.

FINDING SOLUTIONS

In the difficult first few months adapting to life as an impoverished 'rump state', the NCP's economic gurus realised they didn't have many options. Raising taxes wouldn't help, because the economy was doing so badly.[29] A political agreement with South Sudan might eventually paper over some of the cracks. This would involve setting a fee for the new country's use of the pipelines, refineries and the export terminal on Sudanese soil, as well as South Sudan handing over a sizeable amount of money to compensate Sudan for the loss of its oil. However, the two Sudans took over a year to agree on a deal, and even longer to get it to stick even partially.[30]

So Khartoum adopted a two-pronged economic strategy:[31] the first was to boost income and reduce spending, to stabilise the economy. In essence this was designed to tide the government over until the political tensions created by the southern region's secession ebbed a little. The second part of the strategy was serious structural reform, to readjust the economy to the depressing new realities. The short-term tactics rested on two main planks: touring friends to ask for loans; and imposing austerity measures. Throughout the oil years Khartoum had been able to get substantial loans, in particular from Asian countries. China gave several worth up to $3 billion each. Satti believes the government used to receive almost as much in loans as it did in petroleum, about $4 billion a year.

With no oil revenue to guarantee the loan, the conversation with the Chinese, an old ally, suddenly became much harder. Finance Minister Ali Mahmoud was able to restructure Sudan's debts to Beijing, reportedly winning a five year grace period.[32] China proved much less amenable to handing over new loans. When one finally came through in late December 2012, the impressive-sounding sum of 300 million yuan was trumpeted on state media.[33] However, this was not translated into SDG, or even the US dollar equivalent of less than $50 million. Peanuts, in other words.

Later that month, Mahmoud announced the China National Petroleum Company (CNPC), the biggest player in oil in Sudan, had agreed to a $1.5 billion loan that would lead to a 'radical change' in the Sudanese economy.[34] There were some suspicions that this was not new money, but an agreement to repay existing debts gradually. That Sudan was short of money was clear: Khartoum was unable to pay an $850 million debt to the oil companies due in 2012.[35]

Faced with these crushing difficulties, the Sudanese looked far and wide for financial help. Senior figures including First Vice President Ali Osman Taha travelled to Libya, Egypt, Algeria, Iran, Saudi Arabia, Qatar and elsewhere, apparently begging for aid. Bashir went to Doha, Tehran and Beijing. From time to time officials suggested 'huge' amounts of money had been secured, though they rarely went into details. Qatar apparently promised $2 billion in 2012, and another $1 billion in late

2013, but there were doubts about whether all this money would actually arrive.[36] Lual Deng, the South Sudanese who was the federal Petroleum Minister as part of the Government of National Unity until Sudan split in two, says he thinks Libya may have helped out too. The Qataris, in particular, were not prepared to see Bashir's government fall; but nobody was prepared to offer the kind of money that would come close to replacing the lost oil revenues. After more than two decades of conflict and disastrous rule, the NCP's credit is all but exhausted.

Austerity measures

However much they recouped from abroad, the NCP leaders knew it was time for some belt-tightening: their own, and those of the people. In the first year after separation, the Sudanese government discussed, trailed and then announced a series of cost-cutting measures. Budgets were trimmed, and reworked. Parliamentarians fought off one attempt to slice fuel subsidies, arguing that the impact on food prices, and so on the poor, would be too painful. It couldn't last.

On 18 June 2012, in the run up to the first anniversary of the disastrous division of the country he has presided over, Bashir went to parliament to detail a sweeping series of austerity measures. More than one hundred federal government posts were cut, including several of his own advisers. Five ministers lost their jobs, and twelve junior ministers. A 45 per cent cut in the state governments' spending was also announced, resulting in more than 260 people being made redundant. Allowances and benefits of those still employed were to be reduced, Bashir said.

More worryingly for ordinary people, he confirmed a partial lifting of fuel subsidies.[37] When the fuel subsidy cut was announced, petrol prices rose by 60 per cent, and diesel by more than 30 per cent.[38] Transport costs as a whole rose by 70 per cent in 2012.[39] The cost of basic foodstuffs rocketed again. In an effort to protect the most vulnerable, Bashir said the number of poor people receiving direct aid would increase from half to three quarters of a million; imported wheat, sugar and flour would continue to be exempt from taxation; and taxes would be lifted from powdered milk, cooking oil, and medicines.

Sudan revolts

Bashir's promises weren't enough. Student protests, which had begun two days before Bashir's speech once it became apparent fuel prices would rise, spread from the University of Khartoum to other universities around the capital, and then the country. 'Sudan is going down the drain', said one female student who took part in the first protests. I met her in the headquarters of a small opposition party, but even here she preferred not to use her name. Perhaps it was wise: several of her friends were arrested after they left the party offices. 'Prices keep going up,' was how she explained her motivation. 'If we had a good president, our economy wouldn't be that bad.'

In a typical scene from one of the early demonstrations, trucks stuffed with riot police in blue combat uniforms roared down Sharia Jamaa, or University Street, in the centre of Khartoum, sirens screaming as they forced other traffic out of the way. Plain-clothes men from national security bashed protesters with long sticks, as tear gas grenades exploded all around.

On Friday 22 June, four days after Bashir's speech at parliament, the protests moved up a level: hundreds of demonstrators marched out of an Umma party mosque in Wad Nubawi in Omdurman, only to be forced back by the truncheons and tear gas of the waiting security forces. In Al Daim, a poor neighbourhood to the south of central Khartoum, young men briefly took control of the streets, pulling together makeshift barricades from rocks, branches, and ripped-out concrete bollards. There were substantial demonstrations in several other towns, including Nyala, Gedarif, Kassala and Wad Madani.

The protests, which were partly co-ordinated on the internet, were live-blogged on twitter by an increasingly enthusiastic, but small, cadre of young revolutionaries. The following week the activists came up with a name for what were now overtly anti-regime protests: 'Elbow-Licking Friday'. This was a mocking reference to Bashir and Nafie's frequent dismissal of the opposition as 'elbow-lickers'—people attempting to do the impossible.

With each protest gathering hundreds rather than thousands of demonstrators, #SudanRevolts, as they were known online, eventually petered out. The protesters hadn't been able to convince enough ordinary people to join in, and hundreds of those who did take part were arrested. To no-one's surprise, the fearless Boushi, the activist who had been filmed criticising Nafie and the NCP, was among those locked up. He and others could not achieve what they wanted, but the crackdown, mass arrests, and desperate attempts to keep the 'Sudanese Summer' out of the news showed how worried the authorities were. Everyone in Sudan is aware that two military Presidents, Ibrahim Abboud in 1964 and Nimeiri in 1985, have been overthrown by street protests.

A NEW (OLD) ECONOMY

Unpopular though they were, the austerity measures were unavoidable. The IMF praised a 'difficult but important' decision.[40] Far more is needed. In years to come, prosperity for Sudan's people will depend to a great extent on the government's success in restructuring the economy. The intention is to develop agriculture, agro-industry, and mining, with a particular focus on gold. Bashir launched the White Nile Sugar Factory in July 2012, an $800 million project which will eventually have the capacity to produce 500,000 tons of sugar a year. Ironically, given the great Sudanese love of sweet things, the bulk of the sugar factory's production will be exported to bring in foreign exchange.

Just over two months later, the President was grinning for the cameras at the opening of the Sudan Gold Refinery, which should eventually serve countries throughout the region. If no major new oil reserves are discovered, the authorities hope gold can keep the economy from collapsing. In 2009, gold revenues represented around $400–450 million. By 2012, they had soared to $2.5 billion.

This came not through heavy investment or a clever development plan, but through 'just good luck', according to Sabir al Hassan, the head of the NCP's economic team, and a former Central Bank governor. Or, to put it in more Sudanese terms, as al Hassan quickly did, 'the Sudanese say "*Allah Kareem*"'—God is generous. (As I listened back to the tape of one of the two interviews I did with him, I could hear the regular click-click-click as he rolled his prayer beads through his hands.) In the period either side of independence, a succession of young men left their homes, and even their fields, to prospect for gold. Some pan for the precious metal in tubs filled with mercury, which isolates the gold, and may also slowly poison the miners.[41] Others wander through likely-looking patches of desert with metal detectors. 'I've gathered gold for about four months and I've already paid for two used cars,' one miner, Mukhtar Yussif, said.

This Sudanese gold rush has been characterised by traditional surface mining, carried out by impoverished men with a glint of hope in their eyes, rather than the heavy machinery and careful calculations of the big mining companies. This unregulated world also leads itself to lucrative attempts to work outside the formal system: the Central Bank believes that at one point as much as 40 per cent of the gold was smuggled.[42] In fact, the Central Bank is so desperate for foreign currency it buys most of the remaining gold. The Bank has an office in Khartoum's gold market, and reportedly purchases nearly $200,000 worth of gold from just one shop owner every week.[43] From time to time the smugglers raise the price, and the Bank is forced to match. According to economists and the NCP's al Hassan, it has printed money to do so. This has further increased inflation.

However, al Hassan believes that gold, which is not so tightly controlled by the government, may benefit the people more than oil; an admission of how little of the oil wealth has actually trickled down.

Oil is concentrated, its impact is very limited on the population because it belongs to the government. But gold does not belong to the government. Gold is in the rural areas. That's why you see the economic activities have moved from the central cities, like Khartoum, to those rural areas where the mining is taking place. And it is not only one place, it is the north, it is in the west, in the east, it is all over.

The flip side of this is that the state's finances will not benefit enough from gold. It is unlikely to be the saviour many are hoping it will be. Put simply, the figures do not add up. Even at its 2012 level, gold revenue is a third to a half of what oil was bringing in during the interim period, and experts think the sector will not expand much further.[44]

Back to the fields

The government's other big hope is agriculture. This is ironic, of course. Agriculture was once the mainstay of the economy, but was woefully neglected when the petro-dollars were flowing freely. Despite the government's focus on oil, a large part of the population makes some sort of living from farming and livestock. The challenge for the government is to make it more profitable. The businessman Osama Daoud's contention is that Sudan could have easily invested in 100,000 acres of agricultural land in every year of the interim period.[45] If that land gave a reasonable return, it would be worth as much as a fully-implemented oil deal with South Sudan, Daoud believes.

Douad's DAL Agriculture is now one of the most productive and cutting edge components of his DAL Group business empire.[46] At Al Waha,

(The Oasis) farm, a blaze of green surrounded by a concrete-coloured desert, DAL has invested nearly $60 million since 2008.[47] The 22,000 *feddan*s (a Sudanese measurement close to an acre) are served by 102 centre pivot irrigation systems, which spray out water brought from the Blue Nile in a neat circle. Al Waha's principal crop, alfalfa, is sold as fodder to the Middle East, having been dried in a 'natural oven'—Sudan's painfully hot sun.[48]

Even with DAL's multi-million dollar budget, there are many constraints on this sort of agriculture. The company has been asking the government to provide electricity since 2008, but has to resort to diesel generators, which account for around 40 per cent of the overheads. A manager also tells me that the country's economic problems mean they have to plan six months in advance to purchase chemical fertiliser, because of the difficulties of obtaining dollars from the bank.

Air-conditioned cows

A few kilometres north along the 'Gaddafi Road'—apparently a gift from the former Libyan leader—is the DAL Integrated Dairy Farm. 2,000 cows have been imported from Australia, South Africa, Germany and Holland, as the local bovine population is not well suited to milk production. The main problem, according to Dr Mohamed Said, the general manager of the project, is the heat, which often flirts with fifty degrees Celsius in the hot season. Still, Dr Said says, 'We are achieving cow comfort!' And how. The cattle live in a roomy barn. Overhead fans spin round 400 times a minute, and the cold air is pumped through water vapour, producing a cooling spray. A similar system is used in the most chic Khartoum cafés, to keep the customers from overheating over their cappuccinos.

That is not the end of the facilities in the cowshed: a special curtain drops down if a current of hot air is sensed. The temperature in the barn is around twenty degrees lower than the air outside. 'If it is too hot, we would have a drastic drop in milk production,' Dr Said says. 'We are approaching thirty litres per cow a day. Without this we would be achieving far less.' Each cow also has an electronic belt around its neck which lets a central computer know if it is getting sick and when it is ready for insemination.[49]

With Al Waha and his air-conditioned cows, Daoud believes he has 'proved that investment in agriculture actually works'. Of course hardly anyone will be able to match this Sudanese super-company's costly cutting edge technology, or the sheer scale of the investments it has poured in over the last few years. DAL's high-tech farms also reduce the manpower needed, though Al Waha takes on 200 seasonal labourers each year.

Failing farms

Mohamed Babikir Alamin's story is more typical than DAL's. He is one of the many farmers who have been forced to find new ways to make money. A thin man with greying hair and a twinkle in his eye, he took me in his spluttering car to what had once been a prosperous farm. His property, which is a short walk from the White Nile river, measures 25 *feddan*s, roughly 900 times smaller than DAL's Al Waha. By the banks of a canal, Babikir has constructed a fish farm, and nearby he used to grow sorghum and flour to sell in his town, Gataina.

'We are a big agricultural country, but we forgot all about it when the petrol came,' Babikir says. Now he finds it impossible to get the loans he needs from local banks. He feels this is because he is not on good terms with the NCP. As a result Babikir hasn't farmed for some time. Luckily some years in France, and a spell working for the French embassy in Khartoum, enabled him to buy two bulldozers. He rents them out to farmers in the Gezira Scheme, to clear the irrigation canals. The canals have lots of silt and weeds, and have been poorly maintained. The farmers struggle to rent Babikir's bulldozers, as the bill used to be picked up by the state; some have to sell their sorghum reserve to cover the cost.

In the Gezira Scheme and elsewhere cotton no longer dominates. Its place has been taken by sesame and livestock, as well as sugar, groundnuts and gum arabic.[50] Gum arabic, a colourless and odourless gum which is a key component in fizzy drinks, carries flavour in food, and can even be used as a lick-able adhesive for postage stamps, is a good indication of the importance of agriculture in rural Sudan. Gum arabic is cultivated in a great band in the south of the country, from Darfur in the west through to the border with Ethiopia in the east, and an estimated five million people depend, at least in part, on the income it brings.[51]

The gum belt is also known as the 'poverty belt'.[52] In a good year, a tapper might earn 3,000 SDG, less than $500 by late 2012 black market rates. In early 2013 the government admitted the gum arabic sector needed substantial local and foreign help.[53] The gum arabic trade also highlights some of the iniquities common in agriculture and the Sudanese economy as a whole. 'There is a type of feudal system where some people go and take a big chunk of land because of their position in the government or state, and they have a monopoly,' explains the former head of the forestry commission, M. K. Shawki. He speaks the precise English of the older generation which went to school before Arabic became the language of education. 'The actual producer is only a hireling, and so they just pay him subsistence, and even that is very little.'

Agriculture in Sudan has been neglected so thoroughly that it will take a long time to reverse its decline. Productivity is low, in part because irrigation schemes like Gezira have not been well maintained. One report suggested as much as 85 per cent of the cultivated area in Gezira and the al Managil extension suffers from a shortage of water.[54] Agricultural schemes in some areas are also short of labour. The South Sudanese have left, and many Sudanese are now prospecting for gold, rather than working for a daily wage on someone else's farm.

The government has also leased out large amounts of land to foreign companies, mainly from the Gulf.[55] Between 2003 and 2008 nearly a million hectares were allocated to foreign investors in nine states, according to the World Bank.[56] There were further deals both before and after separation. Some, like the former State Finance Minister Abda Yahia al Mahdi, see no problem as long as this large-scale auctioning off of Sudan's land leads to jobs for locals, food in the markets, and the development of the local economy. However these conditions are usually not met. Instead there have been complaints that the government has sacrificed the nation's land in return for quick cash. Sometimes rural communities have demonstrated against land deals. In June 2013, for example, landowners reportedly protested against the Sinnar State governor, Ahmad Abbas, accusing him of distributing their land to a group of investors.[57] In early July, the governor even had to be whisked away from a rally in Al Dali, as the farmers were so angry with him.[58]

It is clear that in one form or another, agriculture will be at the heart of Sudan's response to its economic crisis. If it is handled well, the country can fulfil some of its food needs, and boost its exports too. However, it is unlikely agriculture will ever match the gaudy oil revenue which poured new confidence into the Sudanese elite, and transformed Khartoum's skyline.

INTERNATIONAL RELATIONS: HINDERING NOT HELPING

Sudan's economy faces three major external financial drags, all linked to its politics: US sanctions, a crushing debt burden and a trade embargo put in place on South Sudan. The sanctions were first imposed by Bill Clinton in November 1997, by Executive Order 13067, because of Sudan's alleged support for international terrorism and sustained human rights violations.[59] They consisted of a trade embargo, as well as an asset freeze on the Sudanese government. After the Darfur civil war bled its way into the world's consciousness, George W. Bush tightened the sanctions by targeting individuals the US held responsible for atrocities in Darfur. He also excluded the (by then semi-autonomous) southern Sudan region, as well as others areas that had been particularly affected by civil war. Gum arabic importers were able to secure an exemption, since the commodity is vital for Pepsi and Coca Cola. American NGOs are permitted to work in Sudan, with some limitations, but American companies and banks are barred. Dollar transfers are now impossible, and this also affects non-American investors.

As he did at the opening of the White Nile sugar factory, Bashir regularly whips up popular fervour by denouncing the foreign powers trying to bring his country down. Economists complain there is no investment by US companies; and politicians suggest this is hurting the people, not the government.[60] Mustafa Khogali says he was forced to route American goods via Italy and Dubai, adding to the shipping and handling costs. A set of $1,000 drums set him back $5,000 because of this. At a time when the Sudanese are desperate to open their economy up, the US sanctions create a substantial obstacle.

Debt

The external debt is an even bigger problem. It was largely created under Nimeiri, as he tried to finance a succession of ill-conceived agricultural and industrial schemes. In 2013, the total debt had risen to $45.6 billion, according to the IMF. It grows by an average of at least $3 billion a year[61] and the Sudanese are completely incapable of paying it back. This makes new borrowing extremely difficult. 16 per cent of the debt is owed to multinational organisations like the World Bank, the African Development Bank and the IMF according to Abda al Mahdi. This cuts Sudan off from international markets, and forces Khartoum to borrow on bad terms, largely from Asian countries. She also points out that Sudan is often obliged to buy from the lending country, with no control over the quality of what is purchased. Getting the debt reduced or cancelled would have a major impact on Sudan's economic prospects; but as long as the rest of the world follows America and the West's lead on this issue, Sudan's catastrophic political and human rights record makes this unlikely.

Trade

Another political decision which hurt the Sudanese economy was a trade embargo imposed on South Sudan, in May 2011, just before the new country seceded. Inevitably, some people attempted to get round the ban, sometimes with disastrous consequences. In June 2012, Ahmed Abdul Rahman Al Hussein and Mustafa Al Hussein Mohamed were each sentenced to ten years' imprisonment and a 5,000 SDG fine for trying to smuggle sorghum into South Sudan.[62]

The government line was that the embargo was a military decision aimed at securing the borders. Another explanation is that Sudan wanted to stop the South Sudanese using old Sudanese pounds, which it feared might destabilise its economy. In South Sudan the embargo was seen as a punitive measure: economic warfare against their fledgling state. Whatever the truth of the matter, it undoubtedly cost the Sudanese economy dearly, and in particular the already impoverished areas on the border. The Sudanese Ministry of Trade estimates that the Sudanese used to export 180 different commodities to South Sudan on a regular basis.[63] Many of these goods can be exported only to South Sudan, as there would be no demand for them anywhere else.

THE FUTURE

With its economy contracting, and the financial burdens on it mounting, the government came under increasing criticism after secession. The economist and opposition figure Hassan Satti says the government has failed. 'I think now they don't even know what to do. The only thing they know is to stay in power: to spend on themselves, the army, security, and take tough measures against anyone who is against them.'

Looked at more charitably, the crisis means the government is undoubtedly less able to take on the kind of grand projects that characterised the oil boom years; but the investment in infrastructure from this period, patchy though it was, as well as the relatively well-educated population, should stave off the very worst. Yet despite the scrabbling for loans, the austerity measures, the new factories, the 'lucky' gold and the new focus on agriculture, Sudan's economy is unlikely to flourish in the years to come. If the government doesn't adjust its mindset to its new circumstances, and reduce its spending, things could even get worse.

This economic crisis may represent the future. At several points in Sudan's history, economic woes have had serious political ramifications. The NCP would do well to heed Khogali's warning: 'If you look at the first speech made by the president, justifying why they were coming into power, the reasons that he gave then are the exact same situation that we are in today.'

SOUTH SUDAN

The Paloich oilfields wallow in the Melut basin, just south of the border with Sudan. This is some of South Sudan's least hospitable land. The rough road north from the Upper Nile state capital, Malakal, embraces then pushes away from the White Nile; as the palm trees on the banks of the sluggish river recede, the terrain becomes ever more desolate. During the dry season, gorse bushes stick out from blackened topsoil. When it rains most tracks turn to sludge. Each village is just a few grass-thatched huts. There is little sign of the state; certainly no electricity or tarmac. Under the ground lies South Sudan's fortune, as well as the fuel for conflict past, present, and almost certainly future: oil.

It's easy to tell when you're getting near the oilfield. The road sheds its muddy skin, metamorphosing into smooth concrete; metal pipelines thicker than a man's leg snake alongside, raised a few inches above the ground; and giant electricity pylons tower above. The pipelines flow north to Sudan; the road and electricity lead to the oil workers' camp. Security at the camp, which is more of a small town, is provided by the SPLA as well as the oil company's own team. The fenced compound has a mosque, a dining hall and a football pitch. The small airport is nearby. The workers, from South Sudan, Sudan, China, Malaysia and elsewhere, live on site, in the only substantial brick buildings in the area. Even the local police commissioner's office, in a nearby town, is a shipping container.

At night, the glow from the oil company's lights can be seen from many miles away. A short drive from the compound up the well-maintained

road, past one of the many oil rigs, is the oil processing facility: an elon-
gated red and white pyramid pushing out pipes adorned with pressure
gauges. Workers in bright orange bibs bustle past circular storage tanks,
which glint in the sun. The hard edge of modern technology seems to
mock the shacks and huts of the nearby villages, one of which is just a
couple of hundred metres away, next to a pool of foul-smelling water.

The oil curse

Economies that depend heavily on a single source of income are always
vulnerable. Few can ever have been as much in hock to one raw material
as South Sudan. On independence in July 2011, oil accounted for 98 per
cent of the government's revenue, as well as all the central bank's foreign
exchange: this is the oil curse brought to life. Oil has aptly been described
as 'the lifeline of the economy,'[64] yet many, like those living near the oil
facilities in Paloich, have not benefited from it at all. At independence,
the government estimated the GDP per capita at $1200, a figure that
was greeted with disbelief, although technically it was true.[65] Perhaps the
more relevant statistic is that over half the population lives on less than
a dollar a day.[66]

During the long war years, oil did not help southern Sudan at all. The
revenue went to Khartoum, and SAF bombed southern Sudan with weapons bought by proceeds from the southern oil wells. After the CPA was
signed in 2005, the semi-autonomous government of southern Sudan
began to receive 49 per cent of the oil revenue coming from under its soil;
an equal share went to the federal government in Khartoum, with the
remaining 2 per cent going to the oil-producing areas. The billions poured
in, creating tremendously rich individuals, and a nascent petro-state.

On independence day, South Sudan took control of all of its oil; at the
very moment Sudan was facing the collapse of its economy, South Sudan's
already unprecedented income doubled. This was the new country's
chance to make up for decades of underdevelopment, and create a prosperous nation. Yet in January 2012, as part of an ongoing row with Sudan,
the South Sudanese shut down their oil production.[67] This bold move
gave the country a glimpse of its economic future: most experts think
South Sudan's oil revenue will decline seriously from 2020, and some
believe the downward slope is more likely to be reached in 2015.[68]

Limited reserves

There are many different views on just how much oil South Sudan has, in part because the war made proper surveys difficult. In the aftermath of independence, South Sudan was producing around 350,000 barrels per day,[69] all in two states near the border with Sudan, Unity and Upper Nile.[70] The oil experts are working on the basis that the united Sudan had proven reserves of five to six billion barrels, although some believe it could be just a third of this. Even in late 2012, South Sudan wasn't sure exactly how much oil it had inherited.[71]

Juba has great hopes of further discoveries, particularly in Jonglei, the most populous and least stable state.[72] The government thinks there may be oil reserves in Lakes state, and also in Unity and Upper Nile near existing operating oilfields. Jonglei represents perhaps the best chance of a new find of oil in exploitable quantity, though experts worry about the high costs associated with extracting it in such difficult and under-developed countryside.

Some South Sudanese also dispute the international consensus that the oil is probably running out; for example Lual Deng, the former federal Petroleum Minister in the united Sudan and a member of the South Sudanese National Assembly, is convinced that enough commercially exploitable oil will be found to make up the gap. Further gains could be made through better techniques too. The current production is extremely inefficient: only 27 per cent of the oil is recovered. With Norwegian help, South Sudan is trying to improve this figure significantly.[73] Whether new reserves are found or not, for at least the first decade after independence oil is likely to represent South Sudan's greatest, indeed almost only, source of income.

Life outside the oil fields

Oil has a dirty history in South Sudan. Some of the most ferocious fighting in the north-south war involved militias linked to Khartoum carrying out 'egregious human rights abuses, including massacres and mass civilian displacements' to clear space around the oilfields.[74] Many South Sudanese are still very angry about this experience.

Even after peace came, the petro-dollars certainly haven't done much for those who live in the shadows outside the oil facility's lights. Take Paloich. 'We are not benefiting from all these things they are doing here,' says Jok Kaman, an upright man in a dirty checked shirt. He's standing next to that stinking pool of water, which is close enough to the oil workers' compound to reflect its buildings. 'No-one cares for us, for our health, for our education, even for our livelihood,' Jok says. 'We want to live as people, as those who have something. We have nothing at all.'

It's a damning critique, not least of the South Sudanese government, which has been in formal control of this area since 2005, and has earned billions of dollars in oil revenue since then. However the villagers say the real problem is with the oil company. Many locals want jobs, but they often go to more qualified outsiders, either from elsewhere in South Sudan, or from Sudan or further afield. Worse still, the villagers say, the environmental impact of the oil production has been devastating.

Nyang Pal is a man in his forties. Despite the presence of a security guard from the oil company, he is determined to speak. 'The oil and this waste water contaminated our crops,' he says. 'The environment is not good for us.' Pal and others charge that oil production has ruined local water supplies. The governor of Upper Nile state, Simon Kun Pouch, backs them up.[75] In his dimly lit office in the state capital Malakal, he told me water contaminated by the oil is dumped around Paloich, endangering the health of people there.[76] Parliamentary investigations have found 'significant environmental problems caused by unsafe dumping of water, mud and other waste in the open.'[77]

Oil and the village city

Kaman and Pal might find it hard to believe, but in the years since 2005 oil has brought about a limited but impressive transformation—in South Sudan's capital at least. When the peace agreement was signed, Juba was a provincial garrison town devastated by years of war. In one of his short stories, the South Sudanese writer Victor Lugala put it like this:

Our freedom fighters packed their few earthly possessions and said goodbye to the grass curtain, as they trooped to Juba, a city repeatedly raped by zombies and forgotten by time. Welcome to Juba, the village city of heat, filth, shit, booze, grub and raw sex.[78]

The 'village city' is now a fast-growing town (metropolis would be an exaggeration) of hundreds of thousands of people, its borders expanding every day.

In 2009, you could say 'the road' and everyone knew you meant the one good tarmac road in town. By 2012, there were over sixty kilometres of paved roads in Juba. In some neighbourhoods it seems every other building is a hotel, some using shipping containers as bedrooms, each charging extortionate prices. There is a new basketball stadium, a vast cultural centre, and numerous new office buildings. Most of the growth the South Sudanese government can claim over the last few years has been down to oil money, and the investment it attracts.

THE SHUTDOWN, OR SOUTH SUDAN'S 'ECONOMIC DOOMSDAY MACHINE'

When the government decided to shut down its own oil production, the reaction around the world was one of bewilderment. The Sudans expert Alex de Waal wrote that South Sudan had 'set off its economic doomsday machine'.[79] It was a decision created by rage. Since before independence, South Sudan had been exporting its oil through Sudan's pipelines, refineries and export terminal. With negotiations between the two countries going badly, there was no agreement on how much the new country should pay for this use of Sudan's infrastructure.

In December 2011, after months without being paid for facilitating the exports, Sudan started to confiscate part of the new country's oil. This was condemned internationally, and even within the country: Osama Daoud, the Sudanese businessman, says it was 'an unfortunate decision'. The consequences were certainly dramatic. On 20 January 2012, South Sudan instructed the oil companies inside its borders to shut down the wells. Juba justified this dramatic move by saying Sudan had stolen $350 million worth of oil, and prevented ships carrying $400 million worth of oil from leaving Port Sudan.[80]

The shutdown happened so quickly that the oil companies were concerned about long term damage to the pipelines. South Sudan's deputy Minister of Petroleum and Mining, Elizabeth Bol, acknowledges they may well be right, calling the shutdown 'too quick. There were some challenges and some technical mistakes. Even some of our technical staff did not know how to shut it down.' The oil companies had wanted a gradual shutdown, flushing out the pipelines with chemicals, and then water. But South Sudan wanted to act fast.

When a South Sudanese national, the vice president of Dar Petroleum, counselled less haste, he was removed from his position.[81] This was a time of anger. According to my regular but anonymous ministerial source, emotions were running so high in cabinet when the shutdown was discussed that it was impossible to raise a dissenting voice. 'We had no time for considering what the impact would be—if you're angry you think about that sort of thing later. So we will have to put up with the impact of that decision,' The Minister told me a few weeks after the shutdown began.

Paying the price

The consequences were devastating. The South Sudanese government had willingly foregone its only source of income, in a multi-billion dollar game of chicken with Sudan that made both sides poorer.[82] Although the South Sudanese claimed to have stashed away enough money to hold out for three years, few believed them. Even the senior SPLM politician Luka Biong guessed in March 2012 that there were only three months of reserves left.[83] The then-Vice President Riek Machar told me development would be put on hold for thirty months, but basic services would be maintained.

South Sudan's international allies were dismayed. 'They paid a terrible price,' is how the US Special Envoy for the Sudans, Princeton Lyman, put it. 'There are almost three million people in South Sudan who are living off the World Food Programme. We and other donors had to stop development and start buying pharmaceuticals and keeping teachers in school, instead of building roads and teacher training schools and all the things we were doing for development.' At a time when the South Sudanese finally believed they would get the development they had needed for decades, its leaders had put any chance of that in cold storage.

It took a leaked briefing note from the World Bank to make it clear just how ordinary people would suffer because of the shutdown.[84] Marcelo Giugale, the Bank's Director of Economic Policy and Poverty Reduction for Africa, told Kiir and senior ministers on 29 February 2012 that the Bank had never seen a situation as dramatic as the one faced by South Sudan. The meeting convinced him that Kiir and senior ministers simply hadn't understood the economic implications of the shutdown. The consequences, according to the World Bank's analysis, would include a collapse of GDP (not a collapse of growth, as usually happens in a financial crisis); a massive devaluation of the South Sudanese Pound (SSP); an exponential rise in inflation; and a depletion of South Sudan's reserves.

Worse still, the World Bank estimated a further 3.6 million people would fall under the poverty threshold, taking the poverty rate from 51 per cent in 2012 to 83 per cent in 2013. The child mortality rate would double and school enrolment would drop from 50 per cent in 2012 back to its abominably low 2004 wartime level of 20 per cent. As nearly half of South Sudan's food is imported, food insecurity would also rise, quashing hopes that the shutdown would only hurt urban state employees. Kiir was apparently concerned about the food insecurity, but in the end the government's response, as summarised by the World Bank, was that the South Sudanese population had suffered for years, and would be prepared to suffer again.

By August, the South Sudanese pound had collapsed to more than five to the dollar (compared to an official rate of under three), and there were petrol queues in Juba, with a litre costing 25 SSP on the black market, rather than the 6.2 SSP petrol pump rate. Outside the capital, the figure was often considerably higher. Importing food and fuel was difficult because Uganda and Kenya did not want the South Sudanese currency, causing Juba to dip into its precious store of dollars. Inflation soared to a yearly figure of over 80 per cent in June 2012.

Yet despite this rapidly deteriorating situation, the shutdown was initially greeted with great public enthusiasm, as the government had predicted. There were rallies in favour of the government's decision, and phone-in shows on the radio overflowed with positive reactions. The difference with Khartoum was marked: with inflation running at about half the South Sudanese rate, thousands of Sudanese took to the streets to protest. In South Sudan, however, the leaders still had a large store of political credit: these were, after all, the men who liberated the country. Riek described the shutdown to me as the moment South Sudan took its economic independence from Sudan, a politician's bombast, for sure, but also reflective of a wider mood.

Austerity, survival and suffering

Just like their counterparts in Khartoum, the government in Juba announced a series of austerity measures. The salaries of federal civil servants (including the military) were not cut, but benefits and travel allowances were reduced. In some cases housing allowances were halved.[85] This was particularly significant as in some cases allowances make up more than half of the monthly take home pay.[86] The government made a belated attempt to increase taxation revenues, but these remained pitifully small.[87]

The grants to the states also went down. Although the drop was initially only meant to be 10 per cent, Rizik Zachariah Hassan, the governor of Western Bahr el Ghazal, said his remittances from Juba were sliced by 46 per cent, to around $6 million per year.[88] The governor said he was able to avoid redundancies, but everyone had to suffer a little.

If you ask South Sudanese how they are, as a greeting, they will often reply 'somehow', an answer surely born out of years of struggling to get by. Throughout most of 2012, the South Sudanese economy managed to survive, somehow. Kosti Manibe, the Minister of Finance and Economic Planning at this time, was even able to boast halfway through the year that the country had not collapsed, despite the predictions of the economists.[89] As well as the austerity measures, Manibe said South Sudan hoped to raise non-oil revenue to $700 million, though it is clear that even if attained this would hardly make a difference.

The rest of the gap was apparently to be made up with domestic borrowing and foreign loans. My ministerial source said Qatar had provided $100 million. The suspicion is that the government must have received substantially more than this to get by; perhaps money was advanced against future oil revenue, though if this did happen it would have been on disadvantageous terms. Then-Vice President Riek was one of many SPLM leaders who denied that this had happened. Lyman, the US envoy, believes cutting off their oil left the South Sudanese 'in debt up to their eyeballs.'

Enthusiasm for the shutdown waned over the months. In Leer, the small town in Unity state where the cow-herder Gatgong Jiech lives, it was easy to see why. Teachers and policemen complained their salary came late. The policemen's pay packet, when it did arrive, dropped from 640 SSP to 450 SSP, part of a general cutback in Unity state.[90] In the market, a collection of mottled tin shacks rising from rubbish-strewn soil, the price of a bag of sorghum more than doubled, to 700 SSP, around 150 dollars, which was far too expensive for most to afford.[91]

'When the oil was stopped, so many problems happened', complains Peter Nyok, the senior administrator for Leer county. 'The economy went into a downturn. The things we got from oil stopped, and so did the development we were doing in the counties.' Nyok's office is as bare as the shutdown economy: a room with peeling aquamarine paint, a desk and some chairs, but no computer, electricity, or files. Nyok and others would not express any frustration with their party, the SPLM, or the new country, but there was a clear sense of dismay at how hard their lives had become. It was not just in Leer. The price of the staple food, millet, quadrupled throughout the border states.[92] Many simply went hungry. If this is a glimpse of life when the oil finally runs out, it is a tremendously depressing one.

A new pipeline

As soon as the shutdown was announced, the South Sudanese said they would build a new pipeline, either to Lamu on the Kenyan coast, or to Djibouti. The idea, which had first been floated before separation, was to remove Juba's total economic dependence on the old enemy in Khartoum. The shutdown illustrated vividly just how damaging that could be. However experts warned it would take many years and many billions of dollars to finish a new pipeline. South Sudan had neither time nor money. By late 2013, there had been no work on a new pipeline, though South Sudanese leaders frequently said it was still an integral part of their plans.

THE FUTURE IS IN THE FIELDS

Like Khartoum, Juba is aware of the need to diversify its economy; a need that became an absolute imperative once the oil stopped flowing. Here too, agriculture seems like the best option. Despite oil's prominence in the South Sudanese economy, 78 per cent of households live from crop farming and animal husbandry.[93] However, South Sudan doesn't produce enough to feed everyone. When he signed the CPA, John Garang said oil would be used to develop agriculture.[94] So far it hasn't happened, although there is little doubt that South Sudan's future is as an agricultural nation.

According to the Agriculture ministry, more than 90 per cent of South Sudan's land is suitable for agriculture.[95] Sceptics believe this figure is exaggerated. It is clear, though, that only a small proportion of the country's prime land is being used for agriculture. The official figure is 4 per cent. There are other natural resources that help farming: for instance, South Sudan has many rivers, and heavy rainfall for up to nine months of the year. Fishing could also provide a reliable source of income. The world's newest country also has the sixth biggest herd of cows in Africa.

So far South Sudan's agricultural potential is almost totally under-developed. The lack of roads means that even the agriculturally rich pockets of the country cannot get their food out.[96] The economist Peter Biar Ajak points out that 'South Sudan is a net importer of food, including even animals, which is what we are supposed to have in abundance.' If you sit down to eat a steak in Juba, the chances are it came from abroad, despite the vast herds of cattle all over South Sudan. Just as Khartoum concentrated solely on oil once it started flowing, Biar Ajak says Juba should have done much more to develop agriculture during the interim period. 'With six years and a constant supply of $2 billion per year, and you could not manage to develop a concrete agricultural scheme that could become the foundation of your economy! It simply tells you that we were not thinking.'

In Northern Bahr el Ghazal, which borders Sudan, the importance of agriculture is obvious. 'In our state, if it's not 100 per cent doing agriculture, it's 99 per cent because there is no other way,' says Ayii Bol Akol, with a smile. 'Even those working in government are doing agriculture.' Bol should know. He is the state's minister for agriculture and forestry, and he has a farm of his own. In his office, a simple building built by foreign donor money a short drive out of Aweil town, Bol explains that sorghum, groundnuts, rice, maize and sesame are produced in Northern Bahr el Ghazal. The ministry is trying to introduce cassava, which is already grown in neighbouring Western Bahr el Ghazal, and Bol wants to start trials of sugar-cane and sunflowers. Most of the farming relies solely on good old-fashioned sweat and toil, but there are two mechanised schemes in the state. Bol is particularly proud of the Aweil rice scheme, an old project which has become a recent (if limited) success story.

A promising rice scheme

The project was first set up in 1944, during the colonial period.[97] After Sudan became independent, UN bodies and foreign donors developed the infrastructure, raising dykes and improving canals. In the 1970s the scheme started producing. It became such a fundamental part of local life that popular songs were composed about the new crop. It also became, for many in Aweil, a further example of their status as second-class citizens in the eyes of Khartoum. The grade three rice, the worst quality, was kept to feed South Sudan, Bol says, and the good rice, grades one and two, was sent to Khartoum.

When the second civil war broke out in 1983, production in the rice fields stopped. Northern Bahr el Ghazal was one of the areas worst affected by the fighting. By the time the CPA was signed in 2005, the rice fields had been so heavily mined, by both sides, that it was impossible to walk through them, much less farm. In 2008, a grant from the EU got the scheme started again. It took a year to completely de-mine the fields. By 2011, 600 tenants were producing 10,000 bags of rice a year.

Each farmer is allocated two to four *feddan*s which they control, clean and harvest. Raised embankments that serve as roads run between the basins. Small concrete bridges straddle the canals of dirty, peanut-coloured water. Women in knee-length skirts and men in sun-bleached shirts pick weeds to protect the thin vertical green stalks. The women bend from the waist, keeping their legs straight. It is hard work.

Nearby a red Massey-Ferguson tractor is on hand. The government doesn't have enough tractors, so Bol has pushed for farmers all over the state to organise themselves in co-operatives. Twenty-six were set up in the two years after he was appointed in 2010. 'If there is only one tractor for my area, I will use it, because I am the minister, then the MP will use it, then the commissioner, and so on,' he explains. 'The low person who is vulnerable will not use it.' Now groups, including the Aweil Rice Co-operative, get priority for tractors, and for food-for-work schemes run by the World Food Programme.

Marco, a bald man with a moustache, wearing a polo shirt with horizontal stripes, has been given two *feddan*s to look after. In 2011, he was able to produce twenty bags of rice. He sold some, and the rest went to his family, including his five children. 'It changed our situation a lot,' Marco says. 'Now our children are going to school, we can pay the fees, and we have some food to eat. Rice is good.' The farmers turn over 48 per cent of their production to the government, which has provided ploughs, harrowing, the tractor, fuel and a driver, and the water infrastructure. Farmers often complain about paying for the water, as they say it is provided free of charge by God. The minister replies that God may have sent the water, but it was the government that provided the canals.[98]

The scheme has provided jobs, and even changed local habits. Not everyone eats rice in South Sudan, but Bol says it has been a staple food for Northern Bahr el Ghazal since the 1970s.[99] It is also a cash crop. 'Farmers tell me "I married my second wife with the cows I got from rice!"' Bol says. Now the plan is to get foreign investment to develop some of the other basins which are currently unused, and begin to export rice. Here, as elsewhere, the roads are bad, making it difficult to get crops to market. However Bol says the suitable climate, willing workers and large number of warehouses in the state mean it could export rice in large quantities.

Agricultural problems

The history of large state-run schemes is not a glorious one. Rice was produced in Aweil for only a decade or so, before this recent revival. The Zande Scheme, which was set up in what is now Western Equatoria during the Second World War, provides a further warning. It was intended to transform the life of the Azande, largely through cotton cultivation. However it failed, 'at considerable human and financial cost.'[100] Today the Zande Scheme's imposing buildings still stand in Nzara, in a state of advanced decay, a mouldering monument to the failed idea.

Most agriculture in South Sudan will continue to be small-scale subsistence farming, as it has been for centuries. Yet large tracts of good quality land have been sold off or leased to foreign companies. By 2011, an estimated 9 per cent of South Sudan's land was in the hands of foreigners or large domestic investors.[101] This is seen by some as an affront to the new country's sovereignty. Land used by foreign companies is also unlikely to be used for food production for the domestic market, which is of vital importance as so many people struggle to grow or buy enough to eat. There is little evidence that the foreign-owned land has brought much development either.

Some of the deals have been heavily criticised. In one case, in Mukaya *payam* (an administrative district) in Central Equatoria state, 600,000 hectares were leased for forty-nine years, for the incredibly low sum of just over $25,000. Nile Trading and Development Ltd, a company in Texas, signed the contract with local officials. It included the right to exploit the area's natural resources and keep most of the profits.[102] The deal was reconsidered after an outcry by South Sudanese and international groups.[103]

There are also concerns about South Sudan's low agricultural productivity. In 2012, national cereal production dropped by 25 per cent on the previous five years, because of drought in 2011 and flooding in key areas the following year. In general cereal yields are low in South Sudan compared to the East African region.[104] Variable rainfall, and inter-ethnic conflict which displaces tens of thousands of people every year, make farming difficult.

Nevertheless agriculture is undoubtedly the sector with the potential to help the most people in South Sudan. There is clearly lots of room for improvement, and any that comes will affect millions of people, many of whose lives are extremely precarious. It will take sustained investment, particularly using South Sudan's own oil revenue, for the sector to become one which can support the country once the oil runs out.

Making the cows work

Livestock, and in particular cattle, are vital to the South Sudanese way of life, but unlikely to provide much of a boost to the economy. The Agriculture ministry notes there are an estimated 11.7 million cows in South Sudan,[105] more than one for every person. Warlords, ministers and star musicians own huge herds. However, for cultural reasons many South Sudanese prefer to hang on to their cows rather than sell them, even in times of desperate need. Gatgong Jiech, the expert cow horn shaver in Leer, says he is very reluctant to part with his cows, even if he is hungry. Without cattle, a young man cannot marry, or even, in some cases, have much respect in society. One of the country's great assets is thus considered a source of wealth to be conserved, like money in the bank, rather than sold to use as capital.

Foreign experts often argue more economic use should be made of all these cows. They haven't found a way to convince the South Sudanese yet, and are unlikely to any time soon. However, cows do have a substantial impact on the economy, and society as a whole. To give one example, a rise in the bride price, which is often paid in cows, encourages cattle raiding, with devastating effects. International efforts to change this, or any part of South Sudan's relationship to cows, are likely to fail. I once watched a senior UN official lecture a state governor that letting men buy their wives with cows was disrespectful to women. The men present laughed, and moved the conversation on.

OTHER POSSIBILITIES

The oil brings in the money, and people farm, tend animals and fish, but South Sudan has several other possible sources of income. All of them are underdeveloped, which is inevitable after decades of war. The large wildlife migrations in the south-east of the country lead some to dream of making South Sudan a tourist destination, though this would require a massive overhaul of the existing infrastructure. A World Bank report lists the country's resources as fertile agricultural land, hydro-power potentials, gold, diamonds, petroleum, limestone, iron ore, copper, chromium ore, zinc, tungsten, mica, silver, and hardwoods.[106] Already there is concern about the way hardwoods like teak are being exploited.[107]

The latest geological surveys date from the 1970s and 1980s. The Ministry of Petroleum and Mining's copy of one report on gold reserves has been half-eaten by termites.[108] Artisanal gold mining is a feature of the local economy in Western Bahr el Ghazal and the Equatorias. Several international firms are interested in what is reputed to be high-quality gold. In the period after independence, though, the lack of infrastructure, including railways to get minerals out of the country, have dissuaded investors. The mining is largely unlicensed, and much of the gold in Eastern Equatoria, for example, is smuggled over the border into Kenya or Uganda. It will take time for South Sudan to extract revenue from the other riches under its soil in the way it has from oil.

In Juba, but also in big towns all over the country, hospitality is one of the fastest growing sectors. Many senior figures from the government live in hotels, because of the lack of good quality housing. The industry is dominated by Ugandans, Kenyans, Ethiopians and Eritreans. People from neighbouring countries often work as small traders too, particularly in the three Equatorian states in the south of the country. In the small private sector as a whole, a quarter of all paid jobs are held by foreigners, almost entirely Africans.[109] There was a worrying trend of xenophobic attacks in Juba in 2011 and 2012.

In 2010, there were only twenty companies in South Sudan that employed more than fifty people.[110] In general, the lack of foreign investment in the country is a concern. A lot of the small investors who have come in provide services to the government and the international community. The institutions and laws are weak, which tends to attract bad investors.[111] Big multinational companies are wary of the security situation, the poor legal framework, and the general economic instability. Land rights also make investment difficult, because they are often held by communities not individuals, and because documentary proof of ownership often does not exist.

Large foreign companies and even potential domestic investors are scared away by the scale of the challenges in the country. South Sudan falls into all four of the traps the economist Paul Collier contends keep countries poor. It is struggling to emerge from conflict; gets most of its income from one natural resource, oil; is landlocked with bad neighbours; and suffers from bad governance.[112] As a result of some of these factors, only around one in four South Sudanese can read and write, and less than 2 per cent have a post-secondary school qualification.[113] The almost total lack of development in South Sudan has created another barrier to economic prosperity. Faced with these constraints, only donors and a few brave investors will venture in. External help is unlikely to revolutionise the economy. Instead it is up to South Sudan to use what is left of its oil reserves to create a prosperous post-oil future.

* * *

Oil revenues, or the lack of them, defined the economies of the two countries after separation—and even threatened the security of those in power. Sudan lost three-quarters of its oil production when the south seceded. The battle to make up this gaping financial hole—through minerals or agriculture—was almost impossible to win. To further complicate matters, international disdain for Bashir and his politics obstructed the many attempts to cancel debt or sanctions, or obtain sizeable new loans. As the economy slumped, thousands took to the streets to protest, setting Bashir and his regime one of their greatest challenges.

At separation, many South Sudanese believed their oil reserves would create the sort of prosperity decades of rule from Khartoum had not provided. Yet in January 2012 the South Sudanese shut down their oil production, forfeiting almost all of the government's revenue, in a row over how much to pay to export the oil through Sudan's pipelines. The subsequent economic collapse was one of the most dramatic in history. Even after independence, South Sudan's economic lifeline was at Khartoum's mercy. The politicians in Juba are also aware that the oil will not last forever, so like the Sudanese they must diversify their economy, or see it crumble.

4

DEVELOPMENT

WHERE DOES THE MONEY GO?

SUDAN

On a particularly sweltering day in early May 2011, a SPLM-North soldier called Angelo Adam Juju Baba set out to have a drink. It was two months before South Sudan seceded, and just a month before a new war would break out in Angelo's region of Sudan, the Nuba Mountains, though of course he did not know this yet. Angelo walked a few hundred yards along a makeshift path from his *tukul* or hut to a favourite drinking spot in Upper Kauda, one of the three settlements that make up Kauda, a small town in the heart of the Nuba Mountains. As this was an area controlled by the SPLM, *marissa*, the local beer made from sorghum, was openly on sale.[1] Just under a dozen women competed for his business; Angelo eventually settled into one of the almost identical drinking spots, an area of shade created by some wooden poles supporting a roof made with a brightly-coloured square of cloth. He sat down on an uneven wooden bench, and ordered.

Angelo could hardly have been farther from Khartoum's air-conditioned cafés, with their flat screen TVs and iced coffees; apart from anything else, alcohol is prohibited in the areas of Sudan controlled by the NCP. The woman serving him, whom I will call Maha,[2] had spent three days making the *marissa*, a thick, dark liquid, which is so strong that the Nuba often describe it as food rather than drink. Like many women all over Sudan from non-Arab communities, brewing beer was the only work she could find.[3]

On a good day, Maha earns ten Sudanese pounds, around two dollars according to the black market rate of the time. More often than not though, she says with no apparent anger, her husband, her son or one of her neighbours drink part of her brew, cutting into her income. 'I am poor and I need the money,' she explains, so she will keep producing *marissa*, no matter how often her family makes off with it. 'She has no choice,' Angelo butts in. 'There are no jobs here.'

The vantage point of Maha's beer shack emphasises both the beauty and remoteness of Kauda's setting. Rocky hills splashed with vegetation curve away to the horizon. There aren't many concrete buildings in this part of the Nuba Mountains, or health centres, or government offices. The roads in and around Kauda are not made of tarmac, or even murram, a gravel substitute widely used in both Sudans. In the rainy season the tracks around Kauda disappear under water, which pours down the sharply inclined hillsides all around the town. The better tracks are more stones than dirt, and last longer, even though they damage the tyres of the cars that drive on them. If you have a good vehicle, though, it's a relatively easy drive to the Smokin primary school at which Yassir Ajour is a teacher.

There are ninety-four students in his class. Yassir is young and enthusiastic. He says that he would be happier if his class could be limited to fifty kids, because with nearly a hundred he is worried they aren't all taking in the lessons he is trying to share, but of course he will not turn students away. The lessons in this SPLM-controlled area are all in English, and follow the Kenyan curriculum. In the mid-1990s, a great conference of the Nuba people decided that their children should be educated in English. Nagwa Konda, the Nuba development worker, says her people 'didn't want Arabic as a language of education, because it was an Arabised and Islamised curriculum designed to brainwash African people like us. Even the [Nuba] Muslims said this.'

With beer on sale, English as the language of instruction, and the SPLM flag fluttering over the town, it feels like the Nuba Mountains, or at least those areas under the SPLM's control, have opted out of the Sudanese state. The area saw some of the worst fighting in the second north-south civil war, after many of the Nuba joined the southern Sudanese in the fight against Khartoum. They joined the SPLA for two main reasons. First, in the mid-1980s their neighbours the Misseriya were given weapons, but no salaries, as part of Khartoum's counter-insurgency measures against the southern Sudanese rebels. The Misseriya often attacked the Nuba, plundering their homes and farms. Secondly, and just as importantly, according to a Nuba politician, Al Nour Burtail, the government had been confiscating Nuba land since the 1960s, giving it to northerners for mechanised agricultural schemes. The Nuba often ended up as tenants on land they had once owned, and all the harvests and profits went to Khartoum. Even the *zakat*, the alms that Islam specifies each Muslim should give, was collected locally and then donated to people in Khartoum, Burtail said.

The Nuba proved to be among the SPLM's best soldiers, but their area suffered terribly. The fighting in the Nuba Mountains stopped in 2002, and its people did benefit, a little, from the peace that followed. The freshly painted concrete walls indicate that Yassir's school had been constructed recently. Nagwa Konda, who was born not far from Kauda, says there were 300 schools in the SPLM-North areas by 2010, compared with only a handful in 1995.

However the development that finally came was a sticking plaster over a terrible wound. Kauda, like so many areas on Sudan's periphery, had been neglected and exploited by the riverain elite for decades. The first school in Kauda was only built in 1945, and the rural areas all around were totally ignored. Even in the 1980s, Nagwa's cousins had to walk four hours to and from school every day. The Nuba were largely forced to cope without modern health care, and there were so few paid jobs that many people became domestic servants for Arab families.

Although Sudan's GDP per capita was a respectable $1435 in 2011,[4] making it a lower-middle income country by international standards,[5] large numbers of Sudanese are forced to get by on far less than this. Over the course of a year, Maha's earnings in her open-air beer tent probably work out at less than a dollar a day. Most of the teachers in the Nuba Mountains, like Yassir, are actually volunteers, living off the generosity of relatives and occasional handouts. In Sudan as a whole nearly half the population lives in poverty.[6]

As might be expected, poverty rates vary tremendously from location to location. In Khartoum a little over a quarter of the population is below the poverty line, while in North Darfur the figure is more than two-thirds. Of course, there is inequality in every country, but ever since its creation Sudan's failure to spread its wealth in an equitable way has been one of its defining characteristics. Too many of its citizens are poor; too many areas of the country have seen little or no development. This contributed to people from numerous areas of the united Sudan taking up arms against the state.

In the years running up to and immediately after separation, there were three principal reasons for the poverty and underdevelopment that characterise so much of Sudan (though certainly not all of it). Firstly, a large proportion of government spending is dedicated to the military-security apparatus. Secondly, the high prevalence of corruption increases the imbalance between those who have access to the resources of the state, and those who do not. Finally, any money left over has been heavily channelled into the riverain centre, benefiting the towns, agricultural schemes and politically-connected people in and around the Nile valley.

THE MILITARY

The amount spent on the military, and the intelligence and security services, is a highly sensitive matter in Sudan (as in many countries). However some economists, including the former State Finance Minister Abda Yahia al Mahdi,[7] believe that military spending accounts for more than 70 per cent of the budget, often as part of revenue streams that do not show up in the official accounts. Some think that this estimate is too high. Officials won't comment on just how much goes to the military and the security services, but do acknowledge that it is substantial.[8] Quite apart from salaries, the military and security personnel have their own accommodation, hospitals and other benefits. Soldiers and officers are often given help to purchase motorbikes or cars. As lots of people have relatives in the military or security forces, these benefits are an effective method of buying support.

In addition to the financial resources allocated to the military and NISS every year, the wars in Darfur, South Kordofan and Blue Nile, as well as the border clashes with South Sudan, have been extremely expensive. (South Kordofan and Blue Nile are important agricultural areas too, so conflict there has a further impact on the economy.) As a result of the military spending, hardly any of Sudan's budget goes to health or education. Abda Yahia al Mahdi carried out a study of state and federal spending on health and education in 2008. She found that these vital areas received less than 1.5 per cent of Sudan's GDP, one of the lowest totals in sub-Saharan Africa. As Sudan has now lost most of its oil revenue, there is little chance of any improvement in this area.

Even the NCP's Sabir al Hassan admits that 'there is always competition for resources between the military and development. We are hoping demand from the military people goes down.' As long as Sudan continues to hand over a large chunk of its limited resources to the military and the security forces, it will be all but impossible to develop a national economy that benefits every citizen. Abda is not against military spending which is used to defend the nation, but she is concerned with 'the security spending that is in place to protect the regime rather than the country'. She and many others would like to see this slashed. Of course, given the nature of the Sudanese state, any sort of reduction in the budget for the military-security apparatus is extremely unlikely.

CORRUPTION

The gangrene of corruption has spread through the Sudanese body politic at an alarming rate in the last two decades. According to one prominent newspaper columnist, Al Tahir Satti, it is 'the biggest threat to progress and prosperity in this country'. He received death threats for expressing strong opinions like that, and writing pointed articles about sensitive cases.[9] Of course, corruption existed before Bashir seized power in 1989, but even senior NCP officials accept that it has increased during their time in power, encouraged by the unprecedented flow of petro-dollars.[10]

Older Sudanese often reminisce about the efficiency and probity of the civil service bequeathed by the British; no-one harbours any such warmth for it today. Transparency International's 2012 Corruption Perception Index placed Sudan as the fourth most corrupt country in the world.[11] Money that should have been used to develop the country has been stolen; cheaper, sub-standard construction work has been carried out in return for back-handers.

The NCP has also adroitly used patronage to keep key interest groups happy, including by stuffing the civil service with its supporters. Access to the state and its resources is not based on the need of an individual or region, but linked instead to the relationship with the Islamist project, perceived loyalty to Khartoum, or ties to individuals in power. This has, inevitably, benefited those in or near the capital, and further disadvantaged the people from the geographical margins, and their areas. In Sudan there is a widespread feeling that politicians are corrupt, using their positions to hand out money to relatives and friends.

I was once interviewing a very senior NCP politician,[12] when his secretary knocked on the door. The politician's uncle had arrived. Once he was shown in, the old man, dressed in a white *jallabiya* and turban, got straight to business, asking his nephew for cash, 26,000 SDG to be precise, around $6,000 by the black market rates of the time. The politician told his relative he would deal with the matter later, watched him leave, and then turned to me. 'Simple people think government is just about giving money,' he said.

State bodies have been implicated in corruption scandals, and the Khartoum rumour mill frequently alleges the president's family is involved in dodgy deals. The area where many of the president's allies live, Kafouri in Khartoum North, is nicknamed 'Hosh Bannaga' by the Sudanese, after Bashir's home village. Alongside a new highway in 'Hosh Bannaga' are what must be the biggest houses in Sudan. My source who has worked with Bashir for many years is dismayed that the president does not speak out, to make it clear that the allegations against some of his family members are nonsense.[13]

A strictly controlled press investigates corruption scandals surprisingly frequently. The columnist Satti points out that although the National Assembly often condemns corruption, no-one ever gets prosecuted. Echoing a common view, Satti says Bashir took power vowing to restore morality, but the NCP has failed to live up to this promise. 'They said they will fight corruption and they will fight poverty and they will fight injustice,' he says, his voice rising with every clause,

but during the twenty-three years they have been in power we did not see anyone who went on trial because of corruption cases, although we have documents which prove that some of them are corrupt. But nothing happened. This proves that the mentality of this regime is not to put anyone on trial as long as he's one of them.

Osama Daoud, Sudan's biggest businessman, was expressing a minority view when he told me 'corruption is not big by African standards'.

By contrast, one market trader explained that predatory policemen extort money so often it's as if 'they don't even take a holiday'.[14] The large-scale graft comes through government tenders and in many dealings with officialdom. Mustafa Khogali, the drumming businessman, says corruption has been institutionalised and internalised to such an extent that

it's become a norm and they've actually, in certain places, made official names for, it calling it *hafiz*. *Hafiz* is like calling it a stipend.[15] Anything you want done in a governmental institution, if you want it done on time you have to pay a little something under the table. Now due to the economic situation that we're in, knowing how much these people get paid in ministries, I can understand, you know? These people get paid [monthly] salaries that I would spend in a day or two or a week.

The result is that the efficiency of the civil service has deteriorated dramatically, and service delivery has become even harder.

THE CENTRE AND THE PERIPHERY

One of the defining characteristics of the different forms of the Sudanese state, from the early nineteenth century to the beginning of the twenty-first, has been the concentration of power and resources at the centre, at the expense of the periphery. Khartoum's economic and political domination is so great that Sudan has been termed 'The One City State'.[16] The capital is actually three cities, linked by bridges. Khartoum itself is the wealthiest town in the country; Omdurman, on the west bank of the White Nile, was once the capital, and is seen by many as the home of the ordinary Sudanese; Khartoum North (sometimes known as Bahri) is an industrial area to the north of the Blue Nile where some of the nouveaux riches also live. Power in the Tri-City has been concentrated in the hands of the Three Tribes.

At street level, the overall impression Khartoum gives can be chaotic: women selling hot drinks sit on knee-high stools under mango trees, boiling up spicy coffee and hibiscus tea, a couple of paces away from expensive coffee shops where a cappuccino costs as much as the tea lady makes in a week. Open-backed trucks giving lifts to men in turbans bounce over the rusting train tracks cutting through the heart of the city. Young boys selling knives and prayer mats and Tupperware cluster at traffic lights, a stone's throw from mosques and malls. However if you soar above the capital you get a totally different impression: the roads, whether tarmac or dirt, are laid out in neat grids, and power cables push in straight lines out to the expanding suburbs. The apparent chaos, at the heart of the city-state, is really under tight control.

The structure of Sudan itself is reflected in Khartoum: wealth fades away the further you go from the heart of the town. The centre's old colonial buildings, now used as ministries, and the gleaming offices built by petro-dollars, are soon replaced by stubby tower blocks, and mansions with small but well-watered gardens. The villas and the flats become more and more thickly interspersed with simple single-storey brick buildings, each with its courtyard sectioned off with a low wall. In public gardens, desiccated palm trees overlook Chinese-built fun-fairs. On the furthest outskirts of the city, the homes have a temporary feel: hastily-constructed huts to provide some shelter from the sun, inhabited mainly by people from the margins of the country. They have come to the capital for a better life, though not all have found it. Here the tarmac has been replaced by dirt tracks, and donkeys drag carts carrying water-tanks. The edges of the Tri-City slowly bleed into the desert.

The historic roots of inequality

The centre/periphery discourse was popularised, though not invented, by John Garang. His argument that the outer reaches of the state and those who live there had been marginalised still resonates with people in both Sudans, even after the split. The dynamic existed long before Garang's time. For much of the *Turkiyya* period (1820–85) 'administration' in the hinterlands consisted of little more than a few *zariba*s or trading forts used as bases to capture slaves.[17]

The heavy-handedness of the *Turkiyya* officials helped raise support for Mohamed Ahmed al Mahdi. He conquered the country and kicked out the colonisers in the mid-1880s. However the Mahdist state, in particular under the Mahdi's successor or *Khalifa*, Abdallahi al-Taisha,[18] made little effort to improve the lives of ordinary people. The energy of the ruling elite was consumed with the battle between the *Khalifa*'s kinsmen and supporters from Darfur and Kordofan, and the *awlad al bahr* or children of the river.[19]

The Anglo-Egyptian Condominium, which ruled from 1898 to 1956, extended the reach of the state, expanding into what is now South Sudan, and incorporating Darfur in 1916. The north and the south were ruled very differently: Christian missionaries were encouraged to make southern Sudan a bulwark against the spread of Islam, the Closed District Ordinances made travel between the two parts of the country difficult, and at times traders were not allowed to sell 'Arabic' clothing in the south.[20] All parts of the country were administered through local chiefs, the famed 'indirect rule', which kept costs low while creating a group of tribal leaders, not all with traditional legitimacy, who owed their positions to the colonisers.

According to one of the leading political figures of the Bashir era, Ghazi Saleheddin Atabani, the British held a meeting in Khartoum in 1938 in which they concluded that real decentralisation was the best way to develop Sudan, but that it would be far too expensive to put in place. It was often easier, they found, to buy off one of the local leaders rather than to provide any services for his people. The British also gave lucrative contracts to the son of the Mahdi, re-establishing the Mahdi family at the heart of Sudanese political and economic life.[21] The Condominium needed a class of educated Sudanese to work in the lower and middle levels of the state bureaucracy; these people became known as the *effendiya*. They were drawn predominantly from the riverain Sudanese, whose geographical location, and in some cases their support for the British forces that overthrew the *Khalifa*, gave them access to education, and in turn positions within the state.

Overall, the period of Anglo-Egyptian rule entrenched a northern elite, while creating 'a wider population excluded from full participation in the political process, [fuelling] half a century of centre-periphery conflicts in post-colonial Sudan.'[22] In fact, the opening shots of the first north-south civil war, which were fired in Torit in 1955, came even before Sudan's independence. In one of the last acts before the end of the Anglo-Egyptian rule, the 'Sudanisation' of the civil service led to around 800 British and Egyptian posts being turned over to Sudanese. Only six went to southerners.[23] It served as a signpost for the inequality to come.

Educational and business opportunities were concentrated in the centre, for the benefit of those in control of the state. The far-flung reaches of what was Africa's biggest country, at over a million square miles, had no voice in Khartoum, and saw no meaningful development. The full effects of this in South Sudan will be considered later in the chapter. In short, however, when it achieved independence in 2011, the new country was considered one of the least developed in the world.[24]

Darfur

The lack of state involvement was no less nefarious in Darfur. When the British left in 1956, no new boys' schools had been opened for almost a quarter of a century, there were no provincial agricultural officers (despite this being a common post elsewhere in Sudan), and the first provincial judges and education officers had only arrived in 1947, more than thirty years after Darfur came under British control.[25] In the decade after Sudan's independence, two technical schools were set up, and the railway was extended to Nyala, in what is now South Darfur, both under General Ibrahim Abboud. However, the general 'then proceeded to redirect Sudan's wealth for the benefit of Central and Northern Sudan.'[26]

That pattern continued, whoever was in charge in Khartoum. When Hawa Ibrahim, the Darfuri woman from Zalingei, was growing up in the 1970s and 1980s, her brothers used to walk for a day to get to their Koranic school in Wadi Azom. 'There was no transport,' Hawa says. Schools were free at the time, but her family were so poor they kept her at home to work on the land. In 1973 and 1984–85, Darfur suffered through major famines, part of a series going back centuries.[27]

During the Bashir years, discontent over the lack of development can be highlighted by the failure to build a modern road from Khartoum to North Darfur's capital, El Fasher. Darfuris were hopeful it would strengthen the economic and social ties with the rest of the country. In the planning stage, it had been named the '*Ingaz*' road, after Bashir's 'Salvation' revolution, and it was intended to be a sign of the NCP's commitment to Darfur. Darfuris contributed money towards it, but by separation—twenty-wo years after Bashir's coup—it had not been built, continuing the region's isolation.[28] According to a senior NCP source, security was a problem even before the Darfur civil war began, but more importantly most of the money allocated for the road was stolen.[29]

This economic underdevelopment often went hand-in-hand with political marginalisation. Abdallah Khalil, one of the riverain ruling class and one of Sudan's first prime ministers, was elected as a member of parliament for the Um Kadada constituency, in what is now North Darfur. He had never been there.[30] Darfuris set up a committee (this is one of the perennial Sudanese political steps) to militate against the centre imposing parliamentary candidates like Khalil on their region. As the years went by, anger at the lack of development and political influence was one of the factors fuelling inter-ethnic clashes and local uprisings in Darfur.[31]

A just war?

When the Darfur civil war broke out in 2003, it was a 'just war' according to Tigani Seisi, an intellectual who eventually became the leader of a rebel movement.

If you compare Darfur with the rest of the country you would realise there are huge differentials in all terms. Economically Darfur is much more deprived, and all the development projects were more or less concentrated in the centre. In Darfur you could count the number of development projects in the region. If you compare services and social indicators there were marked differentials. The health indicators were terrible, education was incomparable, and Darfur had been politically marginalised since independence. And therefore there were genuine grievances in the region.

Although the causes of the war in Darfur are numerous, if the region had not been so badly neglected, the conflict, one of the world's worst in the first decade of the twenty-first century, might well have been avoided.

Development and Sudan's racial and religious hierarchy

Sudan's vast size and challenging geography make it a hard place to develop, and this was even more true before separation. When Sudanese leaders say it is challenging to improve the lot of people hundreds of kilometres away through the desert or the southern forests, they have a point.[32] Nevertheless, it is no coincidence that the least developed areas in the country fit in with Albaqir Alafif Mukhtar's classification of Sudan's loose racial-religious hierarchy: the lower down that list a Sudanese group comes, the more likely it is that their area has been marginalised.[33]

Some of the development indicators for eastern Sudan, home to the Beja and Rashaida among other ethnic groups, are frighteningly bad. The UN describes the region as having chronically high food insecurity, and the rates of acute malnutrition in the three eastern states are all above the World Health Organisation's 15 per cent emergency threshold. Red Sea state's 2010 acute malnutrition rate of 28.5 per cent was the worst in Sudan,[34] astonishing considering the ongoing conflict in Darfur.

Perhaps unsurprisingly, political movements from the area have called for greater autonomy for decades,[35] and a long-running rebellion only came to an end in 2006. The Eastern Sudan Peace Agreement (ESPA), like similar deals for Darfur and southern Sudan, promised stratospheric sums of money to develop the region.[36] In its corruption and self-interest, the Sudanese centre has consistently sent the message that the only way to attract the attention of Khartoum is to take up arms.

PEACE AND BUILDING

By the time the CPA was signed in 2005, ending the north-south civil war, the centre/periphery dynamic was well established both in practice and in people's minds all around the country. It had become painfully clear that the neglect of certain areas had led to conflict. The oil boom, and the relative peace and stability brought by the CPA, did allow Khartoum to invest in some development. Ghazi Salaheddin of the NCP calls it 'unparalleled in the history of Sudan'.

Five bridges were built in the Khartoum area and tarmac roads multiplied in and around the capital. In the country as a whole, the road network almost doubled between 2000 and 2008.[37] (Famously, Osama bin Laden had built roads during the 1990s, including the highway linking Khartoum to Port Sudan, when he lived in Sudan as a guest of the government). Indeed one Sudan scholar believes 'the strongest card of Sudan's NCP—aside from the formidable security services—is a successful economic record.'[38]

A sizeable middle class was created, largely in and around Khartoum, and its interests became intertwined with those of the NCP, extending the party's political base.[39] But the oil boom spending was inordinately concentrated in cities, as even the head of the NCP's economic division, Sabir al Hassan, admits. Worse still, the oil revenue went on 'the kind of infrastructure that is not very productive,' he says. There is not much economic point in a rural road if the agriculture scheme it is meant to serve has been completely run down; and development in Khartoum only reinforced the existing inequalities.

One major plank of the NCP's economic strategy was dam-building. Dams can provide hydro-power, and increase the amount of irrigated land in the country, and are seen as crucial to Sudan's long-term prosperity. The Merowe Dam in the north of the country took up almost 40 per cent of total public investment in national development projects between 2005 and 2008.[40] It doubled Sudan's electricity generation, but displaced more than 50,000 people, according to campaign groups.[41] It wasn't the first time. In late 1964, the construction of the Aswan Dam resulted in thousands of Nubians being transported to Eastern Sudan;

their homeland vanished under the waters. The forced displacement around Merowe was more violent. In August 2007, a senior UN official said he had received reports of 'shooting of unarmed demonstrators, arbitrary arrests of activists, and repressive measures against the press when journalists have attempted to cover the events'.[42] His call for the dam construction to be halted was ignored.

In late 2011 and early 2012, members of the Manasir ethnic group protested for more than 100 days in front of River Nile state buildings in Ad-Damar. They, along with the Amri and Hamadab, had been affected by the construction of the Merowe Dam. The protestors said they had not received the compensation they were owed, and all the promises to develop their new areas had not been kept. Opposition politicians and journalists were blocked from attending the peaceful sit-in. The demonstration, part of a pattern of local opposition to the dam-building programme, was given added urgency by the government's continued reliance on new dams to provide electricity.

On 1 January 2013, Bashir celebrated the anniversary of Sudan's 1956 independence at the Roseiris Dam, just outside the Blue Nile state capital Damazin. The dam had been heightened to increase its capacity. The project had been five decades in the making, Bashir said, and would benefit the people of Blue Nile, even those who had been displaced to make space for the dam.[43] All the same, rural areas, even those near dams, often do not have electricity. One Damazin resident complained, pointing at Roseiris, 'the dam is right there, but we do not have regular power here. It is all going to Khartoum.'[44]

Capital struggles

Although the Tri-City capital is by far the wealthiest part of Sudan, there are and always have been many people living in desperate poverty there. In the 1970s the Sudanese poet Ali al Mak tackled the subject in his long homage to Omdurman, *A City of Dust*:

> He smelled an aroma of roasting meat,
> The scent of meat being toasted by fire…
>> And, because of hunger
> His stomach plunged into his backbone,
> For hunger could be very painful…

> Be patient! She said…
> "Tomorrow is another day"
>
> [...]
>
> Still he cried, till tears filled him…
> Filling the silver of space
> Where his stomach nursed, at the curve of his back.[45]

Not much has changed since then. Hawa Ibrahim, the Fur farmer who moved to Khartoum in the early 1980s, makes a couple of dollars a day as a tea lady, so little she can't afford to keep all her children in school.

Hawa lives in Haj Youssif, an area of Khartoum North where a lot of people from the peripheries have settled.[46] One of her neighbours, Mohamed Abakr Idriss Ahmed, is a fellow Darfuri who works as a bus driver. On average he earns fifty SDG a day, around seven dollars by the late 2012 black market rate. Following the death of his father, he has to support eighteen people with this tiny amount of money. The school fees are not that high, but they are more than he can manage. One of his sons is working, in a factory that makes clothes for the military. He helps his dad when he can, but he worries he won't have enough money to get married, when the time comes.

As the prices of food and fuel increased following South Sudan's secession, Mohamed simply did not know how he could feed, clothe and educate everyone in the family. When I visited him one evening in May 2012, he gave me a prime seat on a bed placed in the shade in the middle of a courtyard, and sent one of his sons to buy a few cokes, as Sudanese hospitality dictates. The drink was deliciously cool, but I realised Mohamed's generosity had cost around a quarter of the money he had earned that day.

Sharing out the dividends of peace

The wealth-sharing component of the CPA included a section on the establishment of a Fiscal and Financial Allocation and Monitoring Commission which was intended to ensure 'transparency and fairness' in the way money was shared out between the regions.[47] Like so much of the CPA, it was largely ignored: a great chance missed. Khartoum and Gedarif, two of Sudan's seventeen states, receive over 36 per cent of the money allocated to the states (as opposed to the federal government).[48]

Although Khartoum has the largest population, and brings in the most tax revenue, it is also the richest. A truly just system would have allocated the most money to the least developed and poorest states. Kordofan, Darfur, and some parts of the east missed out the most.

The situation is exacerbated by the fact that there are seventeen states, a large number. They all struggle to generate any money, and most of what they do collect simply goes to their own bureaucracies. Khartoum usually sends money for salaries, but not always for development work, so often state employees are paid to sit around doing nothing. All this keeps the states weak, and unable to challenge Khartoum's dominance.[49] The centre-periphery trope is also repeated within each state: the state capital receives most of the resources, and the smaller municipalities next to nothing.[50]

Ghazi Salaheddin said the failure to allow the Allocation Commission to work properly was a terrible error, one he attributed to 'bad government'. At the time he said this, he was a presidential adviser, as well as a very senior MP.[51] But Ghazi admitted money was allocated to the states in uneven ways that boosted the influence of individuals, and there had been a lot of 'unnecessary political spending on the tribes and on the political parties,' an admission of the weight the NCP has given to patronage networks in the regions. All these errors, he said, have 'given rise to many complaints from the states, and the feeling they have been discriminated against. We could have developed in a better way.'

South Kordofan

Abdelaziz Hussain, the half-Misseriya half-Dinka cow-owner, is one of the millions of people from the periphery who can attest to Ghazi's words. He lives in South Kordofan, the state which contains the Nuba Mountains. Abdelaziz's part of the state has always been under government control, but that hasn't brought it very much. 'We don't have many people who have had a good education, and we have no good facilities, no hospitals and roads and schools,' he complains. The Misseriya, like many groups on the periphery who speak Arabic as a mother tongue, have been both ignored by Khartoum and manipulated in the name of a presumed common identity.

Many Misseriya have served in the PDF and other paramilitary groups, as Khartoum trusts them more than the nearby Nuba or South Sudanese. But the military service provided by the Misseriya could not totally overcome their physical distance from the centre, and their unimpressive position in Sudan's racial hierarchy. Although he now lives just a short journey from an international border, and needs to travel to South Sudan every year with his cows, Abdelaziz has no passport. 'We have nothing. We have no documents. How can you get a passport? We live here, outside of Khartoum. No-one in Meiram has a passport, because there is no government, no office, nothing there. What can we do?'

A few kilometres away in Kauda in the Nuba Mountains, in that sunny week in May 2012, a mood of qualified optimism prevailed. Everyone I spoke to was convinced that the SPLM-North's candidate would win the election for state governor, which had taken place that week. People were nervous about what would happen after the results were announced, in a very divided state; but the years of peace had brought undoubted benefits. The war, added to the lack of government interest sustained over decades, had resulted in high levels of illiteracy; but a local radio station broadcast important messages about land-mines, health and community issues from a small new brick building. New schools, including the one Yassir Ajour taught at, had been built, along with boreholes and mills to grind sorghum. Mahmoud Badawi, a prominent local, had constructed Kauda's first hotel, a simple set of rooms around a courtyard just a short stroll from Maha's beer shack.

All this progress came because of the peace agreement, although in the continued absence of the government almost all of the development was financed by foreign NGOs.[52] It wasn't nearly enough, Nagwa Konda said, sitting in her office. Women often walked for an hour to a water pump, and then had to queue for just as long; children in the primary school were forced to travel to the cities each holiday to earn some money for their school fees, or to give to their family; and many of the Nuba who had fled the area during the war returned, but left again when they realised there were very few services. It would clearly take a long time for the people of the Nuba Mountains to attain a reasonable standard of living. All the same, the development of the previous few years was a lot better than anything the area had seen before. A month later, though, Kauda was under attack.

SOUTH SUDAN

'Even before the ravages of war could set in, our country never had anything worth rebuilding. Hence we characterise our post-conflict mission as one of construction rather than reconstruction...'

President Salva Kiir, in his first ever address to the UN General Assembly, 23 September 2011.[53]

Towards the end of a rainy-season afternoon in September 2012, almost exactly a year after President Salva's speech, four boys pushed a wheelbarrow down the main street in Leer, a small town in Unity state. The sky above their heads was a mix of cobalt and slate grey, and along the length of the street pedestrians started to walk a little faster, aware that the clouds might burst at any minute. Several weeks of rain had turned the dirt road into an almost impassable mix of puddles and cloying mud. The very few people in Leer who owned vehicles were mainly keeping them at home, because driving was extremely arduous, and petrol far too expensive. The boys struggled on with their heavy wheelbarrow, weighed down with bright yellow jerry cans of water; they were the only traffic on the road. As they made their way home, they loudly imitated the low thrum of an engine, transforming the wheelbarrow into the car of their dreams.

In Leer, the evidence of decades of war, underdevelopment and neglect can be seen everywhere. The town is far from unique. These are the sort of challenges facing people, and their leaders, all over South Sudan. As Salva pointed out in his speech to the UN, South Sudan started with nothing.

Leer in war and peace

During the war years, Leer was sacked by Paulino Matip's militia, and fought over by the SPLA and the Sudanese army. You can still see bullet holes in the walls of the hospital, which is run by the NGO Médecins Sans Frontières (MSF). Gatgong Jiech, the Nuer pastoralist, lives a twenty-minute walk away, past the airport which is used by NGOs to transport goods and their staff. He says almost all the buildings in town were destroyed during the fighting. War obliterated what little infrastructure there was in South Sudan, and made development all but impossible.

Sitting outside his *luak* or cow barn, with his sorghum crop peeking over the fence, Gatgong is thankful the fighting ended; but he is frustrated that there has been little development since the South Sudanese took control of their own destiny. Gatgong still farms with a hoe, though he would love to have the chance of using modern equipment. When people are really struggling, NGOs hand out food, he says, but 'the government gives us nothing.' However, he is glad that he has been able to send his children to school, an opportunity he never had.

The rapper Emmanuel Jal, one of the best known South Sudanese around the world, has rehabilitated two schools in Leer. One of them is named after Emma McCune, the British aid worker who adopted him and who is buried in Leer.[54] During my visit in September 2012, the secondary school was flooded, so all the pupils had moved to one of the two primary schools, a run-down building next to the market. There is no road to the school buildings, so the children have to skip through puddles and mud.

In one classroom, Simon Bol is teaching maths, even though he qualified as an engineer and hoped to work in the oil industry. He says his salary isn't enough to cover all his needs: sometimes he can't afford to buy himself breakfast. During the oil shutdown, his salary arrived late for two straight months. Like many educators around the country, Bol and his colleagues in Leer are not professional teachers, and, Bol adds, 'we haven't been trained well'.

The kids Bol are teaching are privileged though: fewer than one out of every fifty South Sudanese children are enrolled at a secondary school, among the very lowest rates in the world.[55] Adult literacy is only 27 per cent, and it's much worse for women: only around one in six can read or write.[56] Salva and his government, as Gatgong Jiech acknowledges, have made some steps forward. Primary school enrolment has more than doubled in the years since the peace deal.[57] In time, many of these young pupils will go to secondary school, boosting the literacy rate, and increasing the number of qualified people entering the job market.

The academic Alfred Sebit Lokuji points out that although more children are going to school, the quality of education has not improved: 'the child is at school but he faces hunger, sickness, and a lack of care,' he says. 'It's like being in base training camp, rather than an environment exposing the child to the vast wonderful world of knowledge.' Emma Secondary School, with its borrowed buildings, over-crowded classrooms, lack of textbooks, and teachers who haven't eaten since the day before, illustrates the point. All the same, far more South Sudanese are getting an education than at any time in history.

The hardships of an oil-producing state

Leer is in Unity state, where much of South Sudan's oil industry is concentrated. The CPA allocated each oil-producing state 2 per cent of the revenue from its own oil production. Unity should be rich. Roads have been built, including one from the state capital Bentiu to Adok, a river port near Leer; but these were mainly murram roads, which are less durable than tarmac. In fact, the South Sudanese have found out, murram tends to disintegrate during the heavy rains.

Dol Mading, a village elder, points out that the town now has two mobile phone towers, which have revolutionised people's lives. Previously the only form of telecommunication was the satellite phone, and these were usually only owned by warlords. Other than this, it is difficult to see where Leer's share of the oil billions has gone. 'I can see only fields and cows,' Dol says. He is wearing a cream safari suit with long sleeves, and the legs of his trousers are rolled up to the knees to keep them dry. 'In the past the Arabs used to block aid to us,' he says. 'Now we're an independent country. We want to see what the government will get for us.'

The Leer county commissioner's office, on one edge of Freedom Square, is one of the visible signs of the state. It's a brick building covered in fading green paint, with a tin roof, and virulent green mould eating its way up the wall. The building has no electricity. In one of the rooms, the mud-brown carpet has been chewed up, revealing plastic sheeting covered in Arabic lettering underneath. The senior administrator, Peter Nyok, says the first priority is development, and in particular health, education and clean water. He would love a proper all-season road up to the state capital Bentiu. He doesn't mention electricity, as if it is too far-fetched a possibility even to enter his mind. However, he admits there simply isn't the money for any of the things he hopes for, so Dol Mading and Gatgong Jiech are likely to be disappointed.

Outside Nyok's office, the local chiefs sit under trees, trying any cases that are brought before them. The chiefs are elected by the community, and paid a salary by the government.[58] Mostly they judge cases of fighting between the local youth, and instances where young men have refused to pay a dowry. The punishment is usually imposed in cattle; up to 100 for some types of murder.[59] Preventing those sorts of incidents in Leer county is the responsibility of police Colonel David Gatluak. He works in a makeshift office, its walls covered in maroon cloth, on the other side of Freedom Square.

Colonel Gatluak is well respected in the town, but faces an extremely difficult job. He has 186 policemen under his command, a mixture of former SPLA soldiers like him and recruits from the local community. His force was promised a car, but it hasn't arrived, so they have to cover the sixteen *payam*s by 'footing', as it is described in South Sudan. Worse still, his men are short of ammunition, and have only five Motorola radios between them, not nearly enough as the cell phone network doesn't cover the whole county. After a cattle raid, Col Gatluak's men have to chase after the thieves on foot, out of contact with their base. A cattle thief must pray not to get caught, as there is no jail. The colonel admits he has to keep his prisoners in a shipping container.

BUILDING A STATE FROM THE RUINS OF WAR

The shipping container, a temporary and far from perfect solution to an almost universal lack of means, is an apt image for much of the work of the South Sudanese government in the interim period from the signing of the CPA in 2005 until independence in 2011. Even the usually critical Minister, who was in despair about the lack of a proper plan or programme, told me this period was not 'a complete failure', and some positive things had been achieved.[60] The most important was the reduction in poverty.

By one estimate 90 per cent of the southern Sudanese lived in poverty in 2004, although there were no accurate figures. By 2011, government statistics suggested 51 per cent of the people were below the new nationally-agreed poverty line. It is impossible to compare the figures directly, but it is clear many people's living conditions did improve in the interim period. However, almost all that progress was lost when South Sudan opted to shut off its oil production at the beginning of 2012. In that year alone, nearly two and a half million people received food aid, around a quarter of the population. Perhaps as many again were living close to this edge.[61]

Poverty reduction, however temporary, wasn't the only government success. In the interim period 5,000 kilometres of murram roads were built, children were immunised, and many more went to school. The pace of change may have been slow, but it would have been unrealistic to expect much more, given the circumstances South Sudan inherited.[62]

The murram roads provided limited benefits, but the road network between the different states was still completely inadequate, leaving even state capitals cut off during the rainy season. South Sudan's leaders realised that making up for decades of war, and Khartoum's neglect, would be a lengthy process. They drew up a ten year road-building plan to construct at least 7,000 kilometres of roads, including main highways linking up the state capitals, and others heading to the borders, to boost trade.

In one of the many ironies thrown up by South Sudan's complicated history, Major General Gier Chuang Aluong had been in charge of 250 engineers during the war, overseeing the destruction of twenty-one bridges between Juba and Kapoeta, near the border with Kenya. Now, as minister of roads and bridges, he was in charge of rebuilding them.[63]

Aluong's road-building scheme, had it happened, would have cost nine to ten billion dollars, and been a major part of the country's development plan.[64] A 192 kilometre tarmac road, from Juba to Nimule, was opened in September 2012; it was funded by USAID. The new road, South Sudan's 'first paved highway', cut the driving time to Nimule, a town on the Ugandan border, from eight hours to three, speeding up the flow of goods from the Kenyan port at Mombasa.[65] But the oil shutdown stymied any chance of carrying out the rest of the ambitious road-building plan straight after independence. Nor was it just roads: schemes to generate more electrical power were also postponed because of the shutdown.

Health in crisis

Improving the health service is another area that will take many years. During the time of the united Sudan, the southern region was almost totally abandoned, and hospitals were sometimes targeted during the fighting.[66] At independence, only one in five South Sudanese had access to water sanitation facilities, almost half did not have access to clean water, and many were out of reach of even basic health care.[67] These are terrifying figures. Northern Bahr el Ghazal state, home of Governor Paul Malong and Ayii Bol's rice scheme, is one of the worst-affected parts of the country.

Dr Garang Thomas Dhel is the director of Aweil hospital, the only one in the state. Sitting on the terrace outside his office, he explained that many sick people simply could not make it to a hospital or clinic in time, due to the lack of health facilities near their homes and the terrible road network. Some go instead to traditional healers, who are often frauds. Many die before they receive any treatment. Even those who reach the hospital are not yet safe: Dr Garang said one of his biggest problems was the lack of a regular drug supply from Juba. The cheery, well-built doctor also complained there weren't many qualified medical personnel in the country, and most end up working for NGOs because the pay is so much better.[68] In fact, a lot of the health service has simply been turned over to foreign aid workers. MSF already runs the paediatric and maternity departments of Dr Garang's hospital.

In autumn 2012, the Aweil hospital had to deal with a rush of malaria cases: the numbers were triple what they had been the previous year.[69] South Sudan is also home to many of the world's rarest diseases, including the still-unexplained nodding syndrome.[70] Maternal mortality is particularly gruesome: South Sudan has the highest maternal mortality rate in the world.[71] In Aweil, as elsewhere in South Sudan, almost everyone knows a mother who died in childbirth. I met Mary Chong Deng at a clinic for malnourished children on the outskirts of Aweil. Her child was severely malnourished, because of Mary's unemployment and the seasonal hunger gap.[72] A friend of Mary's had recently passed away while giving birth, and members of her family had died this way too.

Later, I saw a heavily pregnant woman stumble, then fall to the floor just outside the Aweil hospital, her red dress splaying out around her. She had apparently walked for several hours to get there, and collapsed at the end of the journey. She was helped into the hospital, and survived. Given access to medical facilities, most mothers will; but there are still far too few clinics and hospitals.

If physical ailments test the creaking health system, mental problems simply aren't dealt with at all. On one trip to Bentiu, in Unity state, I saw a naked man with unkempt hair wandering through the town, muttering and then shouting to himself. The sight is relatively common throughout South Sudan, although this man was unusual. He was once, I was told, a powerful minister, before he went mad. After decades of war, a high proportion of the South Sudanese suffer from depression or Post-Traumatic Stress Disorder.[73] Decades of conflict have led to high levels of violent behaviour and heavy drinking, according to Dr Robert Napoleon, the former administrative director of Juba Teaching Hospital. Even today it is not uncommon for drunken SPLA soldiers to open fire in crowded places; Juba has become increasingly dangerous, and in 2010 the sale of alcohol during work hours was banned in Rumbek, the capital of Lakes state.[74] According to Dr Napoleon, South Sudan has only one qualified psychiatrist.[75] Although there is a mental health ward at Juba Teaching Hospital, it is run by paramedics who have little training and limited drugs. Violent patients are simply transferred to Juba's Central Prison, where they are often chained up.[76] The broader issue, of the psychological needs of a war-scarred population, simply hasn't been addressed.

Back—but to what?

In the five and a half years from February 2007, 1.8 million South Sudanese exiles returned home.[77] They had fled the war, or left to get a better education. They came back because of the most sustained period of peace that many of them had ever known, and, of course, from a simple desire to live in their own country. Although they are sometimes distrusted by those who stayed behind, they often bring a superior range of skills and qualifications. They tend to snap up well-paid jobs with NGOs, but struggle to make much headway within the SPLM, because of the perception that they did not fight for the liberation of the country.

One interesting example of the benefits brought by returnees is the Woyee Film and Theatre Industry.[78] It was founded by refugees who were taught theatre skills by an NGO in the Kakuma refugee camp in Kenya. When they returned to Juba, Daniel Danis and more than fifty others devoted their earnings from making short films for UN agencies into buying a camera and editing equipment. The key roles—director, cameraman, actors, soundman—are rotated among the group, and the youthful energy of the Woyee members overcomes any technical limitations.

They produced what they proudly claim is the first fully South Sudanese movie, *Jamila*, the tale of a young woman, her boyfriend and her older and richer suitor. In December 2012, they organised the country's first film festival. The Woyee team have also made a number of shorter dramas about issues affecting the South Sudanese, including the problems people returning from Khartoum and elsewhere face in reintegrating into South Sudanese society.

As those Woyee short films suggest, the influx of so many returnees weighed heavily on the already sparse resources of the South Sudanese state. For example, nearly 150,000 came back to Warrap state, and many decided to stay in the state capital Kuajok.[79] They were given land, doubling the area of the town, and increasing the problem of providing services for all of them, as well as the million people already living in

Warrap.[80] Many of the children had previously been living in Khartoum, and they struggled at school, because they spoke Arabic, not English, the official language of the state.

Settlements for the new arrivals were built, but thousands spent part of the 2011 rainy season sleeping outdoors while their houses were built. Some people died of malaria, having lost any resistance to it during their stay in the Sudanese capital or elsewhere. The adults struggled to get work, and locals complained that they brought big city crime to Kuajok, a sleepy little town. One of the returnee settlements was called Khartoum Jadeed—New Khartoum. However any returnee expecting the same living standards as the Sudanese capital was in for a shock. 'There is no medicine, and no food. We don't even have shelter, or a proper house,' Chief Manyang Alin Akol said.

Foreign help

Chief Manyang and his people were receiving some help from the UN. With the state unable to provide much development, the onus has fallen on NGOs and foreign donors to make up the gap. 114 NGOs and UN agencies asked for $1.16 billion in 2013 to carry out their many humanitarian and development projects.[81] Foreign organisations, along with their smaller South Sudanese counterparts, have built schools, set up hospitals, drilled boreholes, and given agricultural advice. However the drastic nature of many of South Sudan's crises, whether they concern failing harvests, an influx of refugees from Sudan, or inter-ethnic fighting, push most of the foreign involvement towards short-term humanitarian interventions rather than long-term development. In Warrap state, for example, foreign NGOs have drilled boreholes and provided food to those in need. But they have not built roads, or provided electricity. This pattern was exacerbated by the oil shutdown: foreign donors were forced to switch their funds to humanitarian projects to avoid total collapse. Much-needed development was put on hold.[82]

TAKING THE TOWNS TO THE COUNTRYSIDE; OR THE CENTRE AND THE PERIPHERY, AGAIN

The South Sudanese leaders inherited an awful situation, and have certainly brought about some positive change. Unfortunately, there are signs that they are repeating some of the errors made by the Sudanese leaders against whom they fought so fiercely. Just as the bulk of Sudan's resources were concentrated in and around Khartoum, Juba has developed at a rapid pace. In itself Juba's growth is no bad thing: 'It is beautiful to see!' says Bishop Paride Taban.[83] There has been some growth in the state capitals, too, in places like Kuajok, albeit from a very low base.

However, as in the Sudanese model, South Sudan's ten states are almost entirely dependent on Juba. The 2011 budget of Northern Bahr el Ghazal state, for example, was just over 150 million SSP, slightly over 30 million dollars at the black market rate of the time.[84] Well over 90 per cent of this money came from Juba. The total was clearly insufficient to develop the state, which has a population of over a million people.[85] This situation is repeated all over South Sudan.

Although it desperately needed more money, the state government in Aweil was simply incapable of raising any more. Less than a million dollars came in through taxes, and local MPs were forced to admit they couldn't collect a range of duties, including household tax and property tax, as the laws simply hadn't been voted in.[86] This was due in part to the limited experience and educational qualifications of many of those in government, or to put it in the jargon of UN agencies and international NGOs, a 'lack of capacity'. The weakness of the governments in South Sudan's ten states is structural, and replicates that of the federal government: just as the latter's revenue comes almost entirely from oil, the states' come from a transfer of funds from Juba.

In any given state capital, the state government tends to hold tight to the money it receives, leaving the other areas under its control with next to nothing. Peter Nyok, the senior administrator in Leer county, did not receive the funds he needed to develop his area. Political favour plays a role too: Leer voted heavily against Taban Deng, the Unity state governor, in the disputed 2010 elections, so until he was sacked in 2013 it was less likely to receive substantial support than other areas of the state.[87]

A rural population

When John Garang signed the CPA, he made a firm commitment to developing rural South Sudan, and with good reason: 83 per cent of the population lives in rural areas, and on average they are much worse off than those in the cities.[88] 'The SPLM vision, policy and slogan shall be to take the towns to people in the countryside rather than people to towns, where they end up in slums,' Garang said.[89] Sure enough, 'taking the towns to the people' became one of the great slogans, repeated by everyone from Salva down; but although it was enshrined in policy documents, it did not seem to bring any change on the ground.[90] Local government institutions were set up, but they didn't provide many services. In that same speech, Garang promised that the government would construct 'windmills all over rural Sudan to provide clean drinking water and build micro-dams for generating small scale hydro-electric power for rural towns'. Neither has happened: instead, money and resources have been concentrated in the federal capital, and to a much lesser extent the state capitals.

A quarter of the population needs food handouts to survive.[91] A report by the South Sudanese think tank, the Sudd Institute, suggests food insecurity prevails because of widespread violence, flooding, short or intermittent rainfall, outdated agricultural methods, 'unambitious culture', the shutdown and the austerity measures, and the poor roads network.[92] Some of those problems are out of the state's control. Nevertheless, there is no doubt there was not enough investment: less than 5 per cent of the budget goes to agriculture.[93]

The Sudd Institute report concludes that those in power have forgotten those who helped them get there:

the SPLA survived long and tumultuous years together with the people; because it relied on the local economy led solely by agriculture. A simple payback to the people would have been a focus on agriculture in order to increase both food production and accessibility. So far, people are still waiting at least for a bite of the national cake.[94]

As so many of South Sudan's people live in rural areas, and as only the state, rather than the private sector, is present there, rural people are particularly affected by the limited state investment.

A new capital?

On 2 September 2011, South Sudan's cabinet voted to build a new capital in a place called Ramciel, in Lakes state, not far from where the corset-maker Mary Padar grew up. Ramciel is near the geographical heart of the country. The decision was taken after protracted consultations with communities and local authorities in Central Equatoria, where Juba is situated. Federal authorities and investors have found it difficult to obtain sufficient land in Juba, as much of it is owned by the local community. Representatives of the Bari people are reported to have asked the government to relocate the capital.[95] Many Equatorians have complained that their land has been 'stolen', largely by Dinka and Nuer with connections to the government. Ramciel would be created in relatively underdeveloped land, which would probably be declared as federally-owned. However, many people wondered whether the new country would be wise to spend billions of dollars building a capital, when the needs elsewhere are so evident. By late 2013, the project had not advanced substantially, in part because of the oil shutdown.

CORRUPTION

Some of the failures of the interim period can be ascribed to a lack of experience among those newly in charge, and the small pool of qualified workers able to take on key roles. Those in government were, after all, former rebels who had often spent most of their lives in the bush. Their people had seen their education disrupted by conflict. Two million died, and all were altered by the war.

However, another reason for the failure to develop agriculture properly, or to provide services throughout the country, is corruption. Although the word 'corruption' does not exist in some South Sudanese languages,[96] in the years after the CPA it was not that rare to see two hulking Hummers in the parking lot of the same Juba restaurant, despite South Sudan's unenviable status as one of the least-developed countries on earth. The oil billions flowed in, and, presented with this unimaginable wealth, people helped themselves.

From the very earliest days of the then government of southern Sudan, in 2005, corruption scandals made the news. A grain purchasing scheme to avoid food shortages ended with tonnes of grain mouldering in warehouses, or simply never bought at all. The scam may have been worth up to $2 billion.[97] The awarding of mobile phone licences was also considered suspect in some quarters.[98] Some money was probably siphoned off to prepare for a possible future conflict with Khartoum. Nevertheless, the Auditor General's reports for 2007 and 2008 revealed hundreds of millions of missing dollars—and suggested what might have been done with them: the Ministry of Education's 'weekend allowance' could apparently have paid for the monthly salaries of 855 teachers.[99]

Sometimes the corruption was incredibly visible. A foreign consultant witnessed a senior official at a ministry receive a brown envelope, count a wedge of cash around three inches thick, and then tell the person who had handed him the envelope 'That's fine, you will get the contract on Monday.'[100] Three factors facilitate corruption in South Sudan: the overall lack of institutional strength made graft easy; the country's money came from oil, and opaque extractive industries are notorious for the corruption possibilities they present;[101] finally South Sudan inherited, to an extent, Sudanese bureaucracy, which was desperately tainted. However, the SPLM Secretary General Pa'gan Amum rejects the notion that oil is harmful to a country like South Sudan. 'Believe me, oil is one of the blessings,' he said. 'It's a curse when you are stupid! The curse is the human condition, it's greed.'[102]

Sometimes local attitudes to corruption are not as disapproving as might be imagined. One minister had a box of money half the height of his desk, and he would see fifty people a day, or until the money ran out, according to someone who worked with him. 'He would pick a different community or area every day, and give them money. That's what he saw as his job,' his former colleague says.[103] Ministers and other officials face family and community pressure to share out the state's resources. The rapper and former child soldier Emmanuel Jal puts it like this: 'If you're corrupt in this country, you are considered clever. If you are not corrupt as a leader, you have no support, even your family will not support you because you are not able to get money' to help them.

Many people who fought in the war and suffered so much feel they should be compensated now they are in charge. Not everyone agrees. Steven Wondu, the Auditor General, tells a powerful story about the fallacy of entitlement. 'I have a different interpretation: if you sacrificed so much to create this nation, you should be the last who does something to hurt this nation,' he says. His story is about an African family that is desperate for children. 'They go to see witchdoctors in Zanzibar, witchdoctors in Lamu, to Congo, finally they went to Cameroon,' he says, warming to his tale. 'After twenty years of childlessness they were rewarded with a child. Now you don't expect those parents to make mincemeat out of that child, do you?'

DEVELOPMENT: WHERE DOES THE MONEY GO?

'If you ate stolen food, you will vomit it!'

President Salva Kiir.[104]

In his short story *Vomiting Stolen Food*, published in 2010, Victor Lugala wrote about the growing stench of graft.

When peace embraced the village city there was a stampede to scramble for a piece of the liberation cake. People with sharp appetites fell over each other to feast on the overflowing plate of peace. The eating chiefs indulged their appetites and celebrated the dawn of peace in grand style. They gorged themselves and belched like volcanoes, as if to taunt those who didn't participate in the armed struggle: *where were you when we were fighting?*[105]

By its conclusion, Lugala's story has attained an almost prophetic status. In order for the people to reach redemption, fifty thieves, most of whom 'had fat stomachs like Japanese wrestlers' are separated from the masses. They are forced to vomit up all the food they had stolen, a reference to Salva's memorable phrase promising to make the corrupt pay: 'if you eat stolen food, you will vomit it!'

In fact, Lugala's fifty culprits was a slight underestimation. Less than a year into South Sudan's life, President Salva Kiir wrote an accusatory letter that was sent to seventy-five senior officials. Dated 3 May 2012, and signed with the president's distinctive double loop, the letter revealed the staggering extent of corruption. 'An estimated $4 billion are unaccounted for or, simply put, stolen by current and former officials, as well as corrupt individuals with close ties to government officials,' Salva wrote.[106] By some calculations, this was equivalent to a third of all the oil revenue South Sudan had received from the CPA in 2005 to independence in 2011.[107]

'Most of these funds have been taken out of the country and deposited in foreign accounts,' the letter continued. 'Some have purchased properties, often paid in cash.' The letter announced that a bank account had been set up in Kenya, and urged the recipients of the letter to return 'these stolen funds (fully or partially) to this account' as 'the credibility of our government is on the line'. It was an astonishing letter—as much for the presidential acknowledgement of the problem as for the scale of the wrongdoing uncovered.[108] Incredibly, the $4 billion figure may actually be an understatement.[109] To anyone wondering why Leer's schools are falling down, and the road cannot be used in the rainy season, here is a large part of the explanation.

The anguished tone of the president's letter provided a damning indictment of the SPLM's first few years in power. 'We fought for freedom, justice and equality,' it said. 'Many of our friends died to achieve these objectives. Yet, once we got to power, we forgot what we fought for, and began to enrich ourselves at the expense of our people.' The letter said that measures would be taken if the money was not handed back. Yet unlike Lugala's fifty thieves, who vomited up what they had stolen, hardly anyone pays the penalty for corruption in South Sudan. Money is usually not recovered. Ministers have been sacked, and suspended, and lower-ranking officials have spent time in jail, but only very rarely are they prosecuted. The leaders' self-interest is not the only reason: going after anybody, in this ethnically-divided and fragile country, risks alienating that person's extended community.[110]

THE BIG (MILITARY) STATE

South Sudan, like the country it seceded from, has a large military. By one estimate, 46 per cent of government spending goes to the armed forces.[111] Many of the people the state has employed were rebels who fought against the SPLA. They were brought in as part of Salva's Big Tent strategy, but in general lack both any interest in developing the state, and the ability to do so. Of course, this applies to many SPLA loyalists too. Officials don't want to give the exact number of men in uniform— but many politicians have learned to talk the international community's language of 'right-sizing the military' by getting rid of many people on the payroll.

In fact, whatever the foreign advisers think, this is unlikely to happen. 'Let's not forget the fact that, at this moment in time, the government of the Republic of South Sudan is probably the sole employer and will be the sole employer for some time to come,' the then Minister of Foreign Affairs, Nhial Deng, said a year after independece. A report for the World Bank established that 80 per cent of those with a paid job in South Sudan are employed by the state, although not all of them are in the armed forces.[112] With so few other opportunities to find work, and as South Sudan is already a militarised society, the government is unwilling to cut people loose. As a result, the majority of the government's spending goes to salaries, and especially to the bloated military.[113] In essence, the state is using its money to pay off individuals, rather than on development, while hoping that some of this wealth will trickle down.

'Right now we value peace very, very highly,' Auditor General Wondu says.

Bad as it is, we have never had it so good in our history, and we are holding it with both hands, at a very high social cost to our society. When we came out of the war, we had some of our citizens who were on the other side of the war effort, we had to absorb them, and give them attractive titles and ranks. In real terms, when resources are limited, it's a zero sum game right there.

The former minister Lual Deng believes that soldiers could be steered into farming, and eventually taken off the payroll.

Nevertheless, for many years after independence Wondu's judgement is likely to hold true: 'Society bought peace—and gave up social services, gave up infrastructure development, gave up key things like improvements in education and health services.' The problem is that while Salva's Big Tent strategy kept the peace, more or less, it has done nothing to create the development that will ensure the peace lasts. So much money is spent on the military and the civil service that there is hardly any left over to develop the country.

* * *

Despite the money brought in by irrigated fields, gold nuggets, and oil wells, Sudan is a desperately under-developed country. It is also a very unequal one. Wealth and services have been concentrated in the centre, around Khartoum. The peripheries, which were marginalised politically, and whose people were often looked down on racially, were not developed at all. The CPA brought a brief flurry of construction, but this too was largely in the centre. All this inequality has sparked rebellions in the periphery. The wars are a drain on the economy, and the staggering military spending means there is little money left over for health or education. The high levels of corruption and patronage also siphon money away from development.

The southern region was perhaps the least developed part of the united Sudan. The SPLM has built some schools and roads since the CPA was signed. However South Sudan's challenges are daunting. The health service is in tatters, classrooms are overflowing, and there is only one good tarmac road outside Juba. The politicians seem to be making many of the mistakes they once criticised in Khartoum. Development is centralised, the spending on the armed forces and the civil service is colossal, and corruption is widespread. Drawing a new international border has not yet allowed South Sudan to erase many of the iniquities of the past.

5

INSECURITY

SUDAN

The sound of the blast enveloped us, a deep rumble that created its own tremor in our limbs. Then the screams started. A bomb had landed. We ran in different directions, taking pointless, panicky cover behind thin tree trunks. Above our heads the sun glinted off the wings of a plane, which flew off to the north. 'Antonov!' someone shouted.[1] In the space of a few minutes, the plane had dropped four bombs in total. SAF has been accused of many human rights abuses, but this was an unusual transgression. The bombs had landed in a refugee camp, across an international border.

Tens of thousands of people lived in the camp, in Yida in Unity state in South Sudan. They had marched for many days to get there, fleeing a new Sudanese civil war when the air raids and the lack of food got too much. Skinny kids had trailed behind their weakened mothers on a walk of desperation, before arriving in the apparent safety of the camp. Then, on 10 November 2011, the bombs landed. On this occasion nobody was hurt, but many of the traumatised refugees felt they could take no more. Would they ever be safe? Their outrage reached the UN Security Council. The US Ambassador, Susan Rice, confronted Sudan's envoy, calling him a liar when he denied the bombing.[2]

Sudan has been at war for most of its history. Khartoum fought against generations of southern Sudanese rebels before separation; a rebellion in the east only came to an end in 2006; and the Darfur civil war reached a dispiriting ten-year anniversary in early 2013. South Sudan's independence was the ultimate reminder of the possible consequences of a civil war. Yet in the months just before and after separation, Khartoum found itself fighting two new internal conflicts.

The terrified refugees who were bombed in Yida were from the Nuba Mountains in South Kordofan, where a war broke out in June 2011. Some of them came from Kauda, Nagwa Konda's small town. Three months later another civil war began, in Blue Nile state. Both areas had suffered through some of the heaviest battles in the second Sudanese civil war. Many people from the Nuba Mountains and Blue Nile had fought for the SPLA, only to be left north of the border at separation. Now they were fighting Khartoum again. These new Sudanese civil wars also show how Sudan and South Sudan's destinies are still interwoven: Khartoum is convinced Juba is directing the rebellions, and SAF's bombs land in South Sudan.

THE TWO AREAS: SOUTH KORDOFAN AND BLUE NILE

When the SPLA began fighting Khartoum in 1983, it was keen to show that it was a national movement, not merely a southern Sudanese rebellion. John Garang's reforming New Sudan vision appealed to people all over the country, and in particular in poor areas with large non-Arab populations. The iniquities of racism, religious discrimination and uneven development, and the concentration of power in the centre, were felt just as much in the northern areas of South Kordofan and Blue Nile as they were in southern Sudan. Soon the SPLA had recruited fighters from the Nuba Mountains in South Kordofan, and from non-Arab groups in Blue Nile.[3]

Under the 2005 CPA, southern Sudan became semi-autonomous, and was granted a referendum on secession. This did not apply to Blue Nile and South Kordofan, which were indisputably in the north.[4] Instead the SPLM rebels there were allocated a share of local political power, and both areas were given the right to hold 'popular consultations' on their future. In these, citizens would give their views on how they should be governed, the relationship between the state and the centre, and the share of wealth and power the CPA had allocated to them.[5] However, the popular consultations did not allow the people of South Kordofan and Blue Nile the choice of splitting away from Sudan.

To the surprise of many, the January 2011 referendum happened on time, and its results settled southern Sudan's future. This was not the case further north: the popular consultations had not finished in Blue Nile and had not even started in South Kordofan.[6] The NCP had shown little interest, and the southern Sudanese majority in the SPLM was not prepared to compromise secession by insisting that the process be completed. The international community, concerned by the potential of a new north-south war, kept quiet.

Just before South Sudan's independence, the northern wing of the SPLM broke away, forming SPLM-North as a Sudanese party. SPLM-North still had tens of thousands of soldiers from South Kordofan and Blue Nile in uniform. As Sudanese citizens their place was north of the border; but integrating them into SAF, which they had fought against so recently, would be politically and militarily hazardous. Allowing the SPLM-North troops to remain as an armed force outside the national army was not something Bashir was prepared to accept. He argued that if they wanted to live in Sudan they would have to disarm. However, SPLM-North did not trust the president or his intentions.

SOUTH KORDOFAN

South Kordofan embodies many of Sudan's contradictions.[7] It is rich in oil, but one of the country's least developed areas. It is home to, among others, semi-transient pastoralist Arab groups like the Misseriya, and the African Nuba, who farm on the slopes of the Nuba Mountains. Arab and African groups have many common concerns, but have also clashed with each other. The fighting in the Nuba Mountains, between the Nuba SPLM members on one side and SAF and Misseriya PDF on the other, was some of the most bitter of the second north-south civil war.

After the CPA, a fragile truce held. Security was improved, and roads built. This was the brief period of peace and stability in which, the aid worker Nagwa Konda said, her region had benefited from unprecedented development. In the last years of the interim period, the NCP Governor Ahmed Haroun worked relatively well with his SPLM-North deputy, Abdel Aziz al Hilu.[8] Delayed elections in March 2011 increased the tension. In the run-up to the polls, it became clear that neither side was prepared to lose.[9] The NCP couldn't afford to let this oil-producing area slip out of its control, and SPLM-North needed to assert its strength as a political force before southern Sudan seceded.[10] Abdel Aziz expected that he would have to fight whatever the result of the elections.[11] On 15 May, Haroun was announced the winner of the gubernatorial vote.

The Carter Centre, the only international election observers, endorsed the results.[12] To nobody's surprise, Abdel Aziz claimed that he had been cheated of victory.[13] Now Khartoum faced an angry opponent with a large army under his control. This would have been a difficult situation for any state, let alone one in as much trouble as Sudan. A solution might have been found through dialogue, but this was not Khartoum's preferred path. In a meeting in May 2012, President Bashir told the AU mediator Thabo Mbeki that a decision had been taken: he intended to resolve the situation militarily.[14] SAF leaders, emboldened by their takeover of Abyei,[15] apparently believed they would be able to overcome SPLM-North's forces with little difficulty.[16]

A new war in South Kordofan

Both sides flooded troops into the area.[17] The SPLA's 9th Division, made up of Nuba soldiers, deployed from its base on the border into South Kordofan, according to a confidential AU report, which also concluded that Khartoum sent in additional SAF, PDF and NISS forces.[18] On 23 May SAF Major General Izmat Abdel Rahim Zain al Abdin ordered all SPLA units to withdraw south of the 1 January 1956 boundary line, into what was shortly to become South Sudan. The letter he sent also announced that the mandate of the JIUs, the joint SAF-SPLA units established by the CPA, would finish at the end of May.[19]

This attempt to remove all the Nuba SPLA soldiers from South Kordofan, within a week, felt to SPLM-North like a declaration of war. Sure enough, within two weeks a devastating new conflict had broken out. Just before six pm on Monday 6 June a single shot ran out in Kadugli, the state capital. There was an awful pause, and then the firing began in earnest.[20] The war in South Kordofan had begun. Before long it had spread throughout the state.

Khartoum's forces, which were better armed than the rebels, quickly took control of Kadugli. Hundreds, perhaps thousands, of supposed SPLM-North supporters were detained. Many of them were killed. A UN staff member reported seeing 'an estimated 150 dead bodies of persons of Nuban descent scattered on the grounds of the military compound' at Umbattah locality.[21] A UN human rights report included allegations of mass graves in at least three different places in and around Kadugli, and a satellite monitoring project funded by the Hollywood star George Clooney also identified apparent sites of mass graves in the town.[22]

Presumed SPLM-North supporters were picked up at roadblocks manned by the PDF and other paramilitary forces. 'On the first day they were targeting SPLM—it was the security in Kadugli—they knew the SPLM', one Nuba man says. 'In the coming days, forces which came from outside did not know. They just targeted any Nuba'. The damning internal UN human rights report agreed: 'the SAF and allied paramilitary forces have targeted members and supporters of the SPLM/A, most of whom are Nubans and other dark skinned people.'[23] To the disgust of those who needed their help, the United Nations Mission in Sudan (UNMIS) peacekeepers largely sat tight in their base. According to several reports, people were allegedly even taken away from just outside the UNMIS camp, and executed.[24]

Right from these early days of war, the people of the Nuba Mountains tasted one of Khartoum's favourite counter-insurgency tactics: aerial bombardment. In many cases this involved crude bombs being rolled out of the back of Antonov transport planes. These attacks were incredibly imprecise, but as well as spreading fear, they maimed and killed civilians.[25] Bodies were ripped in half by shrapnel. The low hum of the Antonov is feared all over Sudan's war-zones: they have been used in South Sudan and Darfur, and many people in the Nuba Mountains remembered the terrible effects of the bombings that continued until the 2002 ceasefire in their area. In 2005, the South Sudanese writer Victor Lugala published a poem about the Antonov, a 'shameless creature' which was 'born in Russia/And raised in the Sudan', and 'defecates rotten eggs' in schools, hospitals and markets.[26]

Kauda, as one of the main SPLM-North strongholds in South Kordofan, was a prime target for the Antonovs. The first bombs landed on its airstrip on 9 June, three days after the war began. On 22 June, Kauda residents reported that a woman, Zainab, was killed, and two men and four children wounded in an Antonov attack. There would be many more. 'Most of the victims [throughout the Nuba Mountains] are women and children,' says Nagwa Konda, the Nuba development worker, 'because when an Antonov comes to bomb, mothers look for their children and children look for their mothers.'[27] If you lie on the ground, or better still under rocks or in a foxhole, the odds of being hit are low. In the panic of an air raid, not everyone remembers this. The children Yassir Ajour taught at Smokin, on the outskirts of Kauda, can no longer use the new school buildings, which are too obvious a target from the air. The students take their classes in the natural shelter provided by nearby rocks.

The bombings have forced tens of thousands of people to live in caves, and throughout the Nuba Mountains farming has been made impossible by the air raids. In addition to this, Khartoum stopped international humanitarian organisations from entering areas of South Kordofan controlled by SPLM-North. Without any emergency food aid, many struggled to survive. In April 2013, Amnesty International concluded that 'Indiscriminate bombings, lack of humanitarian assistance and massive displacement which has severely disrupted agricultural production, have all conspired to place civilians […] in an extremely precarious situation.'[28] It seems to many Nuba as if their own government is trying to starve them to death.

Often Sudanese officials claim that no air raids have taken place. However, the senior NCP politician, Ghazi Salaheddin, is more frank:

I don't deny it actually. I object to the criminalization of bombing generally because the United States is bombing in Afghanistan and Iraq all the time, and in Yemen for that matter. […] It's not illegal. It's illegal when you bomb civilians deliberately, for instance, but if you bomb military targets that's within the law. The condemnation of bombing appears to me as a means for the United States in particular to take back from Sudan its advantage over the SPLA, so this has dubious motives.

Nevertheless, in the Nuba Mountains civilians have born the brunt of the air raids, according to human rights groups and eye-witness reports.[29]

Khartoum's air power was backed up by ground assaults led by SAF and paramilitary forces. Nuba activists have complained that villages have been destroyed, and many civilians killed. In one case, which was captured on a cell-phone camera, PDF burned the village of Um Bartumbu.[30] Fighting a rebellion using air power and unruly ethnic militias is an old tactic in Sudan. In Darfur, it has been called 'counter-insurgency on the cheap'.[31] As with Darfur, this was not a case of a local response to a problem spinning out of control. Khartoum was completely in charge, and the politicians in the capital were sometimes more belligerent than those in South Kordofan. On 19 June Bashir, in one of his more aggressive speeches, said 'anyone who looks in our eye, we will poke his eye'.[32]

A short-lived agreement

Despite the rhetoric, on 28 July, less than two months after the fighting began, Khartoum signed a cessation of hostilities with SPLM-North, in part because of international pressure. The deal prepared the ground for a fuller agreement. Khartoum agreed to recognise SPLM-North as a political party, and many of the rebels were to be integrated into SAF or other security forces. Malik Agar, who until this point had kept the other SPLM-North stronghold Blue Nile out of the fighting, signed on behalf of his movement. Nafie Ali Nafie, the NCP Deputy Chairman, scrawled his signature for the government.

Within a few days Bashir tore up the landmark agreement, following outbursts from hardliners, including his uncle Tayyeb Mustafa.[33] This was a very 'public slap' for Nafie.[34] The blow to those in South Kordofan who hoped for peace was considerably more severe. Khartoum's competing centres of power had been unable to agree. One theory is that Ali Osman Taha helped torpedo the deal, as part of his semi-open succession struggle with Nafie. Another, which is perhaps more credible, is that the military felt they could overcome SPLM-North quickly, and resisted any sort of agreement which would see the rebels join the army. Whatever the case, the fighting rumbled on.[35]

A messy war

The South Kordofan Governor Ahmed Haroun was central to the government's effort to defeat the rebels militarily. Haroun has prominent cheekbones and a receding hairline just starting to go grey, and although he is not loud he appears extremely self-confident. He is from the Borgo, an ethnic group mainly found in Darfur, which migrated from Chad—so he is in no way a member of the northern riverain elite. The Nuba still have bitter memories of Haroun from their first conflict with Khartoum, which came to an end in 2002. Haroun subsequently played a key role in Khartoum's dirty war in Darfur. He is wanted by the ICC on fifty-one counts of alleged crimes against humanity and war crimes in Darfur.[36] When Khartoum appointed him governor of South Kordofan, in May 2009, it was seen by many as a deliberate provocation. Now Haroun was in charge of another uncompromising campaign against rebels from the periphery. Haroun expressed dismay about the state's return to war, after years of relative stability and modest progress;[37] but few people in the Nuba Mountains believed his regret was genuine.

The war in South Kordofan has often been presented as a simple battle between good rebels and an evil government; the heroic freedom fighters against the devilish Bashir and Haroun. It has even been described as a 'genocide' against the Nuba people.[38] The reality is more complex than this. Some Nuba fight on the side of the government. Kafi Tayara, a government chief, was accused by fellow Nuba of carrying out 'most of the notorious things done in Kadugli'[39] from his base in Masani, the industrial area.[40] There is substantial evidence that government troops targeted Nuba on the basis of their ethnic identity in the first days of the conflict in Kadugli, yet by and large Nuba elsewhere in Sudan were not affected. There are Nuba judges, civil servants, and tea ladies carrying on with their lives in Khartoum. The government has, however, displayed the utmost ruthlessness in attacking areas held by SPLM-North, or where civilians who are perceived to support the rebels live.

SPLM-North is not blameless either. In April 2012, I went with a government delegation to Talodi, a key town that the rebels had made several attempts to capture. Several parts of Talodi, including civilian areas, had been shelled by the rebels from the nearby mountains. A fuel tank at a power plant had been hit: petals of twisted metal bloomed from the hole, and the rest of the tank had been blackened by the resulting fire. Elsewhere huts had been totally destroyed. Haroun said thirty-five people were killed, fifty-four wounded, and more than 28,000 were forced to flee because of the rebels' attack. It is impossible to verify these numbers independently, but the UN confirmed many people had been forced out of the town.

One of Talodi's residents, Hamid Tir, told me that his two brothers had died in a car crash, in the desperate rush to escape the SPLM-North assault on the town, and he himself had been injured. Although he was a Nuba, he had absolutely no affection for the rebels. In October 2012, the UN condemned an incident in which SPLM-North shelled Kadugli, calling it 'reprehensible', and against international law.[41] Here, too, the safety of civilians seemed to have been disregarded in the rush to strike a military blow. On 14 June 2013 a UN peacekeeper was killed as Kadugli was shelled again.[42] Perhaps more seriously, SPLM-North's leaders were prepared to fight, despite knowing the price the civilians in their areas would pay. Other parts of Sudan have been politically and economically marginalised, but have not taken up arms against the state.

This is not to say there is any moral equivalence between the rebels and the government. Khartoum's tactics—the air raids, and its decision to rely on poorly trained paramilitary forces—have caused far more misery than the SPLM-North fighters have. Khartoum's policy of arming friendly ethnic groups has also increased ethnic tensions.[43] At the end of the visit to Talodi, I asked Haroun if he was worried about facing more ICC charges for his role in the South Kordofan war. He had been caught on video allegedly urging his soldiers to crush the rebels, and not bring any of them back alive.[44] Haroun, like most Sudanese politicians, is usually charming. There was a small, frosty, pause. 'I don't care about that. It's a political court, it is not professional,' he said.

Holed up in their well-defended hills

To the surprise of Haroun and SAF, the rebels have seized control of more territory than they ever took during the first war, in the process capturing large quantities of weapons and ammunition. In particular, they overran government positions in some eastern parts of South Kordofan. This is a strategically important area as it is not too far from the major town of El Obeid and the road to Khartoum.[45] The Nuba are hard to dislodge from their own hills. Part of the reason is that SAF has been weakened. In the past, many of its soldiers came from southern Sudan, Darfur or the Nuba Mountains. Now it can no longer recruit South Sudanese, and SAF doesn't trust Darfuris or Nuba much because the fighting is taking place in their areas. In contrast to the first war in the Nuba Mountains, the Misseriya have not fought in any great numbers on Khartoum's side either. Misseriya leaders say their people have been neglected by the government and so they refused the call to arms.[46] Some Misseriya have even joined SPLM-North.[47]

The intensity of the fighting fluctuates with the seasons: during the long months of rain, it is almost impossible to move tanks or other heavy vehicles, and the conflict simmers rather than boils. Despite the rebels' relative successes, the war has been a bloody stalemate. SPLM-North have been unable to seize small towns like Talodi, let alone Kadugli, the state capital. The rebels' boasts that they will be able to march on Khartoum are little more than hot air. Bashir's claim that he would say his Friday prayers in a liberated Kauda was no more accurate: SAF and its allied forces simply cannot retake the hills. And so the conflict rolls on, damaging the economy and killing civilians, but with little sign of either side achieving its objectives.

BLUE NILE

Nganyofa Agar Eyre Nganyofa, the son of an Ingessana chief in Blue Nile state, was unaware that he was a Muslim until he reached the age of eight. Then he went to Baw Elementary school. The headteacher told him his name was Malik and whatever he had thought before he was now a Muslim. If he spoke his native tongue, rather than Arabic, he would be lashed. From that day on, the little boy was called Malik Agar Eyre. Malik says that he only found out that he was different from the Arabs when he went to intermediate school in Damazin, the Blue Nile state capital. Later he became frustrated at the racism his people suffered from.

The Ingessana, like the other African groups in Blue Nile, were very low down in Sudan's loose racial hierarchy, though perhaps not at the very bottom, since many are Muslim. When Malik was growing up, only a small number of the Ingessana were educated, and so they were unable to take advantage of the few opportunities the state offered. Most did not even question their place in society. In the mid-1980s, Malik Agar went into rebellion for the first time.[48] His elder brother complained: 'if you fight the Arabs, who will sell us salt?' He owned enough cows to purchase his own salt-trading business, but the idea never crossed his mind: that sort of commerce belonged to the Arabs. Despite his brother's disapproval, Malik soon became one of the SPLA's most prominent commanders, working closely with Salva Kiir. In the 2010 polls, he was elected governor of Blue Nile state.[49]

When the conflict began in South Kordofan, it seemed only a matter of time before Blue Nile descended into war. On 21 August 2011, Malik flew with the then Ethiopian Prime Minister Meles Zenawi to Khartoum, for a meeting with Bashir that lasted four hours. Malik, a giant man with a grey beard and watchful, lively eyes, says he talked for most of it. 'Sudan's problem is one of diversity management,' Malik told Bashir. The president, according to Malik, offered to set up committees to look into the matter, a typical Sudanese approach to any political disagreement. The meeting ended inconclusively. Less than two weeks later, Sudan had a new civil war. The shooting began in the Blue Nile state capital, Damazin, on the evening of 1 September. Malik fled, still wearing his slippers.[50]

Three days later, I went to Damazin. Military vehicles raced around town at frightening speeds and nervous soldiers cocked their guns when a journalist tried to take a picture. 'We're going to clean the state,' a triumphant soldier shouted. SAF officers displayed dozens of prisoners, some wearing South Sudanese military uniforms, and showed us South Sudanese money apparently taken from the rebels when they were captured. When one new prisoner was brought in, a soldier leapt forward and began slapping him. An officer realised I was watching, and shouted at him to stop. Another soldier proudly showed off Malik Agar's driving licence, which he had stolen from the governor's residence.

The government achieved considerably more initial success in Blue Nile than it had in South Kordofan. On 3 November, two months into the war, SAF took Kurmuk, the largest town under SPLM-North's control in Blue Nile. This time, unlike in South Kordofan, Bashir was able to fulfil his promise to perform his Friday prayers in a captured rebel stronghold. SPLM-North had withdrawn when it became clear they would not be able to hold the town.

The fall of Kurmuk did not mean the end of the war. By mid-2013, the rebels controlled the southern-most part of the state, had a presence near the state capital Damazin in the north, and had made a concerted effort to cut the road between Damazin and Kurmuk.[51] On several occasions in 2013 the rebels attacked Kurmuk's airport, a few kilometres from the town, before being chased out of the area, unable to cope with the heavy artillery fire from SAF's base in the town. Blue Nile does not offer the same geographical advantages as the Nuba Mountains for guerrilla fighters and SAF has often been able to make its advantage in weaponry pay. SAF also used air raids liberally, making farming impossible and killing and wounding many civilians.[52] Malik told the Ingessana and other groups to leave, as it was too difficult to protect them.

A desperate exodus

Osman and his family followed Malik's advice, and left their home in the Ingessana hills. When I met him, Osman took me to see four recently dug graves. This makeshift cemetery was in Yusuf Batil, one of four vast refugee camps in Upper Nile state in South Sudan, each made up of thousands of white tents scattered across a flood plain. The earth tombs sketched a line of misery which was repeated at depressingly short intervals throughout the camp. In the second of the four graves, Osman's seven-month-old nephew had been laid to rest.

Osman was among the 110,000 refugees from Blue Nile who managed to escape into neighbouring South Sudan by the end of 2012.[53] Thousands more went to Ethiopia. Life in Blue Nile had become unbearable, because of aerial bombardments and the rampaging Sudanese military. Osman and his family walked at night to escape the bombing raids, eating leaves to survive. After six painful and hungry weeks, they arrived in South Sudan. Not everyone made it: one family member died on the way. Shortly afterwards, Osman's baby nephew passed away too. In the camp, malnutrition rates were extremely high, and the rainy season spread diseases. The refugees were so weak that many succumbed. Everyone in Yusuf Batil knows someone who died. The same is true of Yida camp, where more than 70,000 refugees from South Kordofan had arrived by the end of 2012.

DARFUR

In another camp for displaced people in another Sudanese war, in Darfur, Maryam Mohamed Mokhtar stares out from behind a metal grille, which casts a lattice shadow on her face. This is not a prison, just a fence around a borehole, where Maryam has gone to draw water. All the same, she feels trapped. She has been here, in Abu Shouk camp on the outskirts of the North Darfur capital El Fasher, since 2006. She escaped to the camp after her husband and her son were killed, as the violence in Darfur, Sudan's western region, reached a horrifying peak. Like so many other victims they were civilians, not fighters. Mariam begins to cry at the memory.

In March 2013, a decade after the Darfur war began, 1.43 million people like Maryam were living in camps for internally displaced people and surviving from food handouts.[54] Nearly 300,000 more Darfuris were living as refugees across the border in Chad.[55] Their lives and their region have been altered forever by the conflict. For years the Sudanese government has been asking them to return to their shattered homes. Some have gone back. Maryam is one of the very many who think that it is simply too dangerous to leave the camps. There is no end in sight to the war, one of the most deadly in African history, and Darfur has done more than anything else to ruin Sudan's international image.

A war without end

Even before the civil war, Darfur had been unstable for years. It faced many of the problems southern Sudan, the Nuba Mountains and Blue Nile had experienced: the region was dramatically underdeveloped, and lacked political clout. Religious tensions were not a factor: almost everyone in Darfur is Muslim. However most people were poor. Recurrent droughts had led to sustained periods of hardship. Inter-ethnic clashes, often sparked by squabbles over land and the *hakurat* (land grants), were a feature of life.

In the late 1980s, an Arab supremacist movement emerged, in part stirred up by Libya.[56] An Arab-Fur conflict broke out around this time, and in the 1990s there was an Arab-Masalit war. In both, an African group (the Fur, and then the Masalit) fought against Arab groups. African groups like the Fur, Zaghawa and Masalit felt increasingly hard done by, as Khartoum appeared to support the Arabs against them. On 21 July 2001, a large group of Fur and Zaghawa swore on the Koran to thwart Arab supremacist policies in Darfur.[57]

It is usually stated that the Darfur war broke out in February 2003, although there had been clashes even before that.[58] The news only really made it outside of Sudan's borders in April of that year, when the rebels launched a surprise attack on El Fasher airport.[59] SAF was struggling to cope, in part because many of its soldiers were Darfuri Africans. The NCP turned to ethnic militias, and in particular the Janjaweed, a militia drawn from loyal Arab groups, whose fighters often rode into battle on horses. The vengeance meted out on Fur, Zaghawa and Masalit villages, in response to their apparent support for the rebels, shocked the world. Whole villages were burnt, women were raped, and civilians were brutally slaughtered. Just like the subsequent conflicts in South Kordofan and Blue Nile, the militias and the military were supported by air raids.

Brendan Bromwich states that the war was conducted on three levels:

Local level fighting between different groups in Darfur, which is generally defined on a tribal basis, is the first level. Secondly, at the national level, a confrontation between Darfur rebel movements and the government constitutes the next level of conflict; and finally, the regional rivalries amongst Sudan, Chad, Central African Republic and Libya, are implicated.[60]

At the local level, competition over scarce resources was a key factor. In the early days of the war, pastoralist Arab groups were pitted against sedentary African farmers, who supported or joined the rebels. Both needed good land, and there wasn't enough of it. This environmental dimension had been exacerbated by population growth, and the impact of many years of declining rainfall.[61] Before too long the lines became blurred, with Arab and non-Arab groups fighting on both sides, or simply caught up in the generalised chaos.

There is also a fourth, international level, which involves great power rivalries. The Darfur rebels came to believe they had the support of the US, and were convinced Washington would impose a no-fly zone on Darfur, or even intervene militarily. Khartoum has relied on China to block hostile resolutions in the UN Security Council.[62]

In 2008, the UN estimated that at least 300,000 people had died because of the Darfur war.[63] The US and many activist groups accused the government of genocide. In 2010, President Bashir would be charged with just that by the International Criminal Court.[64] The indictment has harmed Sudan's image, particularly in the West, and made it impossible for Sudan to get debt relief, or normalise relations with America. To Bashir's supporters, this was just another example of the fourth level of the conflict: the West was determined to bring Bashir down.

All efforts to return peace to Darfur have failed. The 2006 Darfur Peace Agreement (DPA) was only signed by one rebel faction, led by Minni Minnawi. He later returned to rebellion. On 14 July 2011, a minor rebel group, the Liberation and Justice Movement (LJM), signed the Doha Document for Peace in Darfur (DDPD). The agreement, which was pushed by the Qataris, had provisions for power and wealth-sharing, as well as compensation for those affected by the war. However the three most significant rebel groups refused to sign.

LJM's leader, Tigani Seisi, became the head of a new Darfur Regional Authority (DRA). He said the Doha agreement had calmed the conflict down somewhat, and claimed many of the displaced people had gone back to their home areas to farm, even if they had not moved back permanently. Yet in the year since the agreement, Tigani had become frustrated. When I talked to him in mid-2012, he complained the government had not released the funds the DRA needed to operate. Without the money, he said, the agreement would collapse. In truth, without the presence of the major rebel groups it was close to worthless anyway.[65]

Rebel groups

Three major groups continued to fight the government in Darfur after the DDPD was signed. The Sudan Liberation Army–Abdul Wahid faction (SLA-AW), named after the Fur lawyer Abdul Wahid al Nour, controls much of the Jebel Marra highlands. It has been unable to advance out of this limited base. One of Khartoum's point men on Darfur, Amin Hassan Omar, considers Abdul Wahid to be a 'voice that doesn't carry, a ghost from the past'. Most of Abdul Wahid's soldiers are Fur, and in the first few years of the war he had considerable support among Fur and other IDPs throughout Darfur, though it has decreased since then. A SLA split-off, commanded by Minni Minawi and including many of his fellow Zaghawa, joined the government after the DPA, but subsequently returned to war. Khartoum believes Minni is more dangerous and less predictable than Abdul Wahid. Minni's forces have been accused of numerous human rights abuses.[66]

The third rebel group, the Justice and Equality Movement (JEM), mainly draws its forces from the Zaghawa Kobe subgroup. Its leaders had been supporters of the Islamist Hassan al Turabi, and Bashir's inner circle is convinced Turabi was behind JEM. The Darfuri rebels and Turabi himself have always denied this. JEM carried out the most spectacular action of the war, a 2008 raid on Omdurman. Hundreds of fighters in camouflaged vehicles crossed 1,500 kilometres of desert in three days.[67] The surprise assault failed to take the capital, but it announced JEM as a major force.

Government forces frequently attack all the rebel groups by air and land. Air attacks in Darfur are in violation of UN resolution 1591.[68] JEM's leader Khalil Ibrahim was killed in an air raid, on 24 December 2011, though this took place in North Kordofan, one of the states which borders Darfur.[69] Khalil's brother Gibril took over as JEM's leader. All the rebel groups are divided, allowing the government to encourage key individuals to split away. In April 2013 a JEM faction led by Mohamed Bashar signed a deal based on the DDPD with Khartoum. Bashar was killed in an ambush as he made his way back to Darfur a month later, reportedly by forces from mainstream JEM.[70] However, despite their many weaknesses the rebels have fought the government to a standstill over more than a decade. A map of the areas they operate in shows an archipelago of no-go areas throughout Darfur.

A shifting warscape

Over time, the nature of the conflict in Darfur has changed. Criminal gangs make money kidnapping international peacekeepers and aid workers, or stealing cars. In some years, more people are killed by inter-ethnic fighting than in clashes between rebels and the government. Much of this is local conflict, with little national, regional or international relevance. One Darfuri friend, Abbas, returned to his home village in 2008 after many years' absence. His area in West Darfur had not been that badly affected by the war, so he was shocked to find a heavy machine gun on display in the middle of the village.

The researchers Jerome Tubiana and Claudio Gramazzi have identified three phases to the war:

First, between 2003 and 2005, most of the violence in Darfur involved attacks by largely Arab, government-sponsored militias against non-Arab groups that were systematically regarded as supporters of the rebellion. [...] Second, after the signing of the DPA in 2006, Arab groups turned increasingly against the government, and even more so against each other. [...] A third phase has emerged as Arab groups have become more reluctant to fight on behalf of the government, notably due to the violence they themselves suffered in 2008–10. As a result, the government has shifted to forming and backing non-Arab militias for its counter-insurgency strategy.[71]

In this latest phase, Tubiana and Gramazzi conclude, small non-Arab groups like the Bergid, Berti, Mima, and Tunjur have been used against the Zaghawa, who dominate JEM and SLA-Minni Minnawi (SLA-MM).

However, the war is difficult to divide into neat categories. Many Arab militias are still loyal to Khartoum; the inter-Arab fighting ebbs and flows, and is not always linked to the civil war; and the rebels have continued their struggle against the government throughout. In early 2013, more than 800 people died in clashes between the northern Rizeigat and the Beni Hussein over a gold-mining area, Jebel Amir.[72] Members of the paramilitary Border Guards were reportedly involved.[73] Hundreds more were killed in East Darfur in August 2013 in clashes between the southern Rizeigat and the Ma'aliah.

Whenever the war does come to an end, it will take many years for Darfur to return to normal. When Hawa Ibrahim, the Fur tea lady, went back to visit her parents, she found their homes had been burnt to the ground. They were living out in the open. 'The war in Darfur has created problems for everyone', she says. 'Since the war people do not trust each other. It has changed everything.'

THE SUDAN REVOLUTIONARY FRONT

On 11 November 2011, the four major rebel groups battling with Khartoum, JEM, SLA-AW, SLA-MM, and SPLM-North, agreed to form an alliance. They called it the Sudan Revolutionary Front (SRF). The alliance was bad news for Khartoum: from this point on the rebels in Darfur, South Kordofan and Blue Nile were committed to working together to bring down Bashir's regime. Up until then, their differences had kept them separate. The Darfuri groups do not get along, and there is an ideological divide between JEM, which has Islamist roots, and the other three groups, which have secular leanings.[74]

On 20 February 2012, SPLM-North's Malik Agar was named SRF's head.[75] Less than a week later, spokesmen from JEM and SPLM-North said their forces had combined to win SRF's first victory, in Lake Abyiad in South Kordofan, near the border with South Sudan. The formation of SRF did not immediately revolutionise the military picture, since each group already had well-established areas of operation that they have largely kept to. Even together, there is very little chance of the rebels overthrowing the state. All the same, SRF's potential for combined operations was a concern for SAF, which was already seriously overstretched.

SRF's stated ambition is to topple the government 'using all available means, above all, the convergence of civil political action and armed struggle.'[76] This is easier said than done. In mid-2012, anti-government protesters took to the streets in Khartoum and elsewhere.[77] Many of the protesters were from the northern elite, and were supporters of the traditional opposition parties. They did not necessarily trust the rebels from the periphery. It was noticeable, too, that in general the Nuba and Darfuris living on the outskirts of the capital did not join in the protests, just as the northern elite had not demonstrated against the wars in Darfur or South Kordofan.

The rebels got a little closer to their goal of uniting Sudan's marginalised outlying areas with the political opposition in the centre in early January 2013. The SRF and several well-known figures from Sudanese opposition parties and civil society held talks in Kampala. Many of those who attended signed the New Dawn Charter.[78] The charter stated how this disparate group would like to see Sudan governed, including the separation of religious institutions from state institutions (which tiptoed round the idea of removing *sharia*), and affirmative action to ensure regions wrecked by war would benefit from as much power and wealth as the centre.

The charter terrified the government: if the rebels could make common cause with the opposition, including its leaders from the northern heartland, the NCP would be vastly outnumbered. Six opposition politicians who had attended the talks with the rebels were arrested.[79] Under great pressure, the main opposition parties backed away from any link to the charter, including by suggesting their representatives had only been authorised to attend the talks, but not to sign.[80] A further attempt to bring the armed and unarmed opposition together, in Geneva in July 2013, was scuppered when NISS stopped political opposition leaders from leaving Sudan. Opposition politicians promised they would try again.

Nevertheless the major leaders of the unarmed opposition all had objections to parts of the SRF's vision. Discussions in Kampala had stumbled over whether Sudan should be an Islamic state, the future status of the army, and how much power regions like South Kordofan and Blue Nile should have if Bashir was overthrown and a new system put in place.

Malik Agar realises the SRF rebels need the support of at least part of the northern elite: 'Nile people have ruled these areas, they have committed a lot of atrocities, they think we are seeking vengeance, so they are unnecessarily protective,' he says. 'We want to educate them that we are not a danger to them.' However, the SRF has not been able to articulate a position that satisfies its natural constituency on the peripheries, and wins over the centre to its cause.

Abu Kershola

In late April 2013, the SRF launched its first major combined operation. Two joint SRF battalions, including troops from all the four rebel groups, attacked Abu Kershola, and the nearby town of Um Ruwaba, which is in North Kordofan, on the road to Khartoum. This strike towards the riverine heartland brought the realities of the war home to many Sudanese in the capital. Their anxieties only grew when the SRF were able to hold onto Abu Kershola for several weeks. Some MPs called for the Defence Minister, Abdel Rahim Hussein, to be sacked. He rode out the storm, thanks to Bashir's support. Nevertheless, this latest proof of SAF's weakness cheered up the rebels tremendously. 'We saw how vulnerable the regime is, militarily,' Malik Agar said.

Abu Kershola could not, however, mask all the tensions between the SRF's members. The leaders of the three other rebel movements distrusted JEM's Islamist background—'We're sleeping with the enemy' one rebel commander said—and accused JEM soldiers of carrying out abuses in its new base in the Nuba Mountains. Equally, JEM and SPLM-North leaders were not particularly impressed with Abdul Wahid al Nour: 'his movement is a table with three Thurayas [satellite phones] on it, nothing more', is how one of them put it. The SRF is very clearly a marriage of convenience, but its value to its members may well outweigh their misgivings for some time.

Piecemeal solutions for sweeping problems

The NCP are skilled at using divide and rule tactics. The rebels are dealt with separately. Khartoum says it will only negotiate with the Darfuris in Doha, on the basis of the DDPD, while talks with SPLM-North stutter and stumble from time to time in Addis Ababa. The SRF would like one set of negotiations with the government, with a wide-reaching mandate; but as this book went to press this was not on the cards. 'Who are the SRF? We do not recognise them,' Amin Hassan Omar says. Powerful Western countries will not push for joint talks in part because they do not wish to antagonise Qatar, which sponsors the Darfur negotiations.

Yet if Sudan is ever to find peace, all its rebellious areas and all its governance failings will have to be addressed, in one forum. The people will have to agree on a new constitution, though historically this has proved difficult. The armed and unarmed opposition will have to be involved in the process, and civil society too. The result would not remove the NCP from the political map, but it would undoubtedly reduce its role in governing the country. It would take a poweful concoction of increased rebel miliary successes, domestic pressures including massive demonstrations, and concerted international prodding to force the NCP to accept. In the period immediately after separation, those factors were not present.

SOUTH SUDAN AND THE SUDANESE REBELS

The rebels fighting Khartoum in Blue Nile and South Kordofan were once comrades in arms with the men now in power in South Sudan. Malik Agar served as Salva Kiir's deputy during many hard-fought battles with SAF. Abdel Aziz al Hilu was one of the SPLA's most respected commanders. It would have been unrealistic to expect all contacts to be cut once South Sudan seceded. Indeed, many South Sudanese soldiers believe they have a moral duty to help their former colleagues in the Two Areas. Because of this, Khartoum regularly accuses South Sudan of equipping and even directing SPLM-North.

There is no clear public evidence to back up Khartoum's allegations that South Sudan has supplied arms to SPLM-North in large quantities. The rebels held on to the weapons they had been given when they were part of the SPLA, before secession. This includes tanks, artillery and RPGs.[81] SPLM-North leaders say that they subsequently captured everything else they needed from SAF.[82] Nevertheless, even Western countries which are well disposed to South Sudan, like the US and Britain, believe Juba is providing some level of support to SPLM-North. Khartoum has also accused Uganda of supporting SPLM-North, though this too has been denied.[83] The rebels are clearly getting help from somewhere. SPLM-North's Yassir Arman admits that 'as a guerilla movement, we can always survive in the shifting sands of regional and international politics'. Helpfully for the rebels, Khartoum has plenty of enemies.

Khartoum also accuses SPLM-North of using refugee camps like Yida and Yusuf Batil as rear bases for its soldiers. The bombing of Yida that I witnessed in November 2011 may well have been in revenge for SPLM-North's attack on Talodi, over the border in South Kordofan, though this would in no way excuse bombing civilians.[84] Certainly the refugee camps are full of the families of the SPLM-North fighters, and often the soldiers can be seen nearby. A senior US official has accused the rebels of forcibly recruiting soldiers, including children, in Yida.[85] Malik Agar denies this, and the charge that his soldiers use Yida and other camps as part of their military campaign. He says it is a 'human right' for the soldiers to visit their families.

There is undoubtedly great sympathy in South Sudan for SPLM-North. South Sudan's Riek Machar told me that in his last meeting with Bashir before separation he warned the Sudanese president not to resolve the problems of South Kordofan and Blue Nile by force. Khartoum will always be convinced that the emotional ties between the SPLM and SPLM-North are supplemented by military aid, and so the tensions between South Sudan and Sudan will last as long as the wars in South Kordofan and Blue Nile do. Vital negotiations between the Sudans often foundered over allegations of support to rebel groups.

The SRF

South Sudan extended its support once the SRF was formed.[86] Sudanese rebel leaders are regularly seen in Juba (as well as the Ugandan capital Kampala). More importantly, South Sudan has let Darfuri rebel groups use bases on its territory. The main camp was, for a time, near Bentiu, the capital of Unity state. A UN Panel of Experts said it had

obtained clear and compelling evidence, including eyewitness statements, that, in 2012, JEM used a base for some 800 fighters in a former chicken farm situated between the town of Rubkona and the Bentiu airstrip (at N9°18'27" E29°47'24.5"). [...] The Panel has also received multiple testimonies that another JEM base functioned in South Sudan, notably at Timsaha in Western Bahr el-Ghazal State.[87]

Both Bentiu and Timsaha are near the border with Sudan. South Sudan has rejected the accusation, but even in his denial the Unity state deputy governor reportedly let slip that 'JEM are no longer in our territories'.[88]

In July 2012, at a critical point in the negotiations between Sudan and South Sudan, a JEM convoy of around 105 vehicles assembled near Aweil, in South Sudan, according to a source close to the AU mediators between the two countries.[89] Sudan was dissuaded from attacking the vehicles inside South Sudan by the British and the Americans. After the convoy reached the border area, heading into Sudan, it was 'bombed heavily'. One air raid dropped six bombs just south of the border. The international outrage was directed at Sudan, for another 'unprovoked' attack on South Sudan.[90] The new country was not criticised, despite the fact that the Darfuri rebels were based on its territory.

South Sudan's relationship with SPLM-North was forged by many years of fighting alongside each other for a common goal. However, Juba's decision to help JEM and other Darfuri rebels is, at best, a defensive response to Sudan's own backing for South Sudanese rebel groups. At worst, the new country is lowering itself to Sudan's standards. From the point of view of the SRF's rebels, their South Sudanese bases are useful, allowing them to strike within Sudan, then duck across the border to relative safety. Nevertheless, they are running a risk: how long will South Sudan's support last?

The conflicts in South Kordofan and Blue Nile, and the formation of the SRF, have shown how Sudan's internal security is still affected by South Sudan. The perception of South Sudanese support for Sudanese rebels plays a major role in the tensions between the two countries. However, Sudan's civil wars are not a South Sudanese creation; they are crises with long roots in the political, economic and social marginalisation of many areas of the country.

SOUTH SUDAN

The rebels

The first thing you notice about Stephen Gatwech is his smile, and the delighted chuckle that often follows it. He is particularly engaged by a trumpet made of shiny paper, which sets him into convulsions of laughter every time he blows it. The second thing you notice is that this cheerful boy, who must be five or six years old, is missing most of his left leg. Stephen's foot was reduced to ribbons of useless skin, each roughly the dimensions of his home-made trumpet, by an anti-tank mine in Unity state, not too far from the border with Sudan. His leg was amputated in a hospital in the state capital, Bentiu. The mine had almost certainly been planted by the South Sudan Liberation Army (SSLA), a rebel movement with close ties to Khartoum.[91] It destroyed the vehicle Stephen was travelling in, and killed several of the passengers, including Stephen's grandmother.

At South Sudan's independence, the new government already had several rebel groups to deal with. Most operated near the border with Sudan, in Unity state and Upper Nile state, while another was based in Jonglei. All attempted to portray themselves as angry voices from South Sudan's own neglected periphery, whatever their real motivations. Some rebellions had been started by frustrated losers in the 2010 elections, who believed the polls had been rigged against them. Others, like the leaders of the SSLA, had fought for Khartoum during the north-south civil war. Juba accuses Khartoum of supporting all of these rebels.

The South Sudanese rebel groups are not particularly strong: none has the ability to bring down the state on its own. Even if they united this probably would not change. Immediately after separation they were too divided to form one movement, despite several attempts to do so. Unlike the rebels in Sudan, none of the South Sudanese groups control large amounts of territory. Nevertheless, their impact in the areas they operate in is real enough, as Stephen Gatwech's amputated leg shows. In the first two years after separation, the two most significant rebel groups were the SSLA and the Murle force led by David Yau Yau.

The South Sudan Liberation Army

Bapiny Monytuil, one of the SSLA's leaders, is from Mayom, in Unity state in South Sudan, and the SSLA claimed to be based near there. Bapiny was never in Mayom, however. To meet him you had to go to Khartoum. He had set up his headquarters in the south of the Sudanese capital, in an area called Kalaka Wihda. Lots of poor South Sudanese and Darfuris live nearby, but Bapiny was based in a large house in a fairly prosperous area. I visited him there several times. On each occasion a Hummer and a Land Cruiser were parked outside. Once, a couple of members of the group standing guard by the house were carrying AK47s. Most of the guards were Nuer, judging by their facial scars. Bapiny himself, and many of his rebels, are from the Bul Nuer subgroup.

Bapiny is a tall man, but he moves with a little difficulty, the result of a serious beating a few years previously. In some ways, Bapiny is a very modern rebel: he communicates by text or Skype, and hands over amateur footage of his rebels and their new weapons on USB keys. He has spent a large portion of his life at war, most of the time against the SPLA. All the same, Bapiny still has close ties to several SPLM leaders. Taban Deng, the governor of Unity state until July 2013, married Bapiny's daughter, and still talks to his father-in-law on the phone. One of Bapiny's stated objectives was to conquer Unity state, and overthrow Taban. These connections between apparent enemies are very common in both Sudan and South Sudan.[92] 'It's family, not politics!' Bapiny says.

At separation, the SSLA was led by Peter Gadet, another Bul Nuer general. Gadet announced the formation of the SSLA via the Mayom declaration on 11 April 2011 and fighting was initially concentrated in this area. The SPLA were accused of burning nearly 8,000 *tukuls* or huts as they attacked the rebels.[93] The offensive did not succeed in defeating the SSLA, and Gadet and his troops quickly became one of the rebel groups that caused the biggest headache for the government.

However, Gadet has made a career of switching sides; he has fought both for and against the SPLA. In the memorable phrase of the Sudans expert John Young, 'Gadet is said to wash only one side of his face at a time so that he can always keep an eye open.'[94] In August 2011, a month after independence, Gadet changed sides again, accepting an amnesty offered by President Salva Kiir. Gadet wasn't able to convince all his soldiers to follow him, and the SSLA continued to fight. James Gai Yoach was named the leader, and Bapiny his deputy.[95] The following month, as if to prove their continued relevance, the SSLA attacked Mayom town. Although this was trumpeted as a great victory for the rebels, they were, in fact, chased away after a couple of hours of fighting.[96] All the same the SSLA was taken seriously by Juba, because its troops operated near the Unity state oilfields, and as it often seemed to coordinate its attacks with SAF.

Although Khartoum officially denied any links with the SSLA or other South Sudanese rebels, defectors tell a different story. In March 2012, I met Jacob Nyier, one of the political leaders of the SSLA, at Bapiny's headquarters in Khartoum. Later that year he fled to Juba. He said he had quit the rebels in disgust at the way they were being used by the Sudanese. 'The reason why we are in Khartoum is not because they think we will overthrow the government [in Juba]. It is because Khartoum want us to fight on the borders, so they can tell the world community these people cannot run themselves, they are just fighting a tribal war.' In Khartoum, Nyier and Bapiny had told me that their new weapons, including multiple rocket-launchers and machine guns mounted on trucks, had been bought from Ukraine. In fact, Nyier later admitted, 'that was not true. We got them from [Sudanese] national security.' Other defectors made similar claims.[97]

The more media-savvy members of the SSLA, including its spokesman, Gordon Buay, insisted the rebels were fighting because of corruption and bad governance in South Sudan. Commanders like Bapiny, however, sometimes let slip the sort of argument used to convince poorly educated Nuers in the villages to fight. 'We the Nuer with oil under our feet, we never even get one clinic and one school, even water sanitation, even food, agriculture', he said. 'They take the revenue from our oil, they divide it in two, one for Dinka, one for Arabs.' Part of the SSLA's relevance came from its Nuer base: the Nuer are South Sudan's second biggest ethnic group.

Nyier confirmed that the rebels tried to convince the Nuer that they were fighting against Dinka domination. However, he said, outside of a few villages in Bul Nuer territory around Mayom, hardly anyone supported the SSLA. In 2011 and 2012, the SSLA even ran so short of soldiers that they had to press-gang hundreds of South Sudanese in Khartoum and Omdurman. I spoke to many South Sudanese who were terrified they would be abducted and sent to the front line. Church leaders and construction workers were among those kidnapped.

The Sudanese government denied it was happening, but it seemed to many South Sudanese that the SSLA could not have acted as they did, in a foreign country, without Khartoum's permission. In May 2012, the UN reported that twenty-four men had been abducted in Kalakla Wihda, not far from Bapiny's headquarters.[98] Bapiny had already dismissed accusations that he was involved as 'lies'. He admitted that bus-loads of South Sudanese heading to the border were his soldiers, but he claimed that they had been in Khartoum for medical treatment.

David Yau Yau

David Yau Yau was one of the losing candidates in the April 2010 elections, in his area near Pibor in Jonglei state. He believed he should have won the Gumruk seat in the Jonglei state legislature. Yau Yau took up arms the next month. In a series of calls from his satellite phone, he complained to me about abuses against the Murle, his ethnic group, and made grandiose statements about his military ambitions, none of which were ever realised. Just before separation Yau Yau signed an agreement with the government in Juba. He was given a military rank, a car, money and a house, according to Majak D'Agoot, who at the time was the deputy defence minister.

Despite his new wealth, in April 2012 Yau Yau took to the bush again.[99] 'He got a higher bid from Khartoum,' D'Agoot says. The second time round Yau Yau, who took to calling his forces the South Sudan Democratic Army (SSDA) Cobra faction, achieved more military success.[100] On 22 August 2012, his men ambushed the SPLA near Nanam river, reportedly killing over a hundred of them.[101] In the following months, the Cobra faction regularly clashed with the SPLA at Likuangole, at Gumruk and even near the county headquarters, Pibor.[102] Yau Yau's second rebellion was fuelled by the increased dissatisfaction of the Murle, who were angry at what they saw as the state's failure to stop inter-ethnic fighting in which hundreds of Murle died.[103]

South Sudan says the Sudanese have flown in weapons to Yau Yau. On 22 September 2012, UN peacekeepers observed a white fixed-wing aircraft dropping packages near Yau Yau's base, not far from Likuangole, though the UN could not confirm what had been delivered.[104] In March 2013, the SPLA announced it had captured several airbases at which Yau Yau had allegedly been receiving military support from Khartoum.[105] The man leading the combat against Yau Yau, who announced this apparent triumph, was the former SSLA leader turned SPLA general, Peter Gadet. Sudan denies supporting Yau Yau, but at the very least the perception that it does has further poisoned the relationship between Juba and Khartoum.

Dealing with the rebels

Juba's approach to the various rebel groups aligned against it has varied. D'Agoot, a respected strategic thinker, outlines a combination of buying off rebel leaders and applying military force. The signing of the Juba Declaration in January 2006, by Salva Kiir and Paulino Matip, showcased the principle of bringing armed groups opposed to the SPLA into the fold. Matip, who had fought against the SPLA for many years, became its second-in-command. Similarly, Clement Wani was named the governor of Central Equatoria, and Alfred Ladu and Ismail Konyi became advisers to the president. After separation, Gadet was bought off, as was Yau Yau for a time.

Others were dealt with militarily. George Athor, who led a rebellion in Jonglei after he failed to win the gubernatorial elections there, was for some time a major concern. Yau Yau and Athor claimed they were working together, but there was little evidence of any practical collaboration. Like the SSLA's Bapiny, Athor could frequently be spotted in Sudan, and he 'enjoyed direct military support from Khartoum' according to the research group Small Arms Survey.[106] In February 2011, at least 200 people were killed in Fangak, in Jonglei, in clashes between Athor's rebels and the SPLA.[107] Both sides blamed the other for the death of the civilians. In December 2011, Athor was killed. Earlier that year another rebel, Gatluak Gai, was also killed, in mysterious circumstances shortly after he had signed a peace deal.[108]

In late April 2013, Bapiny was one of several rebel leaders who accepted an amnesty offered by Salva. He flew to Juba. His field commander, Matthew Pul Jang, marched over the border from Sudan into South Sudan, accompanied by hundreds of soldiers. The fighters were 'extremely well armed', but had only limited supplies of ammunition, perhaps because their supply chain had been cut off.[109] At a stroke, the security threat in Unity had dramatically reduced. In June, Johnson Olony came in too, to the relief of many people in Upper Nile. It seemed as if efforts to buy the rebels off had succceeded. By September 2013, David Yau Yau, in Jonglei, was the only major rebel leader who had not accepted the amnesty offer.

This sort of dramatic change is not new. The SPLA has splintered numerous times in its history, only for disaffected commanders to return. The most famous dissenter, Riek Machar, almost broke the SPLA/M when he left in 1991, alongside Lam Akol. After he came back to the fold he ended up as vice president.

For officers like Gadet, rebellion appears to be a career move. A spell in the bush is 'rewarded' with a higher military rank on return. Senior officials like D'Agoot are deeply aware of the problem:

It is not sustainable, but its a trap every post-conflict country gets itself in. You have to buy in warlords, some political leaders who may destabilise the country. We have been doing this for the last seven, eight years. Khartoum has also been making things difficult, they are on the other side of the option market.

D'Agoot thinks it will be a few years before South Sudan is strong enough to rise above co-opting rebels. As long as taking up arms against the state brings rewards, either from Khartoum or, eventually, from Juba itself, rebellions will continue to destabilise South Sudan. If relations between the two Sudans get worse, Sudanese support to the South Sudanese rebels could be increased too.

Juba believes its internal security is heavily dependent on Khartoum's intentions. However in the period after separation, South Sudan's biggest internal threat was actually the rivalry between different ethnic groups.

A POISONOUS THORN IN OUR HEARTS

INTER-ETHNIC FIGHTING

In the last hour of darkness the killers arrived, swarming into Pieri village from the east. Kuol Bol, a tall young man with a shaven head, was asleep in his hut. The first gunshots jolted him awake. Even in the murky pre-dawn light, he knew the attackers were the Murle. Kuol's people, the Lou Nuer, were involved in a seemingly endless cycle of revenge attacks with the Murle in this neglected part of Jonglei state. As the shooting grew louder, Kuol knew he had to act fast to save his family. He sprinted to find his young nephews. Too late: two were already dead. Grabbing the third, he raced out of the village, through a scene from hell: burning huts, some with their owners trapped inside, illuminated his way; assault rifles, and the heart-wrenching screams of those too slow to escape, provided the soundtrack.

In one devastating day, 18 August 2011, as many as 600 Lou Nuer were killed in Pieri and other villages nearby. Women, children and the elderly were slaughtered. Babies were hacked with machetes, to save bullets. As well as those killed, 200 children were abducted, and an estimated 25,000 cattle were stolen.[110] Thousands of Lou Nuer fled. Without their cows, they would depend on handouts and local kindness for the foreseeable future. Several days after the attack, I saw one man queuing up for a blanket and some food wearing a white t-shirt with a happy slogan on the back: 'Celebrating the Birth of the New Nation. 9th July 2011'. South Sudan had been independent for just over a month. The attack on Pieri was a brutal reminder that hoisting a new flag would not be a magical cure for all South Sudan's problems. 'They killed my family', Kuol said. 'I want revenge. I will do what I will do.'

Four months later the Lou Nuer took that revenge. As many as 8,000 young men calling themselves the White Army descended on the Murle homeland around the town of Pibor.[111] The White Army cut a bloody swathe through more than twenty Murle settlements. A UN report said at least 623 Murle were killed, and eyewitness accounts quoted by the UN suggested a further 294 people should be added to this gruesome tally.[112] The Pibor county commissioner, Joshua Konyi, a Murle, said the real death toll was more than 3,000, though this seemed exaggerated.[113]

Nyandit was one of those who survived—just. She was shot in the leg, and another bullet grazed her cheek, causing it to swell and giving her face a lopsided look. Her world was similarly unbalanced. Ten members of her family had been killed, and her only child, a three-year-old boy, was abducted in front of her eyes. 'It is very painful. All my family are dead now,' she said, in a flat voice, from her hospital bed. 'My son has been taken. I am all alone now.' But she expressed no surprise. This was life as she knew it. As a young girl she had been shot, in an earlier raid. The Murle would take revenge for what Nyandit had lost, and the cycle would continue. In a group of people waiting for a food handout in Pibor, I saw a young Murle woman. Like the rest of her age-mates, she had a symbol carved into her shoulder. The ritual mark picked out in raised flesh was a tiny AK47 assault rifle.

In 2011, an estimated 3,406 people were killed in conflict in South Sudan and more than 350,000 were displaced.[114] The South Sudanese authorities—and the people—had to deal with fighting between the SPLA and various rebel groups, like the SSLA. Cross-border clashes with SAF were a problem too. Yet most of the clashes were inter-ethnic. The death toll dropped in 2012, to 1,452, but this was still worryingly high. The security forces were confronted with serious problems in Lakes, Warrap, Unity and Upper Nile states. Northern Bahr el Ghazal, Western Bahr el Ghazal and the three Equatorian states were comparatively peaceful. However Juba, which is in Central Equatoria, became increasingly dangerous. Some shootings were blamed on the security forces, either in or out of uniform, and civilians often carried weapons for their own protection. Nevertheless, more than two thirds of the people killed in South Sudan in 2012 were in Jonglei, and the majority of them died in inter-ethnic conflict.

Jonglei—the problem

The inter-communal fighting in Jonglei, and other parts of South Sudan, is in part a consequence of underdevelopment and poverty. 'When the belly is not full, there will be conflicts,' says Emmanuel Jal, the rapper and activist. 'Peace is justice, equality and freedom for all. Those are the issues this country is struggling with now.' Cattle-raiding is at the heart of the problem. Young men, in particular, need cows in order to get married. They have no jobs, and no means to buy cows, so stealing them seems a reasonable option to many. The ready availability of assault rifles means that each cattle raid costs dozens or hundreds of lives. The state is unable to provide security, or justice, so the survivors set out to get revenge for their murdered relatives, and to recover the cows they have lost. These problems exist in many parts of South Sudan, but they are most debilitating in Jonglei.

Jonglei is South Sudan's largest state, and its most populous. According to the 2008 census, more than 1.35 million people live there, though the real figure may be higher than this.[115] The state is perhaps South Sudan's least developed. The lack of roads also means the different ethnic groups don't trade with one another, which increases their poverty and their isolation. Speaking when he was Vice President, Riek Machar said that Jonglei's profile accounted for so much bloodshed: 'It's inhabited by six ethnic groups, they are heavily armed, and there's competition over scarce resources such as water and grazing areas. Sometimes even cattle disease would bring about conflict.' Fighting has been going on for decades, and not only between the Lou Nuer and the Murle. The Dinka Bor, the Anyuak and the Gawaar Nuer have also been involved at different points.

The decades of north-south civil war contributed to the militarisation of society: there are more armed civilians than members of the security forces in South Sudan. The civil war also inflamed ethnic tensions. Many Murle were armed by Khartoum to fight against the SPLA, and as a result the Murle suffer in South Sudan's ethnicised post-independence politics. They do not have a strong voice representing them in Juba, and are disliked by other groups in part because of their perceived support for and from Khartoum.[116] The inter-communal clashes in Jonglei, in particular, have become a litmus test of the new country's ability to resolve the widespread inter-ethnic tensions, and forge a united nation.

Both before and after independence, Juba's stock response to any inter-ethnic fighting was to blame Khartoum. The old enemy was accused of supplying weapons to the Murle, and others. D'Agoot also alleges that the Lou Nuer who attacked Murleland were using weapons Khartoum had originally given the rebel leader George Athor. Athor had apparently distributed them to his Lou Nuer followers. Whatever the truth of the matter, it underlined the extent to which South Sudan's focus, even after independence, was firmly on Sudan; often for very good reason. However, this sometimes impeded the drive to begin resolving the many security and developmental problems in Jonglei and elsewhere.

The government and the peacekeepers fail to cope

The Lou Nuer and the Murle blame each other for starting the series of deadly clashes. A UN human rights report identified the 2009 raids as a turning point, as they 'marked a change in strategy, with direct attacks on civilians, communities as a whole, and state institutions, as well as raids involving armed youth and cattle rustling.'[117] The fighting decreased in scale in 2010, but it was clear it was not over. Then in the run-up to independence in 2011, hundreds of Murle were killed, according to Konyi.

Even more died when the Murle attacked Pieri in August 2011, the raid during which Kuol Bol's nephews were killed. The Murle were taking revenge, and also targeting a Lou Nuer prophet, Dak Kueth, who they believed was coordinating the raids against them. These two massacres, in which perhaps as many as a thousand people died, should have been a wake-up call to the authorities, and the UN peacekeepers. Yet the Lou Nuer's revenge attacks in December 2011 and January 2012, in which hundreds more died, were chillingly predictable. The government was unable to prevent the attacks. Once they began, it couldn't stop them, in part because of the lack of roads: security forces simply couldn't get to the affected areas in time. Some South Sudanese suspected the ethnically divided army was loath to intervene in a messy civilian inter-ethnic conflict.

Archbishop Daniel Deng was part of a church-led process to bring the warring communities closer together. He blamed the SPLA and the UN for not acting more quickly to prevent a tragedy. If they had been on the ground in November 2011, the massacres wouldn't have taken place, he said. The archbishop reported that he was frequently told by people in Jonglei that the fighting was sparked by politicians in Juba:

Our politicians are not on the ground to help their own people who elected them. Our politicians up to now have not shown their nationalism, whether they are nationalists or leaders of the tribes. Always on the ground the people are telling us the politicians are involved.

I heard similar accusations in the Lou Nuer and Murle areas I visited, though the accusers were frightened of naming the individuals they believed to be responsible.

When explaining Jonglei's problems, the leaders in Juba often put the blame on the Murle. Majak D'Agoot, the then-deputy defence minister, told me the other communities in Jonglei were angry with the Murle for child abductions and cattle-raiding. In January 2012, as the Lou Nuer White Army was attacking Murleland, President Salva Kiir appeared on South Sudan Television and 'claimed there were high rates of venereal disease among the Murle which led to low birth rates, causing the tribe to abduct children from their neighbours.'[118] This widely held theory may have been true in the 1960s, the anthropologist Jon Arensen says, but a World Health Organisation campaign cured the Murle, allowing their women to have children.[119]

The Murle do buy children from the Dinka and the Nuer. In some cases they steal them. As Nyandit's example shows, the Lou Nuer and others also abduct children from the Murle. Nevertheless, the Murle are often cast as the scapegoats in the official narrative. Even within the SPLM, though, not everyone agrees with this. 'The Murle are not pro-Khartoum,' my source The Minister says. 'They are just marginalised and suffering.'

Jonglei: defying the state

The White Army attack on Murleland, in late 2011 and early 2012, was a crisis not just for the Murle or Jonglei, but also for South Sudan. Thousands of armed men, operating outside the authority of the state, forced their way to the suburbs of a county capital, Pibor, killing and raping as they went. The White Army had clear lines of command, and was well armed. Many of the fighters wore uniforms of the SPLA or other security forces like the police, prison service or wildlife service.[120] Graffiti left on the walls of destroyed buildings displayed a deep ethnic hatred of the Murle.[121] Children and old people were stabbed, and young Murle men shot.

As the tornado advanced, Vice President Riek flew to the area. At Likuangole, a small town to the north of Pibor, he met the White Army leaders, his fellow Nuer. 'I called upon them to go back to their home states, and also to stop the fighting so that the government can have ways and means of resolving the problem.' They did not listen. The White Army advanced on Pibor, arriving on 31 December. For The Minister, this was a real crisis: the Lou Nuer had defied Riek, and they had defied the state.

The raiders burnt several huts on the outskirts of town, and ransacked the small hospital run by MSF. The town's small SPLA contingent prepared for a fight, with the soldiers on the perimeter digging foxholes to protect themselves. The United Nations Mission in South Sudan (UNMISS) deployed its two armoured cars to ward off possible incursions.[122] The SPLA did not attempt to drive the White Army away. Taking on the thousands of militiamen would have been a 'suicidal act', the SPLA's spokesman said, because his troops were so outnumbered.[123] The SPLA did open fire on 2 January, killing five and wounding two of a group of at least 150 White Army fighters who tried to enter the town.[124]

Other columns of White Army fighters fanned out around Pibor, attacking villages and killing hundreds of Murle civilians, particularly around the Kangen river valley. Mary Boyoi says that she lost fifteen members of her extended family, and many others she knew. In the end, on 3 January 2012, apparently frustrated by their inability to enter Pibor, the Lou Nuer militia headed for home. They left with thousands of cows, and hundreds of prisoners, mainly children, including Nyandit's little boy. Perhaps even worse, this was not the end of the fighting, merely a horrendous beginning to a new cycle. On 8 February 2013, at least eighty-five people were killed as the Murle attacked Lou Nuer near the town of Walgak.[125] Hundreds more died in clashes in the east of Jonglei as the year progressed.

Disarmament and other solutions

There have been many different approaches to ending the Jonglei crisis. The church stepped up a grass-roots peace-building process, making use of its influence throughout Jonglei's communities. Church leaders committed themselves to 'the long-term changing of attitudes and value systems which will eventually lead to a generation free of armed conflict.'[126] Civil society groups, led by John Penn De Ngong, brought youths from all of Jonglei's communities together. The tensions are so high that sometimes he was accused of betraying his own Dinka Bor people. In March 2013, female activists from Jonglei added their contribution too, threatening to leave their men and settle in a neutral area if the fighting continued.[127]

The government's job is to provide security, justice, and development for the area. In particular, the government committed itself to building 'security roads', all weather surfaces which would allow the armed forces to head off trouble. This will take time. A strong justice system seemed an equally remote prospect. Jonglei state is the size of Malawi or Mississippi, and there are only seven judges. None of them are in Pibor.[128] Those who killed Lou Nuer or Murle civilians have not faced trial.

The oil shutdown compromised the government's ability to improve the situation in Jonglei, one of the hidden dramas of this unprecedented period. Forfeiting the oil revenue meant there was no chance of building the security roads, let alone the schools and hospitals Jonglei cannot prosper without. Speaking just a few weeks after the shutdown, in February 2012, the then-Vice President Riek admitted the people deserved better. He promised that after the oil was switched back on, the government would do 'more substantial development' in Jonglei.

In the first couple of years after independence, the most significant attempted remedy applied to inter-ethnic tensions, in Jonglei and elsewhere, was civilian disarmament. This was part of a recurring pattern: since December 2005 there had been five serious outbreaks of civilian violence in Jonglei, and five flawed disarmament campaigns.[129] The 2012 campaign was heavily criticised. Mary Boyoi was one of many to complain that the Murle suffered numerous abuses during the process. Amnesty International found that the SPLA had carried out extra-judicial executions, torture, simulated drownings and rape.[130] Human Rights Watch made similar accusations in a letter to Salva. From mid-March to 31 August, MSF treated ninety-six patients with violent trauma or sexual violence injuries in its clinics in Pibor, Likuangole and Gumruk. All of these people attributed their injuries to the disarmament campaign.[131]

Senior officials insist that the human rights abuses were not widespread, and that anyone found guilty of a crime would be punished.[132] Thirty-one SPLA soldiers were apparently dismissed because of their behaviour during the campaign.[133] There can be no dispute that the disarmament campaign, in Jonglei and elsewhere, was violent. Jok Madut Jok, the university professor and under-secretary in the Culture Ministry, believes there was no specific targeting of the Murle. Instead, he says, every community across South Sudan that was disarmed, including his own, suffered at the hands of the soldiers.

Unfortunately, the bloody disarmament campaign in Jonglei did not succeed: many civilians are still armed. Majak D'Agoot admits that Dak Kueth, the Lou Nuer prophet, was able to flee to Ethiopia, along with many armed men; lots of Murle also crossed the border to avoid giving up their weapons. Areas where some communities are armed and others are not are among the most dangerous in South Sudan. In late January 2012, at least seventy-four people were killed in one attack in Warrap state, according to Governor Nyandeng Malek. They had been disarmed, but their rivals in neighbouring Unity state had not.

There is no doubt that civilians right across South Sudan will need to be disarmed if the country is to become peaceful. But as long as the military is not able to provide security, or, worse still, is seen as taking sides in inter-ethnic conflicts, this objective will be impossible to achieve.

REBELS AND CIVILIANS

In Jonglei, the civilian disarmament campaign increased the Murle's sense of persecution. Despite the denials of the South Sudanese leaders, it is no coincidence that David Yau Yau's rebellion flared up again after the failure of the state to stop the inter-ethnic clashes, and was fuelled by the flawed disarmament campaign. In the renewed fighting between the government and Yau Yau's rebels in 2013, the Murle deserted many of their main towns, and were often too scared to come to government hospitals for treatment. They simply did not trust the state to treat them fairly. Human Rights Watch said that from December 2012 to July 2013, as many as 100 Murle civilians were killed by SPLA troops during their campaign against Yau Yau's Cobra faction.[134] Many more Murle civilians were killed in clashes with the Lou Nuer. There were also repeated accusations that the Lou Nuer were being armed by SPLA officers, to help them against the Murle. By now, it was extremely hard to disentangle the inter-ethnic conflict from the counter-insurgency.

Many of Yau Yau's grievances, including the political marginalisation of his people and the underdevelopment of Murle-land, are not so different from the triggers for rebellions in Sudan. Bapiny and other rebel leaders could all point to discrimination their people had suffered, even if the rebel commanders' opportunism played a large role too. It is significant that each of South Sudan's rebel movements are based around one ethnic group: Bapiny's supporters were largely Bul Nuer, Yau Yau draws on the Murle, and Johnson Olony's forces were Shilluk, for example. South Sudan's ethnic tensions can create fertile ground for new rebellions to push up, or be created.

Most of the South Sudanese rebel leaders have accepted amnesties, and Yau Yau may too, one day. However, the amnesties are a short-term solution to South Sudan's security problems. The harder task, of developing Jonglei and the rest of South Sudan, disarming civilians, and professionalising the SPLA and the other security forces, is a long-term project. If the government does not succeed in this vital task, South Sudan will not find peace.

A Bishop shows the way

Paride Taban, the campaigning former Bishop of Torit, has been an important part of the Sudan Council of Churches' reconciliation efforts in Jonglei. He has tried to bring the Lou Nuer and the Murle together, and to convince David Yau Yau to sign a peace deal with the government. All these different groups trust him, and often ask for him to lead mediation efforts. In part, this is because of Paride's own work to bring communities together elsewhere. In 2004, Paride set up the Kuron Peace Village, in one of the most remote parts of the country, Kauto Payam in Eastern Equatoria, just over the border from Jonglei. This is an area of South Sudan where there is almost no trace of the state: 'We have no police, no army, no administration,' Paride says. This is the development challenge South Sudan faces everywhere, pushed to its greatest extreme.

Here, in his very own 'garden of Eden', Paride built a village where every community could live together. There is a school, a demonstration farm, a primary health care facility, and a whole range of programmes to build peace. Clashes between the agro-pastoralist Toposa, and their neighbours the Jie, the Nyangatom, the Murle and the Katchipo, have decreased, Paride boasts, though they still continue. Paride is particularly proud that many girls are now going to school, instead of suffering forced marriages.

In February 2013, it was announced that Bishop Emeritus Paride Taban has won the UN's Sergio Vieira de Mello Prize for his work at the Kuron Peace Village. In a very small community, he had achieved the beginnings of what South Sudan as a whole must accomplish: soothe inter-ethnic tensions through education, closer contacts between different communities, and greater development. Of course, it is by no means clear that the peace village can be scaled up to a whole nation. Nevertheless, Paride has given hope that ending South Sudan's debilitating ethnic clashes is not impossible.

* * *

Rebel groups have been fighting the Sudanese state for most of its existence. This is a consequence of political, economic and ethnic discrimination, and the instability at the heart of the political system. The CPA and South Sudan's independence did not resolve these problems. In the period just before and just after separation, new wars broke out in South Kordofan and Blue Nile, to join the long-running conflict in Darfur. In its first months of existence, South Sudan faced its own destabilising rebellions. Both countries blame each other for supporting the rebels. In both Sudans, the rebellions are often inflamed by the legacy of the decades of north-south civil war. This bitter history also exacerbated inter-ethnic conflict in South Sudan. Revenge attacks between well-armed civilians may be South Sudan's biggest internal security threat: in Jonglei alone, thousands were killed in inter-ethnic fighting in the first two years of independence.

6

THE SUDANS AND THE WORLD

SUDAN

George Clooney looked down at the blood-covered bullet, and then at the child it had been dug out of. The boy was lying on his side on a wooden bed in a makeshift hospital. For once this was not a movie, although Clooney was being filmed—by an American activist group.[1] The gruesome sight was in the Nuba Mountains, and everywhere Clooney's handsome face looked there was evidence of the suffering the war had brought: families running from air raids, children cowering in caves, corpses on the stony ground. 'You're a very brave boy,' he said to the young patient, via a translator who was dressed in the military fatigues of the SPLM-North rebels.

Clooney, wearing a beige photographer's waistcoat which he washed every night to wear fresh the next day,[2] travelled illegally into South Kordofan in early March 2012. His goal was to draw attention to the war and the humanitarian crisis there. On his return to the US, the Hollywood star briefed Congress, and then, in a well-publicised stunt, got arrested outside the Sudanese embassy in Washington.

The narrative from Clooney's visit is familiar: Sudan's government is an evil one, doing terrible things to its people. In contrast, those who fight against Khartoum are often viewed as heroes: 'this is a war of retaliation,' Clooney says in the video of his trip, right before footage of the rebels singing and dancing. Being a Sudanese diplomat must be an extremely difficult job. This is not new. Since it became independent in 1956, 'Sudan's foreign relations have [...] largely been reactive, reflecting its domestic instability,' the historian Peter Woodward has written.[3] All that internal turmoil has made it difficult for Sudan to portray a positive image of itself. In addition, in the period after separation Sudan had to contend with Western hostility, wavering support from China, and the consequences of the ICC arrest warrant for President Omar al Bashir.[4]

THE INTERNATIONAL CRIMINAL COURT

For Bashir's supporters, the devil has a name: Luis Moreno Ocampo. The Argentinian's lightly-bearded face is instantly recognisable in Khartoum. Ocampo was the ICC's Chief Prosecutor from 2003 to 2012, and Bashir's fan club accuses him of attempting to destroy their hero and their country, with the backing of America, Israel and most of the West. In March 2009, the ICC issued an arrest warrant against Bashir on counts of crimes against humanity and war crimes allegedly committed in Darfur. In response, the Sudanese government shut down foreign and local NGOs and human rights groups it blamed for supplying the court with information. In July 2010, a second arrest warrant was issued for Bashir, adding charges of genocide. Bashir has denied all the allegations, as have his fellow indictees, who include the defence minister Abdel Rahim Hussein, and Ahmed Haroun, who was responsible for the Darfur file during the most bloody years of the war.

There were serious debates within the NCP about whether Bashir could continue as leader.[5] He won that fight, as he has so many over the years. Then he and his lieutenants proceeded to turn the indictments to his advantage. The ICC helped Bashir enormously in the 2010 elections, Ibrahim Ghandour of the NCP said; indeed, the president frequently referred to Ocampo and the ICC during the campaign. Many Sudanese believed that the ICC was infringing their country's sovereignty. 'Down, down with Ocampo' they shouted at NCP rallies, in English to make sure the international journalists got the message. 'Ocampo is the Satan!' one man yelled at a particularly turbulent gathering, holding a photo of the ICC chief prosecutor to drive home the point. At Bashir's inauguration, following his victory in those flawed 2010 elections, an entire page of the glossy brochure was devoted to mocking Ocampo. The Sudanese president was clearly taking it very personally.

The ICC indictments have made it difficult for Bashir to travel abroad. In the first couple of years after the initial arrest warrant was issued, much of Sudanese foreign relations appeared to be reduced to a search for reliable friends who would oppose the ICC. The Arab League and the African Union denounced the international court, suggesting it was targeting Bashir. Not all the member states agreed. An AU summit in July 2013 was switched from Malawi to Ethiopia at the last moment, after Malawi refused to invite Bashir to Lilongwe.

However, several African and Arab countries, as well as China and Iran, have hosted Bashir, to the annoyance of the ICC and Western countries. Every trip to a country which agreed not to arrest Bashir and turn him over to the ICC was celebrated in the official Sudanese media. Every setback, like when Bashir was forced to abort a flight to Beijing in June 2011, was a cause for fury. Officials close to the president stuttered and stammered as they tried to explain why he had not arrived in China.[6] It was suggested that the president's team were concerned that his aeroplane could be intercepted by US jets over Afghanistan or Pakistan. In July 2013, Bashir left Nigeria earlier than scheduled, according to reports because he was worried about being arrested.[7]

The president's personal struggles attracted the headlines, but the real damage to Sudan was elsewhere. The ICC charges meant it was almost impossible for Sudan to obtain relief for its crippling debt. They also focused the anger of American politicians and activists, ending any hope of the US removing sanctions or the US's designation of Sudan as a state sponsoring terrorism. American and Western diplomats will not interact with Bashir at all. One low-ranking Western official who was sent to Bashir's inauguration was clearly mortified when he had to shake hands with the Sudanese leader. In mid-2012, several Western ambassadors were due to attend the opening of the massive Al Waha (Oasis) mall in central Khartoum. At the last moment they found out that Bashir was going to preside over the ceremony, so they were all forced to pull out.[8]

AMERICA AND THE WEST

Many Americans care deeply about Sudan. Darfur was an important foreign policy issue in the 2008 presidential elections, for example. Princeton Lyman, the US Special Envoy for Sudan and South Sudan until early 2013, puts America's long-standing involvement down to three main factors: firstly, the concern felt by US religious groups (particularly the Christian right) and the Congressional Black Caucus (CBC) over the treatment of southern Sudanese, starting from the mid-1980s; secondly, the scale and timing of the Darfur conflict, which began in the run up to the tenth anniversary of the Rwandan genocide, when the mantra of 'never again' had particular resonance; thirdly, the impact of the north-south Sudanese civil war on its neighbours. Kenya, Ethiopia and Uganda, in particular, had to host hundreds of thousands of southern Sudanese refugees. Sudan has attracted attention from both Democrats and Republicans; it has been one of the few issues both sides of American political life can agree on.[9]

Throughout the 1970s and the 1980s, Sudan was the biggest recipient of US foreign aid in Africa.[10] The CBC and others expressed their concerns for years, but America's relationship with Khartoum did not substantially change until the early 1990s, when Turabi began supporting extremists like Bin Laden. In 1997, Bill Clinton imposed the first sanctions on Sudan and in 1998, the Al Shifaa factory in Khartoum North was attacked by US cruise missiles. The supposed chemical weapons factory turned out to be a pharmaceutical plant.[11]

Pressure from George W. Bush, whose engagement with Sudanese issues apparently flowed from his connections to the right-wing Evangelical movement in the US, played a large role in the signing of the CPA, which eventually led to Sudan splitting in two. Many Sudanese hold America responsible for this. US grass-roots activism on Sudan reached a high point over the war in Darfur, with students, human rights groups and churches leading the charge. Colin Powell famously said that the Sudanese government had committed genocide in Darfur,[12] but this was not followed by any meaningful American action. The former US Assistant Secretary of State for Africa, Jendayi Frazer, told me that the Bush administration she served in seriously explored the possibility of imposing a no-fly zone in Darfur, but calculated that after Afghanistan and Iraq the risks of intervening in another Muslim country outweighed the rewards.[13]

In the US and the West, Sudan's problems are now largely viewed through the activist lens wielded by Clooney and others.[14] This infuriates many Sudanese. The social commentator Nesrine Malik wrote that most of her compatriots took 'eye-rolling offence' to Clooney's campaign, and she herself was concerned 'because the view Clooney is presenting to the world is not an accurate one.'[15] Even some of the most vocal enemies of the NCP, like the opposition group Sudan Change Now, have expressed their concern about the way American activists push a simplified view of

Sudan's problems.[16] However, the complaints of the Sudanese are not often heard in America. A strong anti-Khartoum line is an easy win. The US Congress is deeply hostile to the NCP, and Frazer says Congress members 'grandstand' on Sudan to please their domestic constituencies.

In the other corner are the pragmatists. They think that if the US wants peace between Sudan and South Sudan it needs to engage with both. The pragmatists are dismissive of the activists and their impact. 'By and large their policy recommendations were ill-informed,' says Cameron Hudson, who worked at a high level with a succession of US special envoys. The activist-pragmatist tussle is reflected within the US State Department. 'These two lines of policy,' Lyman admits, with a degree of understatement, 'sometimes rub up against each other'. The stance that the US takes on a particular Sudanese issue matters: the Americans believe, with some justification, that the CPA would not have been signed, and South Sudan would not have seceded, without US pressure.[17]

Sudan and America

The NCP politicians are convinced that America is working to overthrow them, perhaps because they are Muslims, or at any rate because they are Islamists. America's support for South Sudan is seen as clear evidence of Washington's intentions towards Sudan. NCP loyalists frequently shout anti-American chants in rallies. In fact, many Sudanese leaders know America well, certainly far better than the Americans know Sudan. Nafie Ali Nafie, the NCP's deputy chairman, was one of several to study in the US. Just as Americans who deal with Sudan often think that the Islamists are irredeemable hardliners, the NCP politician Amin Hassan Omar says that American critics are 'ideologues: we can't change their position'.[18] President Bashir frequently criticises America and the West in his speeches. The Islamist intellectual Ghazi Saleheddin Atabani has said that Hollywood stars have discovered that 'it is easy to bash Sudan and get credit for that,' but in fact the NCP does exactly the same with America.

Despite this, America and Americans are much more popular in Sudan than might be imagined. The politicians may score points by criticising the US, but you can get your hair cut at the Obama barbershop or the Oprah Saloon in Khartoum, or buy your clothes at a store called Arizona. Sudanese love American wrestling, and you can hear men and women discussing the stars from World Wrestling Entertainment, which is available on satellite television. The anti-US rhetoric is 'political propaganda', according to the artist Rashid Diab; he believes that the NCP dreams of attracting big American investors to Khartoum. This is currently impossible because of the US sanctions on Sudan. The US-educated businessman Mustafa Khogali says that in a globalised world, an anti-American stance carries less weight than it used to. Even the NCP's most loyal supporters are ready to accept the West, Khogali says, if this improves their quality of life.

Despite the angry speeches, Bashir's government has actually worked quite closely with the US on counter-terrorism.[19] Soon after the attack on the World Trade Centre on 11 September 2001, NISS and its then head Salah Abdallah 'Gosh' began drip-feeding information on bin Laden and other extremists who had lived in Sudan to the CIA.[20] This was not given much publicity in Sudan, because of the disconnect between what the leaders said about America and how they behaved. Sharing the intelligence certainly helped the NCP. They were characteristically skilful in using this leverage to keep the regime safe: according to LeRiche and Arnold, 'when the violence in Darfur was at its worst over 2003–4, Khartoum used its supply of intelligence on terrorism to dilute Washington's critiques of the regime.'[21]

Moving the goalposts?

Sudan's leaders feel betrayed by the US. The constant Sudanese complaint is that America makes promises and then 'moves the goalposts'.[22] In the early 2000s, the US said that it would cancel Sudan's debt, help its economy, and remove it from its 'state sponsors of terrorism' list if Khartoum agreed a peace deal with the SPLM.[23] The CPA was signed in 2005, but the Sudanese complained that the US went back on its word. Similar promises were made by the US to get Khartoum to sign the DPA, and then in the run-up to the referendum.

Hudson was with the US Special Envoy of the time, Scott Gration, as he laid out the sticks and carrots in Khartoum in mid-September 2010. A package of incentives was offered, including trade, investment, debt relief and full diplomatic normalisation, if Sudan resolved outstanding issues such as Darfur and the referendum on southern Sudan's future. The special envoy threatened further sanctions if targets were not met.

Gration was 'really naïve' to believe that the US would ever be able to implement the roadmap, Hudson says, since Congress was unwilling to sign off on anything perceived as a present for Bashir's regime, and because the Sudanese were always likely to start fighting again. However, according to Hudson, Gration 'did believe it, and by believing it he was able to sell it to [the NCP]. He was just as duped as they were'. Gration had already said that calling Sudan a state sponsor of terror was a 'political' decision,[24] yet even this damaging designation was not removed after the referendum, to the great fury of the NCP.

The American reasoning is simple: Darfur exploded just as the CPA negotiations were drawing to a close; the wars in the Two Areas stopped the US normalising relations after secession. Frazer accepts that the US has not kept its promises, but puts the blame firmly in the barrel of Khartoum's guns:

We haven't been able to deliver not because of us, but because of the Sudanese, and that's what they don't understand. We say if you sign the north-south agreement and end the war in the south, we'll take you off the list of state-sponsors of terror. And they take that literally—which means 'we can kill in Darfur and that's OK because you said north-south.' And what we mean is stop killing people, and they don't get that.

Furthermore, many of the US sanctions are linked to Darfur, not north-south issues. Some of the sanctions do not even have an exit clause.[25]

Over time, the US's leverage has been considerably reduced. Sanctions could be tightened, but it is unlikely that many more could be added. Khartoum is desperate to have its debt cancelled, but as long as Bashir is president, the ICC charges against him make this very unlikely. Debt relief is tied to good governance, and the US and others feel that Bashir needs to leave office for Sudan to demonstrate it is making political progress. The US still speaks out about Khartoum, but the NCP no longer believes American promises will be kept. The only threat it truly fears, military action, was not on the cards in the period after southern secession. Gration used to joke that 'the only carrot is no more sticks, and the only stick is no more carrots.'[26] The activists complain vociferously, but very little changes. Now that Sudan is no longer top of the international agenda, in the way it sometimes was in the mid-2000s, America's reaction to Sudan could be summed up as appalled impotency.

This is even more true of other Western countries. Britain, Sudan's former colonial master, is listened to politely but carries little weight.[27]

The British sent several high-level delegations to Khartoum in the period before and after separation, to stress that London was not abandoning Sudan. One minister, Andrew Mitchell, told me that twenty million people had died in the north-south civil war that led to separation. As this is ten times the usual estimate, his considerably better-informed aides looked horrified as he spoke. The UK is one of several countries which have appointed a special envoy for Sudan and South Sudan. In practice, all the envoys tend to follow the lead of the American, who has the most clout.[28]

A humanitarian emergency

In the years after separation, the US has acted decisively (and discreetly) in one key area. Once the wars broke out in South Kordofan, in June 2011, and Blue Nile, in September of the same year, Khartoum blocked humanitarian access to the rebel-held areas. Anyone who wanted to travel there, like Clooney, had to sneak over the border. The lack of humanitarian aid, to places being bombed every day, put hundreds of thousands of people's lives at risk. In response, the US began to provide substantial funds to get food and emergency items into the Two Areas.[29]

Nagwa Konda, the Nuba development worker, was a key part of the programme. In the early days of the war, relief supplies were brought in by air to Kauda and other airstrips, but this stopped after the Sudanese government obtained a radar system. From this point on, food (largely sorghum, beans and oil) as well as soap, jerry cans, cooking utensils, blankets and mosquito nets, were flown to the north of Unity state in South Sudan. Then Nagwa's aid organisation, NRRDO, drove its trucks over the border and through the Nuba Mountains to distribute the goods. 'If it had not been for that aid, I think a good deal of the population would be dead by now,' Nagwa says.[30]

US officials have been reluctant to talk publicly about what is, in essence, a secret programme to deliver humanitarian aid against the wishes of a sovereign state. All the same, Special Envoy Lyman confirmed to me that the US had provided 'indirect assistance' in South Kordofan: sending food and other items up to, but not over, the border, just as Nagwa described. When I spoke to him in November 2012, Lyman estimated that no more than two-thirds of the people in need had been reached. The programme 'helped avoid colossal famine' in South Kordofan, he concluded, but it was not enough.[31]

According to Lyman, he and other American officials informed Khartoum about the indirect assistance that they were paying for. The programme infuriated the Sudanese leaders. They saw bringing in aid as providing support to the SPLM-North rebels, fuelling their belief that Washington wants regime change in Sudan. Lyman said the US had received some guarantees that the food wasn't going to the rebel soldiers. However, in practice the US has no control over the goods it provides once they go over the Sudanese border.[32]

CHINA AND THE EAST

At the end of a side street in Riyadh, one of the more opulent Khartoum suburbs, basketball shoes screech on a concrete court and the players cry out in triumph when they hit a good shot. The court was built by a Chinese company which has its main Sudan office nearby. The majority of the players are Chinese, with a sprinkling of Sudanese; all are dressed in the international basketball uniform of baggy shorts and sleeveless tops. Wherever they are from, they talk and taunt in affected American accents: 'Get off me, bitch!' 'Good shot, yo!' Most of the time, however, the Chinese play their game at one end of the court, and the Sudanese hold their own contest at the other.

Chinese and Sudanese officials frequently laud the long history their two nations share.[33] However, this did not develop into particularly strong economic or political ties until the late 1990s, when the CNPC began operating in Sudan. It quickly became the biggest player in the oil industry, which revolutionised the Sudanese economy at the start of the millennium. The relationship was important to China too: in the decade after 1999, Sudan provided China with 5.6 per cent of its oil imports.[34] Malaysia and India also bought stakes in the oil industry, after Talisman, a Canadian company, was forced to sell under pressure from Western activists.[35] Campaign groups had accused the firm of funding the Sudanese government's human rights abuses in southern Sudan. Asian compagnies have not faced similar levels of domestic or international pressure.

China's CNPC built oil infrastructure, including pipelines and refineries, to the extent that 'Sudan first and foremost is a key investment destination' for CNPC.[36] Chinese firms have also built roads, bridges, and most notably dam infrastructure, such as the Merowe dam and hydroelectric power station. In the period after separation, there was talk of greater Chinese investment in gold and agriculture. It is no exaggeration to say that from the 1990s China, and to an extent other Asian countries, helped keep the NCP afloat at a time when it was regarded as a pariah in America and elsewhere. 'With the unjust policies of the West,' the NCP's head of external relations, Ibrahim Ghandour, says, 'China is Sudan's chief partner'.

The NCP, like many other governing parties in Africa, particularly appreciates China's policy of non-interference in the internal politics of sovereign states. Much like the scene on that Chinese-built basketball court, the Chinese brought development, but didn't concern themselves too much with what the locals were doing.[37] The NCP has relied on China to block hostile resolutions in the UN Security Council. This was particularly successful in the early years of the Darfur war.[38] Sometimes international pressure has forced China to moderate its support: the phrase 'Genocide Olympics', coined by activists about the 2008 Beijing Games because of China's refusal to condemn Khartoum's behaviour in Darfur, was particularly damaging.[39]

Chinese people have sometimes paid the price for their work in Sudan's more dangerous areas: workers were kidnapped in South Kordofan in 2009 and 2012, and in Darfur in 2013. However, this hasn't diminished China's support for Sudan, which is 'unflagging' according to the NCP's Ghandour, who travels frequently to the Chinese capital. This backing has also extended, over more than two decades, to selling weapons to the Sudanese. Sudan is under a UN embargo, which theoretically prevents any nation selling arms which will be used in Darfur. However, UN experts' reports have found new Chinese-made weapons and ammunition in Darfur on several occasions.[40] Ghandour is frank: 'Do you expect us to fight with sticks?' he asked when I raised the matter.

There was concern in Khartoum that China would lose interest in Sudan following separation, since most of the oil is in South Sudan. Bashir visited Beijing in the run-up to South Sudan's independence, which was seen in Khartoum as a strong sign that the old relationship would continue. It has not entirely worked out that way. China has been keen to be perceived as even-handed in its dealings with Sudan and South Sudan. This is a marked change from the unconditional support it gave Khartoum before separation. Equal treatment for Sudan and South Sudan is, in fact, a strategic defeat for the NCP. When Sudan began confiscating South Sudan's oil in November 2011, China's Ambassador in Khartoum, Luo Xiaoguang, described the decision as 'very serious and unjustified'.[41] This was the moment the NCP knew it could no longer count on China's unqualified backing.

ARAB AND MUSLIM COUNTRIES

Sudanese officials often describe the country as the crossroads of the African and Arab worlds, and a link between the two. Yet this attractive rhetoric is not matched by many of the Sudanese's own perceptions of who they are. Rather than creating a positive blend of its different cultures, Sudan's leaders have favoured an Arab identity over an African one. The country's foreign policy follows many of the tenets of this internal trajectory, with particular emphasis given to Muslim and Arab countries with which Sudan has, or likes to think it has, a close relationship. Sudanese leaders travel to Arab-speaking countries regularly, but hardly ever to sub-Saharan African ones.[42]

To the north, the Islamists come to power

The Arab Spring transformed Sudan's relations with North Africa. Islam and the Arabs came to Sudan from Egypt, Libya, Tunisia and even Morocco, the NCP's Ghandour points out, so there were already robust historical and family ties. However, Hosni Mubarak in Egypt detested Bashir and the NCP, as did Muammar Gaddafi in Libya. Mubarak's dislike of all Islamists was well known, and he blamed Turabi for trying to assassinate him in 1995.[43] In the dying days of Mubarak's regime, the head of the Egyptian foreign relations committee described Bashir's rule as 'the worst in Sudan's history'.[44] Gaddafi supported the Darfur rebels and intervened in Darfur intermittently for more than two decades. The NCP was understandably delighted when the Arab Spring overthrew Mubarak and Gaddafi, and Islamists rose to prominence.[45]

Egypt has a common past with Sudan, having ruled over it with the British. One of Sudan's main political parties, the DUP, was initially set up—prior to Sudan's independence—to argue for permanent union with Egypt, though it has long since abandoned this objective. There are many contemporary bonds. Nubian people live either side of the Egypt-Sudan border, and if you drive down Africa Road next to the airport in Khartoum, most of the fast food joints with the neon signs are owned and operated by Egyptians. They are taking advantage of the 'Four Freedoms' agreement, which allows Egyptians and Sudanese to travel to the other state, and work, live and own property there. Sudan follows the agreement to the letter, but Egypt is more selective, a reflection of the power dynamic between the two.[46]

In foreign policy terms, Egypt's principle concern is to maintain control over the Nile waters. Agreements signed between Cairo and Khartoum in 1929 and 1959 dictate how much water each state is allowed to use, allocating the vast majority to Egypt and Sudan, to the frustration of up-river countries like Ethiopia and Uganda. Any reduction in the flow of the Nile waters to Egypt has traditionally been seen by Cairo as a *casus belli*.[47] In this matter, Sudan has usually been Egypt's faithful ally, even when Bashir and Mubarak were on the worst of terms. Yet things are changing. Egypt was furious when Ethiopia began constructing the Great Ethiopian Renaissance Dam on the Blue Nile in May 2013. Cairo wanted Sudan's unconditional support, but for once Khartoum hesitated. The Sudanese realise that the dam should bring them substantial benefits.[48]

All the same, Khartoum's renewed friendship with Cairo, based on shared Islamist principles, was confirmed when Egypt's president, the Islamist Mohamed Morsi, made a two day visit to the Sudanese capital at the beginning of April 2013. The Sudanese Islamist daily *Alwan* claimed with breathless exaggeration that it was 'no less historic than the October victory and liberation of Sinai', a reference to the 1973 Arab-Israeli war. The tensions during the visit about the Hala'ib Triangle, a slice of desert on the border which is claimed by both countries, were brushed aside by both camps. The NCP were dismayed when the Egyptian army subsequently ousted Morsi: a fellow-traveller had been replaced by generals who are likely to be much more hostile to Bashir and the Islamists.

Sudan's relationship with Libya dramatically improved once Gaddafi was killed. After the Darfuri rebels JEM were kicked out of Chad in 2010, they had moved to Libya, adding to Sudan's distrust of Libya's leader. Some sort of diplomatic contact between Khartoum and Tripoli has always been needed, since many Sudanese move to Libya to find work.[49] Khartoum was not just a happy spectator when Gaddafi was overthrown. The Sudanese armed the Libyan rebels, and SAF troops apparently even fought against Gaddafi's army, notably in the southern town of Kufra, near the border with Sudan.[50] The Libyans have publicly thanked Sudan for its military support.[51]

The NCP's battle to survive in the post-separation era has been helped by a much more favourable regional context than the party faced in the 1990s. As a result of all this sweeping change in the region, Sudan's northern neighbours are now considerably better disposed to Khartoum, even if Morsi's fall may change Egypt's stance somewhat. However, it seems that in general Khartoum's improved standing has not led to much financial support, although the Libyans may have handed over some money.[52]

The Middle East

Several Arab states have allowed Bashir to visit, despite the ICC indictment against him, and the Arab League held an extraordinary session in El Fasher, Darfur, in 2010, to underscore its backing for Bashir and Sudan. Arab leaders and opinion writers often portray South Sudan's secession as part of a Western-initiated plot to weaken Sudan and the Arab-speaking world. The ICC indictments are seen as another manifestation of this. Yet many Arab countries have offered Sudan only superficial support, at best: when Sudan desperately needed money after separation, its appeals often went unanswered. It is tempting to recall Albaqir Alafif Mukhtar's contention that while Sudanese 'consider themselves Arabs, the "real" Arabs in the Arab World, especially in the Gulf and the Fertile Crescent, do not recognise them as such'.[53] However, the NCP's own failings over many years, as well as some regional suspicion about Islamist governments, might be just as much to blame.

Of all the Gulf countries, Qatar played the biggest role in Sudan in the years before and after separation. This was a consequence of Qatar's desire to expand its international role, and Sudan's need for allies, preferably wealthy ones. The Qataris have invested in finding a solution to Darfur: negotiations between the Sudanese government and various Darfuri movements take place in Doha. Amin Hassan Omar, who has been in charge of the Darfur file for the NCP, says that the Qataris know the Sudanese better than any other Arab state, even Egypt. Historically, this certainly wasn't true; the statement reflects, then, Qatar's current level of support for Sudan and the NCP. Qatar's commitment to the Darfur negotiations, in which the NCP is a key player, is one of the reasons it wants the Sudanese government to survive. On two occasions after the split, the Qataris made pledges of at least $1 billion to tide over the Sudanese government, though there is some scepticism about whether all the money ever arrived. It is clear, though, that Qatar does not want the NCP to fall.

The same is true of Iran. Sudan and Iran's close relationship developed because the two share a mutual enemy: America. This is an example of an isolated Sudan looking for friends in unlikely places: Khartoum had previously backed Iran's great enemy Saddam Hussein, and the Sudanese follow Sunni Islam, while most Iranians are Shiites. Nevertheless, Sudan's Bashir travelled to Tehran in June 2011, and then again in August 2012, annoying the Americans and supporters of the ICC. When Iran's then-President Mahmoud Ahmadinejad came to Khartoum in September 2011, he addressed a meeting of NCP loyalists, and soon had them chanting anti-American slogans. They loved it when Ahmadinejad denounced Israel. They got even more excited when he questioned why there was no pressure on Western countries to hold referendums in separatist regions, like the Basque country in Spain. During Ahmadinejad's meeting with Bashir, the two discussed co-operating against 'the conspiracies that had been woven by the super-power states'.[54] Beyond the rhetoric, the Israelis and the Americans believe that Iran is funnelling weapons to Hamas through Sudan.[55] At the end of Ahmadinejad's two-day visit, however, the Iranians did not offer the financial aid the Sudanese had been hoping for. Nevertheless, there are strong indications that the Sudanese are getting military help from Tehran. A major study by international arms experts found 'growing evidence to suggest that Sudan's security forces also deploy Iranian materiel'.[56]

It seems that the growing rapport between Khartoum and Tehran has antagonised Saudi Arabia, which is on terrible terms with Iran. Sudanese leaders often boast of their warm friendship with the Saudis, but this seems to have the insincere glow of public relations. Pro-government newspapers in Saudi Arabia have criticised Sudan's decision to allow Iranian warships to dock in Port Sudan, and in August 2013 Bashir's flight was forced to return to Khartoum when he not allowed to enter Saudi airspace.[57] There were competing accounts of why permission had not been granted, but many Sudanese believed it was linked to Khartoum's ties to Tehran. All this may have financial consequences. One senior NCP official told me that he was very disappointed that Sudan received less than two per cent of the financial support the Saudis give to foreign countries.[58] Despite their frustration, NCP leaders are careful to limit any public criticism of the Saudis, in part because they still hope for Saudi funds, and in part because of Saudi Arabia's religious significance for all Muslims. Sudanese politicians, including Bashir, regularly travel to Mecca on pilgrimage.

The short trip across the Red Sea is one made by many other Sudanese, some for religious reasons and others in the hope of earning far more money than would be possible in Sudan. There is a similarly well-worn path to the United Arab Emirates. Sudanese doctors and businessmen headed to the Gulf in great numbers after separation, as the economic situation at home worsened. Nearly 100,000 emigrated there in the first half of 2013.[59] Expat Sudanese communities socialise together, and the more wealthy fly over famous Sudanese singers for their weddings. In the other direction, remittances from the Gulf keep many Sudanese families going, though as this money doesn't come through official channels it doesn't benefit the government much. Salafist ideology also blossomed in the Gulf, and in particular Saudi Arabia. It spread to Sudan, in part through Saudi-sponsored or trained religious teachers. Salafism is a growing part of Sudanese religious and political life.

Like most of the Arab League countries, Sudanese leaders frequently use Israel as a convenient target, to be blamed for many of Sudan's problems. NCP leaders rail about 'Zionist conspiracies' threatening the country and keeping it poor. They have also accused Israel of carrying out a succession of aerial attacks in eastern Sudan, which apparently targeted convoys of arms being delivered to Hamas.[60] Several Western diplomats told me they believed the accusations against both Sudan and Israel were probably true. In October 2012, Israel was blamed for an attack on the Yarmouk arms factory in Khartoum.[61] By this point it was clear that Sudan would not retaliate, despite the NCP's bluster, and there seems to be no way to protect Sudanese territory from these air raids.

SUB-SAHARAN AFRICA

Before separation Sudan was the biggest country in Africa, and it still likes to proclaim itself as a diplomatic force on the continent. However the country's own political history, which is perceived by many as Arab domination over African groups, has made this difficult. In addition to this, many leading NCP politicians look first to the Arab world, and distrust African countries, because of their perceived support for South Sudan and America. In March 2013, Foreign Minister Ali Karti complained that politicians from within his party were attempting to stop him developing good relations with African states. 'Some voices are jamming our efforts to develop a strategy towards Africa saying that we can't depend on African countries because, according to them, these countries are "puppets of the West". But facts on the ground belie these misgivings,' he was quoted as saying.[62]

Around the time of this interview, Karti inaugurated an embassy in Rwanda, and there were reportedly plans to open embassies in Angola, Mozambique and Burkina Faso in 2013, to join many others in sub-Saharan Africa.[63] Karti, among others, saw the need to strengthen relations on the continent. The UN Security Council is heavily influenced by the AU, so changing Sudan's image in Africa became one of the NCP's tools to survive. Bashir's indictment by the ICC has seemed to make this easier, as the AU and most African states have supported Bashir over the charges. African solidarity has often trumped what other heads of state feel about Bashir as a leader. This has permitted the Sudanese president to travel to Chad, Eritrea, Kenya and elsewhere without being arrested and sent to The Hague.

Neighbours

At many points in its history, Sudan has interfered in the internal politics of its neighbours, particularly through supporting rebel groups. The NCP has helped rebels in Chad, Ethiopia, Eritrea and Uganda, among others, in the years since it came to power. The major Sudanese armed movements who have fought against Khartoum have also all received external support, mainly from bordering countries. However, in the period just before and just after separation Sudan's position in the region got considerably better, largely through its own diplomatic efforts.

In 1990, Idriss Deby was helped to power in Chad by Khartoum.[64] He was so grateful that he named one of his children after Omar al Bashir. Deby is from the Zaghawa, an ethnic group which is found in both his native Chad and Sudan. When the Zaghawa rebels began fighting in Darfur, Deby was expected to back his kinsmen. Initially he ignored the pressure, because of his debt to Bashir. However, after what has been described as a 'quasi-coup' carried out against him by Chadian Zaghawa officers in May 2005, Deby changed course and began supporting the rebels, and in particular JEM.[65] Soon Khartoum followed suit. 'Chad was availing support to the [Darfur] rebellion. At that time Sudan did the same with some some Chadian rebel movements,' Ghandour acknowledges. Chadian rebels backed by Sudan attacked Ndjamena in 2006 and 2008, and in May 2008, JEM drove through the desert to strike at Omdurman, Khartoum's sister city.

Following secret meetings by senior officials, on 8–9 February 2010 President Deby visited Khartoum. This would have been inconceivable even a few weeks previously.[66] Sudan and Chad agreed to stop supporting each other's rebels, a commitment they have largely kept; the proxy war was over. The military of both countries started joint patrols along the border. The Central African Republic (CAR) came on board too, signing a tripartite agreement. This was a diplomatic master-stroke. It shored up Sudan's western borders, and considerably weakened the Darfur rebels, above all JEM.

Sudan has used a similar strategy with Eritrea. At various points Asmara had supported rebels in the east of Sudan, which borders Eritrea, and even Darfuri rebels from western Sudan. Some rebel leaders were based in the Eritrean capital. All this was apparently in response to Khartoum's support for Muslim Eritrean rebels.[67] However, after the CPA was signed Sudan moved to make peace with the Eritreans, and Bashir's visit to Asmara in 2005 went a long way to achieving this. The borders were opened, allowing people and goods to move freely. The Eritreans stopped aiding the Eastern Front (EF), the coalition of Sudanese rebel groups in the area. As the EF had also lost the support of the SPLA, it was no longer viable as a military force.

The ESPA was signed in Asmara on 14 October 2006, ending the war in eastern Sudan. The agreement has not brought the development and investment it promised, and frustrations are growing rapidly in the region. The NCP is concerned about a new war there. In October 2012, the NCP's Ghandour said that he did not think Eritrea was prepared to support a new rebellion 'at the moment'. As long as the Eritreans do not get involved, any eastern rebel movement would probably not get very far. This gives Sudan an incentive to stay in Eritrea's good books. Bashir regularly meets his Eritrean counterpart Isaias Afewerki, even though Afewerki has been shunned by most of the rest of the region.

In 2011, it was estimated that every month nearly 2,000 Eritreans crossed into eastern Sudan as refugees.[68] They were fleeing the harsh conditions at home, including compulsory military service. Most of them pay traffickers to help them continue their dangerous journey to Europe. Others stay on in Khartoum, or in the desolate refugee camps near the border, where sand blows through the large tent set up for new arrivals. Sometimes the refugees are kidnapped by a network of smugglers led by the Rashaida, an ethnic group which lives on both sides of the Eritrean-Sudanese border. The kidnappers' victims are beaten up, and the women are often raped. They are usually released when their relatives send money, typically the equivalent of thousands of dollars.

One woman I spoke to said that she had been gang-raped. 'There were six of them,' she said, working hard to control her voice. 'It lasted for five hours.' Members of her church in Asmara eventually collected money for her ransom. Another woman told me she was only freed after four months when it became obvious that her rapists had impregnated her. She wound a pink scarf around her face to hide it from the camera, and cradled her baby on her lap. As she talked about the rape, she started crying into the scarf.

The Sudanese authorities seemed to make little effort to prevent these crimes. They do not wish to antagonise the Rashaida, many of whom fought against Khartoum until the ESPA was signed. The Eritrean opposition has also accused Sudan of turning a blind eye when opposition leaders are killed in the refugee camps, apparently by Eritrean security officials, although Asmara denies this charge.

Eritrea's great rival Ethiopia is keen to play the role of regional superpower. Until his untimely death on 20 August 2012, the Ethiopian Prime Minister Meles Zenawi was active in trying to resolve the problems between Sudan and South Sudan, including by sending Ethiopian peacekeepers to the disputed Abyei region.[69] In 2011, as the previous chapter described, Meles travelled with the SPLM-North leader Malik Agar to Khartoum to meet Bashir, in a failed attempt to prevent conflict in Blue Nile state. When the war began there, tens of thousands of people escaped into Ethiopia.[70] Many had already lived as refugees in Ethiopia during the first round of fighting in Blue Nile, which was ended by the CPA. Meles' successor as prime minister, Hailemariam Desalegn, seems keen to continue helping out, brokering talks in Addis Ababa between Salva Kiir and Omar al Bashir in September 2012 and January 2013. He does not yet have the depth of experience of Meles, which gives him less diplomatic clout. Sudan is vital for Ethiopia, which is landlocked; Ethiopian businessmen make considerable use of Port Sudan. Ethiopia could help the Sudanese economy too. Meles' vast dam-building programme may also one day produce cheap electricity for Sudan.[71]

South of South Sudan

South Sudan's secession shortened Sudan's borders considerably. Since 9 July 2011, the DRC, Kenya and Uganda are no longer direct neighbours, and the frontier with both the CAR and Ethiopia has been reduced. In general, the Francophone countries (DRC and CAR) had been afterthoughts in Sudanese foreign policy circles. Kenya is usually seen as the most neutral country in East Africa: the CPA was negotiated there, with the help of a Kenyan General, Lazarus Sumbeiywo. Many of the SPLM leaders moved their families to Nairobi during the war years, and bought property in Nairobi. However, the Kenyans did not support the SPLA/M militarily, to Khartoum's satisfaction.

The relationship has had tense moments. On 28 November 2011, a Kenyan court ordered that Bashir should be arrested if he set foot on Kenyan soil, and handed over to the ICC.[72] The NCP was furious, and it took a visit by Kenya's foreign minister to Khartoum to smooth things over. The March 2013 election of Uhuru Kenyatta, who like Bashir has been charged by the ICC, may allow Khartoum and Nairobi to bond over mutual grievances. However, Bashir did not attend Kenyatta's inauguration, perhaps to spare Kenya's newly elected politicians the need to overrule the country's judiciary, the only alternative to arresting him.

Sudan's relationship with Uganda is antagonistic. Kampala supported the SPLA, and Khartoum propped up the Lord's Resistance Army (LRA), the cult-like Ugandan rebel group led by Joseph Kony. After the secession of South Sudan, the hostility has continued. Many of the Darfuri rebel leaders, like Abdul Wahid al Nour and Minni Minnawi, live in Kampala. JEM's leader, Gibril Ibrahim, reportedly travels on a Ugandan passport.[73] Sudan also believes that the Ugandans are supporting SPLM-North. One American journalist saw Ugandan ammunition crates in a SPLM-North controlled-area in the Nuba Mountains.[74] The organisation Small Arms Survey found proof that Ugandan-owned ammunition ended up in the hands of SPLM-North soldiers. It concluded that either Uganda supplied it directly to the Sudanese rebels, or it went to South Sudan's SPLA, which sent it on to its old allies.[75] The New Dawn Charter was also signed in Kampala. The NCP has no regrets that Sudan no longer directly borders Uganda.

THE UN, AND THE INTERNATIONAL PRESENCE IN SUDAN

When the UN Security Council discusses Sudanese matters, Khartoum often receives support from China and Russia. Moscow has named a special envoy to Sudan, and is on good terms with Khartoum. In fact, Russia has been accused of supplying weapons that have been used by SAF in Darfur, in defiance of the arms embargo.[76] In the Security Council, Russia, like China, opposes anything it considers detrimental to Sudan's sovereignty. In March 2013, Russia's ambassador to the UN strongly criticised his American counterpart, Susan Rice, saying she had made 'outlandish accusations', in essence ones that ran contrary to Khartoum's interests.[77] The NCP's sense that Russia is in its corner, rather than Juba's, was reinforced when the South Sudanese army accidentally shot down a UN helicopter, killing its Russian crew, on 21 December 2012.[78]

Despite Russia and China's sympathetic position, Khartoum's diplomats have to fight constant battles in the Security Council, and in particular against the American- and British-drafted resolutions condemning Sudan. When the Security Council visited Sudan in October 2010, in the run-up to the referendum, the Sudanese saw their chance to make a point. Buses brought in a rent-a-crowd to Sharia Qasr or Palace Street, which runs up to the presidential palace and is the traditional spot for protests. 'Down with America!' they chanted, while some accused the UN of trying to divide Sudan. Before long, I and the only other foreign journalist present were chased away by screaming protestors.

During the interim period there were two peacekeeping missions in Sudan, but the government asked UNMIS, which was responsible for north-south issues, to leave Sudanese territory at separation.[79] The other peacekeeping mission, UNAMID, which operates in Darfur, is hindered at every step. At one point UNAMID was allowed almost 26,000 uniformed personnel,[80] but it has had only a limited impact in protecting civilians. Its patrols are regularly stopped by SAF from going to hotspots, despite in theory having complete freedom of movement. The Sudanese government also makes it difficult for UNAMID to bring in equipment and even personnel.[81] Many contributing countries have wondered whether the nearly $1.5 billion UNAMID costs every year is money well spent. The mission correctly argues that violence has declined in Darfur since the early years of the war. However, to what extent this was because of the peacekeepers—who, in their defence, do not have a peace to keep—is very much open to question.

Many Sudanese come into contact with the wider world through international NGOs and UN agencies. The government generally tolerates development aid like building schools or improving medical services. Islamic NGOs, which are often funded by the Gulf countries, are particularly welcome. Western humanitarian aid is another matter. After the Darfur war penetrated the world's consciousness it was called the 'world's greatest humanitarian crisis'. Foreign NGOs flooded in to provide food, water and medical care, in particular to the more than 2.5 million people who had been displaced by the conflict. Under huge international pressure, Khartoum had no choice but to let the humanitarian workers in. It did so through gritted teeth, and made every effort to control them. Even ten years after the Darfur war began, Khartoum's Humanitarian Affairs Commission (HAC) vets short-lists for new posts within NGOs, and sits in on their recruitment interviews. UN and NGO staff believe their organisations have been infiltrated by NISS employees, who feed back information on the foreigners' activities, conversations and movements.

In one respect it is in the NCP's interests to be suspicious: NGO workers were among those who supplied information to the ICC, which then issued the arrest warrants for Bashir, Abdel Rahim and Haroun. Khartoum is convinced it will not receive a fair hearing from Western-dominated organisations. When the fighting in South Kordofan and Blue Nile broke out, Sudan decided to stop international NGOs from going into rebel-controlled areas entirely. People have died because of this. The NCP drew the wrong conclusion from Darfur: rather than working to ensure there were no more conflicts, it made it hard for outsiders to find out just how bad the new wars were. The international outcry has been muted, compared to the deafening demands for access to Darfur a few years previously. The world has not cared enough about the fighting, and those dying, in the Two Areas. Libya, Syria and other crises have taken precedence, and Khartoum can only be influenced by the most concerted external pressure.

SOUTH SUDAN

If you want to know who South Sudan's closest friends are, you only need to stroll through the centre of Juba. On almost every street corner, there are brightly coloured clues for sale. Hawkers carry dozens of plastic flags on short white poles, splayed out like porcupine quills to catch the eye of prospective buyers. Each bunch includes Kenya, Uganda, Britain and Norway, but according to one street salesman, two flags outsell the rest: America and Israel. The US has been South Sudan's biggest supporter: without American help the new country might never have been born. Israel's role in South Sudan's independence was less obvious. I asked Angelo, who proudly displays an Israeli flag on the dashboard of his car, why he had chosen it. His answer was simple: 'the Israelis hate the Arabs, just like us.'

At independence, South Sudan had a considerable amount of good-will around the world, and many outright supporters among its neighbours and Western nations. Some of this was the result of a rather simplistic worldview: anyone opposing Khartoum's 'evil regime' must be worthy of praise. For others, a new country recovering from decades of war deserved all the help it could get. Nhial Deng, the new country's first foreign minister, was the man responsible for turning these warm feelings into solid diplomatic ties. The foreign ministry was formed from South Sudanese diplomats who had represented Sudan in the pre-secession days, and staff from southern Sudan's Ministry of Regional Co-operation, a sort of ersatz foreign ministry set up during the interim period.

Starting from before separation, the diplomats received training in the Netherlands, South Africa and Eritrea, which allowed 'the personnel to be exposed to the basics of diplomatic work', according to Deng. His new team oversaw applications to join the UN, the IMF, and other international bodies. South Sudan also wishes to join the East African Community, though there are concerns that the regional free market could be damaging for South Sudan's economy, which doesn't produce much.

Some complain about the foreign ministry's lack of resources.[82] Nevertheless, like every part of South Sudan's government, it is in fact overstaffed, especially at the highest level. 'We have more than ninety ambassadors,' Deng says, 'which is superfluous for a country the size of South Sudan. We have a problem finding productive assignments for everyone, in particular the ambassadors.' The plan had been to establish thirty-three embassies, but South Sudan started with twenty-two, for financial reasons.[83] Diplomatic missions were set up in the five permanent members of the Security Council and in countries with which South Sudan already had strong political or economic ties. Austerity measures hit hard here, as everywhere, making it difficult to expand beyond the initial number of embassies. This means that three-quarters of the well-paid ambassadors do not have a post abroad.

So, who are South Sudan's new international representatives? Juba's man in Washington DC, Akec Khoc, does not like the cold. Every time the thermometer drops, his shoulder hurts—a reminder of his war wound. There can't be many accredited ambassadors to the US who have been shot in combat. Khoc taps his shoulder as he remembers: his scapula was broken, and his lung damaged, by a 'nice shot' he took in the early days of the war. Khoc was a medical doctor who was providing treatment to SPLA soldiers and communities near the front line. Medical facilities, including his own, were targeted.

He had joined the SPLA because of injustice. Khoc had good relations with the northerners at medical school—but every so often one would refer to him as *abid* (slave). 'This thing did not work so well for me', he says, with some understatement. In 1991, he was appointed the rebels' envoy in Paris. After the CPA in 2005, he was brought into the Sudanese foreign ministry. Khoc was posted to New York, and then Washington, but he hated having to defend Khartoum's war in Darfur. Separation freed him. First Khoc was part of the committee that set up South Sudan's ministry of foreign affairs, and then he was posted back to Washington, this time as the ambassador of his new country.

'WE ARE NOT NEUTRAL'—THE US AND SOUTH SUDAN

The relationship with the US is vital for South Sudan. Luckily for the SPLM, it has benefited from strong American support for years, largely because of American disdain for Khartoum and its policies. The journalist Rebecca Hamilton has detailed how a group of Washington insiders met every week to help South Sudan obtain independence.[84] The men called themselves 'The Council', and gave each other nicknames like 'The Emperor' and 'The Spear Carrier'.[85] The Council was not a lone voice. Jendayi Frazer, the former Assistant Secretary of State for Africa, is among South Sudan's strongest defenders: 'The fact of the matter is that in this conflict we are on the side of south,' she says. 'I don't think we need to put ourselves in any kind of position as neutral—we are not neutral. There are others who can be neutral.'

Frazer has advocated providing South Sudan with air defence capabilities, and says the US should devote more money to developing the new state. One of her successors as America's point person on Africa, Johnnie Carson, told me Americans 'genuinely want to see South Sudan succeed' because of the devastating wars and underdevelopment its people have suffered from. Carson and the current US policy makers have not gone as far as Frazer would have liked, but there is no doubt that South Sudan began its existence with America's best wishes. The US backed its fine words with financial support too: over $1 billion was pledged for 2011–13.[86]

A bad meeting with the most powerful man in the world

Not long after South Sudan's independence, the US started to become frustrated with the SPLM.[87] The trigger was Juba's alleged support for SPLM-North's rebellion against Khartoum. The SPLM has consistently denied backing its old ally, but US officials don't believe them. 'We were up against a flat denial, which just ran against what the realities were,' is how the US Special Envoy Lyman described it.

On 21 September 2011, Barack Obama met Salva Kiir on the margins of the UN General Assembly. It was an historic moment for the new country. However during the meeting Obama challenged Salva to stop supporting SPLM-North, US officials including Lyman told me. Salva denied the accusation, and apparently suggested the US satellites needed to be checked for accuracy if they were the source of Obama's information. 'Obama turned to his people and basically declared the meeting over', according to Hudson, who was briefed on what happened. 'Obama has very little tolerance for blatant lying to the president of the United States.'

South Sudanese officials either deny that the whole incident ever happened, or do not wish to talk about it. Khoc, the ambassador to the US, does say that 'there is that talk about a difficult meeting, which certainly negatively impacted on the level of relationship between the two countries. But with time things have started to change for the better.'

After the Obama-Salva meeting, Lyman was part of a high level delegation, including the US's then Deputy National Security Adviser Dennis McDonough, which flew to Juba. Salva had apparently sent a letter explaining that he had received more information about the matter Obama had raised, which he was prepared to share. However, when the president met the US delegation he stuck to his original denial of support to SPLM-North. It was all 'totally amateurish', Hudson says. It took a conference introducing South Sudan to businesses and investors, in Washington in December 2011, and a meeting between Hillary Clinton and Salva that took place there, to restore some of the trust. Nevertheless, Lyman and others grew concerned with the scale of the human rights abuses being committed in South Sudan, some of them as part of the government's response to the Jonglei crisis.[88] The SPLM's autocratic style grated too. Just over a year after independence, the US's ambassador to South Sudan, Susan Page, wrote a critical open letter titled 'Democracy is a Fragile Thing'.

It is easy to become impatient with the pace of change and imperfect democratic processes, and want to force that change along by undemocratic means. Such a path will not only crush the dreams of a young nation, but it will also lose the support of the United States, one of the strongest supporters of South Sudan and its people.[89]

In the letter, Page explicitly threatened the removal of the American financial assistance if 'democratic principles' were disregarded.

The tone of Page's letter irked the SPLM leaders. Then-Foreign Minister Deng told me that it was a boilerplate message the US frequently sent to African countries, and South Sudan was 'not to be lectured on democracy', even by the US. The letter, and other public American and Western expressions of concern, came as a nasty surprise to the SPLM, which had been the darling of the West for so long.

Hudson contends that America's 'love affair with Juba is anachronistic' and points out that many of Juba's biggest American supporters, including Frazer and the former Special Envoy Andrew Natsios, are no longer in decision-making positions, or in the case of Congressman Donald Payne have passed away.[90] However, the Americans do feel a sense of responsibility towards South Sudan, having helped in its creation, and will not abandon it completely. There was no immediate sign of Page's threat being carried out.

Even South Sudan's greatest cheerleaders became concerned about the country's trajectory after independence. In July 2013, as the new nation celebrated its second birthday, four members of the self-styled 'Council', the influential informal American group which had campaigned so hard for South Sudan's independence, wrote their own open letter. Ted Dagne (the 'Emperor'), Eric Reeves (the 'Deputy Emperor'), Roger Winter (the 'Spear Carrier') and John Prendergast (the 'Council Member in Waiting') expressed their concern to Salva that abuses and corruption meant that 'without significant changes and reform, your country may slide toward instability, conflict and a protracted governance crisis.'[91] Most

American activists are still firmly behind the new country,[92] but Juba's own behaviour means this backing may not last forever.

The rest of the West

The relationship with Britain, a former colonial power, is a complex one. Many South Sudanese still object to what they saw as preferential treatment for the north during the Anglo-Egyptian period. The British also decided to administer southern and northern Sudan together, and grant them independence as one country, despite having considered attaching southern Sudan to British colonies in East Africa.[93] This was one of the causes of the two long civil wars that southern Sudan suffered through. However, more than half a century after the colonialists left, some South Sudanese say they are glad that at least the British brought Christianity.[94]

In more recent times, the British were one of the main international backers of the CPA, which boosted Britain's reputation. Several South Sudanese leaders, including Nhial Deng and Barnaba Marial, who has had several ministerial portfolios, have lived in the UK. After separation, the British ambassador, Alistair McPhail, was among the most active foreign envoys, frequently meeting senior officials, including the president. The British, along with the US and Norway, made it clear they were dismayed by the oil shutdown and would be unwilling to maintain their level of support until oil started flowing again.[95]

There cannot be many countries around the world where Norwegians get a warmer welcome than in South Sudan. Norway was the third member of the Troika, with the US and the UK, which pushed through the CPA. Just as importantly for many ordinary South Sudanese, however, Norwegian NGOs stayed even during the worst years of the war. Norwegian People's Aid is particularly popular; it is sometimes nicknamed 'Norwegian People's Army' because it clearly decided to support the SPLA during the war years rather than profess neutrality, as so many international organisations tend to do. Norwegian experts have also advised Juba (as well as Khartoum) on maximising its oil reserves.

Western countries have been some of the most generous donors to South Sudan ever since the CPA was signed. Canada, Denmark, the Netherlands, Norway, Sweden and the UK, combined as the Joint Donor Team, contributed more than $400 million in the interim period.[96] In the run-up to the referendum, the European Union also pledged 200 million euros of development funds.[97] South Sudan has had 'a long-standing relationship' with the US and the West, Deng said, and this goes beyond financial aid.

However, Deng worries that his country has become too dependent on Western support, and is concerned that the West believes it can dictate to the South Sudanese. 'On the side of our partners, there are people who have not seemed to realise this long-dependent entity called South Sudan should be given space to choose our own path,' he says. The talk of South Sudan shaking itself entirely free from exterior guidance came to an end with the oil shutdown, which left the new country terribly dependent on outside support, once again. In April 2013, the US organised a donor forum to save the South Sudanese economy from complete collapse. Donors said that they would add up to $300 million to the $1.3 billion already pledged to South Sudan for 2013.[98]

CHINA

For many years, China's backing for Khartoum infuriated the SPLM. After the split, however, China's objective is to be seen to be fair to both Sudan and South Sudan, favouring neither. One month after South Sudan's independence, the Chinese foreign minister, Yang Jiechi, visited both Khartoum and Juba. Given China's historical support for Khartoum, even equal treatment is a considerable gain for Juba. Many South Sudanese are still bitter about China's role during the civil war. The focus of the anger was on the apparent collusion of the oil companies (which were part-owned by China's CNPC) with SAF and its allied militia groups. Nevertheless, after the CPA China began to subtly alter its policies, like many countries around the world.[99]

Salva visited Beijing in 2007, and apparently stressed to the Chinese that most of the oil was in the south, and southerners would soon have a referendum on their future.[100] A Chinese consulate was then opened in Juba in 2008. The South Sudanese have sometimes overplayed the support that they are likely to receive from China. Salva visited Beijing in April 2012, and afterwards the minister Barnaba Marial announced that China had agreed to loan South Sudan $8 billion for development projects.[101] This confused the Chinese. After a suitably diplomatic pause, China's Special Envoy to Africa, Zhong Jianhua, said it simply wasn't true.[102]

All the same, China's focus is no longer exclusively on Khartoum. By mid-2012 there were more than fifty Chinese companies in South Sudan, a reasonable amount given the small size of the new country's private sector. The consulate, which was turned into an embassy, has registered several hundred Chinese citizens.[103] They chiefly work in oil, communications and construction companies, and own hotels and restaurants. In September 2012, I met Wang Jianchao, the boss of Jemins International Co. Ltd, which imports 4x4s from Dubai. Over cups of Chinese tea, he told me that he had invested $3 million in just over a year. At the time of our meeting he was running at a loss. In the nine months since the oil shutdown, he had sold only ten cars; sales were down fivefold on the previous year. Wang was optimistic, however: he saw South Sudan as an expanding market, and was convinced his investment would pay off.

Victor Lugala points out that China's presence in South Sudan is not entirely new. Lugala himself was treated by Chinese doctors in Juba in the 1970s. This was the first time he had seen acupuncture needles. Lugala is wary about China's motives, since just a few years ago the Chinese 'were helping Khartoum bomb us'. He sees them, in South Sudan and throughout Africa, as 'the new colonialists, the economic imperialists'; their goods have flooded the markets. However, Lugala says the Chinese build things that everyone can see or use, while the Westerners just bring ideas. Like everyone else, he noticed their increased interest in South Sudan just before and after independence.

The South Sudanese leaders are realistic about the imperatives behind this new dynamic. 'We know what the Chinese are like: they are only interested in our oil and resources' is how my regular source, The Minister, puts it. His colleague Nhial Deng, who was foreign minister until the 2013 reshuffle, likes the fact that the Chinese are now trying to support both Sudans, but regrets that in his country there is little Chinese investment outside the oil sector. It will take time before South Sudanese are ready to welcome China with open arms, but Beijing's policies in the period leading up to and immediately after secession have certainly brought that day closer.

AFRICAN NEIGHBOURS

South Sudan's longest and most important shared frontier is with Sudan.[104] It also borders Ethiopia, Kenya, Uganda, the DRC and the

CAR. Several of South Sudan's ethnic groups are also present in these countries, creating cultural and economic ties which often ignore the lines on the map. Ethiopia, Kenya and Uganda were all close to the SPLM at one point or another during the liberation struggle. Juba's regional relationships are informed by this historical fact. In practice they tend to focus on security issues and economic ties. There are local tensions on the borders, often related to inter-ethnic confrontations, but most of the time these do not cloud the strong relationships between South Sudan and its southern neighbours.

Uganda's President Yoweri Museveni openly supports Juba against Khartoum. At the first anniversary of South Sudan's independence, Museveni delighted the crowd by telling them he understood their 'struggle with the short man from Khartoum' (a derogatory reference to Bashir). He told the South Sudanese their sisters and brothers in Uganda would support them.[105] It wouldn't be the first time. During the first north-south Sudanese civil war, Uganda helped Israel supply weapons to the Anyanya insurgency.[106]

Museveni and John Garang were at university together in Tanzania in the 1960s, which undoubtedly contributed to Museveni's decision to help the SPLM during the second war. Indeed, according to LeRiche and Arnold, Kampala's backing was vital in the bleak years after the SPLM was kicked out of Ethiopia, and Riek Machar and Lam Akol split away: 'it was Uganda's military support that helped the SPLA to recover and drive home a stalemate with the SAF'.[107] Subsequently, Juba allowed Ugandan troops, and after independence a regional force, to carry out the hunt for the remaining LRA rebels from a base in Nzara, in Western Equatoria state.[108]

Nhial Deng says that there is lots of good will between South Sudan and Uganda, and describes Museveni as a 'key supporter'. At South Sudan's one-year anniversary celebrations, Museveni also called on the South Sudanese to toughen themselves up 'because the world likes strong people,' and warned them only to accept a fair deal with the Sudanese, however much outside pressure there might be. Deng concluded that Museveni 'spoke for most of us if not all of us'. However, the opposition leader Lam, a former foreign minister in the united Sudan, says the relationship with Uganda highlights the weaknesses of South Sudan's foreign policy. Despite the theoretical strength of the ties, he told me in mid-2012, there was no formal treaty linking the two countries.

There are, however, many ethnic and historical links, in particular between Equatorians and northern Ugandans. Many southern Sudanese lived in exile in Uganda in the two wars, and Ugandans looking for business came to Juba and elsewhere after the CPA. In 2010, Uganda had the biggest number of foreign residents in southern Sudan, and was the region's biggest trading partner.[109] Tensions do occasionally build up on the borders. In one post-independence incident, the South Sudanese local authorities reportedly complained that Uganda had built a market and other permanent structures in a village they considered part of South Sudan.[110] In August 2013, Ugandan MPs protested when South Sudan decided that foreigners were no longer allowed to drive motorcycle taxis, known as 'boda bodas'. Many Ugandans left the country immediately after the decision. Squabbles like these do not alter the fact that Uganda is South Sudan's most reliable friend in the region.

There are similarities with South Sudan's relationship with Kenya. The CPA was negotiated in Kenya, and many of the South Sudanese elite live or have lived in Nairobi. Their less fortunate compatriots made do with the refugee camps in the north of the country. The northern Kenyan town of Lokichoggio also served as a logistics base to transport food and other vital supplies into southern Sudan during the war years.

After the CPA, perhaps the most striking thing about the relationship between Juba and Nairobi is the economic ties. Kenya is the region's economic powerhouse. South Sudan's banking sector is dominated by Kenyan banks, after the SPLM made it clear they didn't want Islamic banking. In 2010, Kenya was southern Sudan's second biggest economic partner, only marginally behind Uganda. Kenyans are very visible in the hospitality and transport sectors in Juba. As South Sudan is landlocked, many of its goods are brought in from Mombasa, Kenya's major port. South Sudan would like to export its oil through a new pipeline, to remove its dependency on Sudan. One option would use the port at Lamu, on the Kenyan coast, although the South Sudanese have also considered going through Djibouti. A new pipeline would be extremely costly, however. Construction hadn't started by late 2013.

The relationship has had its share of low points. Kenya has protested over the death of its citizens in Juba;[111] there is also a long-running territorial dispute over the Ilemi triangle, which is administered by Kenya. By October 2012, this had not been discussed officially by the new government in Juba, according to Deng. Despite this dispute, and occasional 'local misunderstandings on the border', including clashes between Kenya's Turkana and South Sudan's Toposa peoples, on the 'macro level there are no real problems', Deng says.

Ethiopia was crucial to the early growth of the SPLA/M, and was perhaps in part responsible for the left-wing ideology of the movement's early days. Things got tougher for John Garang when the Derg was overthrown in 1991. Meles and his allies had been supported by Khartoum, and when they came to power they chased the SPLA/M out of their camps near the Sudan-Ethiopia border. Mary Boyoi was one of the many South Sudanese who fled. 'When the Ethiopians chased the South Sudanese, we ran', she remembers. She and her companions, refugee boys and child soldiers, had to escape across the Gilo river. Most didn't know how to swim. 'Most of my colleagues were drowned in the river', she says. Thousands of the children lost their lives.

Over time, Meles' Ethiopia became markedly less hostile to the SPLA/M. Meles, and his successor Hailemariam Desalegn, have been perceived as fair mediators between Khartoum and Juba. South Sudan is keen to return the favour: Deng says South Sudan could help to broker peace between Ethiopia and Eritrea, as it is one of the few countries in the region on good terms with both. South Sudan has its own all-consuming problems, and in the first couple of years after independence this outsized ambition remained unfulfilled. Within the new country, it is not unusual to see Ethiopians and Eritreans working together, despite the animosity between their homelands. Most run hotels or small restaurants.

The SPLM never received much support from South Sudan's Francophone neighbours, the DRC and CAR, and haven't paid much attention to them after coming to power. However, the Azande, one of South Sudan's biggest ethnic groups, spills across the border into both states. Many Azande have lived in the DRC, particularly during the second north-south civil war. Deng said his diplomats intended to develop better relations with the Francophone nations, despite the language barrier. In early March 2013, South Sudan and the DRC signed a joint communiqué on bilateral co-operation, which included a desire to make their common border safer.[112]

ISRAEL, EGYPT AND THE ARAB WORLD

For decades, southern Sudanese fought against Khartoum's Arabising policies. Most Arab countries supported the Sudanse government against the rebels, some morally, others with financial or military aid. Given this history, it is little surprise that an independent South Sudan is hesitant about the Arab world. It also goes some way to explaining why Juba is so keen to develop its ties with Israel.

South Sudan's relationship with Israel has a strong symbolic value. The practical benefit of the friendship, in terms of aid and other forms of support, is more open to question, much like Sudan's relationship with Iran. President Salva made a flying visit to Jerusalem on 20 December 2011, less than six months after independence. He met President Shimon Peres and Prime Minister Benjamin Netanyahu. Salva said that without Israeli help his country 'would not have arisen', and praised his hosts: 'As a nation that rose from dust, and as the few who fought the many, you have established a flourishing country that offers a future and economic prosperity to its children.'[113]

The visit unleashed a cascade of negative stories in the Sudanese press, and the spokesman of Sudan's foreign ministry expressed his concern about the trip. Khartoum still remembers the military support that Israel provided to the southern Sudanese rebels during the first civil war, and is worried that this could be repeated. John Garang was among the officers to receive Israeli training. Nhial Deng says the Sudanese shouldn't be scared, as the Israeli officials who have visited Juba mainly talk about agriculture and telecommunications.

Khoc, South Sudan's ambassador to the US, is less guarded. When I asked him if South Sudan had military links with Israel, he said 'not yet, but why not? We hope they could develop in the future.' He is one of many South Sudanese hoping to go on a pilgrimage to the Holy Land, something that was illegal when they were Sudanese citizens. Khoc believes that the fundamental reason to develop good ties with the Israelis is because they are close to the Americans, South Sudan's most important foreign partner (apart perhaps from Sudan). Juba is therefore trying to be a 'strategic ally' for both the US and Israel.

South Sudan's relations with Israel are not always sunny. There was some dismay when Israel began deporting hundreds of South Sudanese refugees, on the grounds that they were no longer at risk of persecution in their new home country. South Sudan also voted in favour of upgrading Palestine to observer status at the UN in November 2012. The South Sudanese diplomats, having recently celebrated the birth of their own country, felt they could not vote against a people so desperate for their freedom. The decision was not universally praised by the South Sudanese.[114] The speed at which Israeli flags are snapped up on the streets of Juba gives an indication of the genuine popular support for the country.

Israel's mass appeal is matched—perhaps even created—by widespread anti-Arab sentiments, and Juba's friendship with Israel does not improve Arab countries' perception of South Sudan. Parts of the Arab world do have long-standing links with South Sudan. In the 1970s, Kuwait built a hospital in Juba, and Cairo began paying for southern Sudanese to study in Egypt. The opposition leader Lam Akol argues in favour of closer ties with the Arab world, not least because many South Sudanese speak Arabic, rather than English, the official language of the new country.

Ambassador Khoc agrees. Developing friendships with countries like Qatar, the UAE and Kuwait would serve several purposes, he says. Firstly, it would dispel any thoughts that South Sudan's problems with Sudan were fuelled by anti-Islamic or racist feelings. Secondly, it might counteract any negative actions against Juba in the Arab League and international fora. Finally, the rich Arab nations might invest in South Sudan, or contribute funds for development. As part of this strategy, the then-Vice President Riek Machar travelled to the United Arab Emirates in March 2013. He invited Gulf firms to build a new international airport and hospital.[115] Nevertheless, many people in South Sudan's foreign ministry are not keen on strengthening ties with the Arab world, and this reticence may be more closely aligned with the sentiments of the majority of South Sudanese.

Egypt is the Arab state with the most at stake in South Sudan, because of its obsession with the Nile waters. Many South Sudanese have studied in Egypt, though they often complain that they were victims of racism there. For many years, Cairo seemed blind to the interests of the SPLM and the feelings of the southern Sudanese. As late as 2010, Egyptian diplomats were dismissive about the chances of southern Sudan seceding. They did not want another country with partial control over the Nile, and they seemed to take their desires for reality.[116] Once it became clear, even to them, that the southern Sudanese were going to vote for independence, the Egyptians increased their efforts to woo Juba, including by making 'generous' promises of economic aid.[117]

This will probably not be enough to win South Sudan's support over the Nile waters. Cairo got a nasty surprise when South Sudan's Water and Irrigation Minister at the time, Paul Mayom, reportedly said in late March 2013 that 'South Sudan does not recognise—and underline does not recognise—the content of the 1959 agreement' on how much Nile water each country can use.[118] South Sudan's position is that it is not bound by an agreement signed by the united Sudan. Juba also feels that South Sudan and other upstream countries like Ethiopia, Uganda, Kenya, Rwanda and even the DRC should benefit from a greater share of the Nile. South Sudan has plans to build a dam on the White Nile, near Nimule on the Ugandan border. This is sure to antagonise the Egyptians; yet it is difficult to see why South Sudan should not exploit the river running through its own soil. 'Nobody should dictate anything on our land,' Khoc says.[119]

THE UN AND THE INTERNATIONAL PRESENCE IN SOUTH SUDAN

South Sudan is a weak state which is dependent on foreign aid and diplomatic support; but Juba also wishes to assert its new-found sovereignty. Salva found the perfect man for the difficult job of South Sudan's representative to the UN in Francis Deng. He is the new country's most highly regarded intellectual, and he knows the UN system, having previously been the UN Secretary General's Special Advisor on the Prevention of Genocide. If anyone can defend South Sudan's position, solicit support, and assert his country's independence, all at the same time, it is Francis Deng.

Inside South Sudan, the most visible sign of the UN is the peacekeeping mission, UNMISS. Salva asked for the peacekeepers to stay on after independence, in sharp contrast to Bashir's decision to kick them out of Sudan. The mission is permitted up to 7,900 uniformed personnel. At her opening press conference in Juba on 13 July 2011, UNMISS' Norwegian head, Hilde Johnson, stressed that the new mission had the mandate to protect civilians if the government was not able to.[120] This raised the expectations of many South Sudanese, but confidence in UNMISS did not last long.

In December 2011 and January 2012, hundreds of Murle were killed by the Lou Nuer's White Army in Jonglei, as was described in the previous chapter. South Sudanese wanted UNMISS to intervene; instead the mission told the Murle to run. When I went to Likuangole, the first stop on a trail of horror, I saw charred outlines of what had been huts less than fifty metres from the barbed wire of the UNMISS camp. Half a human skull grinned up from the burnt grass. UNMISS had not been able to deploy sufficient military force to take on the several thousand White Army members. If this was the case, many wondered, what point did the peacekeepers serve? South Sudan's government shared some of these concerns. It also criticised UNMISS's failure to protect civilians from air and ground attacks by SAF. Furthermore, Juba is uneasy with UNMISS' Chapter VII mandate, which in theory allows it to take military action to restore peace, and which South Sudan sees as an affront to its sovereignty.[121] South Sudan's growing ambivalence about the peacekeepers is another sign of the young nation's desire to fully exercise its freedom.

International NGOs are responsible for many public services in South Sudan; they also provide the most sought-after jobs. In Leer in Unity State, for example, the MSF hospital serves the town and the surrounding area. It employed 247 people in late 2012. 'There are no other jobs here,' said one MSF worker, Mayen Chop, so everyone wants to work at the hospital. Even a security guard, who earns 500 SSP a month (a bit more than $100 at the rate of the time), was better off than a policeman, and more likely to be paid on time.

South Sudanese communities rely heavily on aid. Some aid workers, and politicians including state governors, talk of a 'dependency culture' among the people.[122] Others point out that the South Sudanese would never have survived the war years, when the aid was intermittent, without a strong streak of resourcefulness. There are signs that the authorities are keen for more control over the NGOs, following Sudan's model.[123] In the first couple of years after separation, however, this did not go too far. South Sudan knows it needs international support, both politically and to develop the country.

* * *

Sudan has an image problem, which has serious consequences. For many countries, in particular in the West, Bashir has made his country a pariah state. This impression was reinforced by the ICC charges against the Sudanese president, which dominated Sudan's foreign relations in the period after separation. Yet Sudan could count on support, from China, Arab countries and some African states too, even if the Sudanese elite's focus on the Arab world cost it some friends in the neighbourhood.

At independence, South Sudan was swaddled in goodwill. America and other Western countries felt they had played a role in its creation, and China was attracted by South Sudan's oil. This enviable position rapidly lost some of its shine. As the country's inexperienced diplomats tried to build ties without enough money to do so, Juba's own political problems began to frustrate some of its allies. Just like Sudan, its own domestic instability hinders its foreign relations.

7

THE SUDANS

When he fell in love, Garang Thomas Dhel knew that his life had suddenly got much harder. The woman his heart chose lived on the other side of an ethnic and cultural divide that many considered an unbridgeable gulf. It was a gap so big that it split a country in two. Garang would not let that scare him away. Garang, the son of a famous southern Sudanese rebel,[1] was then a young medical student in Khartoum, and his beloved, Hiba al Makki, was also training to be a doctor. They met at university in the late 1990s, and soon became inseparable. Unfortunately for Garang, Hiba was from the northern Sudanese elite.[2] Hiba's family would not contemplate her spending her life with a Dinka, a southerner. 'Here big tribes don't give their daughters to strangers,' Garang says. 'And when the man is a southerner…' His sentence grinds to a halt. 'It became a long story.' The story took a decade to come to its conclusion.

Four years after Garang fell for Hiba, and just as he was about to graduate, he made it clear to the Makki family that he intended to ask for their daughter's hand in marriage. Garang was told not to even think about it. Despite the disappointment, Garang and Hiba did not give up. Hiba made it clear she would marry Garang, and no-one else. 'My lady was a strong lady, a very strong lady.' Garang's pride is evident. 'She sent a message to her family: "OK, if you're rejecting him I will not marry, and I will still be there waiting for him." She had chosen me, and that was all.'

Garang has a receding hairline and a round face, and his moustache stretches past the end of his lips. He is serious, measured, and passionate. In 2006, after the CPA was signed, the doctor became the director of the hospital in Aweil, in what was then southern Sudan. Over the years, Garang made several fruitless efforts to convince Hiba's family. In 2008, ten years after falling in love, he decided to try one last time. If he failed, he was prepared to elope with Hiba, perhaps to Australia. As well as this threat, Garang had another weapon: his northern relatives. Garang's maternal grandfather was a northerner, a wealthy trader who had lived in Aweil. The son of a southern rebel had northern blood running in his veins.

Like Hiba, Garang is a Muslim, although this is just one station on his spiritual journey: 'I was brought up to be a Christian minister in Aweil. I escaped to be a Muslim. I am now close to being a non-believer.' Much like the united Sudan itself, and the two countries that have succeeded it, Garang is a complex mix of identities. Garang made use of this, calling on his northern relatives to provide part of the delegation he sent to Hiba's family home. This time Garang's committee was let inside the door, but the answer was still the same: marrying a southerner, even a Muslim one with some northern blood, would be impossible.

Undeterred, Garang went to meet 'the big man, the lion, the father of my madam.' They talked for hours. Garang wondered what the family had against him; surely after years of proposals they realised he was serious? Hiba's father told him it wasn't personal, but he belonged to a tribe, and what could he tell his tribe if he married his daughter off to a southerner? Nevertheless, Garang was convincing: by the time he left the lion's den, he had got his way. In February 2008, Garang and Hiba, a southerner and a northerner, were married in Khartoum.[3]

After so many years and so much disappointment, married life was wonderful. All the same, Garang and Hiba had to overcome the suspicion of relatives and friends. 'Nobody thought we would succeed,' Garang admits. For once, Sudan's politics helped: this was the interim period, the gulp of stability before separation, a time when the Sudanese had to get used to many new ideas. 'The days of peace were hopeful, people were very happy, there was no stress,' Garang explains. Even those who did not like the idea of the mixed marriage accepted it as part of the 'blessings of peace'. Soon Garang and Hiba were celebrating further blessings: first a son, Monty, and then a daughter, Azal.

Garang could be forgiven for wishing the interim period had lasted for ever. Three years after the wedding, South Sudan's independence placed an international border between him and his family. Dr Garang runs his hospital in Aweil, in South Sudan. Hiba works for the Ministry of Health in Khartoum. Monty and Azal are with her, because the schools and healthcare are better in Sudan. As the two Sudans began to squabble, and then fight, the pressure on the couple grew; friends told Hiba her husband would move her to South Sudan, and they would never see her again.

Through all this adversity Garang and Hiba's commitment remained strong. 'We love each other, we know each other in and out, we know what we are doing,' he says. But the separation, of the couple and the country, has been hard to accept.

It is painful. Because of politics and psychopaths and all this failure we are now seeking many papers, many stamps and many signatures to see each other. I miss the people I like and love: not just my wife, but also my mates, my colleagues, students. I had a great relationship with them.

In late 2012, more than a year after their country had split in two, making their marriage a long-distance one, Garang flew to meet Hiba. They went on holiday to Egypt, a neutral place in which they could finally spend some time together.

Two lungs in the same body

Garang and Hiba's love affair is extraordinary, both for their determination to be together, and because marriages between the citizens of what are now Sudan and South Sudan have been rare.[4] In another sense, though, their relationship is emblematic of the many ties, sentimental and practical, ethnic and commercial, historical and still-developing, which bind the people of the two Sudans even after separation. The people of Mali and Guinea, West African countries linked by ethnicity and history, are frequently described as 'two lungs in the same body'.[5] The relationship between the Sudanese and the South Sudanese, and their countries, is not nearly as harmonious; nevertheless, they are even more dependent on the other than the West African pair.

If one of the Sudans fails, then the pressure on the other will be enormous. Largely this is due to a shared history. The people were subjects of the same colonial masters. One of the first Sudanese national heroes, a man who called for independence from the British and Egyptians, Ali

Abdelatif, was a Dinka. There is a street named after him in Khartoum. After independence was eventually achieved in 1956, the united Sudan of a million square miles, which stretched from Wadi Halfa in the north to Nimule in the south, lasted only fifty-five years. Yet it may well take another half century to disentangle the people of the two nations, who have lived, worked, socialised—and married—across what is now an international border. The geography of the two countries argues in favour of close ties too. The White Nile flows north from Juba to Khartoum, its path now mimicked by oil pipelines; and Sudan's creeping desertification pushes more and more people towards South Sudan's pastures. Separation was an angry divorce, after which the two parties will be forced to maintain some sort of relationship.

After the split, hundreds of thousands of South Sudanese stayed in Sudan, mainly in and around Khartoum. Equally, there are Sudanese traders in the markets of almost every major South Sudanese town. In the *tamazuj* or 'intermixing' zone, the eleven states on the border of the two countries in which there are more than 13 million people,[6] prosperity still depends on the neighbours, in much the same way as it has for decades. In particular, South Sudanese still rely on Sudanese businessmen for food and many manufactured goods. All over the new country, but above all in the border states, South Sudanese are often more comfortable speaking Arabic than English, their new national language.[7]

Sudanese bring their cattle into South Sudan every year, spending many months in what is now a foreign state, seeking better grazing. Abdelaziz, the half-Misseriya half-Dinka cow owner, is one of these men. His route passes just to the west of Garang Thomas Dhel's home in Aweil. Often the relationships of the people living either side of the border are conflictual. Nevertheless, they are an inescapable part of life in both Sudans. Said al Khatib, one of Sudan's main negotiators with South Sudan, says there is no hope of prosperity for both countries unless they work together: 'trying to survive without this co-operation—maybe it is possible but it is one degree above suicide.'

OLD WARRIORS SCRATCHING THEIR SCARS

The politicians know that their countries are economically interdependent, and that working together would bring benefits to both; but it is not easy to move past the bitterness created by so many years of war. The scar tissue runs deep. The political elites in both Sudans are still obsessed with, and to an extent defined by, their relationship with the other country. State television in both countries frequently carries interviews with officials lambasting their old enemies across the new border. My source The Minister told me that 'there will never be peace with Sudan, because the Arabs want to dominate us'. The feeling is mutual: Ghazi Salaheddin Atabani, the leading NCP intellectual, says 'the prevailing feeling among the NCP is that there is no way you can reach peace with the SPLM'.

The profound mistrust between the political elites sometimes blinds them to the other challenges their states face. Princeton Lyman, the US Special Envoy for Sudan and South Sudan until early 2013, met regularly with the political class in both countries. He says each of the two Sudans believe that the other is the biggest threat, whereas the greatest challenges are actually internal: governing a diverse country, in Sudan's case, and building a state up from nothing, for South Sudan. Lyman concludes that old animosities still drive many politicians: 'There are people in both camps who live on the tension and the conflict with each other'.

In the period after separation, emotions were still high. South Sudan's leaders often spoke about the feeling that Bashir was 'humiliating' them, or treating them as if South Sudan was still a province ruled by Khartoum. Sudanese leaders were dismissive about what they saw as a lack of sophistication in South Sudan. Even politeness often prepared the ground for an accusation. I noticed that whenever a Sudanese or South Sudanese politician was about to be particularly critical, he would preface the statement by calling his target 'brother': 'Our brothers in South Sudan', one would say, and then accuse them of wanting to overthrow Bashir; a South Sudanese politician would use the same device: 'Our Sudanese brothers do not want our country to succeed.'

On 8–9 October 2011, President Salva Kiir visited Sudan for the first time since South Sudan's independence. The visit temporarily reduced some of the tension between the two countries. For once, the word 'brother' seemed heartfelt. As a dutiful host, President Bashir went to the airport to see Salva off. Both delegations sat with the heads of state in the airport's presidential terminal, drinking sugared fruit juices and pecking at biscuits. Deng Alor, one of the most senior South Sudanese politicians, told a succession of jokes, and the laughter of the leaders of both countries filled the room. In many cases, these are men who have known each other for years: Deng, for example, went to school with the NCP's al Khatib in the town of Wad Madani.

All the same, after the South Sudanese had flown back to Juba the usual verbal hostilities resumed. This is a very Sudanese (and South Sudanese) trait, according to Garang Thomas Dhel:

When they are far from each other, they are more aggressive. When they are near they are more emotional, they are more accepting. When they are negotiating, they laugh, but when they come to the media, they criticise. This is the way the people live on the ground too.

Even after separation, the leaders of the two Sudans would have plenty of opportunity to laugh together, and to criticise each other: they met regularly to negotiate a number of unresolved issues, which at several points threatened to start a new war.

OUTSTANDING ISSUES

Remarkably, at separation there was no agreement over where Sudan ended, and where South Sudan began. The borders were disputed, with several areas claimed by both sides. The borderlands are where the ethnic groups of Sudan and South Sudan overlap and mingle. Cattle-herders drive their cows to the south, as they have done for hundreds of years. Sudanese peoples, like the Misseriya and the Rizeigat, believe that the territory on which they hold these long-established grazing rights should remain within Sudan. South Sudanese ethnic groups like the Dinka Malual look after their own herds in areas claimed by Sudan. Ethnic homelands have shifted over the years. Throughout the disputed borderlands, there are places where ancestors are buried and battles have been fought. For the two national capitals, the fact that the border area is where all the major oilfields are situated is perhaps of greater importance.

As part of the CPA, the SPLM and the NCP had accepted that the 1 January 1956 boundary between northern and southern Sudan would become the border between Sudan and South Sudan. This meant that emotional and ethnic arguments about where the border should be would not be relevant.[8] Everything would depend on the geographical location of the boundary line left by the Anglo-Egyptian colonisers at their departure in 1956. However, as the historian Douglas Johnson, who studied the problem, has pointed out, 'There is no single authoritative source stating precisely what those boundaries were on that date. Much of the boundary area was unsurveyed, and even the most detailed contemporary maps often do not record significant topographical features along the boundary lines.'⁹

As a consequence, by separation Khartoum and Juba had not been able to agree on the exact location of the border in several areas. These included part of the dividing line between South Darfur in Sudan and Northern Bahr el Gahzal in South Sudan; the mineral-rich Kafia Kingi area, which South Sudan claims, but which has been administered from South Darfur since 1960; the oil-rich Heglig area, which was under Sudan's control; and several smaller areas along the boundary line of Upper Nile state in South Sudan. The issues that had been raised initially were called the Disputed Areas. Others that were added later, such as Heglig, were named the Claimed Areas. The distinction was between territories that both sides agreed were in dispute (the Disputed Areas), and areas where one side, in most cases Sudan, said that there should be no argument (the Claimed Areas). Immediately after separation, Khartoum's position was that it only wanted to discuss the Disputed Areas.

These differences were a constant source of tension. The security dossier was a key concern for both countries, and for the AU-appointed mediators, led by the former South African President Thabo Mbeki. In addition, both Khartoum and Juba had strong links to rebel groups which operated in the border regions, as the Insecurity chapter showed. This damaged the relationship between the two Sudans. The mediators hoped to find a way of damping tensions on the border, and to convince both sides to cut their ties with the other's rebels.

Abyei

The Abyei region, which is wanted by both Sudans, is mainly unremarkable savannah dotted with small villages. There is just one settlement of any size, which is called Abyei Town. Even here most buildings are mudbrick huts, with the exception of a few official or religious buildings and a UN base. Yet this small and impoverished region has been in the national—and international—spotlight for years. In May 2008, fighting between SAF and SPLA in Abyei Town threatened to drag northern and southern Sudan back to war. Three years later, as southern Sudan prepared to declare its independence, the lilac walls of the Catholic church were still pockmarked by bullet holes, and Abyei's status was still unresolved.

Abyei is known historically as the area of the nine Dinka Ngok chiefdoms. It used to be part of southern Sudan, but in 1905 it was transferred to Kordofan in northern Sudan. The Dinka Ngok, a Dinka sub-group, see themselves as South Sudanese. Abyei is also claimed by the pastoralist Misseriya, who are Sudanese, and who have been grazing their cattle in the area for centuries.[10] They rely on passage through the region in order to feed their cattle during the dry season. Tensions in Abyei were high in the run-up to separation. In January 2011, I travelled with a UN patrol to the north of Abyei Town. When we arrived in a Misseriya village, angry men, some carrying AK47s, made it clear they didn't want us there. We quickly left.

Abyei is north of the 1 January 1956 line, but the CPA granted the people of the area a referendum on whether to join southern Sudan or remain part of Sudan. The 1972 Addis Ababa agreement, which ended the first north-south civil war, had given Abyei the right to make a similar choice. However this was never implemented. This time round, the Dinka Ngok were determined that the vote would happen. The first obstacle was obtaining consensus on Abyei's borders. Khartoum rejected the conclusions of the Abyei Boundary Commission (ABC), which had been set up by the CPA. International arbitration was sought. In 2009, the Permanent Court of Arbitration (PCA) in The Hague gave its verdict. The borders demarcated by the PCA were smaller than those suggested by the ABC. Most significantly, the oilfields in Heglig were placed outside Abyei, to the annoyance of southern Sudan. From this point on, the area defined as Abyei by the PCA ruling did not have substantial (known) oil reserves.

The Dinka Ngok have several representatives in the senior ranks of the SPLM, including Deng Alor, Luka Biong and Edward Lino, and South Sudan's Ambassador to the UN, Francis Deng, is the son of the legendary Dinka Ngok chief, the late Deng Majok. This gives Abyei particular prominence in South Sudanese politics. The Misseriya traditionally supported the Umma party, and haven't always seen eye to eye with the NCP, but Khartoum is keen not to antagonise them. The Misseriya often describe the importance of Abyei in the most expansive terms: 'For us, Abyei is a matter of survival,' exclaims Sadig Babo Nimr, the brother of the Misseriya paramount chief. The Misseriya fear that a denial of grazing rights in the region could destroy their livelihood.

Dinka Ngok and Misseriya leaders often say that if only the politicians in Juba and Khartoum would leave them alone, they would be able to work out their problems between them. This is, perhaps, an over-optimistic assessment, although at many points in the past the Dinka Ngok and the Misseriya were able to resolve their conflicts peacefully.[11] In any case, a purely local solution is no longer likely: Abyei has become a national issue for both Sudans.

Abyei's referendum had been scheduled simultaneously with the vote on southern Sudan's future, in January 2011. Despite numerous conferences and high-level negotiations, Khartoum and Juba could not agree on whether the Misseriya would be eligible to vote. The sticking point was whether the semi-nomadic Misseriya counted as residents. If the Misseriya were allowed to participate, the Dinka Ngok feared that the referendum would result in Abyei remaining a part of Sudan. As there was no consensus, the vote was postponed indefinitely. Not for the first time, the interests of the people of Abyei had been sacrificed in the hope of maintaining the peace between northern and southern Sudan.

Throughout the first half of 2011, tensions rose between SPLA and SAF troops stationed in Abyei as JIUs, and between the Dinka Ngok and the Misseriya. There were several small-scale clashes. On 19 May, a SAF convoy escorted by UN troops was attacked by the SPLA, a fact confirmed by a UN internal report and the SPLM.[12] This was the excuse Khartoum was looking for: the following day it sent its tanks into Abyei, routing the small southern Sudanese force. SAF was followed in by Misseriya militias, who looted and burned most of Abyei Town. The SPLA did not respond, judging that the risk of jeopardising independence, which was less than two months away, was too great.

Over 110,000 Dinka Ngok fled to southern Sudan. Some survived by cooking leaves. In a camp near Wau, I saw a young girl swinging on a water pump. Her slight body weight wasn't enough to bring water to the surface. 'I just want to hear Abyei will be part of South Sudan,' her mother Afath Deng said. On 27 July 2011, the UN Security Council authorised a new peacekeeping mission, and shortly afterwards a force largely made up of Ethiopian troops moved in to Abyei. Eventually the Sudanese soldiers pulled out, and some Abyei residents went back to rebuild their homes. Sudan's controversial military action had only postponed, rather than made, the decision on Abyei's future. In the period after separation Abyei remained one of the biggest sources of friction between the two Sudans.

Citizenship

At separation, citizenship presented challenges too. Millions of southern Sudanese had moved to the north during the second civil war, often fleeing the turmoil in their home areas. A smaller number of northerners lived in the south. The southern Sudanese leaders had to decide who would qualify as citizens of their state, and the Sudanese needed to determine how they would treat South Sudanese living on their territory. In the end, the conditions for obtaining South Sudanese nationality were broad. Ethnic southern Sudanese, anyone with a parent or recent ancestor who was born in South Sudan, and even people whose parents or grandparents had lived in southern Sudan since before 1956 were eligible for a South Sudanese passport.

Sudan decided it would revoke the Sudanese nationality of all those it considered South Sudanese. This was a punitive measure. The Sudanese constitution allows citizens to have two nationalities, and several leading NCP politicians have British passports. The South Sudanese, uniquely, would not be allowed dual nationality. That was not all. All South Sudanese civil servants lost their jobs, and Sudanese officials threatened that the South Sudanese would no longer have the right to live or work in Sudan. They were given until 9 April 2012 to sort out their papers, but in practice this proved impossible.

For people like Carlo Musa, a tailor, this was a disaster. A South Sudanese who had lived in Sudan for more than four decades, Carlo had few memories of his ancestral home. He and his family left their house in Omdurman, and joined a small community of his compatriots in makeshift huts on the outskirts of the Sudanese capital. When I met Carlo in April 2012, he and thousands of others were sleeping rough while they waited for someone to give them the money to go to South Sudan. In total, more than 900,000 South Sudanese returned to their country in 2010–12.[13] They no longer felt welcome in Sudan.

Separation also created many difficulties for those with links to both countries. Garang and Hiba, the two Sudans couple, initially found it impossible to obtain Sudanese nationality for their children, Monty and Azal. 'It seems to be the coming conflict for families like mine,' Garang says, sadly. South Sudanese women with light-skinned children were accused of kidnapping them. One South Sudanese woman, who had adopted a Sudanese baby, was arrested as she travelled to the new country. She was allowed to continue her journey, but the authorities held on to her child.[14] People with Sudanese fathers were in a stronger position. The cow-owner Abdelaziz Hussain, whose father was Misseriya and whose mother is Dinka, was able to keep his Sudanese nationality, since Sudan is a patrilineal society.

The whole process altered lives forever. A distraught South Sudanese who lived in Khartoum asked me to tell the SPLM Secretary General, Pa'gan Amum, that he and others were suffering. As early as November 2010, the AU mediator Mbeki lost his cool in a meeting with Sudanese and South Sudanese leaders, including Pa'gan. Mbeki usually keeps his emotions on a tight rein; not this time. 'It is not right,' he kept repeating. He was outraged by the lack of concern shown by the politicians on both sides for the ordinary southern Sudanese people, many of whom had been born in the north. Khartoum took away their nationality, and Juba did not fight for their rights.

'I honestly think this is inhuman,' Mbeki said, according to a person who attended the meeting. 'We are imposing a pain on ordinary people who are not responsible for any of these decisions. Why? It is not right.'[15] The politicians on both sides seemed to agree that one of the prices South Sudanese would pay for seceding would be losing their existing Sudanese nationality. Instead of questioning this, the post-secession negotiations concentrated on agreeing on the conditions in which Sudanese and South Sudanese could live and work in the other country.

Economic issues

At separation there were several unresolved economic issues too. South Sudan's oil could only be exported through Sudan's infrastructure: the pipelines, the refineries and the export terminal. Optimists hoped this apparent economic interdependence would encourage the two states to work together. This did not happen in the first year after separation. In particular, the two sides could not agree on how much the South Sudanese should pay to export its oil through Sudan. The impasse resulted in constant public arguments. Debt was also tricky: Juba objected to the idea of assuming some of Sudan's debt, of around $40 billion, saying the money had been used to buy weapons to fight the war in the south.

South Sudan did agree to the principle of 'creating two viable states', which meant, in effect, paying Sudan compensation for the loss of its oil reserves. Both countries accepted that the gap would be made up in three ways: firstly, measures taken by the Sudanese government itself; secondly, an international contribution; and thirdly, South Sudan would make its own contribution, which became known as the Transitional Financial Assistance (TFA). There was a lack of clarity over whether the TFA would be in the form of oil fees or should be a separate payment. The negotiations both before and immediately after independence foundered on this dispute, and on just how much the three components should amount to.

Talks, *tajility* and the 'enemies of peace'

To many around the world it seemed extraordinary that so much could be undecided on South Sudan's independence day. However, strategic delay has been a key part of Sudanese politics for decades. In the 1930s, the British colonisers coined a term for this, 'tajility', from the Arabic word '*tajiil*', which means to forestall or delay.[16] The mediators and the leadership of both sides had committed to resolving all the outstanding issues before separation, though this was never likely. Khartoum delayed, probably to give it the option of postponing the referendum, though in the end under international pressure it allowed it to go ahead. Juba realised it would be in a stronger negotiating position once South Sudan had become an independent country.

Long after the independence celebrations, the negotiations dragged on. Frequent meetings were held, usually in the Ethiopian capital, Addis Ababa, but they often seemed to make no progress at all. A Sudanese leader and a South Sudanese politician both told me a joke about local attitudes to timekeeping that seemed to apply to the talks: 'Let's meet at two. I will call at four to say that if I am not there at six, you can decide at eight to leave at ten.'

The post-referendum talks, like the CPA negotiations before them, did not include a broad range of political actors. Nhial Deng, South Sudan's foreign minister until the 2013 reshuffle, even admitted that 'these negotiations were designed to be between political parties, between the SPLM and the NCP'. Opposition parties and civil society had no role. The negotiating teams reflected many of the flaws of their respective governments. Sudan's delegation was headed by Idriss Abdel Gadir, a minister, but different factions held sway at various points. When Said al Khatib played a prominent role, the mediators felt compromise was more likely. At other times the military seemed to be calling the shots, led by

Defence Minister Abdel Rahim Hussein, who is wanted by the ICC. Abdel Rahim is a stubborn man, with a burning drive not to concede any ground to South Sudan. In this he did not always prevail.

Over several years of talks, individuals in key positions changed their stance considerably, reacting to what seemed to be acceptable to their domestic constituency. In this precarious period, it was difficult for a Sudanese politician to appear too sympathetic to South Sudan. Many put on the clothes of a hardliner. Al Khatib, exceptionally, admits that there are 'enemies of peace' within the Sudanese political elite. These are people who are determined to bring South Sudan down, either through conviction or because continued conflict serves their narrow interests. Al Khatib also believes that many of the SPLM are enemies of peace too, because they still dream of overcoming Bashir and his system.

South Sudan's negotiators were led by Pa'gan Amum, who was one of John Garang's disciples.[17] Pa'gan is a Shilluk, though his enemies claim that he does not have a particularly strong ethnic support base. He is a gifted modern politician, who is deeply aware of the requirements of the media age: he gives long press conferences, in both Arabic and English, in his rich, confident voice. Pa'gan has a startling gift for antagonising the NCP, which is appreciated by many South Sudanese. He also tends to keep his strategy to himself, which sometimes frustrated the rest of the South Sudanese negotiating team. The talks became Pa'gan's power base, the area of South Sudanese political life in which he exercised the most control. He was regarded as unpredictable and sometimes unreasonable by the mediators, who also often despaired at the slow pace of the talks. *Tajility* was employed by both sides, and the longer the negotiations stalled, the more the tension grew.

THE SHUTDOWN

South Sudan's decision to shut down its own oil production, in January 2012, will be remembered as one of the most startling negotiating tactics ever, anywhere. The shutdown deprived the South Sudanese government of 98 per cent of its revenue, at a time when the new country desperately needed to build something out of the rubble of the war years. Cutting off the oil ushered in an extremely difficult period for both Sudans. The shutdown was, as has been discussed in the Economy chapter, a direct consequence of the failure to agree on how much the new country should pay to export its oil through Sudan. Khartoum's 'confiscation' (or theft, as Juba saw it) of oil in lieu of transit payments was the moment the South Sudanese were pushed into an unstoppable rage. The anger was channelled into a strategic decision. By cutting off its oil production, Juba hoped to exert pressure on Bashir and his regime. With the oil no longer flowing, Khartoum had no immediate prospect of boosting its economy with oil transit fees, and the diplomatic spat meant there would be no agreement on the multi-billion dollar TFA payment either. Juba hoped that this would bring benefits at the negotiating table, or, potentially, send Sudan's economy into such a tailspin that popular protests would remove Bashir from power.

The veteran SPLM politician Lual Deng, an economist who had been the federal petroleum minister before separation, warned his colleagues in Juba that it would not work. They were 'naive' to believe the Sudanese state was so weak that Bashir would fall in six months, he told me; and the shutdown was 'a classic case of incompetence in decision-making'. The Sudanese, despite their initial fury, quickly saw the possibilities the shutdown brought: South Sudan was considerably more dependent on oil than they were, and living without the oil revenue might bring radical change at the top in Juba. 'Khartoum was waiting for us to collapse,' South Sudan's then-Finance Minister Kosti Manibe said.[18]

As Salva and Bashir settled down to wait for each other to be overthrown, African mediators and influential countries like the US and China tried to get the South Sudanese to change their mind. On 27 January, just before an AU Summit in Addis Ababa, Kenya's President Mwai Kibaki and Ethiopia's Prime Minister Meles Zenawi met Bashir and Kiir. Mbeki's team, the African Union High Implementation Panel (AUHIP), had prepared a salvage plan, which laid down the broad outlines of a deal on oil that they would hope be acceptable to both sides. It included a transit fee of $3 per barrel, and set a range of $2.6–5.4 billion for the TFA payment. At the bottom end of the range, this was similar to the deal that the South Sudanese eventually agreed to later in the year.

Privately the AUHIP team worried that the proposal was too close to South Sudan's demands to be palatable for Sudan. Nevertheless, during the meeting Meles seemed to have convinced both Bashir and Salva to accept. Bashir said that he would stop unilaterally taking the oil, and both Bashir and Salva agreed that they would sign AUHIP's document, according to al Khatib.[19] This was confirmed by other sources at the talks.

That afternoon, Meles announced the good news to a gathering of regional heads of state. Following the applause, Salva stood up and told the bemused presidents that he wasn't sure that he would be able to sign the agreement after all.[20]

This was extremely embarrassing for Meles. He made several efforts that evening and the following day to convince Salva to sign, but eventually was forced to accept defeat. After a last meeting with Salva and Pa'gan, Meles told collaborators that the SPLM was better informed about the consequences of the shutdown than he had thought—and more reckless. Several sources present at the time believe Pa'gan was the man responsible for the about-turn; according to one, he shouted at Salva, completely undermining him.[21] The failure of the summit meant that both Sudans would wait for the other to disintegrate: the shutdown was now a showdown.

War, again

There is a photograph that perfectly encapsulates what happened next.[22] In the picture, a dead SAF soldier is stretched out in a pool of oil, his feet pointing towards a leaking oil installation. In the photo's subdued light, the drenched corpse and the oil have the same dull sheen. The photo was taken at Heglig, the largest oilfield under Sudanese control, and a major part of the Sudanese economy. The South Sudanese call it Panthou, and believe that it is part of their country. By the time the picture was taken, the oilfield had been overrun by the SPLA. On 26 March 2012, South Sudanese troops pushed up to Heglig,[23] sending SAF running. The SPLA were responding to an attack on their position by SAF, who were backed up by Bapiny Monytuil's SSLA rebels. Salva announced the news, to wild cheering, at a SPLM conference in Juba.[24] On this occasion the South Sudanese withdrew.

Two weeks later, on 10 April, the scenario repeated itself: Sudanese aircraft and ground troops bombarded the SPLA. The South Sudanese fought off the attackers, and chased after them, and this time the South Sudanese did not stop until they had seized control of Heglig.[25] The proxy war had become a real conflict. Before long, SAF had been pushed back to twenty-five kilometres north of Heglig, according to Mac Paul, South Sudan's deputy head of military intelligence.[26] This was a stunning military victory for South Sudan: Sudan had lost control of one of its major sources of income, Heglig, and previous assumptions of SAF's military superiority had been called into question.

This was not a simple conflict between Sudan and South Sudan. Sudanese rebels fought alongside the South Sudanese army, and some believe that they actually reached Heglig before the SPLA. SPLM-North fought within South Kordofan, near to Heglig. JEM, who were originally from Darfur, struck north from their South Sudanese base in Unity state. They had arrived there a month before the conflict, according to a well-connected Bentiu resident. JEM soldiers could be seen walking in Rubkona market, not far from the former chicken farm identified as their base by a UN report.[27] Two journalists had their cameras confiscated by a JEM fighter, and had to negotiate with a SPLA commander to get them back.

The South Sudanese military had also brought up an elite unit of commandos to Bentiu, as they had 'intelligence' Sudan was about to attack.[28] This combination of Sudanese rebels and South Sudanese elite troops were able to overrun Heglig. Sudan, in turn, used the South Sudanese rebels, the SSLA, to fight back. The SSLA defector Jacob Nyier confirmed that the rebel group fought alongside SAF around Heglig, and also carried out attacks near Pariang junction in Unity state, South Sudan, behind the front line. The SSLA captured several JEM fighters, and handed them over to SAF. Nyier said more than 100 SSLA fighters were wounded, and sent to Khartoum for treatment. It was a hint at just how badly the fighting went for SAF and its South Sudanese rebel allies.

Painful words

In Sudan, there was profound dismay. Many wondered how SAF could have allowed the SPLA to penetrate to Heglig once, withdraw, and then take the vital oilfield on the second attempt. There were some limited calls for the defence minister, Abdel Rahim, to be sacked, but his close relations with Bashir meant that this was never likely to happen. The president's response to the crisis was typically aggressive. In a speech at the NCP headquarters, on 18 April, he said the South Sudanese people needed to be 'liberated' from the 'insects'. SPLM leaders said this was tantamount to a Rwandan-style call for genocide.

In fact Bashir had made an ugly pun on *haraka*, which means 'movement' in Arabic, and is a part of the SPLM's name; *hashara*, the word Bashir used, means 'insect'. Bashir wasn't calling for the South Sudanese people to be wiped out; he had asked for their governing party to be crushed. Some saw that as a particularly fine distinction. In his address, Bashir also delivered a hard message to the SPLM: 'either we end up in Juba and take everything, or you end up in Khartoum and take everything.' That sounded to many around the world like a return to outright war. Nationalistic chauvinism swept both countries.

While Bashir fired off insults about insects, South Sudan's military triumph in seizing Heglig was rapidly turning into a debilitating diplomatic defeat for the new country. The AU condemned what it called 'the illegal and unacceptable occupation by the South Sudanese army of Heglig, which lies north of the agreed borderline of 1/1/56.'[29] The UN Secretary General later echoed the criticism.[30] Salva was asked to withdraw his troops by the UN, the AU, the EU, and individual countries including America and South Africa. The president was personally telephoned by Barack Obama, Ban Ki Moon, and many other world leaders.[31]

As this concerted international diplomatic effort intensified, Salva convened a meeting of the National Security Council. On Friday 20 April 2012, ten days after seizing Heglig, South Sudan announced it would remove its troops. The Vice President of the time, Riek Machar, admitted that his country had no choice but to bow to the international pressure: 'We are not a pariah state. We don't want to be isolated from the rest of the world. We don't want sanctions against South Sudan, so we decided to withdraw.' By 22 April, all South Sudan's troops were out of Heglig. It had held the oilfields for less than two weeks.

Stick or twist?

Sudan claimed that it had won a military victory. Bashir flew to Heglig, and the pictures of him shaking his swagger stick in front of jubilating soldiers were broadcast all over the country. It is not clear to what extent the South Sudanese left of their own accord, and to what extent they were forced out by SAF. Sudan's advantage in air power certainly put pressure on the SPLA troops in and around Heglig. The day after the South Sudanese relinquished control of the oilfield, dozens of injured men were unloaded from a truck in the grounds of Bentiu's main hospital, groaning with pain at every movement. They were left under some trees in the courtyard, as the wards were full.

A little further north, on the road from Bentiu, as vehicles brought troops back from Heglig, and civilians returned with goods they had looted from the oil facility, a straggle of soldiers filed past me. 'Many people have died,' one soldier said to me, out of the corner of his mouth, then moved on. Exactly how many South Sudanese troops were killed is a controversial subject. When a journalist in Bentiu wrote an article suggesting that the border fighting had created more than 500 South Sudanese widows, he was arrested.[32] The military intelligence general, Mac Paul, told me 240 South Sudanese troops had been killed, in itself an admission of sizeable losses. He also said that more than sixty SPLA troops were missing in action, and 360 had been injured. He estimated SAF's losses at 800. The real figures will probably never be known.

For a while it appeared as if SAF might make good on Bashir's threat, and march deep into South Sudan. On Sunday 22 April there was further ground fighting. In the evening, several bombs narrowly missed oil installations in Unity state. Mac Paul said that it was the heaviest bombing he had experienced since 1995. The air raid seemed to be in retaliation for what had happened in Heglig. By the time SAF had regained control of the oilfield, the oil installations were in ruins.

Sudan blamed South Sudan. The head of NISS, Mohamed Atta, held a press conference in which he said his agents had intercepted an incriminating phone call. The transcript allegedly revealed that the Unity state Governor, Taban Deng, had ordered two JEM commanders to destroy the Heglig oilfield.[33] Juba retorted that the damage had been done by SAF's air raids. Either way, Heglig's oil production capability was considerably reduced. A senior official in Sudan's petroleum ministry, Awad al Fateh, said almost everything had been damaged, including the pipeline and the oil processing facility.

The next day, Monday 23 April, the Unity state capital Bentiu was hit from the air. The target was the bridge between Bentiu and Rubkona, which allowed the SPLA to bring troops up to the front line. A series of explosions rolled around the town, and SPLA soldiers and civilians answered back with small arms fire. A man next to the hotel I was staying in sprayed the sky with his gun, and laughed when we took cover as the planes flew overhead. He had decided that it wasn't his day to die. The air raid did not take out the bridge, but at least one civilian was killed in the nearby market. However, this was one of the final flourishes of the oil war. The ground fighting stopped, though Sudan continued bombing border areas. It seemed as if Sudan did not have the strength to fight on another front, as SAF was already preoccupied with rebels in Darfur,

South Kordofan and Blue Nile. Khartoum was also subjected to heavy international pressure to stop the fighting.

The consequences of the short oil war

In the short term, both Salva and Bashir benefited from the border battles. South Sudan's initial military victory was hugely popular in the new nation: the old enemy had been given a bloody nose. If nothing else this stoked South Sudanese pride. In Sudan, the opposition rallied to the cause: the Umma party's Sadig al Mahdi visited injured soldiers in the military hospital in Omdurman, and dodged questions about whether this meant he supported the president. When Sudan regained control of Heglig, people took to the streets all over Sudan to celebrate. Even those who did not like the NCP joined in. 'That's guaranteed another five years for Bashir,' one friend texted me.

In both countries, national fervour overcame any other emotion. Mustafa Khogali, the Khartoum businessman and cultural activist, said lots of his friends volunteered to fight. It wasn't because they loved Bashir, he explained, it was because they felt their country was under attack. In South Sudan, there were rallies in support of the military, and several communities donated money or goods. One afternoon I saw a herd of cattle wandering through the military barracks in Rubkona, not far from where the South Sudanese military leaders were sitting, directing the war; the cows had been given to the SPLA by patriotic citizens.

The oil war reminded both sets of leaders that renewed hostilities could be a short-cut to domestic popularity. Yet the fighting inflamed the tensions between the two Sudans, and set back any chance of a political agreement. It also emboldened hardliners in both countries. The 'enemies of peace' in Sudan 'carried the day' for a while, the NCP's al Khatib admitted, and it was the same in South Sudan.

Heglig: a costly claim

The international condemnation of their military action was a deep shock to the South Sudanese. They regarded Heglig, or Panthou, as part of South Sudan. At the beginning of the negotiations, well before separation, South Sudan's position was that Heglig was in Abyei, and this was accepted by the ABC. However, the 2009 PCA ruling placed the oilfields outside Abyei's borders. For a while, it appeared to the AUHIP mediators as if Juba had given up on Heglig. Five border areas were designated as Disputed, and Heglig was not one of them. According to a source close to AUHIP, it was repeatedly reaffirmed in meetings of the Joint Political Committee between the Sudans that only the five Disputed Areas would be looked at.

Then the wind began to change. In November 2010, the NCP's Salah Gosh warned the SPLM negotiators that he would not accept altering the technical wording on the border disputes 'because otherwise you would start claiming Heglig'. In fact, South Sudan did just that. After some heated arguments, Heglig was one of several areas designated as Claimed, even if Khartoum did not accept the premise.

The South Sudanese say Heglig was administered as part of Unity state in southern Sudan until 2004. On 14 June of that year, Nafie Ali Nafie apparently sent a letter and a hand-drawn map to the NCP-appointed governor of Unity, telling him that the area was in the north.[34] The map is not detailed enough to provide much illumination. Juba believes Khartoum transferred oil-rich Heglig to the north once it became apparent that the negotiations which led to the CPA would give southern Sudan almost half of the oil revenues from its territory.

However, in 2010 southern Sudan's own experts on the Technical Ad Hoc Boundary Committee appeared to reject Juba's claim to Heglig as a 'tribal' one, made by the Ruweng Dinka, when their mandate 'was only to adopt the administrative boundary, determined by geographical description based on the coordinates of latitudes and longitudes.'[35] South Sudan may be able to argue that the demarcation process on the ground would place some of the Heglig area within its border, but it is not thought that this would extend to the oilfields. In early 2012, before the oil war, Juba surprised Khartoum and the AUHIP mediators by producing a 'tribal map' from 1954, which showed Heglig as Dinka territory. This ethnic justification appeared to contradict South Sudan's previous commitment to the 1 January 1956 administrative borderline as the border between the two Sudans.

Whatever the truth of the matter, South Sudan's real mistake, in the eyes of the international community, was sending its troops across the line of control: Heglig was administered by Sudan, at least until negotiations or some sort of international arbitration decided otherwise. The AU and the UN considered an attack across this de facto border as a grave mistake by South Sudan. This seemed deeply unfair to the South Sudanese: after all Sudan had bombed border areas of South Sudan dozens of times since separation.

Senior South Sudanese officials, including Riek Machar and Nhial Deng, argued that conquering Heglig (albeit temporarily) had allowed South Sudan to promote its claim to the region to foreigners unaware of the complexities of the Sudans. This does not hold water. South Sudan's actions were met with dismay; Juba's cause certainly wasn't helped. On 2 May 2012, the UN Security Council unanimously adopted resolution 2046. This called on Sudan to stop its aerial bombardments of South Sudan, and on both countries to stop harbouring rebel groups from the other state. It demanded that the Sudans restart negotiations, and warned that sanctions might be imposed if these were not concluded within three months. Sudan had faced international opprobrium for years, but the impact on South Sudan was profound: less than a year into its life, it was already being threatened with international sanctions. The South Sudanese opposition politician Lam Akol's verdict was politically motivated, but accurate: 'South Sudan, which was the darling of the international community, was overnight being seen as an aggressor.'

'A BONY FISH WORTH CHEWING': THE SEPTEMBER AGREEMENTS

In the end, it took the Sudans almost five months to sign a deal, and a partial one at that. In the heat and heightened feelings of the post-separation period, the Sudanese and South Sudanese leaders simply weren't able to agree on a comprehensive solution to their problems. Negotiators had made some progress by late September, so Salva and Bashir travelled to Addis Ababa for what was intended to be a one-day summit. The plan was that the presidents would confirm the final details, then sign. Instead the talks dragged on for nearly a week. Towards the end of the first full day of negotiations, the media were let into a small room to film the historic meeting between the heads of state. Mbeki turned to Bashir: 'You said this would be finished by six o'clock.' There was a pause, then the presidents began to laugh.

The atmosphere wasn't always so jovial. The South Sudanese accused the Sudanese of sending weapons to the rebel David Yau Yau in his Jonglei hideout, on the eve of the talks. There were heated disagreements about security, and the border region. At one point Deng Alor and the NCP's Ahmed Dirdiry had a furious argument over Abyei. My source close to President Bashir told me that he was dismayed at the lack of leadership from both camps, including from his president. 'The hardliners on both sides don't want a deal,' he said.

However, despite the squabbles some sort of agreement was always likely. The two countries were under the threat of sanctions, and the economies in both were deteriorating rapidly. The only sensible solution was some sort of political compromise. In the end, the two presidents accepted a number of deals. These were signed on 27 September, and Bashir and Salva were able to milk the applause of their delegations. 'This is a great day in the history of the region,' Salva said.

Security

One of the key sticking points had been the creation of a demilitarised buffer zone, extending ten kilometres either side of the de facto border. The idea was that it would be monitored by Sudanese, South Sudanese and foreign observers, which would reduce the chances of fighting or cross-border support to rebel groups. The buffer zone would be based on the existing areas of control, rather than on what would eventually be agreed on as the final border between the two states.

Sudanese opposition centred on the 'Fourteen Mile' area, south of the river known as Arab in Sudan and Kiir in South Sudan. Sudan believed that the border between the two countries should be the Munro-Wheatley line, fourteen miles south of the river.[36] However, South Sudan was in control up to the Arab/Kiir river (and, Sudan claimed, even to the north of it; the US Special Envoy Lyman made similar allegations). South Sudan had accepted the AUHIP map of the de facto borderline. The Sudanese rejected the map, because they were concerned that the de facto border of the river would end up as the actual frontier. The AUHIP mediators said this was not the case, but struggled to persuade the Sudanese negotiators. Many in the Sudanese government, and in particular the military, wanted to look 'patriotic', according to al Khatib. In the end, the Sudanese relented, and accepted the map.

As the two delegations made their way back to their private quarters at the Sheraton hotel, the Sudanese defence minister Abdel Rahim bounded up to the South Sudanese negotiating team. 'So, did we get peace and stability?' he roared, and then laughed loudly. The South Sudanese looked uncomfortable. According to someone close to the talks, the South Sudanese had never expected the Sudanese to agree to the buffer zone. Abdel Rahim was laughing at their unhappiness that their bluff had been called. The demilitarised area would now be set up.

The South Sudanese negotiators knew they would find it difficult to convince their own people that they had made a good deal. As Mac Paul, the deputy head of military intelligence, acknowledged, the land south of the Kiir river was not just important for grazing. Over the years, the Dinka Malual had seen their cattle stolen, been forced into slavery, and died in the act of defending the land. The SPLA also disliked the idea of withdrawing several miles south of the river. The Addis Ababa signing ceremony was delayed for a day after furious generals, who were in the South Sudan delegation but had been kept in the dark by the lead negotiator Pa'gan, read the text and objected. Eventually they gave way.[37]

Of all the nine agreements signed in Addis,[38] the security arrangements (which set up the buffer zone) caused the most tension in South Sudan. The residents of Northern Bahr el Ghazal, Paul Malong's state, hated the fact that the area south of the Kiir river would be demilitarised. Who would protect them from Arab raiders or Sudanese military incursions? Malong objected to the idea of removing the SPLA from the land south of the river, and said there was no way he would allow the Fourteen Mile area to end up as part of Sudan.[39] The Northern Bahr el Ghazal community sent a letter to Salva, copied to AUHIP and the UN Security Council, expressing its 'indisputable displeasure and outrage'.[40]

Oil

There were reservations on both sides about the other agreements, but not more than might be expected in such difficult negotiations between hostile parties. An understanding on oil and financial arrangements had been agreed in principle at the beginning of August, and was then signed with the other deals on 27 September. It set the fees for South Sudan exporting its oil through Sudan at $11 per barrel for the oil produced in Unity state, and $9.10 per barrel for Upper Nile.[41] South Sudan also agreed to pay $3.028 billion as the TFA, to compensate Sudan for the economic damage secession had caused. This would be paid at $15 per barrel, to act as a further incentive for Sudan to allow South Sudan's oil exports to continue uninterrupted.

This formula allowed both countries to claim a victory. Sudan had demanded $36 per barrel: it ended up with $24.10 or $26 per barrel, depending on the pipeline. Sabir al Hassan, one of the NCP's chief negotiators, was happy. He pointed out that in 2011, Sudan had budgeted for $24 per barrel, so he considered this a slight improvement. In fact, by the time the oil companies' share was removed, the Sudanese government would receive a few dollars less than the budgeted sum. South Sudan, on the other hand, was able to boast that the transit fee had been set at $1 per barrel, only a slight jump from the $0.63/$0.69 its negotiators had been offering.

In the end, this financial agreement was relatively simple to conclude: both governments desperately needed the money it would bring. The Sudanese negotiator al Hassan said that the South Sudanese had finally seen the light: why would anyone voluntarily lose $20 million every day? This was his estimate of the cost of the shutdown. For ordinary people living near the border, the agreement to restart trade was potentially just as important. The oil wealth hasn't trickled down in either of the Sudans, but cross-border trade is vital for millions of people. In time, trade will take on more significance for the governments too, as the oil in both countries will not last forever.

The Four Freedoms

The people of both Sudans also stood to benefit considerably from the agreement on nationals of the other state. Each country undertook to grant the other's citizens the so-called 'Four Freedoms': freedom of residence; freedom of movement; freedom to undertake economic activity and freedom to acquire and dispose of property. This meant that the hundreds of thousands of South Sudanese still living in Sudan could work, and keep their houses (though most had already sold them), and the smaller Sudanese population in South Sudan could keep their businesses.[42] The Four Freedoms had been resisted fiercely by Sudanese hardliners, led by the president's uncle, Tayyeb Mustafa. He believed the SPLM intended to infiltrate South Sudanese soldiers into Sudan, in order to bring down Bashir. Tayyeb's hatred of the South Sudanese was legendary. Perhaps not coincidentally, his son had been killed fighting against the SPLA in 1998. The Four Freedoms had been initialled by the negotiators in March 2012, at an earlier round of talks. Bashir and Salva were due to sign the document when the Sudanese president travelled to Juba a few weeks later. Bashir's choleric uncle Tayyeb protested. He was furious about the Four Freedoms, and what he saw as his nephew capitulating to the South Sudanese. Senior South Sudanese politicians believe Tayyeb and hardliners in SAF subsequently sparked the Heglig conflict, in order to stop Bashir travelling to Juba. In any event, the summit was cancelled as soon as the Heglig fighting broke out. What Tayyeb didn't seem to understand was that Sudanese would benefit from the agreement too, including traders and the pastoralists who wished to travel to South Sudan with their cattle. The Sudanese negotiators had a better grasp of these realities, and the Four Freedoms was finally signed in Addis Ababa at the same time as the other deals.

Implementing the agreements

John Akec, a South Sudanese professor and blogger, described the September Agreements as 'a bony fish worth chewing'.[43] Both sides took some time to swallow; none of the agreements were implemented for months. The new Ethiopian Prime Minister, Hailemariam Desalegn,[44] brought Salva and Bashir to Addis for crisis talks in January 2013. Eventually, in March 2013, the two Sudans agreed to an implementation matrix: a timetable for fulfilling the commitments they had already made.

Finally things began to move. By mid-March, both armies had begun to withdraw their troops from the border, the first step in setting up the demilitarised buffer zone. South Sudan ordered the oil companies to start production again, and Sudan confirmed that it would transport its neighbour's crude to the world market. It would take some time for South Sudan's oil production to return to its 2011 level, but it seemed like the shutdown was finally over. The economies of both countries badly needed the injection of revenue. There was hope on both sides that once the oil started flowing, and trade began again, trust would slowly be built up. On 11 April Bashir travelled to Juba, for his first visit since separation.

The growing sense of optimism lasted less than two months: Bashir threatened to stop South Sudan exporting its oil again, by closing the pipelines. The trigger, once again, was South Sudan's alleged support for the Sudanese rebels. Once more it seemed Bashir was making policy up as he went along: my source close to the president said the first he had heard about this major decision was when Bashir announced it in the middle of a fiery speech.[45] In the end, the crisis was averted, thanks to international pressure and another presidential visit. This time Salva flew to Khartoum, on 30 August 2013. He was able to smile with Bashir, and both committed themselves once more to the September Agreements, crowning an unlikely if partial reconciliation.

AN UNFINISHED STORY

Thabo Mbeki called the September Agreements a 'great step'; however, it was one of only several the Sudans needed to make to bring about a reasonable working relationship. In Addis Ababa, the two negotiating teams were unable to agree on the status of Abyei, or make much progress on the disputed and claimed border areas. Abyei has the greatest potential to bring about a new war. Khartoum can't risk antagonising the Misseriya further, particularly as some have already joined rebel groups in South Kordofan.[46] South Sudan is unlikely to back down either, since several Dinka Ngok have important positions in the SPLM. 'The Misseriya are calling the shots in Sudan [...] while the Dinka Ngok are wagging the whole of South Sudan' is how al Khatib characterises it. In fact, some of the anger in South Sudan about the September Agreements came because Salva and the negotiating team had agreed to restart oil production without getting a favourable deal on Abyei.[47] In other words, Juba had given up its main leverage for little reward.

Over the years, there have been many attempts to resolve the impasse on Abyei. Before South Sudan's independence, it was suggested that Abyei be divided in two, with the northern part remaining in Sudan and the southern section being transferred to South Sudan. After UN resolution 2046 was adopted in May 2012, AUHIP put forward its proposal to decide the final status of Abyei. The mediators called for a referendum, in October 2013, in which only the Dinka Ngok and permanent residents of Abyei could vote. Both countries would have to respect the rights of the Dinka Ngok and the Misseriya, whatever the result of the referendum. If adopted, the proposal would certainly result in Abyei joining South Sudan, so it was enthusiastically welcomed by the South Sudanese. Sudan rejected it.[48]

The referendum did not take place in October 2013. The Dinka Ngok held their own vote, but this was rejected by the AU, Sudan, and even the South Sudanese government, conscious that supporting it would simply antagonise Khartoum for little benefit. A continued stalemate seems probable, as the AU is very unlikely to impose its solution on two sovereign states. A new conflict over Abyei is possible, given the tensions, which the considerable anger about the 4 May 2013 killing of the Dinka Ngok paramount chief, Kuol Deng Kuol, vividly illustrated.

The September Agreements only made slight progress towards resolving the border disputes. The two Sudans agreed that an AU Panel of Experts would examine the arguments over the Disputed and Claimed areas, but the panel's recommendations would not be binding. Sudan finally conceded that the Claimed Areas could be addressed, but only after the Disputed Areas are dealt with. If a negotiated solution to all the border disputes is not possible, international arbitration will be needed, though Khartoum has resisted this. Neither side is prepared to cede ground. To take two potential outcomes, Juba would find it difficult to accept losing Heglig/Panthou, having spoken so loudly about its claim to the area, and Khartoum would not want to give up Kafia Kingi and its mineral wealth. The issue is not just economic: patriotism plays a big role. Either country could inflate a disappointing decision over the border line into a *causus belli*, particularly if this serves the political imperatives of the moment.

The Two Areas

The September 2012 Addis Ababa negotiations did not even address the wars in South Kordofan and Blue Nile. The Two Areas were 'really the spoiler here,' according to Lyman: 'you can't really go ahead and demilitarise the border as long as that conflict is going on, because it spills over.' The SRF, the loose alliance of SPLM-North and several Darfuri rebel groups, says it controls 40 per cent of the border area. Neither country will trust the other while suspicions of support for rebel groups persist.

The SPLM-North leaders were present in Addis Ababa, on the margins of the September talks. The then-governor of South Kordofan, Ahmed Haroun, came too. He keenly shook hands with every Westerner he could find, aware that most felt awkward about any contact because of the ICC arrest warrant against him. More significantly, Haroun spent a good part of one evening in an animated chat with Yassir Arman, the Secretary General of SPLM-North. The scene was utterly typical of

Sudanese politics: two men at war with each other, who speak of the other's deeds with the utmost disgust, sat and talked amicably for well over an hour. The meeting did nothing to reduce the intensity of the fighting in South Kordofan. In January 2013, the AU Peace and Security Council called on Sudan to open direct negotiations with SPLM-North. As this book went to print, a few preliminary discussion had been held, but no progress had been made. Everyone is aware there will be no peace between the Sudans as long as the Two Areas are on fire.

A new generation to solve old problems

The problems between the two Sudans after separation were perhaps inevitable.[49] South Sudan's deputy defence minister until the 2013 reshuffle, Majak D'Agoot, sees similarities with Ethiopia and Eritrea, who fought on their disputed border after Eritrea seceded. He makes a more positive comparison too: eventually the US and Great Britain were able to develop the fabled 'special relationship', even though the post-independence period was tense and the two countries went to war in 1812. 'It will take time until both [Sudans] see their interest in mutual respect,' D'Agoot says. Some believe that this will happen sooner rather than later. 'The people are intermingled, the interests of the people are not separable,' the Sudanese politician Amin Hassan Omar says. 'The governments will find solutions.' The September Agreements may just have been a first step along this road.

A few go further: Yassir Arman, the SPLM-North politician who is a firm believer in John Garang's New Sudan ideology, hopes that the two Sudans will one day form a Sudanese Union, along the lines of the EU. This is inconceivable, at least in the short term. The tensions between the two countries are still extremely high. Victor Lugala, the South Sudanese writer, expresses the views of many when he says 'that group of NCP are very difficult. Even if they are given honey they will spit it out!' Bashir's supporters are no more complimentary of the 'Insect', as the president called the SPLM.

There is an argument, made by D'Agoot among others, that it will be almost impossible to forge a good relationship if it does not happen soon after separation. 'At least this generation can communicate with one another, the barriers are not so wide,' D'Agoot says. 'Take the [upcoming South Sudanese] generation, which will have less contact with Sudan.

They will not speak Arabic,' and are already moving closer to East Africa. In Sudan, too, younger people have little first hand experience of South Sudan, because of the war.

All the same, the scars of the war years may still be too deep to expect Bashir and Salva, Abdel Rahim and Pa'gan, and many others, to fully embrace their 'brothers' across the border. What is more, neither the NCP nor the SPLM has shown enough consideration for the people they govern. The NCP's disastrous period in power, and the SPLM's record since independence, give little indication that they are prepared to make the necessary sacrifices to reconcile their two nations. Perhaps a more likely route to harmony lies in the softening effects of time. The next generation of leaders, in both countries, will surely be more pragmatic, even if they didn't attend the same schools, speak the same language, and fight in the same battles.

The half-Misseriya half-Dinka Abdelaziz Hussain wants to bring his cows into South Sudan, without having to fight his way past his distant relatives to the best grassy pastures. Gatgong Jiech, the Nuer cow-herder, hopes the Sudanese traders will bring sorghum, driving down the prices in the market. Garang Thomas Dhel wants to be able to meet the love of his life, his wife Hiba al Makki, without struggling through administrative red tape, and battling deeply-ingrained suspicion from everyone around them.

Garang and Hiba talk on the phone almost daily, about 'politics, what is facing our countries, our lives, dealing with markets and schools. Life is becoming expensive, more and more.' With a love as strong as the one he shares with Hiba, Garang has no regrets; but he is sad about the path Sudan took. Eventually, he feels, the politicians will not have the energy to continue their squabbles: 'you know these people, they are like fighting cocks, they will be exhausted.' Garang dreams that the conflict between the Sudans will come to an end. It is to be hoped that one day a generation of Sudanese and South Sudanese politicians recognise the needs of their people, and make a lasting peace.

* * *

It is not easy to escape the weight of history. The dissolution of the united Sudan created two countries, but could not break their dependence on each other, or the numerous and complicated bonds that link their peoples. It may not last forever; but in the years after the split, the Sudans were palms trees swaying in the same breeze. Sudanese travelled south with their cows; South Sudanese hung on in Khartoum; married couples were separated by the new line on the map. The people often got on better than their leaders. The politicians met frequently to negotiate the numerous issues left outstanding at separation. When the talks went badly, they attempted economic sabotage, before finally fighting an outright war, in April 2012. Since then there has been some gradual improvement, but the threat of mutual self-destruction still flutters in the wind. Sudan and South Sudan's divorce is bitter, and incomplete.

CONCLUSION

Splitting Sudan in two did not resolve its many problems. The period after separation was a bloody one for the rump state and the new country. Both struggled to keep the peace, as new rebellions flared up and inter-ethnic clashes multiplied. It was the problems between the two Sudans that attracted the most attention, however. Khartoum and Juba tried to bring each other down economically, and then clashed on their disputed border. There seemed no way to remove the poisonous thorn from their hearts. Yet the September Agreements, which were signed in 2012, hinted that a more harmonious future was possible, if not altogether likely. A real improvement in the relationship depends on the NCP and the SPLM improving the way they govern their own countries, and changing the way they view each other.

SUDAN

Sudan's crisis of governance is older than the state itself. The pattern of an exploitative centre sucking the resources from the outlying areas was first established during the *Turkiyya*, and continued, with varying levels of intensity, through the *Mahdiyya*, and the Anglo-Egyptian Condominium, and then after Sudan became independent in 1956. Sudan has never been easy to govern, because of its size, poverty, and multitude of different ethnic groups, but a succession of leaders have made a particularly bad job of it. Sudan's people deserve better. Nevertheless, Sudanese society must accept its share of the responsibility: the attitudes of racial and religious superiority that have so damaged the country developed among the people, even if they were then exploited by politicians.

Sudan's history has shown that Khartoum only truly listens to the people of the marginalised periphery when they are carrying guns. Sudan's rebels, even those who took up arms for local reasons, now insist on fundamental change in the centre. SPLM-North's Malik Agar concludes that narrow projects based around Arabism, Islamism or Christianity cannot unite Sudan. He says that the NCP's Islamists must choose: 'do you want an integrated Sudan? Or a disintegrated Sudan?' In the run-up to South Sudan's independence, there was speculation that Darfur could also break away. This seems unlikely: Darfur would struggle to exist as an independent state, and in fact many Darfuris support the government. But Sudan's civil wars are unravelling its coherence as a state. Eastern Sudan could be the next crisis area. Up until late 2013 it remained peaceful, but as one of the most underdeveloped regions of the country, and one in which rebel groups fought Khartoum until 2006, it is being watched very closely.

One of the problems of the many peace processes in Sudan has been the fact that they have been limited to one conflict, rather than addressing all of the country's fundamental governance issues. The DPA and the DDPD dealt only with Darfur. Even the so-called Comprehensive Peace Agreement, which addressed wealth and power-sharing issues, ignored the fighting in Darfur and eastern Sudan, and ultimately did not resolve the problems of South Kordofan and Blue Nile either. The CPA promised a national democratic transformation, but did not achieve this aim. The 28 July 2011 agreement signed by Malik Agar and Nafie Ali Nafie will surely one day serve as a blueprint for peace in South Kordofan, and Blue Nile. It will not, however, solve the problems of Darfur.

The NCP has resisted any broad attempt to address all Sudan's crises in one forum, because this would necessitate serious reform of the centre—and loosen the party's hold on power. Sudan's civil wars will continue, and new ones will erupt, until the country faces up to all its problems. Power and wealth must be shared equally among Sudan's people and regions. Hafiz Mohamed of Justice Africa Sudan correctly states that local institutions should be strengthened, and local politicians must owe their loyalty to their constituents, not Khartoum. A political model which supports religious minorities, while addressing the desires of the Muslim majority, might be the hardest step of all.

Omar al Bashir is not the man to bring about these sort of changes, but he will not be in power forever. His long period in charge has been perhaps the most catastrophic in the country's history: there has not been a single day of peace since he launched his coup in 1989. Bashir will be remembered as the first sitting head of state to be indicted by the ICC, and he presided over South Sudan's secession. To his credit, he allowed the South Sudanese to secede, although the suffocating international pressure contributed to this decision. Separation weakened Bashir considerably. He survived because of a repressive internal security apparatus, the lack of a widely-accepted alternative from the NCP or the opposition, the fact that he is personally more popular than many in the West believe, and, perhaps, because of the stronger support he received from around the region following the Arab Spring.

The president himself has said that he will not run in the 2015 elections (though some doubt his word); internal dissent, in both the party and the military, and the frustrations created by the deteriorating economy suggest a more dramatic exit is always possible. Yet however and whenever Bashir leaves office, Sudan's decades-long crisis will not end unless there is a fundamental shift in the way the country is governed. This is not an abstract concern: millions of Sudanese have been displaced by conflict, and even more live in unnecessary hardship. Hawa Ibrahim, the Darfuri tea lady, has completely given up hope. 'We are people with no aspirations,' she says. 'I just want a quiet life, before I die.' Sudan's leaders have utterly failed their people.

SOUTH SUDAN

In Juba, sunsets never last long. This close to the equator, the disappearance of the gorgeous late afternoon light is extremely sudden. The glow from South Sudan's independence celebrations faded almost as quickly. Within a few weeks, the extent of the challenge facing the government was clear: Pieri was the first warning shot, a day of inter-ethnic slaughter in Jonglei state in which hundreds died. Revenge attacks would kill even more over the next few months. The inter-ethnic fighting, while not a new phenomenon, highlighted both the difficulties of constructing a nation out of so many dissimilar building blocks, and the state's inability to protect its citizens. The people of South Sudan also suffered in less dramatic ways: the lack of hospitals, and schools, and roads, a hangover from Khartoum's neglect, made daily life a struggle. After so many years of war, all this was inevitable, even if it dimmed the joys of independence a little.

The government has made the situation considerably worse. The oil shutdown may have been provoked by Sudan, but it halted development for well over a year, and did not even help Juba obtain a significantly better economic deal with Khartoum. The SPLM's autocratic governing style, its tendency to centralise power, and the widespread human rights abuses, reminded some within the country of the successive Sudanese governments they had fought so hard to escape. In the post-independence period, South Sudan's international image suffered too. When the SPLA rumbled into Heglig in April 2012, South Sudan ate into its credit with countries around the world. The South Sudanese leaders were genuinely surprised to be criticised for what the AU called an illegal occupation of the oilfield, which had been under Sudan's control. As a result, less than a year into its existence South Sudan was threatened with UN sanctions. Night had fallen quickly.

South Sudan is suffering from the 'liberation curse' diagnosed by the SPLM's own Luka Biong. The character of a liberation movement, which must fight against those in power and crush any signs of its own frailty, is very different from the responsive, collaborative qualities needed to govern a state. South Sudan owes a debt to the liberation heroes. It is paying it in full. The rebels are now in charge, and will be for the foreseeable future. 'Where were you when we were fighting?' is the refrain, as the writer Victor Lugala puts it. Too many of the former fighters see the resources of the state as their reward for the long years in the bush. The pervasive corruption has begun to erode the bond between the leaders and the people.

Independence has yet to bring the benefits millions hoped for. The most senior members of the SPLM realise that the South Sudanese are upset with the slow pace of development. My regular source, The Minister, says that 'there has to be a change' in the way South Sudan is run. He is concerned that this is most likely to come through violent means, because there is no real democracy. The Minister believes that any uprising or coup would almost certainly be driven by ethnic alliances: 'since there are no ways except the tribal channel, it will take that line.'

President Salva Kiir's July 2013 decision to sack Vice President Riek Machar, and the rest of the cabinet, highlighted the fragility of the state. The episode reminded the South Sudanese of one of the lowest points of their struggle against Khartoum, the 1991 split in the SPLA in which Riek broke away from Garang. This divided the rebellion along ethnic lines, with the Nuer largely following Riek, and the Dinka sticking with Garang. Many thousands of civilians died when these elephants clashed.

CONCLUSION

In 2013, Salva and Riek's power struggle stoked fears that history might repeat itself.

The period after separation was always going to be difficult. With time, the SPLM may well adapt to the new challenges it faces. Mary Boyoi is one of many who point out that independence is still a blessing. Despite the deaths of several of her relatives in the Jonglei inter-ethnic clashes, she believes that secession was the best thing for her and her compatriots. 'We will find a way to live together,' she says. Alfred Lokuji, the Juba University professor, agrees. 'It's not about whether in a year or five years we will all have three bed apartments in high-rises all over the villages,' Lokuji argues. 'That is not the basis of the joy. The basis is we are finally, incredibly, rid of Khartoum.'

Nevertheless, South Sudan needs better governance; freedom will not be enough for ever. 'We need a generational change,' the economist Peter Biar Ajak says. 'We need the liberation generation to give way to a developmental generation.'

THE SUDANS

The decades of hostility between northern and southern Sudan did not end when they were formally separated: the animosity goes far too deep for that. Too many politicians on both sides still dream of bringing down their old enemies over the border. Sometimes the resulting conflict in the period after separation has been economic; at one key moment it was outright war. In addition to this, Sudanese aircraft frequently carried out air raids on South Sudanese territory, and both Khartoum and Juba supported the rebels of the other country. If Sudan and South Sudan make peace, it will be much easier to resolve the countries' internal wars.

The September Agreements were a rare positive step, even if they were not implemented straight away. The end of the oil shutdown, which was a consequence of one of the September deals, gives some hope that the economies of both countries will be able to recover from the disastrous post-separation period, and that, in time, solutions can be found for the many outstanding political disputes. Yet the absence of trust between the politicians leaves both sides vulnerable, as Bashir's June 2013 threat to shut down the pipelines again highlighted. All the same, the September Agreements were a much-needed foundation for a new relationship.

The reason for this apparent détente? Khartoum and Juba both realised that the economic crisis provoked by the shutdown would not cause the other state to collapse. The Sudanese economy had suffered after losing so much oil revenue, but it was much more robust than Juba had believed. The 'Sudan Revolts' protests in mid-2012, which were provoked by the deteriorating economic situation, were nowhere near large enough to threaten the NCP's hold on power. The international efforts to support South Sudan, culminating in the donors' forum in Washington in April 2013, convinced Khartoum that America, in particular, would not let its protégé implode. Given those circumstances, both Sudan and South Sudan decided it was better to improve their relationship, get the oil flowing again, and begin rebuilding their economies.

Dramatic changes in international relations do happen from time to time, as Sudan's overnight rapprochement with Chad in 2010 demonstrates. As long as the oil flows, both Sudans have obvious financial reasons to get along, and the longer this lasts the more mutual trust could grow. Politicians on both sides could decide to emphasise the smiling, back-slapping part of their relationship, which is sometimes on show during the negotiations, rather than the outright hostility that the elites of both countries often display when they are not in the same room. When Salva named a new cabinet in July 2013, he removed some of the ministers who were most hostile to Khartoum, and included Riek Gai, the former head of the NCP in South Sudan, and Abdallah Deng Nhial, who worked with Bashir and then Turabi for years.[1] Sudan saw this as an encouraging sign.

Nevertheless, it would be no surprise if Sudan and South Sudan did not live up to their better intentions. A money-making pact about oil and trade does not, in itself, make it any more likely that the two countries will be able to agree about Abyei, or the exact location of the border. These issues, which were unresolved as this book went to press, could easily raise the temperature between the two Sudans. A return to war, of some sort, remains a possibility. Both political elites will need to accept almost unimaginable changes if they are to make a lasting peace with the other, and inside their own borders. Yet both countries would be considerably better off, economically, politically and socially, if they found a way to put the past behind them. Here, too, a new generation of politicians may be needed.

CONCLUSION

THE WAY FORWARD

In numerous parts of the South Sudanese countryside, murram roads push through the bush, their burnt orange colour standing out from the surrounding greenery. The effects of the rains and heavy lorries on these uneven surfaces make the potholes seem larger than the road. Finding a solution to the problems of the Sudans is a little like this: the route is clear enough to see, but it is a difficult one to drive down. Sudan must respect the diversity of its peoples, and political rights and economic growth should benefit all, not just those in the heartland. Sudanese society needs to overcome its racism. South Sudan has to stop its march in Sudan's dirty footsteps, and Juba should spread wealth and power as it has promised to do. The politicians must put the nation before their own personal ambitions. The South Sudanese need to coalesce into an inclusive nation, rather than a collection of very different ethnic groups. Both countries must cut any contact with the other's rebels, and both should pay more attention to their border populations, who bear the brunt of any tension. Neither of the Sudans can prosper if the dominant narrative is one of hostility to the other.

AFTERWORD

On 22 September 2013, President Omar al Bashir announced the removal of more subsidies. Fuel jumped from 12 SDG per gallon to 21 SDG, and the price of many other basic goods rose too. Protests broke out in Wad Madani, and the following day thousands of people took to the streets in Khartoum, Omdurman, Bahri, Nyala and towns all across Sudan. These protestors were the angry and the dispossessed, mixing but not coordinating with the committed opponents of Bashir. 'We felt like we controlled the city!' one demonstrator in Khartoum said.

The economic crisis had produced one of the greatest threats to Bashir's rule in the quarter of a century since he seized power: a tide of anger in the heart of the Three Cities. Then the security forces opened fire. Doctors and human rights groups said over 200 people were killed. For once, the bullets, funerals and wailing relatives were concentrated in the capital, not in the peripheries. For once, the elite were caught up in the chaos. Salah Sanhouri, a young pharmacist, was among those who were shot dead. The Sanhouris are a well-known and well-off Khartoum family. They were still struggling to cope with their loss when I visited them, a couple of weeks after Salah's funeral. As Salah's sister choked back tears, Salah's uncle, El Shiekh, made a plea that has echoed vainly through Sudan's history: 'We need justice. I am not just talking about Salah—there are hundreds of Salahs', he told me.

Mustafa Khogali, the Khartoum businessman, witnessed some of the protests. 'The sheer force they were met with was horrendous', he said. Mustafa had voted for the NCP in the 2010 elections, though not with any real enthusiasm. Never again, he swore. The violence in the Tri-City affected him, and many others, in a way the fighting in Darfur, South Kordofan or Blue Nile had not. 'There's a big difference between hearing about it and seeing it,' he said. 'This really hit home. Everyone has a relative or friend' who was caught up in it.

In the short term, the crackdown in the capital worked: the protests stopped. The political repercussions continued. The Islamist intellectual, Ghazi Salaheddin, and thirty other prominent NCP members quit to form their own party. They said that they were outraged at the treatment of the protesters. Bashir's long term opponents wondered where their moral scruples had been when civilians in Darfur and the Two Areas were under attack.

After a period of consolidation, Bashir announced a major reshuffle, on 8 December. Out went Ali Osman Taha as first vice president, replaced by Bashir's faithful military companion, Bakri Hassan Salih. Nafie Ali Nafie was removed as presidential assistant too, in favour of Ibrahim Ghandour. Bashir had sidelined the main pretenders to his position. The politicians now close to the centre of power, like Ghandour, are not seen as a threat to the president in the way Taha or Nafie were. By appointing Bakri as his deputy, and keeping Abdel Rahim as minister of defence, Bashir confirmed the victory of the military faction over the Islamists and the securocrats. The president also knows that even if he steps down at the 2015 elections, Bakri or whoever is chosen to replace him would be unlikely to hand him over to the ICC.

As Bashir shuffled the deck in Sudan, political tensions in South Sudan were building to a climax. On 6 December 2013, Riek Machar, Pa'gan Amum, Rebecca Nyandeng, Deng Alor and several other senior SPLM figures held a press conference in the SPLM House in Juba. They accused Salva of 'dictatorial tendencies', and of taking almost every decision under the influence of 'regional and ethnic lobbies and close business associates.'[1] The SPLM heavyweights also accused Salva of sidelining SPLM leaders who had been active in the liberation struggle in favour of politicians with close links to Khartoum. Local media were warned by security officers not to report the remarks.

Just over a week later, a much-delayed National Liberation Council meeting was held. Riek and his somewhat unlikely political allies tried to push through legislation on secret ballots, which they felt would make it easier to vote against Salva's leadership at the forthcoming National Convention. They were defeated. Several of them did not attend the second day of the meeting, on 15 December.[2] That evening, heavy shooting broke out in Juba. Presidential guard members loyal to Salva clashed with those who supported Riek. As the fighting intensified, Riek's house in Juba came under siege. The reinforced metal door of his compound buckled. He fled the capital, though many of his bodyguards were apparently killed.

The following day, Salva addressed the nation live on state media. He had swapped his suit and cowboy hat for military fatigues. Salva told the nation that 'soldiers allied to the former Vice-President Dr Riek Machar Teny and his group' had attacked the SPLA general headquarters near Juba University, in an attempt to overthrow him. Subsequently, Pa'gan, Deng Alor, Majak D'Agoot and many of the leaders who had given the 6 December press conference were arrested. The eleven detainees rejected the accusation. They said that Salva was using the fighting as an excuse to get rid of the main dissenters within the SPLM. Peter Adwok Nyaba, the former minister, wrote that an attempt was made to disarm the presidential guard members from Riek's Nuer ethnic group, while allowing the Dinka (who were loyal to their kinsman Salva) to keep their weapons.[3] The full story will undoubtedly take some time to emerge. In the early days, however, Salva's version of events did not convince many people outside of the country. The US assistant secretary for African affairs said that 'We've not seen any evidence that this was a coup attempt'.[4]

Salva's forces retained control of Juba. Shortly afterwards, however, the fighting began to spread, as SPLA units elsewhere in the country defected, and swore allegiance to Riek. Peter Gadet, the serial turncoat, abandoned the army again, and took control of Bor, the capital of Jonglei state. The town changed hands three times in the next month, at the cost of hundreds (and possibly thousands) of lives. James Koang grabbed Bentiu, and declared himself the military governor of Unity state and its oilfields. He said he was loyal to Riek, and the former Unity state governor Taban Deng. Riek, Taban, Gadet and Koang are all Nuer. Other largely Nuer troops fought loyalists for control of Malakal, in oil-rich Upper Nile state. I spoke to Riek, who was hiding in an undisclosed location 'in the bush', over a satellite phone. There had been no coup attempt, he insisted, but he was now forced to fight against the government. Less than two and a half years after independence, South Sudan had sunk into civil war.

The new country's worst fears had been realised. The political tensions between the president and his former vice president, the growing dissatisfaction with South Sudan's direction and the militarised and ethnically divided society had all combined to plunge the new country into conflict.

In a camp for the newly displaced, I saw a familiar face. I had interviewed David in Khartoum, before separation, as he prepared to make his way to South Sudan for independence. Several months later, I saw him again in Juba. He hadn't been able to find a job, and his frustration was growing, but his joy about South Sudan's birth still shone brightly. Now, with the death toll mounting and new battles breaking out every day, David was in despair. He had fled to the camp, leaving everything he owned behind, convinced that his life was in danger.

The trigger of this conflict was a political crisis, with protagonists from many communities, but the fighting quickly exacerbated ethnic tensions. Nuer soldiers and their families were killed in Juba by Salva's troops at the very outset of the crisis. More than 20,000 people sought refuge in two UN bases, almost all Nuer. David was one of them. 'It is because we are from the same tribe as Riek', one Nuer man told me. 'They want to kill us.' Human Rights Watch researchers 'documented widespread killings of Nuer men by members of South Sudanese armed forces in Juba, especially between December 15 and 19, including a massacre of between 200 and 300 men in the Gudele neighborhood on December 16.'[5]

Elsewhere in the country, Nuer soldiers and civilians targeted Dinka, apparently in revenge for what had happened in Juba. Dinka workers were killed in the oilfields of Unity state, and Dinka soldiers near Bentiu. In Bor, rebels allegedly killed patients in the main hospital, and many other Dinka civilians in the town and the surrounding area.[6] Human Rights Watch saw 'scores of bodies and fresh graves' in Bor, among them many women and children.[7] For many, this felt like a gruesome re-run of the 1991 Bor massacre, which was carried out by largely Nuer troops apparently under Riek's command. This time, at least 80,000 terrified Dinka fled over the river to Awerial, where a makeshift camp grew into the size of a small town. Both sides committed terrible abuses, very often against civilians.

This is not, as it has sometimes been described, an ethnic war. When the fighting broke out, many Nuer remained loyal to Salva, including SPLA Chief of Staff James Hoth Mai, and Foreign Minister Barnaba Marial. Bapiny Monytuil's largely Nuer SSLA, the former rebels who had recently accepted Salva's amnesty offer, stayed loyal to the president and fought against the new rebellion. Deng Alor and Majak D'Agoot were among the Dinka politicians initially accused of trying to overthrow Salva. Yet the ethnic fractures so evident in South Sudanese society could not be completely escaped either. Most of the soldiers who defected to join Riek in the early days of the war were Nuer. Riek told me that the White Army, the militia from the Lou and Gawaar Nuer subgroups which had been fighting the Murle, was now 'part of' his forces. White Army members joined Peter Gadet's mutineers to retake Bor from the government at the very end of December 2013, and took part in the fighting in Malakal. The government mobilised troops from communities it considered loyal. The fighting deepened already existing ethnic tensions, exploding the fragile cohesion of the South Sudanese nation. Even many of those not involved in the fighting joined in, keyboard warriors who spewed hostility at each other over the internet.

South Sudan's neighbours quickly got involved. Uganda's President, Yoweri Museveni, sent troops to South Sudan, ostensibly to protect key infrastructure and Ugandan civilians. He also threatened to 'defeat' the rebels militarily if they did not come to the negotiating table. He said he was speaking on behalf of the regional body the Intergovernmental Authority on Development (IGAD), although of all the regional leaders Museveni was by far the most prominent in his support for Salva. When Salva's forces retook Bor from the rebels for the second time, on 18 January 2014, they were helped by Ugandan troops. Museveni himself acknowledged that his forces were involved in the fighting.[8] Riek told me he was dismayed at Museveni's 'interference' in South Sudan's affairs, and asked the international community to 'restrain' him. His pleas had little effect. Right from the beginning of the crisis, IGAD, and Barack Obama, made it clear they would not recognise anyone who came to power in South Sudan by force.

Faced with this international pressure, Riek sent a delegation to Addis Ababa for talks, which began in early January 2014. The negotiations were brokered by IGAD, with the backing of the AU and Western countries, and in particular the US. Salva named a large negotiating team designed to show he represented all South Sudanese. It was led by the former foreign minister, Nhial Deng, and included ministers, generals, a judge and even the opposition leader Lam Akol. Riek's chief negotiator was Taban Deng. Riek had initially attempted to name Rebecca Nyandeng, John Garang's widow, to lead his team. She had become a fierce critic of Salva. However she refused the post. Her son, Mabior Garang, did join Riek's delegation, to the fury of many of his fellow Dinka Bor.

Riek would not accept a cessation of hostilities before the talks began, arguing that a verification mechanism would need to be set up first. He also demanded the release of the eleven political leaders, who were still detained in Juba. Salva said they would have to face justice first. Both sides had their bargaining chips clearly marked out. Salva was strengthened by the Ugandan military support. On the day I interviewed him, in late December, Salva appeared confident, and unwilling to compromise. He told me a political solution was possible, but he would not consider power-sharing: 'it is not an option', he said. 'If you want power, you do not rebel.'

On the battlefield, the tide began to turn against Riek. His troops were unable to hold onto Bentiu, pulling out before the SPLA loyalists arrived on 10 January. Eight days later, the SPLA and the Ugandans took control of Bor again. Shortly afterwards, Riek's rebels were pushed out of Malakal. At the beginning of the war, Riek had taken three state capitals. Now his troops were left without a single major town. This was not a total defeat: as the SPLA itself had shown in the long war with Khartoum, a rebel movement can prosper by controlling rural areas; but it was a damaging blow. The government got one more piece of good news in January. David Yau Yau, the Murle rebel leader who had been fighting the SPLA since April 2012, long before the Riek-Salva confrontation, agreed to stop fighting and talk. Paride Taban's prolonged peace-making efforts appeared to have paid off.

On 23 January 2014, after nearly three weeks of negotiations in Addis Ababa, Salva and Riek's delegations signed a cessation of hostilities. The agreement called for both sides to stop fighting. Over three quarters of a million people had been displaced,[9] often to areas where it was too dangerous or too remote to bring in aid. The agreement required both sides to allow humanitarian access, and to withdraw 'allied forces' from the battlefield. The latter was a response to the rebels' demand that the Ugandan troops should leave South Sudan, although not one that completely satisfied them.

The chief negotiators, Nhial Deng and Taban Deng, also signed a statement on the eleven detainees, Riek's political allies. However, this did not commit Salva to release the men. Nevertheless, on 28 January the justice minister announced that seven of the detainees would be set free, and sent to Kenya, although it was suggested that they could be brought back if new evidence against them came to light. The four remaining prisoners, Pa'gan Amum, Majak D'Agoot, Oyai Deng and Ezekiel Gatkuoth, were accused of 'treason', alongside Machar, Taban Deng and the former minister Alfred Ladu Gore, who were at large. The US and others publicly called for the remaining detainees to be released.

Despite the cessation of hostilities agreement, the fighting rumbled on. There were clashes in Jonglei, Upper Nile and Unity, the three areas where the rebels had their strongest presence. Both sides accused the other of carrying out attacks. On 1 February, more than a week after the agreement came into effect, government troops swept through Leer, Riek Machar's home town. Staff at the MSF hospital had already fled into the bush, taking the most ill patients with them. The rebels said the government soldiers had 'burnt down the whole of Leer town', simply because Riek was from there.[10] The little shoots of peace and development the cow herder Gatgong Jiech had praised after the CPA had been trampled into the dirt. It was the same in many other places in South Sudan: Bor, Bentiu and Malakal were all disfigured horribly by the fighting.

Signing the initial agreements set the stage for talks on a broader political settlement, which were due to begin shortly after this book went to press. The talks were threatened by the treason charges against the four detainees, and the continuing fighting.

In the end, both Salva and Riek will have to compromise. Some sort of agreement between the warring parties would not be enough, however, to restore harmony. The political detainees, many of whom are not Riek's natural allies, represent a potential third force, and their views will need to be taken into account. The deeper political failings will have to be addressed, as will the preponderant role the military plays in South Sudanese society. The crisis underlined how the SPLA was more a collection of militias, each with its own loyalties, than a coherent army. This was one of the consequences of Salva's Big Tent strategy. Many South Sudanese called for a genuine process of national reconciliation, to examine the fresh wounds created by this conflict and the scars of the past. Perhaps most importantly of all, the South Sudanese will have to defuse the ethnic and community tensions that were made worse by the fighting. Diverse and divided communities will have to build a real nation. This will take time, and effort, but is indispensable if South Sudan is to have a harmonious future.

On 6 January, Omar al Bashir flew to Juba. The old enemy came, he said, as a friend. He had fought against Salva Kiir, and worked alongside him; he had supported Riek Machar, when he broke away from the SPLA in 1991. He knew both men well, he pointed out. On this occasion, Bashir threw his weight behind the South Sudanese president. The improvement in the relationship between Juba and Khartoum over the previous few months must have been uppermost in his mind. Sudan needs South Sudan's oil to keep flowing, to keep its own economy ticking over. Bashir surely hoped South Sudan would cut any ties to the SRF in return for his backing. Yet many people in South Sudan are sceptical about Bashir's intentions. 'Riek might get support from Bashir again', The Minister told me. The turmoil in South Sudan is just the latest test of the relationship between the Sudans, and one more proof of their shared destinies, even after separation. Peace in both countries seems a long way off.

London   *2 February 2014*

NOTES

INTRODUCTION

1. They would describe themselves as nationalists.
2. It appears that the term 'Sudan' was first widely used, at least within the country, during the Anglo-Egyptian period.
3. After the revolution, Egypt's new rulers believed the only way for Sudan to escape from British rule was for Egypt to give up its own claim. This hastened the end of the Anglo-Egyptian Condominium. One of the leaders of the Egyptian revolution, Mohamed Naguib, had been born in Khartoum, to a Sudanese mother. He became Egypt's first president. There is a major street in the Amarat neighbourhood of Khartoum named after him.
4. Some in both Sudans put the start of the first civil war as 1963, when rebels began to take to the bush in large numbers. But it is more common to give the start date as 1955, when the Torit mutiny was brutally put down, even if the following few years were relatively quiet. For more see Poggo, Scopas, *The First Sudanese Civil War: Africans, Arabs, and Israelis in the Southern Sudan, 1955–1972*, New York: Palgrave Macmillan, 2009.
5. For a fuller discussion of this paradox, see LeRiche, Matthew and Matthew Arnold, *South Sudan: From Revolution to Independence*, London: Hurst, 2012.
6. When Nimeiri made this speech, Eritrea had not yet seceded, so he mentioned eight neighbouring countries.
7. Quoted in a speech by the former South African President, Thabo Mbeki, in Khartoum on 5 Jan. 2011 four days before the referendum on southern Sudan's future.
8. The politician was Tayyeb Mustafa, the uncle of the Sudanese President Omar al Bashir, and the leader of a hardline political party, the Just Peace Forum.

1. PEOPLE AND IDENTITY

1. 'Sudan: Dreams, Ghosts, Nightmares', *The Guardian*, 15 May 1998. Quoted in Scroggins, Deborah, *Emma's War: Love, Betrayal and Death in the Sudan*, London: HarperCollins, 2004, p. 79.
2. Ryle, John, 'Peoples and Cultures of the Two Sudans', in Ryle, John, Justin Willis, Suliman Baldo and Jok Madut Jok, *The Sudan Handbook*, London: James Currey, 2011, p. 31.
3. Actually the phrase often used to describe the South Sudanese is 'Christians and animists'. Even though scholars have pointed out that animism does not accurately describe South Sudanese indigenous religions, the wording became a convenient media shorthand to describe the underlying reasons for the conflict.
4. Collins, Robert O., *A History of Modern Sudan*, Cambridge: Cambridge University Press, 2008, p. 41.
5. Assher, Ben, *A Nomad in the South Sudan: the Travels of a Political Officer Among the Gaweir Nuers*, London: H. F. & G. Witherby, 1928, pp. 9–10.

6. Ministry of Information, *Sudan: The Land of Opportunities Facts and Figures*, Khartoum: Ministry of Information, 2011, p. 14.

7. Confidential conversation with a Sudanese church leader in Khartoum.

8. James, Wendy, 'Religious Practice and Belief', in Ryle, Willis, Baldo and Jok, op. cit., p. 46.

9. Other brotherhoods, like the Khatmiyya and the Ansar, have played a great role in Sudanese politics; the Khatmiyya form the base of the Democratic Unionist Party, and the Ansar, the followers of the Mahdi and his successors, are the main constituency for the National Umma Party. The two parties, in slightly different guises, took Sudan to independence in 1956, and have kept a central role in Sudanese political life ever since. However Sheikh Yagout, following a warning from one of his aides, decided he did not want to discuss anything more than his spiritual and social role.

10. On 5 Nov. 2012, police intervention was required after Salafists fought with Sufis who were celebrating the birthday of the Prophet Mohamed. This is considered heretical by Salafists. See 'Salafists vs. Sufis: A Simmering Conflict in Sudan', *Al Akhbar*, http://english.al-akhbar.com/node/5193 accessed on 15 March 2013.

11. Often ethnic groups are described as 'tribes', and their clashes as 'tribalism', but I will avoid this in this book. 'Tribe' is a contentious word which is particularly used to describe Africans and other people from the developing world, often with a sub-text, subconscious or not, of savagery or lack of civilisation. A political analysis of Scotland's differences from England hardly ever describes the 'Scottish tribe' or tribes; and the conflict in the Balkans was not referred to as a 'tribal war'.

12. Fadl Hasan, Yusuf, *The Arabs and the Sudan*, Khartoum: Sudatek Limited, 2010, p. 146.

13. Fadl Hasan, ibid., pp. 145–54.

14. Alafif Mukhtar, Albaqir, 'Beyond Darfur: Identity and Conflict in Sudan', available on the website of the Al Khatim Adlan Centre for Enlightenment and Human Development, http://kacesudan.org/articles/byenddarfur.pdf accessed on 17 Jan. 2013.

15. The authors of the Black Book define the northern region as the Northern and River Nile states, two of the twenty-five Sudanese states that existed before separation. In most cabinets northerners were in a majority, even though their region only accounts for around 5% of the population. 'The Black Book: Imbalance of Power and Wealth in Sudan', in Osman el Tom, Abdullahi, *Darfur, JEM and the Khalil Ibrahim Story*, Trenton: Red Sea Press, 2011.

16. In 2005, the former finance minister, Abdel Rahim Hamdi, called for public funding to be concentrated in what became known as 'the Hamdi Triangle', based on the axis of Dongola, Sinnar and Kordofan. This meant giving the priority to the central, Arab areas, at the expense of the periphery. Hamdi wrote in a paper he presented at the NCP conference that 'What is required at the present relates to how to keep the identity of the nation [Islam and Arabism] rather than to how to keep the structure of the state'. In fact the broad lines of this policy were already being applied. For more see 'Sudan: Preventing Implosion', International Crisis Group, Africa Briefing N°68, 17 Dec. 2009, p. 9.

17. Ryle, op. cit., p. 33.

18. The people known collectively as the Nuba are actually numerous distinct groups brought together by a similar geographical location, history and culture rather than a common language or ethnicity.

19. Ryle, op. cit., p. 36.

20. This is not set in stone. The northern Nuba are more likely to speak Arabic in the home, while those south of Kauda tend to speak their Nuban language, according to Al Nour Burtail.

21. This comes from a 2012 assessment of Sudan's progress towards the Millenium Development Goals. It is available at 'Status of MDGs in Sudan in 2012', UNDP, http://www.sd.undp.org/mdg_fact.htm accessed on 15 March 2013.

22. The law is very vague, and could apply to men as well as women. In practice, though, it is only women who are punished.

23. This is common in both Sudans. In addition, lots of people, who do not know their precise date of birth, were given 1 January when they applied for identity documents.

24. Aboulela, Leila, 'Cosmopolitans and Close' in McKulka, Tim, *We'll Make our Homes Here: Sudan at the Referendum*, Khartoum: UNMISS, 2011, p. 29.
25. This is because of Mustafa's ethnicity, but also his educational background. However, the group he comes from, the Jaaliyin, have found it easier to get a good education, and find a well-paying job, than people from the Fur, like Hawa. Gender clearly plays a role in Mustafa's head-start, too.
26. Alafif, op. cit., pp. 19–20.
27. Alafif, ibid., p. 6.
28. Nevertheless, the northern elite, Alafif writes, even have an expression for their tactic of recruiting black Africans into the army or the state-sponsored militias to fight rebels, who are usually other black Africans: *aktul al-'Abid bil-'abid*, 'kill the slave by the slave.' Alafif, ibid., p. 25.
29. Alafif, ibid., p. 51.
30. Shurkian, Dr Omer M., 'The Dynamics of Identification in the Nuba Culture', available at http://www.sudantribune.com/spip.php?article44484 accessed on 18 Jan. 2013.
31. Nagwa believes the fact some Sudanese women use skin-lightening creams reveals an unhealthy perspective on race. This was echoed by a Sudanese blogger in a 'rant' that stirred up the Sudanese blogosphere: 'I'm Black, and So Are You [Rant #2]', http://b45.tumblr.com/post/39829947575/im-black accessed on 18 Jan. 2013.
32. This is an extract from the full poem. I first read the poem on the wall of the SPLM leader in Kauda, Younan al Baroud. The poem had been written out beautifully, framed, and was then displayed in Younan's office. I copied out the poem.
33. This definition comes from Mohamed Haroun Kafi, a Nuba politician, intellectual and writer. Quoted in Shurkian, op. cit., p. 13.
34. Nagwa went to Ahfad in 1997, as part of the first generation of Nuba women to attend this university. However, her scholarship actually came from the wife of the then British ambassador, rather than Gassim Badri.
35. Willis, Justin, Omer Egemi and Philip Winter, 'Land and Water', in Ryle, Wilis, Baldo and Jok, op. cit., p. 16. Insights from this chapter were drawn upon throughout this paragraph.
36. The political and personal impact of the relationship between the Sudans will be examined fully in the final chapter.
37. According to the 2008 census, 12,910,266 people lived in the ten border states. Subsequently hundreds of thousands of South Sudanese returned to the border areas, mainly from Khartoum. South Sudanese officials also believe the census under-reported their people, so the real number may actually be higher.
38. Diab, Rashid, 'Reflections on Sudan', in McKulka, op. cit., p. 47.
39. Diab and others believe the younger generation of urban Sudanese, a more globalised group, care a lot less about narrow ethnic identities.
40. It is not just in South Sudan: it is worth noting that inter-ethnic clashes occur in Sudan too, in particular in Darfur. In some years more people died in this sort of fighting than in the violence directly linked to the Darfur civil war.
41. Deng, Francis, *War of Visions: Conflict of Identity in the Sudan*, Washington: Brookings Institute, 1995, p. 9.
42. This was stated in an interview in Juba, but in this case the minister did not wish to be named.
43. Interview in November 2011.
44. South Sudan Radio Service, 3 Sep. 2012.
45. Deng, op. cit., p. 4.
46. Sudanese officials, perhaps unsurprisingly, dispute this figure. Amin Hassan Omar, for example, told this author it was a gross exaggeration put about by NGOs and others who disliked the government in Khartoum. Nevertheless the figures are widely accepted, internationally.

47. See, for example, Akol, Lam, *SPLM/A: Inside an African Revolution*, Khartoum: Khartoum University Press, 2009, p. 260.
48. Statistic available at http://www.internal-displacement.org/IDMC_IDP-figures_2001–2010.pdf accessed on 4 April 2013.
49. It is also jokingly said in Juba that men far too young to have fought in the war pretend to be former child soldiers to win over impressionable young female aid workers. They have been satirically nicknamed 'infant soldiers'. 'New Vocabulary for New Republic', New Times, http://newtimes-ss.com/?p=1444 accessed on 11 Jan. 2013.
50. 'Lakes State: Revenge Clashes Leave 25 dead and 30 Wounded', *Sudan Tribune*, http://www.sudantribune.com/spip.php?article45232 accessed on 19 Jan. 2013.
51. This will be covered in detail in chapter 5, Insecurity.
52. Broadly speaking, the southern part went to the Anglicans, the north-west to the Roman Catholics, and the north-east to the American Presbyterians. James, op. cit., p. 48.
53. This is the New International Version, as are all the quotes in this section, unless otherwise stated.
54. The Good News Bible says 'God Will Punish Sudan', while the New International Version's translation is 'Prophecy against Cush'. Cush was suggested as a possible name for the new country, before South Sudan was adopted.
55. Young, John, *The Fate of Sudan: The Origins and Consequences of a Flawed Peace Process*, London: Zed Books, 2012, p. 300.
56. 'Peoples' profiles', *Gurtong*, http://www.gurtong.net/Peoples/PeoplesProfiles/tabid/71/Default.aspx accessed on 1 Dec. 2012.
57. Accessed at the official government of South Sudan website http://goss.org on 6 Dec. 2012.
58. The Joshua Project, which helps evangelical Christians identify possible converts, puts the total at 80 South Sudanese ethnic groups. 'South Sudan–people groups', Joshua Project, http://www.joshuaproject.net/countries.php?rog3=OD accessed on 6 Dec. 2012.
59. Bishop Taban's work at his Kuron Peace Village will be covered in more detail in chapter 5.
60. For a thought-provoking look into this aspect of life among the Nuer, see Hutchinson, Sharon E., *Nuer Dilemmas: Coping with Money, War and the State*, London: University of California Press, 1996.
61. South Sudan is now divided into 10 states. However the idea of the three regions still carries some weight. Sometimes they are referred to as Greater Upper Nile, Greater Bahr el Ghazal and Greater Equatoria, to avoid confusion with states of similar names to the old provinces.
62. Ryle, op. cit., p. 40.
63. 'Shilluk (Chollo)', Gurtong, http://www.gurtong.net/Peoples/PeoplesProfiles/Shillukchollo/tabid/230/Default.aspx accessed on 17 Jan. 2013.
64. 'Nya' is a prefix indicating a female.
65. Hutchinson, op. cit.
66. Hutchinson, ibid., contains a brilliant dissection of the worth of cows and their place in the Nuer's universe of values.
67. Hutchinson, ibid., pp. 348–50.
68. Ryle, op. cit., p. 41.
69. The Azande also live in the neighbouring Central African Republic and Democratic Republic of Congo.
70. See, for example, the Azande profile on the Gurtong website: http://www.gurtong.net/Peoples/PeoplesProfiles/Azande/tabid/179/Default.aspx accessed on 6 Oct. 2013.
71. Ryle, op. cit., p. 41.
72. Ryle, ibid.
73. Willis, Egemi and Winter, op. cit., p. 17.
74. Abuk's own poem was rejected as it was judged to be too 'English' and hard to understand.

2. POLITICS

1. It is usually stated that the first civil war cost an estimated half a million lives, and the second civil war more than two million, though of course exact figures are impossible to establish. The estimate for the second civil war comes from, among others, the United States Committee for Refugees, in 1998, drawing on published reports and many aid agencies working in Sudan. It has become a widely accepted figure, at least in the West and in South Sudan. See, for example, 'Millions Dead in Sudan Civil War', *BBC*, available at http://news.bbc.co.uk/1/hi/world/africa/232803.stm accessed on 15 Sept. 2013.

2. Bashir himself did not sign. Ali Osman Taha, the Vice President, signed on behalf of the Sudanese government, and John Garang signed for the SPLM.

3. Tayyeb has his own party, the Just Peace Forum, but he has a lot in common with the hardline wing of the NCP. Often he is able to publicly voice opinions that Bashir and NCP hardliners feel they are not able to.

4. The state's control of the economy, which brings with it the ability to hand out patronage, is another key factor. This will be addressed in chapter 4, Development.

5. The idea of the Venn diagram is borrowed, with apologies, from John Garang, who used it to dissect different aspects of Sudanese political life.

6. I had extensive conversations with a person who has worked with President Bashir for many years, and he will be quoted at several points in the book. The interviewee did not want to be named.

7. Collins, Robert O., *A History of Modern Sudan*, Cambridge: Cambridge University Press, 2008, p. 187.

8. At one point Bashir was based in Kadugli in what is now South Kordofan, near the border with South Sudan. He also served further south, in Mayom. One South Sudanese military source says he had a particularly good relationship with Paulino Matip, the southern Sudanese general who fought for Khartoum against the SPLA, and later became the SPLA's second in command.

9. Gezira University awarded the president a master's degree in Islamic Sharia Science in 2012. This was reported in several Sudanese newspapers on 26 Aug. 2013, including *Al Ahram al Youm*. Gezira University said Bashir attended classes for three years, and presented a thesis on 'Sharia Implementation Challenges in Contemporary Societies'. However many Sudanese were sceptical.

10. The video can be watched at http://www.youtube.com/watch?v=J—qfZE48zU accessed on 5 Feb. 2013.

11. I once attended the election victory party of a leading NCP official: the men and women sat in different parts of the marquee, and there was no question of them dancing together.

12. 'Carter Center Threatens to Withdraw from Sudan Unless Bashir Apologises Publicly: TV', *Sudan Tribune*, http://sudantribune.com/spip.php?article34670 accessed on 1 Feb. 2013.

13. Confidential interview, 2012.

14. This is according to Mubarak al Fadil al Mahdi, an opposition politician who worked with Bashir in the early 2000s.

15. Collins, op. cit., p. 187.

16. The debate over whether Sudan should be Islamic or secular had raged since before the departure of the British in 1956. Sharia was the basis of the 1958 and 1968 constitutions, but it was never really applied. One head of state, Ibrahim Abboud, pursued an aggressive Islamising and Arabising policy, in part in response to non-Muslim separatists in southern Sudan during the first north-south civil war (1955–72). President Jafaar Nimeiri was the one to introduce sharia, by the so-called September Laws in 1983. Nimeiri had initially pursued left wing policies, and subsequently relied on the support of southern Sudanese after he signed the Addis Ababa agreement with the southern Anyanya rebels in 1972, ending the first Sudanese civil war. Five years later he swung to the right, eventually abrogating Addis Ababa, and introducing sharia. Following Nimeiri's overthrow, Sadig al Mahdi

came to power in elections in 1986. In his three years in power he proved unable, or unwilling, to repeal the September Laws.

17. At Turabi's inaugural Popular Arab and Islamic Congress meeting, the 300 Sudanese and 200 foreign delegates, including from Iran and Hizballah, agreed to establish the 'Armed Islamist Internationale', which has been described as 'an umbrella organization for Sunni Islamist international terrorism.' Collins, op. cit., p. 196.

18. *Season of Migration to the North* was recognised as the 'most important Arabic novel of the 20th century' by the Arab Literary Academy in Damascus.

19. Salih, Tayeb, *Season of Migration to the North*, Portsmouth, NH: Heinemann, 1970, p. 79.

20. 'Obituary: Tayeb Salih', *The Guardian*, http://www.guardian.co.uk/books/2009/feb/20/obituary-tayeb-salih accessed on 24 Jan. 2013.

21. The unions had played key roles in the 1964 and 1985 revolutions that overthrew unpopular presidents, and in many cases they were strongly opposed to the Turabi-Bashir coup, so they were particularly targeted.

22. Collins, op. cit., p. 189. A longer version of the quote gives a fuller idea of the horrors of the period. 'Some were arbitrarily imprisoned; others were held in detention centres, the infamous "Ghost Houses" (*bayt al-ashbah*) [...] that acquired a fearsome reputation for bestial interrogation, torture of every conceivable means, and mock executions, as well as the use of drugs, electric shock, and death. Many Sudanese simply "disappeared," their whereabouts unknown, their deaths unrecorded. Others were publicly flogged for the manufacture, possession, or consumption of alcoholic beverages; others were publicly executed for possession of heroin or undocumented foreign currency.'

23. Bashir's father is from the Bideria, who can be found both near Dongola, and in White Nile state. Usually in Sudan's patrilineal society people are associated with their father's ethnic group, but Bashir is popularly known as a Jaali.

24. All the statistics in this paragraph come from 'The Black Book: Imbalance of Power and Wealth in Sudan', in Osman el Tom, Abdullahi, *Darfur, JEM and the Khalil Ibrahim Story*, Trenton: Red Sea Press, 2011, pp. 234–45. The Black Book was written by Darfuris who subsequently took up arms against the government. Nevertheless, even my source close to Bashir did not dispute the accuracy of the figures.

25. On 12 December, two days before the National Assembly was due to vote on legislation proposed by Turabi aimed at curbing the powers of the presidency, Bashir sent tanks and soldiers to surround the parliament. A state of emergency was imposed, and Turabi was sacked as speaker of the Assembly. Collins, op. cit., pp. 226–7.

26. According to Amin Hassan Omar, a senior politician, by the time of the split the 'majority' of the Islamists had forsaken the previously revered Turabi, because of the gap between his grandiose vision and Sudan's needs.

27. The ideologues appeared to lose their way at this point. Turabi's absence also dimmed their international prestige, particularly in the Muslim world.

28. The University of Khartoum professor, Islamist and frequent contributor to Sudanese newspapers Tayeb Zain al Abdin made this point.

29. Many of the five Brigadiers, seven Colonels, two Lieutenant Colonels and a Major who composed the Revolutionary Command Council in 1989 would retain key roles for the next two decades or more. Two of them, Zubeir Mohamed Salih and Ibrahim Shams el Din, were only removed from the equation when they died in plane crashes, the first in 1998 and the second in 2001.

30. This story was told to the author by Mubarak al Fadil al Mahdi, from his time working closely with Bashir in the early 2000s. He is now an opposition politician.

31. One of the sources was the Sudan expert Alex de Waal, who was working as an adviser to the African Union mediators on Sudan and South Sudan: 'according to my information, the military made a démarche to the leadership including President Bashir, saying they would be informing rather than consulting' them, he said.

32. The group making all the decisions is believed to be composed of Bashir, Hassan Salih,

Abdel Rahim, and sometimes Mohamed Atta, the head of NISS. Occasionally Taha and Nafie Ali Nafie are added to this list.

33. 'Bashir Plans Islamic Law if Sudan Splits, Defends Flogging Woman', *Reuters*, http://blogs. reuters.com/faithworld/2010/12/19/bashir-plans-islamic-law-if-sudan-splits-defends-flogging-woman/ accessed on 21 Jan. 2013. It is not clear what the woman's crime was, though some have suggested she may have been convicted of adultery. The video got so much attention that the American Nobel Prize-winning novelist Toni Morrison published an open letter to the whipped woman, admiring her courage in trying to rise after each blow: 'Each cut tearing your back hurts women all over the world. Each scar you bear is ours as well,' Morrison wrote. Morrison, Toni, 'Dignity and Depravity', *Newsweek*, available at http://www.thedailybeast.com/newsweek/2011/09/18/toni-morrison-on-the-injustice-of-a-public-whipping-in-sudan.html accessed on 1 Feb. 2013.

34. Just before and after separation the two main areas with lots of non-Muslims, South Kordofan and Blue Nile, were both fighting Khartoum, as the Insecurity chapter will explain.

35. According to much Islamist theory, including Turabi's, democracy comes through *shura* or consultations. Turabi, Hassan, *The Islamic Movement in Sudan: Its Development, Approach and Achievements*, Beirut: Arab Scientific Publishers, 2008.

36. One of the memos, which was apparently written by people who had held key roles in the Islamist project, went further: having criticised the government for the secession of South Sudan, the war in Darfur and the declining economy, it called for a civil state. This is a formulation designed to avoid the word secular, without differing much in practice from this previously taboo concept. The veteran Islamist politician, Ghazi Salaheddin, believes Islamists have become less scared of secularism in recent times, having observed the position of Muslims in secular states like Turkey and Canada. 'New Islamists Memo Calls for Civil State in Sudan', *Sudaneseonline.org*, http://sudaneseonline.org/cs/blogs/english/archive/2012/01/27/new-islamists-memo-calls-for-civil-state-in-sudan.aspx accessed on 2 Feb. 2013.

37. The word 'fundamentalist' is often misused in the West when describing Islamist and Islamic groups as a synonym for extremist. This is not the intention here. The Salafists want to follow the exact form of Islam laid down by the Prophet Mohamed during his lifetime. Abu Zaid, wary of how Salafists are often portrayed in the West, insisted at the end of the interview that Salafist did not mean terrorist, even though I had not suggested it did.

38. The point was rammed home when the old soldier Bakri Hassan Salih, who is not known for his theoretical sophistication, was chosen as the deputy secretary general of the Islamic Movement.

39. This joke was originally made by a Western diplomat with an occasional sideline in stand-up comedy, in a performance he gave in Khartoum in 2012.

40. During the three years I was based in Khartoum, I was kicked to the ground by plain-clothes security men at a women's rights protest; punched by a man I suspected to be security at a rally against the UN; and thumped twice with a truncheon by a uniformed policeman outside parliament, as SPLA politicians tried to push their case for a referendum law in 2010.

41. Sudan came 170 out of 179 countries. 'Press Freedom Index 2013', *Reporters Without Borders*, http://en.rsf.org/press-freedom-index-2013,1054.html accessed on 3 Feb. 2013.

42. It can be watched at http://www.youtube.com/watch?v=wsS1P95cDkw accessed on 1 Feb. 2013.

43. A few weeks earlier a leading NCP official, Ibrahim Ghandour, had also been jeered off stage at a rally for Syria at the headquarters of the opposition Umma party.

44. Although they are clearly committing numerous human rights abuses, the security forces are, on balance, less violent than they were in the 1990s. Activists and protestors are usually released after a few days, rather than 'disappeared'. It seems the security forces are wary of making martyrs. This too is an indication of the weakness of the government's position.

45. Boushi's experience is far from unusual, as the US's 2011 human rights report on Sudan makes clear: 'The main human rights abuses during the year included the following: govern-

ment forces and government-aligned groups committed extrajudicial and other unlawful killings; security forces committed torture, beatings, rape, and other cruel and inhumane treatment or punishment; and prison and detention center conditions were harsh and life threatening.' All this was carried out with complete impunity: 'Except in rare cases, the government took no steps to prosecute or punish officials in the security services and elsewhere in the government who committed abuses.' Country Reports on Human Rights Practices for 2011: Sudan', US State department, http://www.state.gov/j/drl/rls/hrrpt/humanrightsreport/index.htm#wrapper accessed on 3 Feb. 2013.

46. The video can be seen at http://www.youtube.com/watch?v=k-34FaFn-d4 accessed on 5 Feb. 2013.

47. At one press conference, a visibly furious Sudanese journalist asked one international observer mission how so many irregularities were considered acceptable now, when Sudan had been able to organise credible elections in 1986, after sixteen years of dictatorship. The poll monitors had no answer. The Carter Centre did say the elections didn't meet international standards, but in his press statements Jimmy Carter himself downplayed the significance of this, to the fury of many of his election observers. John Young was a political adviser to the Carter Centre during the electoral period. His conclusion was damning: 'Democracy was traded off in the elections, just as it was countless times during the peace process interim period, in the interests of political expediency.' Young, op. cit., p. 170.

48. Sadig was prime minister in the 1960s and the 1980s, the DUP has been in power several times, albeit often as part of a coalition, and Turabi was, in effect, in control in the 1990s.

49. Both Sadig and Mirghani are personally very wealthy, but their parties are not. Sadig appears to have less control over Umma than Mirghani over the DUP, but in contrast to the former prime minister Mirghani never seems that interested in politics, focusing more on his spiritual and business interests. Umma's power base traditionally came from the west, and from what is now the south of Sudan, on the border with the new country, though it has lost strength in both areas. The DUP's supporters are often from northern and eastern Sudan.

50. Several hardline Salafist groups, including Ansar al Sunna, have flirted with politics too. Sudan's Sufi brotherhoods are also consulted by the politicians, and in some cases paid off to ensure votes or obedience.

51. Although he initially leaned to the left, Nimeiri destroyed the Communist party in 1971, accusing them of carrying out a failed coup attempt against him. The Communists' leader, Abdel Khalig Mahjoub, and the southern Sudanese communist Joseph Garang, were among those executed. For decades the Communists existed underground, publishing tracts to disseminate their views and meeting in secret. They kept some supporters. The revered singer Mohamed Wardi, who died in 2012, is said to have donated money to the Communist party. Their appeal among young Sudanese has dwindled, and critics say the Communists have never been tested in government. They were also weakened by the 2012 death of Mohamed Ibrahim Nugud, who had led the party since 1971.

52. However, SPLM-North was still very much a military threat, as the Insecurity chapter will explain.

53. Since coming to power in 1989 the NCP had managed to split Umma and the DUP, on several occasions giving the leaders of breakaway factions government posts to create the semblance of consensus. Hardly anyone was fooled.

54. Even several months after the decision was made, DUP members were trying to convince Mirghani to pull out of the coalition. 'DUP's Leader Asked to Exit Sudan's Government', Sudan Tribune, http://www.sudantribune.com/spip.php?article41800 accessed on 2 Feb. 2013.

55. 'Bashir has throat surgery in Qatar, in good health–official', Reuters, http://uk.reuters.com/article/2012/10/21/uk-sudan-bashir-idUKBRE89K07V20121021 accessed on 3 Feb. 2013.

56. According to the NCP's Amin Hassan Omar.

57. Sometimes ethnic divisions are said to play a role: Bashir's mother was from the Jaaliyin, and Taha is Shaigi.

58. 'Shattered Dreams of Ali Osman Taha', www.sudaneseonline.com, http://www.sudane-seonline.com/cgi-bin/esdb/2bb.cgi?seq=msg&board=12&msg=1248216044&rn=1 accessed on 10 Feb. 2013.

59. This will be examined in more detail in the chapter on Insecurity, chapter 5.

60. Gosh was demoted to presidential adviser for security affairs, and then apparently further angered the inner circle by holding extensive talks with the opposition. In April 2011 he was removed from his advisory role.

61. 'Sudanese Government Determined to Prosecute "the Plotters"', *Sudan Tribune*, http://www.sudantribune.com/spip.php?article44696 accessed on 3 Feb. 2013.

62. After some time in prison, Gosh was released, to a rapturous welcome in his home village to the north of Khartoum, and a more muted reception elsewhere in the country.

63. On his way to southern Sudan Mustafa caught malaria. Once he got back to Khartoum, his appalled family intervened, and sent him off to America.

64. The complex is called Bilpam, after the place in Ethiopia where many of the SPLA were based at the beginning of their rebellion.

65. For more on this see Johnson, Douglas H., *The Root Causes of Sudan's Civil Wars*, Oxford: James Currey, 2007 and Poggo, Scopas S., *The First Sudanese Civil War: Africans Arabs and Israelis in the Southern Sudan, 1955–1972*, New York: Palgrave Macmillan, 2009.

66. 'S. Sudan Defends Removal of over 100 Senior Military Officers from Active Service', *Sudan Tribune*, available at http://www.sudantribune.com/spip.php?article45558, accessed on 14 Apr. 2013.

67. 'The "Curse" of Liberation', *Sudan Tribune*, http://www.sudantribune.com/spip.php?article45547 accessed on 3 Apr. 2013.

68. Jok himself was beaten up by SPLA soldiers preparing for the arrival of the president at the airport in Wau, even though he is a senior official in the Ministry of Culture. 'Dr. Jok Madut Tortured: "My Encounter with Evil in Wau"', Gurtong, http://www.gurtong.net/ECM/Editorial/tabid/124/ctl/ArticleView/mid/519/articleId/6272/Dr-Jok-Madut-Tortured-My-Encounter-with-Evil-in-Wau.aspx accessed on 7 Feb. 2013.

69. This was the Auditor General, Steven Wondu.

70. 'South Sudan Shoot-out at Unity State Peace Talks', BBC, http://www.bbc.co.uk/news/world-africa-16873273 accessed on 9 Feb. 2013.

71. Corruption will be discussed in full in chapter 4.

72. For more on this see Young, op. cit.

73. The SPLM pulled out of elections in most areas in northern Sudan, and the NCP did not run against Salva Kiir for president of (then) southern Sudan. Neither side complained too much about the alleged rigging carried out by the other, in contrast to what would have been expected. Both parties ended up in complete control of their respective areas, preparing the ground for separation. However, both the SPLM and NCP have denied the existence of any such pact.

74. Lam was previously one of the leaders, with Riek Machar, of the great split in 1991 that almost derailed the entire rebellion, before coming back into the fold. He was never fully trusted again by the SPLM leaders, despite being given senior positions like minister of foreign affairs in the federal government in Khartoum. In 2009 he broke away again to form an opposition party, SPLM-Democratic Change.

75. Young, op. cit., p. 174.

76. Lam doesn't always help himself: spending time in Khartoum confirms many South Sudanese suspicions, and when he was in the Government of National Unity (GoNU) on behalf of the SPLM (before he founded his own party) he was accused of following the NCP line.

77. If Garang had adopted a separatist position at the start of the rebellion he would have alienated Ethiopia, a key supporter, which had its own problems with separatist regions. For all his talk of reforming Sudan, Garang was clear that if this did not happen, secession would be the best option for the south.

78. In March 2001 Salva told John Young that his position was that 'if we capture Juba today we will declare the independence of southern Sudan tomorrow.' Young, op. cit., p. 191.

79. Constitution of the Sudan People's Liberation Movement, 2008, p. 2. Available at http://www.splmtoday.com/docs/SPLM%20docs/2008%20The%20Constitution%20of%20the%20SPLM.pdf accessed on 7 Feb. 2013.

80. SPLM, ibid., p. 2.

81. 'Sudan: Civil War and Famine', *ITN*. The transcript can be read at http://www.itnsource.com/shotlist/ITN/1992/02/27/T27029213/?s=* accessed on 11 Apr. 2013.

82. Amnesty International estimated that 2,000 civilians were killed. 'Sudan: A continuing human rights crisis', Amnesty International, AFR 54/03/92, 15 April 15 1992, p. 17. The Bor community believes the real death toll was much higher.

83. The notes of the meeting record Salva saying, 'There is no code of conduct to guide the Movement's structures. When the Chairman leaves for abroad, no directives are left and no one is left to act on his behalf. I don't know with whom the Movement is left with; or does he carry it in his own brief case?' See the *Sudan Tribune* website at http://www.sudantribune.com/spip.php?article26320 accessed on 3 Apr. 2013.

84. The Senegalese intellectual and novelist Boubacar Boris Diop points out, rightly, that 'good governance' is a phrase usually used only with developing world countries. 'Who talks about good governance in Belgium?' he says, despite the chronic political failures there. Nevertheless 'good governance' regularly crops up in conversations by South Sudanese and foreigners working in the country. 'Mali: le Regard de Boubacar Boris Diop', www.lesenegalais.net, http://www.lesenegalais.net/index.php/actualites/items/mali-le-regard-de-boubacar-boris-diop.html accessed on 9 Feb. 2013.

85. LeRiche, Matthew and Matthew Arnold, *South Sudan: From Revolution to Independence*, London: Hurst, 2012, p. 154.

86. Article 102 (2) states in full 'If the office of the President of the Republic falls vacant prior to the conduct of the general elections, the post shall be assumed by the Vice President pending the filling of this position, within fourteen days from the date of the occurrence of the vacancy, by a nominee of the political party on whose ticket he or she was elected.'

87. There had been a number of inter-ethnic clashes in the state, which some believe led to Chol's sacking. Nevertheless Lakes state is not nearly as badly affected by inter-ethnic violence as Jonglei state, for example.

88. This was a play on the 'one state two systems' the CPA created during the interim period.

89. 'Profile: Southern Sudan Leader Salva Kiir', BBC, http://www.bbc.co.uk/news/world-africa-12107760 accessed on 9 Feb. 2013.

90. Young, op. cit., p. 14.

91. The Auditor General Steven Wondu points out that there is a precedent to bringing political enemies into the centre of power. When the Addis Ababa agreement was signed in 1972 to end the first north-south Sudanese civil war, the southern Sudanese who had negotiated on behalf of Khartoum, Abel Alier, became the first president of the High Executive Council of Southern Sudan. This is despite the fact that in the eyes of many, and certainly the Anyanya rebels, he represented the interests of Khartoum and not southern Sudan.

92. Interview with Akec Khoc, South Sudan's Ambassador to the US. Khoc is from Garang's area in Jonglei state.

93. Arab militias known as the *Murahaleen* attacked the state on many occasions, burning villages and carrying off young boys and women as slaves.

94. The quote is from the opposition leader Lam Akol, who is otherwise critical of Malong.

95. The Dinka made up around a third of the southern Sudanese in both the 1956 and 1983 censuses. Johnson, op. cit., p. 51.

96. However, as the historian Douglas Johnson has pointed out, this was in part because until then they had been under-represented in government service. Johnson, ibid., p. 52. For a fuller discussion of 'Dinka domination' during this period, see pp. 51–3.

97. Johnson, ibid., p. 67.

98. The former minister Lual Deng makes this point.

99. It took nearly seven weeks to choose the twenty-nine ministers, to the surprise of those

who felt the list could have been decided on before independence, and named shortly after it.

100. Greater Equatoria is composed of Western Equatoria, Central Equatoria and Eastern Equatoria. Greater Bahr el Ghazal includes Western Bahr el Ghazal, Northern Bahr el Ghazal, Warrap and Lakes. Greater Upper Nile is made up of Unity, Upper Nile and Jonglei.

101. 'New RoSS Cabinet Consolidates Unity' was the full headline. *Southern Eye*, 29 Aug– 4 Sept. 2011.

102. Confidential interview, 2013.

103. 'South Sudan: Two Years Old But Nothing to Celebrate', *The Guardian*, 4 July 2013, available at http://www.theguardian.com/world/2013/jul/04/south-sudan-two-years-on accessed on 28 Aug. 2013.

104. 'Survey of South Sudan Public Opinon', International Republican Institute, Juba: 2013.

105. In the interim period the 'joint' north-south security forces were based in this building, which was constructed before separation.

106. The government was also blamed for 'arbitrary arrest and detention, including prolonged pretrial detention; and an inefficient and corrupt judiciary' as well as restricting 'freedoms of privacy, speech, press, assembly, and association.' Those responsible were not brought to justice, the US's report stated. 'The government seldom took steps to punish officials who committed abuses, and impunity was a major problem' the report said. 'Country Reports on Human Rights Practices for 2011: South Sudan', US Department of State, available at http://www.state.gov/j/drl/rls/hrrpt/humanrightsreport/index.htm#wrapper accessed on 10 Feb. 2013.

107. One person who spoke out publicly was Joseph Lagu, who led the Anyanya rebels in the first civil war. Lagu said of the security forces that 'Possibly they are influenced by the behaviour of the security in the north. They should know that we fought against the north because of that behaviour of northern security that they don't have to copy here.' 'Sudan: Fight for the Soul of the South', Al Jazeera, broadcast in July 2011, available at http://www.aljazeera.com/programmes/sudanthebreakup/2011/06/201162311444468410.html accessed on 14 Apr. 2013.

108. 'South Sudan Blogger and Government Critic Killed', Reuters, http://uk.reuters.com/article/2012/12/06/uk-southsudan-blogger-idUKBRE8B50LU20121206 accessed on 10 Feb. 2013.

109. The reaction of a Bor community association was typical: 'We took up arms in rejection of slavery, marginalisation, suppression, systematic killing, injustice, extortions and corruptive system amongst many others. We fought for a country where we will be seen as equal citizens, free to express what one sees not going right. A country where one can sleep without lingering doubt of being dragged out in the dead of night and imprudently killed in the manner Isaiah Abraham was slain helplessly.' 'Greater Bor Petition vis a vis Isaiah Abraham's Heinous Death' available at https://paanluelwel2011.wordpress.com/category/press-release/ accessed on 10 Feb. 2013.

110. 'Capt. Mabior Garang de Mabior: a Call for Fundamental Change in South Sudan', *New Sudan Vision*, http://newsudanvision.com/index.php?option=com_content&view=article &id=2669:capt-mabior-garang-de-mabior-a-call-for-fundamental-change-in-south-sudan&catid=1:sudan-news-stories&Itemid=6 accessed on 10 Feb. 2013. All the quotes in this paragraph from Mabior are from this article.

3. ECONOMY

1. James, Laura, 'From Slaves to Oil', in Ryle, John, Justin Willis, Suliman Baldo and Jok Madut Jok (eds), *The Sudan Handbook*, Woodbridge, Suffolk and Rochester: James Currey, 2011, p. 74.

2. It is difficult to estimate percentages because revenues change every year. These figures were

given to the author by Sabir Mohamed al Hassan, the former Governor of the Central Bank and a key member of Sudan's negotiating team with South Sudan; and Abda Yahia al Mahdi, a former State Minister of Finance. Some reports put the budget gap at 36%. Just before separation the IMF estimated oil accounted for half of government revenue, and 90% of exports. Figures available at http://www.imf.org/external/pubs/ft/scr/2011/cr1186.pdf accessed on 14 Apr. 2013.

3. Figures available on the IMF's website at http://www.imf.org/external/pubs/ft/weo/2012/02/pdf/c2.pdf accessed on 29 Dec. 2012.
4. James, op. cit., p. 71.
5. Collins, Robert O., *A History of Modern Sudan*, Cambridge: Cambridge University Press, 2008, p. 119. There is a long history in Sudan of announcements of 'world-leading' projects, making many people sceptical towards the government's post-separation boasts about sugar factories and gold refineries.
6. Quoted in Young, John, *The Fate of Sudan*, London: Zed Books, 2012, p. 32.
7. See Collins, op. cit., p. 232.
8. The statistics come from Abda Yahia al Mahdi, a former State Minister of Finance.
9. James, op. cit., p. 76.
10. Sabir Mohamed al Hassan, in an interview with the author in Addis Ababa in September 2012.
11. This is after the oil companies had taken the share their contracts entitled them to. The source was Sabir Mohamed al Hassan, in an interview in Khartoum in Oct. 2012.
12. The oil from Block 2, in and around Heglig, is known as Nile Blend, has a low sulphur content, and fetches a good price. It is linked to the export terminal at Port Sudan via a pipeline which was originally constructed by foreign investors. By late 2012, it was 70 per cent owned by the Sudanese government, according to the under-secretary at the ministry of petroleum, Awad al Fateh. From 2006, Sudan has also been producing Fula Blend, from Block 6, just to the north of Heglig, though this is poor quality crude for domestic consumption. It subsequently began pumping some light oil from block 6.
13. This will be covered in more detail in the last chapter, which is about the relationship between the two Sudans.
14. For example, according to the petroleum ministry, on 23 Jan. 2011 Sudan's 1,369 wells, of which 1,156 were active, produced 478,289 barrels of oil. Document in the author's possession.
15. Sabir Mohamed al Hassan.
16. 'Sudan inaugurates new oil field in South Kordufan', *Sudan Vision*, http://news.sudanvisiondaily.com/details.html?rsnpid=217452 and 'Sudan launches oil field in South Kordufan', *Sudan Vision*, http://news.sudanvisiondaily.com/details.html?rsnpid=217726 both accessed on 30 Dec. 2012.
17. Reported on the state news agency, SUNA, in July 2012.
18. However, before separation the economy was fairly evenly split between agriculture, services and industry (oil and non-oil), in GDP terms. This breakdown comes from 2009, but did not change substantially before separation. James, op. cit., p. 74.
19. See, for example, 'Sudan takes aim at currency traders as pound hits new record low', Reuters, http://www.reuters.com/article/2012/12/25/sudan-curremcy-idUSL5E8NP31H20121225 accessed on 30 Dec. 2012.
20. These figures were given by the opposition politician Hassan Satti, and confirmed by another economist who works extensively on Sudan.
21. Some economists believe this is because the government imposed artificial exchange rates.
22. The NCP's Al Hassan acknowledged this: 'There was a lot of pressure on the exchange rate because of the scarcity that developed. The deterioration of the exchange rate resulted in inflationary pressures, and so there was a kind of de-stabilisation of the economy.'
23. The exact statistics given by the Central Bureau of Statistics show that prices rose by 83.8 per cent for meat, 45.4 per cent for sugar, and 40.2 per cent for vegetables. 'Food prices in

Sudan on the rise again as wages go up', *Sudan Tribune*, http://www.sudantribune.com/spip.php?article45059 accessed on 5 Jan. 2013.

24. Military expenditure was also extremely high. This will be covered in the next chapter.

25. Dutch disease is named after the effect of North Sea gas on the Dutch economy.

26. Collier, Paul, *The Bottom Billion: Why the Poorest Countries are Failing and What Can Be Done About It*, Oxford: Oxford University Press, 2008, p. 39.

27. James, op. cit., p. 81.

28. Collier, op. cit., p. 38.

29. The government also has long-standing difficulties in collecting tax effectively.

30. This will be fully discussed in chapter 7.

31. This approach was outlined to the author by the NCP's Sabir al Hassan.

32. See, for example, 'Sudanese's [sic] budget deficit amounts to $6.6b', Sudanese Online, http://www.sudaneseonline.com/news/5202-sudanese-s-budget-deficit-amounts-to-6-6b.html?print accessed on 30 Dec. 2012. This achievement lead to Mahmoud being named one of *Africa Review* magazine's 'People to Watch' for 2013.

33. 'Loan of 300 million Yuan to Sudan', *SUNA*, http://suna-sd.net/suna/showNews/XA_kjN-BNO-Pqg3FSQTlEcSKXwug23P6V6U-1XC8jmR4/2 accessed on 30 Dec. 2012.

34. See, for example, 'Sudan receives loan form [sic.] Chinese company', *SUNA*, http://suna-sd.net/suna/showNews/jNVnaAtPJesyPsUZeCiF93f9HCS6YjByw7UYn7h-G0w/2 accessed on 1 Jan. 2013.

35. This number comes from the under-secretary at the Ministry of Petroleum and Mining, Awad al Fatah. He also told the author that the overall debt in the oil industry is many times this figure.

36. 'Qatar to Deposit $1 Billion in Sudan's Central Bank: Report', *Sudan Tribune*, available at http://www.sudantribune.com/spip.php?article48288 accessed on 6 Oct. 2013.

37. One NCP official had tried to prepare the ground by claiming 58 per cent of the subsidised fuel went to international organisations like NGOs and the UNAMID peacekeepers in Darfur–don't worry, you the people won't miss your cheaper petrol, seemed to be the message. This was treated with the scorn it deserved. The story was in the *Sudan Vision* newspaper, 16 June 2012.

38. The source was the economist Abda Yahia al Mahdi, and it was confirmed by conversations with other Sudanese in Khartoum and elsewhere.

39. According to the Central Bureau of Statistics, quoted in 'Food prices on the rise again in Sudan as wages go up', *Sudan Tribune*, at http://www.sudantribune.com/spip.php?article45059 accessed on 5 Jan. 2013.

40. 'IMF welcomes Sudan's new economic policy but urges protection of the poor', *Sudan Tribune*, http://www.sudantribune.com/spip.php?article43369 accessed on 30 Dec. 2012.

41. 'Sudan gold miners vie for desert riches', AFP, http://www.google.com/hostednews/afp/article/ALeqM5gCmQ_KcOqBDUeOvaqdOhPTjAI7tA accessed on 1 Jan. 2013. The quote from the miner is also from this article.

42. According to al Hassan, the former Central Bank governor.

43. 'Sudan looks to fill coffers with gold,' *FT*, http://www.ft.com/cms/s/0/40fe5280-cc34-11e1-839a-00144feabdc0.html accessed on 1 Jan. 2013.

44. The economist Abda Yahia al Mahdi is one of those who believes gold production got close to its limit in 2012.

45. Daoud's calculation is that it costs $3,000 to prepare an acre of land for agriculture, with the latest technology. If 100,000 acres had been prepared every year, Sudan would have 600,000 acres, at a cost of $1.8 billion.

46. The DAL Group operates across six sectors: food, agriculture, engineering, real estate, medical services and education.

47. The figure was correct at the time of my visit, in mid-2012.

48. The Saudis are apparently particularly keen on Sudanese alfalfa. It is more expensive, but better quality than the Spanish version and the US exports, the Sudanese say.

49. The wonders do not end there. Dr Said oversees a programme in which the best cows, the

'elite' as he calls them, are impregnated several times a year. The embryos are then removed, and implanted in lower value cows, allowing the elite to pass down their genes far more frequently than would otherwise be the case. It's expensive to import Western cows, but soon DAL will have produced its own.

50. James, op. cit., p. 74.
51. According to the Gum Arabic Board, the gum belt is around 400 million acres, with over 360 species of acacia trees. Gum Arabic Board presentation, in the author's possession.
52. According to a quote in 'West's sweet tooth gives Sudan gum arabic export success', Reuters, http://www.reuters.com/article/2013/01/02/sudan-gumarabic-idUSL5E8N-U0OG20130102 accessed on 5 Jan. 2013.
53. 'Hilal stresses importance of rehabilitation of gum arabic belt', *SUNA*, http://suna-sd.net/suna/showNews/GDpYCDZFeQSwT_8kxP3IT-NGOBkpv9olaKqJo_FMA_c/2 accessed on 5 Jan. 2013.
54. This point, and the following one about the lack of labour, were made by the Sudanese political scientist Magdi el Gizouli on his blog: http://stillsudan.blogspot.co.uk/2012/10/south-sudanese-labour-refill-kambo.html accessed on 14 Apr. 2013.
55. See for example 'Sudan farmers fear land grab by foreigners', Al Jazeera, http://www.aljazeera.com/news/africa/2012/01/201211142114188969.html accessed on 1 Jan. 2013.
56. Quoted in Mosley, Jason, 'Peace, Bread and Land: Agricultural Investments in Ethiopia and the Sudans', London: Chatham House, 2012, p. 5.
57. 'Sinnar Farmers Present a Petition Against the Governor to the Presidency', Sudan Radio Service, http://www.sudanradio.org/index.php/using-joomla/extensions/modules/content-modules/531-sinnar-farmers-present-a-petition-against-the-governor-to-the-presidency accessed on 25 Aug. 2013. The governor said the land would go to citizens returning to Sudan from South Sudan.
58. *Al Khartoum*, 3 July 2013.
59. The full citation reads 'the policies and actions of the Government of Sudan, including continued support for international terrorism, ongoing efforts to destabilize neighboring governments, and the prevalence of human rights violations, including slavery and the denial of religious freedom, constituted an unusual and extraordinary threat to the national security and foreign policy of the United States.' More details can be found on the official website of the US Treasury, via http://www.treasury.gov/resource-center/sanctions/Pro-grams/Documents/sudan.pdf accessed on 1 Jan. 2013.
60. It is not just the US. Any Western bank that operates in the US cannot work in Sudan. The UK's Barclays Bank was fined 'quite a lot of money' by the US, according to a Western diplomat.
61. According to Sabir al Hassan.
62. Reported in *Sudan Vision* newspaper, 12 June 2012.
63. According to Sabir al Hassan.
64. By Peter Biar Ajak, a former World Bank employee who now runs an economic think tank.
65. LeRiche, Matthew and Matthew Arnold, *South Sudan: From Revolution to Independence*, London: Hurst, 2012, p. 167.
66. According to the South Sudan National Bureau of Statistics, available at ssnbs.org accessed on 4 Jan. 2013.
67. The political consequences of this decision will be discussed in chapter 7, The Sudans.
68. See LeRiche and Arnold, op. cit., p. 168 for more details.
69. Interview with Elizabeth Bol, the deputy minister for petroleum and mining, Juba.
70. Unity's oil is marketed as Nile Blend, the same high quality oil that is produced in Heglig, under Sudan's control. The oil from Paloich and other oilfields in Upper Nile is marketed as Dar Blend, and accounted for 250,000 barrels per day at independence, according to the deputy minister for petroleum and mining. However, it has a high sulphur content: one early batch after production started in 2006 sold for only two dollars per barrel, though the quality and prices have since increased dramatically. This last point was made by Laura James. James, op. cit., p. 76.

71. According to Elizabeth Bol.

72. The French giant Total purchased a concession there in the 1980s. It suspended its work when the SPLA attacked the base of a French company digging the Jonglei canal in 1984. Frustrated by Total not carrying out more exploration, in 2012 South Sudan decided to take Total's licence away, and divided the concession into three blocks. This was confirmed by the Deputy Minister for Petroleum and Mining, Elizabeth Bol.

73. A 2010 study by the National Unity government suggested that this rate could eventually be increased to 42 per cent, and that every additional increase of 1 per cent would raise the proven reserves by 120 million barrels. Quoted in a report for the World Bank, called 'Creating Sustainable Jobs for Peace', in the possession of the author.

74. Moro, Leben Nelson, 'Local Relations of Oil Development in Southern Sudan', in Large, Daniel and Luke A. Patey, *Sudan Looks East: China, India and the Politics of Asian Alternatives*, Woodbridge and Rochester: James Currey, 2011, p. 70.

75. I contacted Dar Petroleum for their response to all these allegations, but they did not respond.

76. It is also telling that the government has been unable to provide clean water for its own people.

77. Moro, op. cit., p. 77.

78. Lugala, Victor, *Vomiting Stolen Food*, Nairobi: Black Rain, 2010, p. 3.

79. 'South Sudan's doomsday machine', *New York Times*, http://www.nytimes.com/2012/01/25/opinion/south-sudans-doomsday-machine.html?_r=0 accessed on 3 Jan. 2013.

80. Press release from South Sudan's Ministry of Petroleum and Mining, 20 Jan. 2012. In the author's possession.

81. Confirmed by Elizabeth Bol, and the former federal oil minister Lual Deng.

82. The political ramifications of the decision will be discussed in chapter 7.

83. At the UK's Overseas Development Institute 'Juba Calling' event, 14 Mar. 2012.

84. The *Sudan Tribune* website, a daily reference point for followers of the Sudans, obtained a copy of the meeting notes, and posted them online at http://www.sudantribune.com/DOCUMENT-World-Bank-Analysis-of,42534 accessed on 3 Jan. 2013.

85. Press briefing by then-Finance Minister Kosti Manibe, 18 September 2012.

86. For example, the minimum monthly salary at the bottom of the government's salary range was 503 SSP in 2012, of which 58.6 per cent was in the form of allowances. The total was a bit more than $100, depending on the black market rate. Figures given in World Bank, op. cit., p. 24.

87. The World Bank noted that even if the government tripled its non-oil revenue, it would be insignificant given the scale of the financial deficit.

88. It is possible the higher percentage is accounted for by the cut in allowances for state postholders. It is also worth noting that the grant from Juba accounts for 90 per cent of Western Bahr al Ghazal's state revenue.

89. At Manibe's September press briefing.

90. 'Unity state to cut salaries by 25 per cent as part of austerity measures', *Sudan Tribune*, http://www.sudantribune.com/spip.php?article44107 accessed on 6 Jan. 2013.

91. Prices were already high because of Sudan's economic blockade. Everything had to be brought in from East Africa, along almost non-existent roads, or the river. The shutdown provided the final blow, as it increased the transport costs dramatically.

92. According to an internal Oxfam document, seen by the author.

93. From the 2009 National Baseline Households Survey, available at ssnbs.org, accessed on 4 Jan. 2013.

94. Quoted in LeRiche and Arnold, op. cit., p. 177.

95. According to a presentation given by the then Minister of Agriculture and Forestry, Betty Achan Ogwaro, in Washington on 31 Oct. 2012. A copy of the presentation is in the author's possession. The other statistics in this paragraph are also from this presentation.

96. This point was made by the economist Peter Biar Ajak.

97. A British district officer apparently noticed the climate was ideal for rice, and started to

grow some. He invited the local chiefs to dinner, according to local legend, and fed them some of his rice. The venerable chiefs said it was delicious, asked where it came from, and were surprised to hear the answer: 'Here!' They gave their permission for local land to be used for further tests.

98. The scheme has attracted casual labourers, who get 10 SSP, about $3 at the official rate, for a long day's work. Bona Malwal, a young man, complains that some days he is not hired, and even when he gets a day's work it is not enough. 'I am poor, we have no cows or sheep in my family,' he says, and, worse still, he has few options to change his situation. He also asked me for money, a sign of just how hungry he was.

99. In one of the two restaurants named after the BBC in Aweil, rice is prominent on the menu, along with Sudanese staples like *fuul* (fava beans).

100. Large, Daniel, 'The International Presence in Sudan', in Ryle, Willis, Baldo and Jok, op. cit., p. 166.

101. 'The New Frontier: a Baseline Survey of Large-scale Land-based Investment in Southern Sudan', Norwegian People's Aid, available at http://www.npaid.org/index.php/News/2011/ South-Sudan-threatened-by-land-grab accessed on 14 Apr. 2013.

102. The contract has been made available online, at http://media.oaklandinstitute.org/sites/ oaklandinstitute.org/files/Lanya%20County%20Land%20Grab—Lease_0.pdf accessed on 14 Apr. 2013.

103. 'Success at Halting Largest Foreign Land Deal in South Sudan', Oakland Institute, http:// www.oaklandinstitute.org/success-halting-largest-foreign-land-deal-south-sudan accessed on 14 Apr. 2013.

104. Average cereal yields in South Sudan over the past years are estimated at 0.9t/ha, which is low compared to Kenya (1.7t/ha), Ethiopia (1.4t/ha) and Uganda (1.5t/ha). World Bank, op. cit., p. 51.

105. According to Agriculture Minister Achan's presentation in Washington.

106. World Bank, op. cit., p. 18.

107. 'Is All Well in the Teak Forests of South Sudan?', African Arguments, http://africanarguments.org/2013/03/14/is-all-well-in-the-teak-forests-of-south-sudan-by-aly-verjee/ accessed on 3 April 2013.

108. 'Gold fever sweeps South Sudan ahead of new mining law', *Reuters*, http://www.reuters. com/article/2012/11/09/us-sudan-south-gold-idUSBRE8A80M120121109 accessed on 2 Jan. 2013. The information in this article was used in the rest of the paragraph.

109. World Bank, op. cit., p. 47.

110. Statistic given in the *South Sudan Statistical Yearbook 2010*, quoted in World Bank, op. cit., p. 25.

111. The point is made by the economist Peter Biar Ajak.

112. Collier, op. cit.

113. World Bank report, op. cit., p. 68.

4. DEVELOPMENT

1. The SPLM controlled large parts of the Nuba Mountains, as well as territory in southern Blue Nile state, during the 1983–2005 war. They maintained this control after the CPA. The SPLM areas were ruled very differently from the other parts of northern Sudan, where the NCP held sway.

2. She did not want her name to be used.

3. Women from other communities often struggle to find work too, but for cultural and religious reasons are less likely to brew alcohol, though it does happen.

4. This is the World Bank figure for 2011, and so includes some of the oil revenue. The number dropped in 2012. Accessed at http://data.worldbank.org/indicator/NY.GDP.PCAP.CD on 8 Jan. 2013.

5. The characterisation is the World Bank's. http://data.worldbank.org/country/sudan accessed on 9 Jan. 2012.

6. The actual UN figure for 2012 is 46.5 per cent. 'Status of MDGs in Sudan', United Nations Development Programme, http://www.sd.undp.org/mdg_fact.htm accessed on 18 Jan. 2013.

7. Abda Yahia al Mahdi was the State Finance Minister from 2002–4. She was one of those given government posts as part of Mubarak al Fadil al Mahdi's party, after he split away from the Umma party, and signed an agreement with the NCP.

8. According to the NCP's Sabir al Hassan.

9. Satti would not reveal who had threatened him.

10. Confidential interview with a senior NCP official.

11. The results are available at http://www.transparency.org/cpi2012/ accessed on 10 Jan. 2012. The ranking is based on local perceptions of corruption, established by several surveys, rather than empirical evidence.

12. The conversation was off the record, so the official will remain nameless.

13. Confidential interview, September 2012.

14. Hassan al Amin sells clothes in a market in Omdurman. He says one day in 2012 the police confiscated all his merchandise, and told him to pay 250 SDG to get it back–or 100 without a receipt. He eventually coughed up all he had on him: 30 SDG. This happens regularly, he says.

15. Another translation might be 'incentive'.

16. Cockett, Richard, *Sudan, Darfur and the Failure of an African State*, New Haven and London: Yale University Press, 2010, p. 7.

17. Collins, Robert O., *A History of Modern Sudan*, Cambridge: Cambridge University Press, 2008, pp. 16–17.

18. The Mahdi died in June 1885, four months after Khartoum was captured.

19. The Sudanese political scientist Magdi el Gizouli has written that 'Abdullahi al-Taaishi, a Baggara from Darfur, completed the transformation of the Mahdist revolution into a state structure, an exercise that demanded the centralisation of power in his own hands. In that context, the Khalifa faced considerable resistance from the riverain elite of the time'. El Gizouli, Magdi, 'Unworthy of Liberation', http://stillsudan.blogspot.de/2011/09/unworthy-of-liberation.html accessed on 9 Jan. 2013.

20. Collins, op. cit., p. 35.

21. Willis, op. cit., p. 59.

22. Willis, ibid., p. 61.

23. Collins, op. cit., p. 65. This decision, although made while Sudan was technically still under foreign rule, was taken by a committee dominated by the Sudanese political elite who ran the country once it achieved its freedom.

24. 'UN admits South Sudan at the 49th Least Developed country', Gurtong Trust, http://www.gurtong.net/ECM/Editorial/tabid/124/ctl/ArticleView/mid/519/articleId/8873/UN-Admits-South-Sudan-As-the-49th-Least-Developed-Country.aspx accessed on 9 Jan. 2013.

25. Collins, op. cit., p. 277.

26. This was one of the conclusions of the Black Book, a document initially produced as a pamphlet in 2000 to highlight the imbalance of power and wealth in Sudan. The Black Book was translated and published at the end of Osman El-Tom, *Darfur, JEM and the Khalil Ibrahim Story*, Trenton: Red Sea Press, 2011.

27. For a fuller understanding of the famines, it is worth reading de Waal, Alexander, *Famine that Kills: Darfur, Sudan*, Oxford: Oxford University Press, 2005.

28. This point was stressed by both Tigani Seisi, the head of the Darfur Regional Authority, and the economist Abda Yahia al Mahdi.

29. Confidential interview with a senior member of the NCP.

30. According to Tigani Seisi, the Fur intellectual who became a rebel leader, and then the head of the Darfur Regional Authority.

31. According to Tigani Seisi.

32. Sudan's various leaders do not appear to have made a concerted effort to develop their own

home towns. Jaafar Nimeiri was from Dongola, but this town on the Nile received no special favours in his decade and a half in power. Bashir's village, Hosh Bannaga, which is near the town of Shendi, also on the Nile, is no better off. Instead, wealth and development have been funnelled into Khartoum and its immediate surroundings, even if it is the northern political elite that has benefited from this.

33. This is not an absolute rule. Prominent figures from the north of the country, like the businessman Osama Daoud, complain their region is every bit as under-developed as Darfur. However, the difference is that the northern elite were able to move their homes and businesses to Khartoum and prosper there. This was not so easy for those from Darfur, or southern Sudanese before the split.

34. These statistics are in the 2013 UN's 'Consolidated Appeals' document for Sudan, p. 15. It can be viewed at https://docs.unocha.org/sites/dms/CAP/2013_Sudan_Workplan.pdf last accessed on 4 April 2013.

35. The Beja Congress was set up in 1958, the same year as the Nuba National Party of Father Philip Gaboush. Young, John, *The Fate of Sudan*, New York: Zed Books, 2012, p. 20.

36. Often, however, eastern Sudanese complained that the money their area had been promised never materialised.

37. World Bank figures quoted in Verhoeven, Harry, 'Blue Gold for Black Gold? Sudan's oil, Ethiopia's water and regional integration', Chatham House briefing paper June 2011, p. 8. The figures include South Sudan.

38. Verhoeven, ibid., p. 7.

39. Verhoeven, ibid., p. 8.

40. Verhoeven, ibid., p. 7.

41. 'Merowe Dam, Sudan', *International Rivers*, available at http://www.internationalrivers.org/campaigns/merowe-dam-sudan-0 accessed on 26 Aug. 2013.

42. 'UN Expert Urges Sudan to Respect Human Rights of Communities Affected by Hydro-Electric Dam Projects', Relief Web, available at http://reliefweb.int/report/sudan/un-expert-urges-sudan-respect-human-rights-communities-affected-hydro-electric-dam accessed on 26 Aug. 2013.

43. Bashir's speech was on Sudanese state TV on 1 Jan. 2013.

44. The interviewee did not want to be named, owing to the sensitive nature of what he was saying.

45. Al-Mak, Ali, *A City of Dust*, Washington: Sudanese Publications Series (number 11), 1982, pp. 3–4. In the English version of the poem the world 'silver' is used 'silver of space'—though presumably the translation should have been 'sliver'.

46. There used to be large numbers of South Sudanese too, but most of them left just before and after separation.

47. Comprehensive Peace Agreement, Chapter 3, clause 8, p. 57.

48. According to the economist and former minister Abda Yahia al Mahdi, who carried out research into the money each state received and spent.

49. Some Sudanese analysts believe that this extends to the popularity of local politicians, too, suggesting that the removal of Qaramallah Abbas in Gadaref and Abd al Hamid Musa Kashir in South Darfur came because their local power base became too challenging for the state. Conversation with a Sudanese political source, Aug. 2012.

50. This point was made to the author by Abda Yahia al Mahdi, Ghazi Salaheddin Atabani and the opposition politician and economist Hassan Satti.

51. Bashir got rid of many of his advisers, including Ghazi, as part of the 2012 austerity measures.

52. According to Nagwa Konda, the director of the Nuba aid organisation NRRDO.

53. The text of the speech is available at '"We are committed to maintaining peace" Kiir assures UN members', Gurtong, http://www.gurtong.net/ECM/Editorial/tabid/124/ctl/ArticleView/mid/519/articleId/5778/We-Are-Committed-To-Maintaining-Peace-Kiir-Assures-UN-Members.aspx accessed on 11 Jan. 2013.

54. McCune married Riek Machar, a rebel leader from Leer who was South Sudan's vice president until mid-2013. For more on this story, see Scroggins, Deborah, *Emma's War*, London: Harper Collins, 2003.

55. The statistic comes from the UN's Consolidated Appeal or CAP, and can be viewed at 'Consolidated Appeal for South Sudan 2013', http://www.southsudancap.info/ accessed on 11 Jan. 2012.

56. 'Statistical yearbook for southern Sudan 2010', Southern Sudan Centre for Census, Statistics and Evaluation, available via http://ssnbs.org/statistical-year-book/ accessed on 11 Jan. 2013.

57. In 2004, 20 per cent per cent enrolled in primary school, while in 2010 the figure was 44 per cent. UN, op. cit.

58. Interview with Chief Peter Gatjeng in Leer in September 2012.

59. According to Chief Peter Gatjeng. If the fighting is between two groups, the killer will typically be forced to pay 50 cows. If it is an act of solitary murder, then the punishment, payable to the victim's family, will double.

60. A senior government minister, who for obvious reasons asked not to be named, provides a number of insights throughout this book.

61. UN, op. cit.

62. Jok Madut Jok, a leading South Sudanese academic, who became the under-secretary at the Ministry of Culture and Heritage. He also says the government was hampered by a desire to appear to be doling out the development equally, meaning those areas most at need did not receive the full attention they deserved.

63. The minister Gier Chuang Aluong himself brought this up at a press briefing he gave on 17 Jan. 2012 in Juba. He was one of the ministers replaced in the 2013 reshuffle.

64. These figures come from a briefing given by the then Minister of Roads and Bridges, Gier Chuang Aluong.

65. 'First paved highway in South Sudan constructed by US AID, officially opened', US AID Press release, http://www.usaid.gov/news-information/press-releases/first-paved-highway-south-sudan-constructed-usaid-officially-opened accessed on 11 Jan. 2013.

66. For example, the hospital run by Norwegian People's Aid in Nimule. LeRiche, Matthew, and Matthew Arnold, *South Sudan: From Revolution to Independence*, London: Hurst, 2012, p. 91.

67. 'Key Indicators for Southern Sudan', Southern Sudan Centre for Census, Statistics and Evaluation, available at http://ssnbs.org/storage/key-indicators-for-southern-sudan/Key%20Indicators_A5_final.pdf accessed on 28 Sept. 2013.

68. A doctor can earn as little as $400 a month, while the NGOs pay more than this.

69. 'South Sudan: malaria cases triple in Aweil', MSF, http://www.msf.org.uk/Malaria_cases_triple_in_Aweil_South_Sudan_20121012.news accessed on 11 Jan. 2013.

70. Nodding disease causes children to nod furiously when they smell food; in their frenzy they don't eat, becoming malnourished, and often suffer brain damage and a lack of physical development. An eighteen-year-old can look ten years younger. There are several thousand sufferers in Western and Central Equatoria, as well as over the border in Uganda. Despite several studies, nobody really knows what causes the disease.

71. 2,054 mothers die for every 100,000 live births. UN, op. cit. The figure comes from 2006 but is not believed to have got considerably better in the years since then.

72. The hunger gap is the period when last year's food has run out, but this year's harvest has not yet matured.

73. 'Post-Conflict Mental Health in South Sudan: Overview of Common Psychiatric Disorders. Part 1: Depression and post-traumatic stress disorder.' *South Sudan Medical Journal*, available at http://www.southsudanmedicaljournal.com/archive/february-2012/post-conflict-mental-health-in-south-sudan-overview-of-common-psychiatric-disorders.-part-1-depression-and-post-traumatic-stress-disorder.html accessed on 11 Jan. 2013.

74. 'Sudan's Lakes state governor bans sale of alcoholic drinks in Rumbek', *Sudan Tribune*, http://www.sudantribune.com/spip.php?article35023 accessed on 11 Jan. 2013.

75. Worse still, he used to work outside the country. However he then accepted a job at Juba University's Faculty of Medicine, according to Dr. Edward Eremugo Luka, the editor in chief of the *South Sudan Medical Journal*.
76. According to Dr. Edward Eremugo Luka and Dr. Robert Napoleon.
77. International Office of Migration statistical report, in the author's possession.
78. 'Woyee', sometimes spelt 'oyee', is a shout of praise. 'South Sudan woyee!' people chanted on independence day.
79. IOM, op. cit.
80. 'Key indicators for Warrap state', *National Bureau of Statistics*, http://ssnbs.org/storage/key-indicators-for-southern-sudan/Key%20Indicators_81.pdf accessed on 12 Jan. 2013.
81. UN, op. cit.
82. This was confirmed by the US Special Envoy for Sudan and South Sudan, Princeton Lyman, and by Nhial Deng, who was Minister of Foreign Affairs until the 2013 reshuffle.
83. However Jok Madut Jok points out the development of Juba has largely come through the private sector, rather than the government.
84. 'Ref: State approved budget 2011 summary on capital expenditure', Finance, Public Accounts and Economic Development Committee, Northern Bahr el Ghazal State Legislative Assembly, 2 Nov. 2011.
85. The 2008 national census established the population of Northern Bahr el Ghazal state as 720,898. This statistic is available at the National Bureau of Statistics' Northern Bahr el Ghazal page, http://ssnbs.org/storage/key-indicators-for-southern-sudan/Key%20Indicators_82.pdf which was accessed on 13 Jan. 2013. South Sudan's leaders believe the census under-represented the South Sudanese people, so the real figure may be higher. According to an International Office of Migration document in the author's possession, 460,150 people are estimated to have returned to Northern Bahr el Ghazal between Feb. 2007 and Nov. 2012. Most these will have returned after the census was conducted, so the population of the state is likely to be above 1 million.
86. 'Budget execution report fy [sic.] 2011', Ministry of Finance, Trade and Industry, Northern Bahr el Ghazal state, Nov. 2011.
87. However, the then Vice President, Riek Machar, is from Leer. His wife Angelina Teny ran against Taban Deng in the 2010 elections, and many people in Leer voted for her.
88. According to the National Bureau of Statistics, http://ssnbs.org/ accessed on 13 Jan. 2012.
89. The full speech can be read at 'TEXT: Garang's speech at the signing ceremony of S. Sudan peace deal', *Sudan Tribune*, http://www.sudantribune.com/article.php3?id_article=7476 accessed on 12 Jan. 2013.
90. 'The local government framework for Southern Sudan', Government of Southern Sudan, 2006, available at http://www.goss-online.org/magnoliaPublic/en/Independant-Commissions-and-Chambers/Local-Government-Board-/mainColumnParagraphs/0/content_files/file0/Local%20Government%20framework.doc accessed on 13 Jan. 2013.
91. UN, op. cit.
92. Awolich, 'Food Security', *Sudd Institute Brief*, 2012, pp. 3–4.
93. Figure given by the then Agriculture Minister Betty Achan.
94. Awolich, op. cit., p. 4
95. 'South Sudan Relocates its Capital from Juba to Ramciel', *Sudan Tribune*, http://www.sudantribune.com/South-Sudan-relocates-its-capital,40027 accessed on 22 Apr. 2013.
96. According to Steven Wondu, the Auditor General.
97. See, for example, this story on *Sudan Tribune*, accessed on 3/1/2012: http://www.sudantribune.com/South-Sudan-ministers-invited-to,39246
98. Leriche and Arnold, op. cit., p. 172.
99. The reports were only published after independence in 2011. 'Special Report: plunder preserves a fragile peace', Reuters, http://www.reuters.com/article/2012/11/20/us-south-sudan-governors-idUSBRE8AJ08N20121120 accessed on 13 Jan. 2013.
100. The foreign consultant did not want to be named.

101. This point is made by Jok Madut Jok.
102. Pa'gan Amum said in this in a press conference in March 2012.
103. The minister's colleague did not wish to be named.
104. Quoted in Lugala, Victor, *Vomiting Stolen Food*, Nairobi: Black Rain, 2010, p. 2.
105. Lugala, ibid., p. 3–4
106. Letter from President Salva Kiir, a copy of which is in the author's possession. All subsequent quotes are from this letter.
107. 'South Sudan Officials have Stolen $4 Billion: President', *Reuters*, available at http://www.reuters.com/article/2012/06/04/us-southsudan-corruption-idUSBRE8530QI20120604 accessed on 15 Apr. 2013.
108. There was subsequently an attempt by some officials to deny that the letter had ever been sent. However two former ministers, Lual Deng and Awut Deng, both came forward in parliament to say they had each received the letter, in an effort to clear their names.
109. Interviews with well-connected South Sudanese and foreigners in 2012.
110. Peter Biar Ajak, the economist, made this point.
111. This is the figure given by Alfred Lokuji, the Juba University professor.
112. 'Creating Jobs for Sustainable Peace', a 2013 World Bank report in the author's possession.
113. Among the central government employees sent to the states and counties, for example, 62 per cent of salaries are what are termed 'other forces' (the police, the fire service, prisons, the wildlife service), who are almost all former SPLA soldiers. In contrast, only 28 per cent are for education, 9 per cent for health, and 1 per cent for agriculture. World Bank report, ibid.

5. INSECURITY

1. People who have survived government bombing raids all over Sudan and South Sudan often identify almost any plane that bombs as an Antonov, though sometimes it is actually another type of aircraft. The Antonov has obtained a sort of iconic, if deeply despised, status.
2. 'U.N Officials Accuse Sudan of Bombing South Sudan', *NY Times*, http://www.nytimes.com/2011/11/12/world/africa/un-officials-accuse-sudan-of-bombing-south-sudan.html?_r=0 accessed on 21 Mar. 2013.
3. A SPLA attempt to bring the war to Darfur in 1991, under the leadership of Daud Bolud, failed miserably. Bolud was captured and executed. For more details see Flint, Julie and Alex de Waal, *Darfur: A New History of a Long War*, London: Zed Books, 2009, pp. 24–5.
4. Both areas are north of the 1 Jan. 1956 boundary line between northern and southern Sudan that was agreed on as the border between the two countries once South Sudan seceded.
5. The focus of the popular consultations was meant to be on 'the constitutional, political, administrative, and economic arrangements related to the structure, the type and the level of decentralised governance, institutions and authorities; the relationship between the state and the centre; the executive and legislative powers; and the share of each of the two states in wealth and national power as detailed in the Comprehensive Peace Agreement.' 2010 People's Consultation Act, Article 3, quoted in Young, John, *The Fate of Sudan: The Origins and Consequences of a Flawed Peace Process*, London: Zed Books, 2012, p. 231.
6. For a full discussion of the popular consultations in Blue Nile, including the way in which they entrenched ethnic divisions, see Young, ibid., pp. 231–42.
7. In July 2013, the state of West Korfodan was created. Its boundaries were not initially clear, but it mainly comprised the western half of the old South Kordofan state. The new West Kordofan is largely inhabited by Arab groups, and contains Sudan's major oilfields. Unless stated otherwise, 'South Kordofan' in this book refers to the state boundaries up until the July 2013 creation of West Kordofan. Ahmed Haroun, the governor of South Kordofan, was also removed from this post and appointed governor of North Kordofan.
8. This assessment comes from, among others, the human rights activist and government critic Hafiz Mohamed, who is from South Kordofan and knows both men.

9. Abdel Aziz's campaign granted a large role to James Wani Igga, the head of the southern Sudanese parliament. This was a strange decision. Wani Igga's region was about to secede, leaving Abdel Aziz on the other side of an international border. Using a southern Sudanese to campaign allowed Abdel Aziz's opponents to portray him as in the pay of southern Sudan, and did nothing to win over those who had doubts about the SPLM-North to the party's cause.

10. Abdel Aziz's village was attacked on the eve of the elections. He told me it was a deliberate attempt to rattle him. At least 29 people were killed, allegedly by a PDF unit. See Young, op. cit., p. 250.

11. Confidential interview, Nov. 2012. There was substantial debate within SPLM-North around the time of the state elections about whether taking up arms was the only possible response to a rigged vote.

12. The Carter Center was set up by the former US President, Jimmy Carter. It has worked in Sudan for many years. 'Vote in South Kordofan is Peaceful and Credible, Despite Climate of Insecurity and Some Irregularities', *Carter Center*, available at http://www.cartercenter. org/news/pr/sudan-051811.html accessed on 16 Apr. 2013.

13. SPLM-North was accused of electoral fraud too. The SPLM in southern Sudan played its part by keeping a Nuba leader who might have challenged Abdel Aziz's popularity, Telephone Kuku, in jail. He was on the ballot, but unable to campaign.

14. Confidential interview, Nov. 2012.

15. SAF troops seized control of Abyei on 21 May 2011. This region is still disputed by both countries, and is a major security worry for both. It will be discussed in more detail in chapter 7, The Sudans.

16. Interview with a military source, Khartoum, March 2012.

17. Already the SPLM had been criticised for not withdrawing all its troops south of the 1 January 1956 border line: 'legally, the SPLA was also in the wrong', according to the political scientist John Young. Young, op. cit., p. 273.

18. 'Mission Report: Kadugli, Southern Kordofan', *AUHIP* Confidential, 24–25 May 2011. A copy of the report is in the author's possession.

19. 'Highly Confidential' letter, entitled 'Ending Mandate of the Joint Integrated Units in the two Areas of Blue Nile and Southern Kordofan', and dated 23 May 2011, addressed to the Chief of Staff of the SPLA, and the Vice Chair of the JIUs. A copy is in the author's possession.

20. The build-up to the fighting was extremely fast. On the morning of 5 June, nine SAF tanks moved through Kadugli, sending panic waves through the town. People were already jumpy after several weapons had been looted from a police station the previous evening. Later that day there were limited clashes in Um Dorain, and at least two other places in the state. SPLM-North said SAF was trying to disarm their troops. SAF blamed SPLM-North. On Monday 6 June the tension seemed to drop a little, as a committee from Khartoum attempted to resolve the election dispute. Then the firing began. The events in this paragraph and the subsequent ones on the beginning of the war are reconstructed from interviews with several Sudanese citizens who were present in the town at the time, but who did not want to be named for fear of reprisals. Most of the interviewees were Nuba.

21. 'UNMIS REPORT on the Human Rights Situation in Southern Kordofan', UNMIS internal report, June 2011. A copy is in the possession of the author.

22. 'Crime Scene: Evidence of Mass Graves in Kadugli, Sudan', Satellite Sentinel Project, http://www.satsentinel.org/report/crime-scene-evidence-mass-graves-kadugli-sudan accessed on 20 March 2013.

23. The UN report also recorded 'indiscriminate shelling of Kadugli town apparently targeting densely civilian-inhabited areas', bombing of civilian areas throughout the state, and extrajudicial killings. UNMIS, op. cit.

24. See, for example, 'UN Accused of Standing by while Sudanese Forces Killed Civilians', *The Independent*, http://www.independent.co.uk/news/world/africa/un-accused-of-standing-by-while-sudanese-forces-killed-civilians-2308896.html accessed on 20 March 2013.

25. 10 weeks into the war, Amnesty International and Human Rights Watch investigated thirteen bombing attacks in Kauda, Delemi and Kurchi, and concluded 26 people had been killed, and at least 45 wounded. 'Sudan: Southern Kordofan Civilians Tell of Air Strike Horror', Amnesty International and Human Rights Watch, 30 Aug. 2011.

26. Lugala, Victor, 'Rotten Eggs', in *Beating the Drums of War*, Accord-Sudan, 2005.

27. Nagwa left Kadugli a couple of days before the fighting broke out, by chance. She was in Kauda when the first bombs fell. Subsequently she was able to leave. She has not been able to go back, but she is in regular contact with Kauda and other SPLM-North areas of the Nuba Mountains, because she is part of the humanitarian operation to provide food and other essential items to the Nuba.

28. 'Sudan: Indiscriminate Bombing Exacerbates Humanitarian Crisis in Southern Kordofan', Amnesty International, available at http://amnesty.org/en/news/sudan-indiscriminate-bombing-exacerbates-humanitarian-crisis-southern-kordofan-2013-04-17 accessed on 19 Apr. 2013.

29. For example, Amnesty International and Human Rights Watch researchers 'witnessed government planes circling over civilian areas and dropping bombs, forcing civilians to seek shelter in mountains and caves.' Amnesty International and Human Rights Watch, op. cit.

30. 'Sudan Forces Responsible for Burning Village of Um Bartumbu, Residents Say', *Nuba Reports*, http://www.nubareports.org/reports/sudan-forces-responsible-burning-village-um-bartumbu-residents-say accessed on 20 March 2013.

31. Alex de Waal used this phrase, a few years before the second war in the Nuba Mountains, about Darfur. 'Counter-insurgency on the Cheap', *London Review of Books*, vol. 26 no. 15 Aug. 2004, pp. 25–7, available at http://www.lrb.co.uk/v26/n15/alex-de-waal/counter-insurgency-on-the-cheap accessed on 20 Mar. 2013.

32. This was translated slightly differently by *Sudan Tribune* as 'anyone who looks our way, we will stab his eyes'. The meaning is obviously the same. 'Sudan's Bashir Threatens a Repeat of Abyei and S. Kordofan "Lessons"', *Sudan Tribune*, http://www.sudantribune.com/Sudans-Bashir-threatens-a-repeat,39269 accessed on 19 Mar. 2013.

33. 'Sudan President Omar al-Bashir Officially Renounces S. Kordofan Accord', *Sudan Tribune*, http://www.sudantribune.com/Sudan-President-Al-Bashir,39459 accessed on 20 Mar. 2013.

34. This was the phrase used by Mubarak al Fadil al Mahdi, the veteran opposition politician, who at one point worked with Bashir and Nafie.

35. Abel Alier, a former Vice President of Sudan and a South Sudanese, once wrote a book called *Too Many Agreements Dishonoured*. By signing and then ignoring the 28 July agreement, Khartoum was following a well-worn path.

36. Under his watch 'regular and irregular forces became virtually indistinguishable.' Flint and de Waal, op. cit., p. 128.

37. Confidential interview, August 2013.

38. For example, in June 2012 the former senior UN official in Sudan, Mukesh Kapila, warned of 'the second genocide of the century' unless the international community acted. 'Former UN Head in Sudan Calls for Urgent Action in Southern Kordofan', *VOA News*, http://www.voanews.com/content/mukes-kapila-act-now-or-it-will-be-too-late/1178687.html accessed on 20 March 2013.

39. Confidential interview with Nuba men who fled Kadugli after the war began, in 2012.

40. Tayara, like many of the actors in this depressing play, is well known for the part he played in the first war in the Nuba Mountains, in which he also fought for Khartoum. He has been described as 'responsible for recruiting to the PDF, organising the administration and carrying out government policies. He is very faithful to the National Islamic Front. [...] Also, Kafi Tayara has a private security force estimated at more than 100 armed men, and a private prison'. De Waal, Alex, and A. H. Abdel Salam, 'Islamism, State Power, and *Jihad* in Sudan', in de Waal, Alex (ed.), *Islamism and its Enemies in the Horn of Africa*, London: Hurst, 2004, pp. 104–5.

41. '"Five Dead" in Rare Sudan Rebel Strike on State Capital', AFP, http://www.google.com/

hostednews/afp/article/ALeqM5hUpjQjbaBgdi8MhlGY_p3gejyk-g?docId=CNG.292dd
cff221210313506b09b3ac3844b.331 accessed on 20 Mar. 2013.

42. 'UN Condemns Shelling of Sudan Base Which Killed 'Blue Helmet,' Injured Two Others',
    UN News Centre, available at http://www.un.org/apps/news/story.asp?NewsID=45175&
    Cr=Sudan&Cr1=#.Uhxiw9JtgSh accessed on 27 Aug. 2013.
43. In Talodi I found members of a newly-recruited militia. They were all from the Awlad
    Shoron Arab group, and they had been armed to fight the Nuba rebels. 'The government
    gave us the guns. Omar al-Bashir gave us the guns,' said Hussein Ahmed Sharif, one of the
    new militiamen. He and his colleagues had received eighty-seven weapons, but no salaries.
    This has often been a short-cut to disaster: armed men plunder when they are not paid.
44. 'Sudan Governor to Troops: 'Take No Prisoners'', Al Jazeera, available at http://www.
    aljazeera.com/news/africa/2012/03/2012331114433519971.html accessed on 4 March
    2013. Haroun said the video was doctored, and he would sue Al Jazeera. As this book went
    to press, this had not happened.
45. Interviews with Yassir Arman, the Secretary General of SPLM-North, and Hafiz Mohamed
    of Justice Africa Sudan, who is from that part of South Kordofan.
46. Interview with Sadig Babo Nimr, the brother of the Misseriya paramount chief Mukhtar
    Babo Nimr, Khartoum 2012.
47. SPLM-North leaders like Yassir Arman dream of history repeating itself: the Mahdi's
    troops, which conquered Khartoum in 1885, included many Nuba, alongside the Baggara,
    a western Arab grouping which includes the Misseriya.
48. He was the head of an 11-man unit, which had only 10 guns between them. They started
    their rebellion by attacking police stations to obtain more weapons.
49. Malik Agar was initially reported as being behind in the count, but was finally announced
    as the winner. Young, who was a political adviser to the Carter Centre, which monitored
    the elections, has written that 'it seems likely that the SPLM leadership in Juba threatened
    to abort the entire election if Malik was denied the governorship, and the NCP felt com-
    pelled to bend.' Young, op. cit., p. 230.
50. Malik says the cultural centre he had set up was one of the first buildings targeted. This
    was, he says, because it threatened Khartoum's Arabising and Islamising narrative.
51. This information in this paragraph comes from interviews with Malik Agar and other
    SPLM-North officials, military sources, international sources, and published reports of the
    fighting.
52. This was confirmed by numerous interviews with refugees from Blue Nile in camps in
    Maban county, South Sudan; medical personnel who treat the victims; and published
    reports.
53. By March 2013 the UN estimated 115,248 refugees from Blue Nile in Sudan were living
    in Upper Nile, over the border in South Sudan. This figure is given at http://reliefweb.int/
    sites/reliefweb.int/files/resources/OCHA%20South%20Sudan%20Weekly%20Humanitar-
    ian%20Bulletin%2025–31%20March%202013.pdf accessed on 5 Apr. 2013.
54. This is an official UN statistic, available at https://docs.unocha.org/sites/dms/Sudan/
    Reports/OCHA_Sudan_Weekly_Humanitarian_Bulletin_Issue_10_%284–10_
    Mar_2013%29.pdf?utm_source=OCHA+Sudan&utm_campaign=893f782341-
    SHB+Issue+10%2C+2013&utm_medium=email accessed on 21 Mar. 2013.
55. The exact figure given by the UN refugee agency, UNHCR, was 288,700 in Sept. 2012. See
    http://www.unhcr.org/pages/49e45c226.html accessed on 21 Mar. 2013.
56. See, for example, Flint and de Waal, op. cit., pp. 47–70.
57. This brief summary of the beginning of the conflict draws heavily on Flint and de Waal,
    op. cit., chapter 4.
58. Sometimes the start of the war is given as 26 February 2003, when Golo, the district
    headquarters of Jebel Marra, was attacked. The Darfur Liberation Front claimed responsi-
    bility.
59. In the raid, 317 rebels destroyed seven planes, and captured the head of the air force, along
    with sizeable amounts of weapons. 'In more than twenty years' war in the south, the SPLA

had never inflicted such a loss on the air force', according to Julie Flint and Alex de Waal. Flint and de Waal, op. cit., p. 121.

60. 'Analysing Resource Constraints as One Dimension of the Conflict in Darfur', *Humanitarian Exchange Magazine*, July 2008.

61. *Humanitarian Exchange Magazine*, ibid. pp. 117–19. Bromwich points out that rainfall actually increased during the war years, but the overall trend over the previous decades saw rainfall decline sharply.

62. The international dimension to the crises in Sudan is the subject of the next chapter.

63. 'Darfur Deaths 'Could be 300,000', BBC, http://news.bbc.co.uk/2/hi/africa/7361979.stm accessed on 21 March 2013. The numbers are controversial. The Sudanese government has put the total at 10,000, though few believed it. However many have died, it is clear atrocities were committed on a huge scale in Darfur.

64. He had already been indicted, for war crimes and crimes against humanity, in 2009.

65. The idea was that the other groups would join in time. In mid-2012 Amin Hassan Omar of the NCP thought of the three major rebel leaders, Minni Minawi was the most likely to sign. He had no hope Abdul Wahid could be convinced. He thought Gibril Ibrahim, whom he described as a friend, might end up by convincing JEM to make peace. All the rebel leaders said they had no intention of signing the DDPD, because they didn't trust Khartoum.

66. See, for example, Flint and de Waal, op. cit., pp. 153–8.

67. Osman el-Tom, Abdullahi, *Darfur, JEM and the Khalil Ibrahim Story*, Trenton, NJ: Red Sea Press, 2011, p. 216.

68. 'Report of the UN Panel of Experts on the Sudan Established Pursuant to Resolution 1591 (2005)', UN Panel of Experts, available at http://www.securitycouncilreport.org/atf/cf/%7B65BFCF9B-6D27-4E9C-8CD3-CF6E4FF96FF9%7D/s_2013_79.pdf accessed on 21 Mar. 2013.

69. According to Amin Hassan Omar, one of Khalil's guards used a cellphone, which was tracked, and the group was then hit from the air. JEM has said foreign powers were involved in the attack, perhaps a reference to Qatar or the French-backed Chadian forces. Both countries have denied these accusations.

70. See, for example, 'Justice and Equality Movement-Mohamed Bashar (JEM-Bashar)', *Small Arms Survey*, July 2013, available at http://www.smallarmssurveysudan.org/fileadmin/docs/facts-figures/sudan/darfur/armed-groups/opposition/HSBA-Armed-Groups-JEM-Bashar.pdf accessed on 27 Aug. 2013.

71. 'Forgotten Darfur: Old Tactics and New Players', *Small Arms Survey*, p. 13, available at http://www.smallarmssurveysudan.org/fileadmin/docs/working-papers/HSBA-WP-28-Forgotten-Darfur.pdf accessed on 21 Mar. 2013.

72. '839 Deaths in Darfur Tribal Clash: Official', *Sudan Tribune*, available at http://www.sudantribune.com/spip.php?article47747 accessed on 28 Aug. 2013.

73. Many members of the Janjaweed were reportedly integrated into the Border Guards, who are often accused of abuses.

74. In fact JEM signed more than three months after the other organisations had agreed in principle to work together, because of these differences.

75. SPLM-North's Abdel Aziz al Hilu was appointed overall military commander. One of the Darfuri leaders should have been appointed head of the SRF, but the three Darfuri factions couldn't agree among themselves which of them should hold this post, so Malik Agar was chosen.

76. Communiqué of the Sudan Revolutionary Front, 11 Nov. 2011.

77. For more detail on this, see the Economy chapter.

78. The leaders of the four main rebel groups in the SRF, Malik Agar (SPLM-North), Gibril Ibrahim (JEM), Abdul Wahid al Nour (SLA-AW) and Minni Minnawi (SLA-MM) all signed, along with members (but not leaders) of some of the main opposition groups. The most prominent were Mubarak al Fadil al Mahdi, the former presidential candidate, and

Siddig Youssif from the Communist party. A representative of the underground youth opposition group Girifna signed too. Youssef al Kauda, the leader of a moderate Islamist party, later signed a separate document with rebel groups.

79. The most prominent were a retired General, Abdel Aziz Khalid, and a moderate Islamist, Youssef al Kauda. Al Kauda actually met the rebels a few weeks after the main talks in early January. 'Sudan: Crackdown on Political Opposition', *Human Rights Watch*, available at http://www.hrw.org/news/2013/02/26/sudan-crackdown-political-opposition accessed on 22 Mar. 2013.

80. However, the former presidential candidate Mubarak al Fadil al Mahdi, who signed the New Dawn Charter as a national figure, said the leaders of the major parties were in constant contact with their delegates at the talks, by Skype. If true, this suggests that they were well aware of the content of the charter, and gave their approval for their representatives to sign it, despite the later denials.

81. Interview with South Sudan's then deputy defence minister, Majak D'Agoot, Juba, July 2013.

82. The organisation Small Arms Survey believes that as of April 2013 'SAF appears to be the primary source of the bulk of military equipment in the hands of the SPLM-N'. 'Comparable SPLM-N Arms and Ammunition Stocks in South Kordofan and Blue Nile, April 2013', *Small Arms Survey*, available at http://www.smallarmssurveysudan.org/fileadmin/docs/facts-figures/arms-ammunition-tracing-desk/HSBA-Tracing-Desk-SPLM-N-April-2013.pdf accessed on 27 Aug. 2013.

83. 'Uganda Rubbishes Sudan Rebel Claims', *New Vision* (Uganda), http://www.newvision.co.ug/mobile/Detail.aspx?NewsID=629608&CatID=1 accessed on 5 Apr. 2013.

84. This was the conclusion of Bapiny Monytuil, the South Sudanese rebel leader, who works closely with Khartoum. He will be discussed later in the chapter.

85. Anne Richard, US Assistant Secretary of State for the Bureau of Population, Refugees and Migration, made the claim. 'Sudan rebels recruit children from S. Sudan refugee camp: US', AFP, http://www.google.com/hostednews/afp/article/ALeqM5joRe5DVTV97zosQxvrX g9NbSD2Pg?docId=CNG.9d9bb5d97241aa39684f8140764984ed.6d1 accessed on 5 Apr. 2013.

86. Khartoum is convinced that the negotiations which led to the formation of the SRF actually took place in South Sudan, not at the SPLM-North base in Kauda.

87. UN Panel of Experts Report, op. cit., p. 18.

88. 'South Sudan's Unity State Denies Hosting Darfur Rebels', *Sudan Tribune*, http://www.sudantribune.com/spip.php?article46183 accessed on 22 Apr. 2013.

89. Confidential interview, 2012.

90. 'UN Investigators Confirm Khartoum's Renewed Bombing of South Sudan: Implications for Negotiations in Addis', Eric Reeves, available at http://www.sudanreeves.org/2012/07/25/un-investigators-confirm-khartoums-renewed-bombing-of-south-sudan-implications-for-negotiations-in-addis/ accessed on 22 March 2013.

91. The SSLA was named after one of the most successful *Anyanya* forces from the first north-south civil war.

92. The SSLA leaders also had close ties with Paulino Matip, who until his death in 2012 was the deputy chief of staff of the SPLA, a position he was given after he made peace with Salva in 2006. Although he was nominally part of the establishment he seems to have kept in contact with rebels like Bapiny Monytuil. Bapiny even described him as 'our legal adviser'.

93. The commissioner of Mayom county was sacked after he repeated this claim. 'Unity State Authorities Deny that SPLA Burnt 7,800 Homes in Mayom', *Sudan Tribune*, http://www.sudantribune.com/Unity-State-authorities-deny-that,39045 accessed on 28 Mar. 2013.

94. Young, op. cit., p. 305.

95. James Gai Yoach was also based in the Sudanese capital, in Fitihab, an area of Omdurman. However, in August 2012 there was a clash in the Kilo 23 camp in South Kordofan in which Bapiny's lieutenant Matthew Pul Jang killed Gai Yoach's supporter, Kolchara Nyang.

From this point on Gai Yoach's power was broken, and Bapiny became the de facto leader of the SSLA. This account was provided by several South Sudanese sources, including the SSLA defector Jacob Nyier, and South Sudan's deputy head of military intelligence, Mac Paul.

96. This is according to state officials, and an eyewitness who was in the town as it was attacked. He did not want to be named.

97. Confidential interviews, 2012.

98. UN OCHA weekly bulletin, 7–13 May 2012, available at http://reliefweb.int/sites/reliefweb.int/files/resources/OCHA%20Sudan%20Weekly%20Humanitarian%20Bulletin%20 7–13%20May%202012_0.pdf accessed on 5 Apr. 2013.

99. See, for example, *Small Arms Survey*, op. cit.

100. Unlike Gadet or Bapiny, Yau Yau did not have a military background; but then again, D'Agoot notes, nor did the majority of those who went into rebellion as the SPLA in 1983.

101. Small Arms Survey, op. cit., p. 2.

102. It is difficult to tell exactly how many fighters Yau Yau has. Small Arms Survey has written that thousands of Murle youth are fighting the state, though not all are loyal to Yau Yau. 'An estimated 20–30 fighters suspected to be linked to Yau Yau were initially sighted in Pibor county in August 2012. Since then, it is estimated that 4,000–6,000 largely Murle youth have either directly joined Yau Yau's ranks, received arms and ammunition from him, are exploiting the current chaos to independently attack the SPLA or other Murle, or a combination of the above.' *Small Arms Survey*, op. cit., p. 2.

103. This will be covered in more detail later in the chapter.

104. 'UN Confirms Air Drop Where South Sudan Says Sudan Dropped Guns', *Bloomberg*, http://www.bloomberg.com/news/2012–09–24/un-confirms-air-drop-where-south-sudan-says-sudan-dropped-guns.html accessed on 27 March 2013.

105. 'SPLA Captures Rebel Bases in Jonglei', *Sudan Tribune*, http://www.sudantribune.com/spip.php?article46058 accessed on 5 April 2013.

106. *Small Arms Survey*, op. cit., p. 1.

107. 'South Sudan Jonglei Attack by Athor Rebels 'Killed 200'', BBC, http://www.bbc.co.uk/news/world-africa-12465366 accessed on 27 Mar. 2013.

108. 'South Sudan Rebel Gatluak Gai Killed After Peace Deal', BBC, http://www.bbc.co.uk/news/world-africa-14261525 accessed on 27 Mar. 2013.

109. 'Weapons and Ammunition of Returning SSLA Forces, Mayom, Unity State, May 2013', *Small Arms Survey*, available at http://www.smallarmssurveysudan.org/fileadmin/docs/facts-figures/arms-ammunition-tracing-desk/HSBA-Tracing-Desk-SSLA-July-2013.pdf accessed on 27 Aug. 2013.

110. All these were figures given by the Jonglei state authorities. Initially the UN said it was able to confirm 339 deaths. It called the figure of 600 dead 'unconfirmed'.

111. The name refers back to previous incarnations of a largely Nuer militia. In particular, the White Army fought alongside their fellow Nuer, Riek Machar, when he split away from John Garang in 1991. They took part in the massacre of the Dinka Bor, Garang's ethnic group, in 1991. According to John Young, who has carried out the major study on the White Army, it 'was an almost exclusively Nuer organization made up of members of the Lou and Gawaar clans of central Upper Nile, the Jikan in eastern Upper Nile, and the small Duk clan of the Dinka, who are culturally close to the Nuer.' The White Army: An Introduction and Overview', *Small Arms Survey*, June 2007.

112. 'UNMISS Jonglei Human Rights Report', UNMISS, p. 12.

113. The UN and Juba both cast doubt on the figure of 3,000 deaths. Both have every interest in downplaying the scale of the tragedy. However, I believe the figure is likely to be too high, because Konyi announced it just a day or two after the attack, when it seemed impossible to know exactly how many had been killed. He has stuck to the figure, however.

114. UN figures based on inter-agency assessments and local authority reports. Document in the author's possession.

115. Statistics available at the National Bureau of Statistics website, http://ssnbs.org. Accessed on 26 Mar. 2013. South Sudan's leaders believe the census, which was carried out before separation, under-represented the southern Sudanese.

116. In fact, it is more complicated than this. Jon Arensen points out that 'After the peace accords were signed in 2005 the Murle people were a split society with the northern Murle having aligned themselves with the Arab government and the southern Murle around Boma having aligned with the SPLA. There was tension between the two sides, but eventually, with the help of Murle pastors, peace was established and the tribe was reunited. However, the neighboring Nilotic tribes continued to see the Murle as traitors, since they had temporarily aligned themselves with the north.' Arensen, Jon, 'Murle Contemporary Issues', paper given at a conference on Jonglei in Nairobi in March 2012.

117. UNMISS, op. cit., p. 6.

118. Young, op. cit., p. 321.

119. Arensen, op. cit.

120. UNMISS, op. cit., p. 15.

121. 'Statement by Sudan Council of Churches of The Current Situation in Jonglei State', Sudan Council of Churches, 18 Jan. 2012. It is worth noting that the SCC kept the name from the time of the united Sudan. The organisation now represents churches in the two Sudans. The statement came from South Sudanese clergy, not their Sudanese counterparts.

122. Unless stated otherwise the information in this paragraph is based on UNMISS, op. cit., and interviews conducted in Pibor.

123. 'SPECIAL REPORT: For the World's Newest Nation, a Rocky Start', Reuters, http://www.reuters.com/article/2012/07/09/us-south-sudan-governed-idUSBRE86806Q_20120709 accessed on 25 March 2013.

124. UNMISS, op. cit., p. 18.

125. The death toll was given by a UN human rights report, in the author's possession. Other reports put the number even higher.

126. Sudan Council of Churches, op. cit.

127. In their statement, they wrote 'We Jonglei State women will leave our homes and convene together as women in a neutral land called "Gadiang" for two months without the men as soon as this resolution is read to them and they continue with the conflict. The men have finished our children in conflicts and we find no need for child bearing any more.' 'Jonglei State Women Communique to the State Government', March 2013.

128. UNMISS, op. cit., p. 30.

129. 'South Sudan: Lethal Disarmament. Abuses Related to Civilian Disarmament in Pibor County, Jonglei State', *Amnesty International*, p. 6.

130. Ibid., p. 8.

131. 'David Yau Yau's Rebellion', *Small Arms Survey*, p. 2. Available at http://www.smallarms-surveysudan.org/fileadmin/docs/facts-figures/south-sudan/armed-groups/southern-dis-sident-militias/HSBA-Armed-Groups-Yau-Yau.pdf accessed on 27 March 2013.

132. Interviews with senior SPLM officials, including Deputy Defence Minister Majak D'Agoot, in 2012; and South Sudan's ambassador to the US, Akec Khoc, in 2013.

133. Small Arms Survey, p. 2.

134. ''They Are Killing Us' Abuses Against Civilians in South Sudan's Pibor County', *Human Rights Watch*, Sept. 2013.

6. THE SUDANS AND THE WORLD

1. Clooney travelled with the Enough Project, a campaign group which works extensively on Sudan. The video of the trip can be watched at http://www.youtube.com/watch?v=p89Ou PODBMM last accessed on 13 Feb. 2013.

2. This bit of celebrity gossip comes from the Enough Project's John Prendergast, who often travels with Clooney.

3. Woodward, Peter, 'Sudan's Foreign Relations since Independence', in Large, Daniel and Luke A. Patey, *Sudan Looks East: China, India and the Politics of Asian Alternatives*, Woodbridge: James Currey, 2011, p. 42.
4. This chapter examines some of the key international relationships for both Sudans. The most important relationship of all is the one between Sudan and South Sudan. This is the subject of the next chapter.
5. Several NCP politicians confirmed this to me.
6. The flight's u-turn was so unexpected that the Sudanese ambassador in Beijing waited around on the tarmac for his boss's jet to arrive. 'Sudan's al-Bashir Goes Missing on Way to China', *Daily Telegraph*, available at http://www.telegraph.co.uk/news/worldnews/africaandindianocean/sudan/8600895/Sudans-al-Bashir-goes-missing-on-way-to-China.html accessed on 4 Oct. 2013.
7. 'Sudan's President Bashir Leaves AU Summit in Nigeria', BBC, available at http://www.bbc.co.uk/news/world-africa-23327830 accessed on 5 Oct. 2013.
8. This is part of a regular pattern, a sort of diplomatic dance, in which Western envoys work out whether they can attend an event, or not. If it turns out Bashir will be present, a low-level diplomat is sent instead of the ambassador.
9. The former US Assistant Secretary of State for African Affairs, Jendayi Frazer, also points out the influence of the many southern Sudanese who fled the war to the American 'heartland'–Nebraska, Iowa, and Ohio–and advocated for their cause there, often in churches. The latter two have been swing states in several elections, which means their concerns are listened to more attentively by politicians.
10. LeRiche, Matthew and Matthew Arnold, *South Sudan: From Revolution to Independence*, London: Hurst, 2012, pp. 206–7.
11. Some people accused Clinton of ordering the air strike to distract attention away from the Monica Lewinsky trial. See, for example, 'They Bomb Pharmacies, Don't They?', *Salon*, http://www.salon.com/1998/09/23/news_114/ accessed on 8 Apr. 2013. This became known as the 'Wag the Dog' theory, after a Hollywood film in which an American president goes to war to distract attention from a sex scandal. However the official report into 9/11 found no evidence to support the theory, calling it a 'slur'. 'The 9/11 Commission Report', p. 118, available at http://www.9–11commission.gov/report/911Report.pdf accessed on 8 Apr. 2011.
12. 'Powell declares genocide in Sudan', BBC, http://news.bbc.co.uk/2/hi/3641820.stm accessed on 8 Mar. 2013.
13. She did not agree with the decision not to intervene, and regrets it was made.
14. The most well-known activists include the Save Darfur organisation, the prolific university professor Eric Reeves, who writes articles suffused with moral outrage, and John Prendergast and his Enough Project. Prendergast, whose long greying hair makes him an unmistakeable figure, is open about his position. 'Is there an inbuilt bias against a head of state wanted for genocide? Sure!' Celebrities like Mia Farrow and Don Cheadle have also raised awareness about Sudan's problems.
15. 'George Clooney Isn't Helping Sudan', *The Guardian*, http://www.guardian.co.uk/commentisfree/2012/mar/19/george-clooney-isnt-helping-sudan accessed on 12 Mar. 2013.
16. Sudan Change Now, a youth movement which is involved in many street protests against Bashir, wrote an open letter to Clooney after his trip to South Kordofan: 'Portraying the regional conflicts in the country as a simplified war of Arabs and Africans concerns us. It does not fully capture the historical and political aspects of the conflict considering that the Sudanese government is a dictatorship and does not reflect the sentiments of the majority of the people. The regional conflicts in Sudan are not simple and are highly political with a strong basis on economic gains such as oil and other resources.' Sudan Change Now Open Letter to George Clooney', Sudan Change Now press statement available on http://www.sudantribune.com/spip.php?iframe&page=imprimable&id_article=41950 accessed on 8 Mar. 2013.
17. Americans often highlight their prominent role in South Sudan's independence, and some

South Sudanese do too. However, it is vital to remember that those fighting and dying for that goal were the South Sudanese themselves; without their sacrifices independence would never have happened.

18. He lists Sudan's enemies as activist organisations like Save Darfur, the Congressional Black Caucus, the Jewish lobby, and Susan Rice, America's envoy to the UN. Rice is particularly disliked by Sudanese politicians, and the feeling appears to be mutual. She has spoken out strongly on Sudan for many years. Even within the State Department, some feel she is more an activist than a diplomat.

19. The anti-US stance is simply 'for public consumption' according to the opposition politician Mubarak al Fadil al Mahdi, who worked with Bashir in the early 2000s. He also points out that even Hassan al Turabi addressed Congress in the 1990s.

20. The CIA thought the Sudanese provided 'good information', according to Frazer, and kept the channel open.

21. LeRiche and Arnold, op. cit., pp. 207–8.

22. Ibrahim Ghandour, the NCP's Head of External Relations, is one official who used this phrase to me.

23. In this instance the list came from the NCP's Ibrahim Ghandour, but it has been repeated by many Sudanese offificials.

24. 'Does Envoy's Approach Hint at US Shift on Sudan?', *NPR*, http://www.npr.org/templates/story/story.php?storyId=111422940 accessed on 14 Feb. 2013.

25. Jendayi Frazer made this point.

26. One of Gration's senior officials, Cameron Hudson, recounted this.

27. Sudanese officials close to Bashir told me they hated British policies towards their government, but they were keen for British teachers to come Sudan to improve the level of English in Sudanese schools.

28. Norway, the third member of the Troika that pushed the CPA, gives advice to both countries on oil but, like the British and the EU, defers to the Americans on most matters.

29. This was confirmed by US officials and their Sudanese partners.

30. One rebel-held area in the western Nuba Mountains, near the town of Dilling, has proved almost impossible to reach, because the government controls the area around it. NRRDO also funnels donor money from at least one European NGO into cash injections into the local economy, as well as medicines, incentives for medical staff, and seeds.

31. Blue Nile was more complicated, Lyman said, because of the logistics. SAF control most of the north of the state, and the areas they do not in the north are very hard to access because of the fighting.

32. For many senior USAID officials, and the veteran activist Prendergast, the operation brought back memories of Operation Lifeline Sudan, which provided food and other goods to desperate southern Sudanese during the second north-south war, and of unauthorised missions to bring food into rebel-controlled southern Sudan in the 1980s and 1990s.

33. The British General Charles Gordon, who fought rebels in China and Sudan and was variously known as 'Gordon of Khartoum' and 'Chinese Gordon', has been used by several generations of Chinese and Sudanese statesmen as 'a shared symbol of both violent imperialism and heroic resistance.' This quotation is from 'Sudan Looks East: Introduction', Large, Daniel and Luke A. Patey, in Large, Daniel and Luke A. Patey (eds). *Sudan Looks East: China, India and the Politics of Asian Alternatives*, Woodbridge: James Currey 2011, p. 5. Gordon led the 'Ever Victorious Army' which put down the Taiping Rebellion in China, before becoming the Governor General of Khartoum, in the pay of the Khedive, who ruled much of what is now Sudan from Egypt. Gordon was brought back to evacuate the Europeans from Khartoum as the Mahdi approached, but instead attempted to defend the city. It fell to the Mahdi's forces in 1885, and Gordon was killed.

34. Quoted in Large and Patey, ibid., p. 16. However, this translated to a much smaller percentage of China's overall fuel consumption.

35. For more on the involvement of Malaysia and India, see Large and Patey, ibid.

36. Large and Patey, ibid., p. 16.
37. This sometimes annoys the sociable Sudanese. The artist Rashid Diab says 'we never see the Chinese. They bring their own food, and sit at home.'
38. See, for example, 'China Blocks Efforts to Sanction Sudan over Darfur Crisis', Canada. com, 30 May 2007, http://www.canada.com/topics/news/world/story.html?id=4bb2ff74–12a6–4a92-a3c4–2bf5c2ec1481 accessed on 17 Feb. 2013. China has abstained from voting on resolutions 1556, 1564, 1591, 1593 and 1672, all of which concerned Darfur. Shichor, Yitzhak, 'China's Voting Behaviour in the UN Security Council', Jamestown Foundation: China Brief, 2006, available at http://www.asianresearch.org/articles/2947.html accessed on 17 Feb. 2013. China also argues the case for non-intervention in Sudan strongly at the Security Council, sometimes alongside Russia.
39. Some analysts even credit the campaign with getting China to persuade Sudan to accept UN troops to beef up the peacekeepers in Darfur, UNAMID. Cosima Budabin, Alexandra, 'Genocide Olympics', in Large and Patey, op. cit., p. 154.
40. The UN reports can be read at 'Sudan Documents: Reports of UN Panel of Experts on Darfur Arms Embargo', Small Arms Survey, http://www.smallarmssurveysudan.org/documents/reports-of-un-panel-of-experts-on-darfur-arms-embargo.html accessed on 15 Feb. 2013.
41. See, for example, 'Sudan Denies Halting South Sudan Oil Exports as China Condemns Move', Sudan Tribune, http://www.sudantribune.com/spip.php?article40861 accessed on 12 March 2013. It was also reported by Sudan Radio Service on 30 Nov. 2011.
42. The exception is Addis Ababa, because it is the headquarters of the African Union, and because negotiations with South Sudan regularly take place there.
43. 'Mubarak Blames Top Sudanese Cleric in Assassination Bid', AP, June 1995, available to view at http://news.google.com/newspapers?nid=1350&dat=19950630&id=eT8xAAAA IBAJ&sjid=ZwMEAAAAIBAJ&pg=6674,9166829 accessed on 22 Apr. 2013.
44. 'Bashir's Regime "Worst in Sudan's History", says Head of Foreign Relations Committee", Al Ahram, http://english.ahram.org.eg/NewsContent/2/8/2882/World/Region/Bashir-regime-worst-in-Sudans-history,-says-head-o.aspx accessed on 16 Feb. 2013.
45. It was not just in Egypt and Libya. The head of Tunisia's leading party Ennahda, Rashid Ghannouchi, used to live in Sudan. However, Tunisia does not border Sudan, and the relationship between the two does not have a great impact on Sudan.
46. Egypt requires Sudanese men under the age of forty to apply for a visa, despite the fact that the principle of freedom of movement between the two countries has been agreed upon.
47. For example, 'In 1970, Egyptian President Anwar Sadat threatened to declare war on Ethiopia over the proposed construction of a dam on Lake Tana, the source of the Blue Nile. Any future plans by Ethiopia to develop the Nile's headwaters could become a new casus belli for Egypt.' This comes from an article written in 1990: 'Nile River Rights Run Deep', Christian Science Monitor, http://www.csmonitor.com/1990/0313/o1wat2.html accessed on 17 Feb. 2013.
48. Many of these tensions rise to the surface in the meetings of the Nile Basin Initiative (NBI), which was set up in 1999 to make better use of the Nile waters.
49. Ibrahim, a student from Darfur, told me in late 2012 that he intended to join his brother in Libya, because he could earn so much more money than in Sudan.
50. One source close to the Sudanese security apparatus told me that Sudanese ground troops had been backed up by forward air controllers. SAF had taken the town of Kufra, he said, and then handed it over to the revolutionaries. The Sudan expert Alex de Waal has written that Sudan 'despatched an infantry battalion and a tank company to help take control of Kufra', adding that JEM units helped the Libyan army to defend the town. Two of the main protagonists of the Darfur civil war were fighting each other in Libya. De Waal also wrote that Sudanese intelligence apparently helped locate Seif al Islam al Gaddafi in the Libyan desert. De Waal, Alex, 'African Roles in the Libyan Conflict of 2011', Chatham House,

pp. 377–8, available at http://www.chathamhouse.org/sites/default/files/public/International%20Affairs/2013/89_2/89_2deWaal.pdf accessed on 4 April 2013.

51. 'Libya's New Masters are Thankful for Sudan's Military Support', *Sudan Tribune*, http://www.sudantribune.com/Libya-s-new-masters-are-thankful,39985 accessed on 16 Feb. 2013.

52. Diplomatic sources believe the Sudanese may have secured some financial help from Libya in the first year after separation.

53. Alafif Mukhtar, Albaqir, 'Beyond Darfur: Identity and Conflict in Sudan', available on the website of the Al Khatim Adlan Centre for Enlightenment and Human Development, http://kacesudan.org/articles/byenddarfur.pdf accessed on 17 Jan. 2013.

54. Quoted on the Sudanese state news agency *SUNA*, 26 Sept. 2011.

55. See, for example, 'With Longer Reach, Rockets Bolster Hamas Arsenal', *New York Times*, available at http://www.nytimes.com/2012/11/18/world/middleeast/arms-with-long-reach-bolster-hamas.html?_r=0 accessed on 8 Apr. 2013.

56. This apparently was demonstrated by 'extensive supplies to armed groups in Darfur and South Sudan, and ammunition found in positions vacated by SAF in southern Sudan.' 'The Distribution of Iranian Ammunition in Africa: Evidence from a Nine Country Investigation', Conflict Armament Research, available at http://www.conflictarm.com/images/Iranian_Ammunition.pdf accessed on 16 Feb. 2013. Sudan denies that it is receiving substantial military support from Iran.

57. 'Sudan Summons Saudi Diplomat as Dispute Over Bashir's Flight Drags On', *Sudan Tribune*, available at http://www.sudantribune.com/spip.php?article47595 accessed on 13 Oct. 2013.

58. The figure comes from the NCP's Ibrahim Ghandour.

59. The NCP's Ibrahim Ghandour put the figure at 95,000.

60. The alleged incidents took place near the Sudanese-Egyptian border (2009) and near Port Sudan (2011, 2012). US embassy cables obtained by Wikileaks also suggested that Sudan was secretly supplying Iranian arms to Hamas in the Gaza Strip.

61. 'Sudan Blames Israel for Khartoum Arms Factory Blast', BBC, http://www.bbc.co.uk/news/world-africa-20050781 accessed on 17 Feb. 2013.

62. 'Sudanese FM Accuses Some NCP Figures of Undermining Country's Policy in Africa', *Sudan Tribune*, http://www.sudantribune.com/spip.php?article45946 accessed on 4 April 2013.

63. 'Good Day: Karti's Visit to Kigali', Sudan Vision, http://news.sudanvisiondaily.com/article.html?rsnpaid=488 accessed on 22 Apr. 2013.

64. Prunier, Gérard, 'Sudan's Regional Relations', in Ryle, John, Justin Willis, Suliman Baldo and Jok Madut Jok (eds), *The Sudan Handbook*, Woodbridge: James Currey, 2011, p. 156.

65. Prunier, ibid., p. 156.

66. This was made possible by an audacious foreign policy initiative spearheaded by the Sudanese presidential adviser Ghazi Salaheddin Atabani. He held secret meetings with Moussa Faki, the Chadian foreign minister, a risky step given the outright enmity between the two sides. Ghazi had the official sanction of the NCP, but some within the party were initially against the decision.

67. The historian Gérard Prunier says Khartoum supported 'a coalition of three Muslim fundamentalists movements that had united under the name of Jihad Eritrea', from 1988 onwards. Prunier, op. cit., p. 162.

68. Briefing by UNHCR, the UN's refugee agency, Feb. 2012.

69. The peacekeepers have been praised in some quarters. The Ethiopian troops are seen as disciplined, and having soldiers from one country only adds to the mission's cohesion.

70. 'UNHCR to Improve Situation of Sudanese Refugees in Ethiopia', *Sudan Tribune*, http://www.sudantribune.com/spip.php?article45372 accessed on 17 Feb. 2013.

71. According to a Sudanese technician, 'a dam in Ethiopia has more benefits for Sudan than for Ethiopia.' Quoted in Verhoeven, Harry, 'Black Gold for Blue Gold? Sudan's Oil, Ethi-

opia's Water and Regional Integration', London: Chatham House (briefing paper), 2011, p. 12.

72. 'Kenya Court Issues Arrest Order for Sudan's Bashir', Reuters, http://www.reuters.com/article/2011/11/28/us-kenya-bashir-icc-idUSTRE7AR0YA20111128 accessed on 16 Feb. 2013.

73. 'Report of the Panel of Experts on the Sudan Established Pursuant to Resolution 1591 (2005)', UN Panel of Experts, p. 3. Available at http://www.securitycouncilreport.org/atf/cf/%7B65BFCF9B-6D27–4E9C-8CD3-CF6E4FF96FF9%7D/s_2013_79.pdf accessed on 17 Apr. 2013.

74. 'Civil War Still Rages in Nuba Mountains', McClatchey, http://www.mcclatchydc.com/2013/01/07/179205/civil-war-still-rages-in-nuba.html accessed on 24 Feb. 2013.

75. 'SPLA-N Weapons and Equipment, Southern Kordofan, December 2012', Small Arms Survey, available at http://www.smallarmssurveysudan.org/fileadmin/docs/facts-figures/arms-ammunition-tracing-desk/HSBA-Tracing-Desk-SPLA-N-SK-Feb-2013.pdf accessed on 12 March 2013.

76. 'Russia and China 'Break Darfur Arms Embargo'', *Daily Telegraph*, http://www.telegraph.co.uk/news/worldnews/1551053/Russia-and-China-break-Darfur-arms-embargo.html accessed on 8 Apr. 2013. Russia denies the accusation.

77. 'Russia and US in Tit for Tat at United Nations over Sudan, South Sudan', Reuters, http://www.reuters.com/article/2013/03/12/us-sudan-un-russia-usa-idUSBRE92B10220130312 accessed on 8 Apr. 2013.

78. 'South Sudan Army Down UN Helicopter in Jonglei, 4 Russians Killed', *Sudan Tribune*, http://www.sudantribune.com/spip.php?article44945 accessed on 8 April 2013. Russia was furious about the incident. The SPLA apologised, but said they had been told by UNMISS that none of the UN's air assets were in the area.

79. This came as a shock to the UN, and even Ban Ki Moon's personal appeal to Bashir to change his mind came to nothing.

80. This was the total number of troops allowed between 31 July 2007 and 31 July 2012, at which point the mandated total was decreased. These and other UNAMID facts and figures can be found on a page on the mission's website, http://www.un.org/en/peacekeeping/missions/unamid/facts.shtml accessed on 16 Feb. 2013. In fact UNAMID never had the maximum number of soldiers and police allowed, and also did not have all the equipment, such as helicopters, that it needed.

81. Equipment is held up for months in Port Sudan, and there are often long delays before visas and travel permits are granted.

82. Jok Madut Jok, the academic who is also the under-secretary at the Ministry of Culture, made this point.

83. The embassies are: the UN, the US, the UK, Belgium, France, Russia, Germany, Norway, Switzerland, Turkey, China, India, Sudan, Eritrea, Ethiopia, Kenya, Uganda, DR Congo, Egypt, South Africa, Zimbabwe and Nigeria. Among South Sudan's direct neighbours, the only country where there is no embassy is the CAR.

84. The group included John Prendergast, Eric Reeves, the Ethiopian-American Ted Dagne, who later became an adviser to Salva Kiir, and South Sudan's leading intellectual, Francis Deng.

85. 'Special Report: the Wonks who Sold Washington on South Sudan', Reuters, http://www.reuters.com/article/2012/07/11/us-south-sudan-midwives-idUSBRE86A0GC20120711 accessed on 21 Feb. 2013.

86. This figure was given in an open letter written by the US Ambassador to Juba, Susan Page. The money was earmarked for 'good governance, agriculture, economic development, education, the environment, conflict mitigation and reconciliation, health, rule of law, human rights, security sector reform, and civil society development.' 'Democracy is a Fragile Thing', Page, Susan D. A copy is in the author's possession.

87. Those who had dealt with the SPLM for years, like Cameron Hudson, had felt for some time that the party was 'hard to love'. This hadn't translated into official policy, however.

88. This has been covered in the chapter on Insecurity. Many of the human rights abuses occurred during the Jonglei disarmament campaign, which was necessary but politically difficult.
89. Page, op. cit. p. 1.
90. Congressman Donald Payne was particularly active on Sudan, championing the cause of southern Sudanese and the victims of the Darfur conflict. He died on 6 Mar. 2012, having seen South Sudan declare its independence as a member of the US delegation that attended the 9 July 2011 independence day celebrations.
91. Open letter available at http://enoughproject.org/files/FriendsofSouthSudanLetter_July2013.pdf accessed on 6 Oct. 2013.
92. The Satellite Sentinel Project, which is part-funded by George Clooney, and promoted by John Prendergast's Enough Project, has released numerous satellite images of Sudanese troop build-ups, and alleged sites of mass graves. However, it hasn't turned its satellites towards the Darfuri rebels who are in South Sudan, in clear violation of several peace agreements.
93. See Holt, PM, and MW Daly, *A History of the Sudan: From the Coming of Islam to the Present Day*, Harlow: Pearson, 2000, pp. 130–1.
94. South Sudan's Muslims are also grateful to what is now Sudan for spreading Islam. However this was not enough to win political loyalty. The southern Muslims made it clear they were in favour of independence in the run-up to the referendum, and most voted for it too.
95. This information comes from South Sudan's then-Foreign Minister Nhial Deng. Only the EU maintained its level of support, he said.
96. 'Fact Sheet Joint Donor Team', Joint Donor Team, available at http://www.jdt-juba.org/wp-content/uploads/2012/02/JDT_fact_sheet_sample-11.pdf accessed on 21 Feb. 2013.
97. 'Council Allocated EUR 200 Million to Southern Sudan', Council of the European Union press release, available at http://www.consilium.europa.eu/uedocs/cms_Data/docs/pressdata/EN/foraff/122152.pdf accessed on 21 Feb. 2013.
98. 'Media Note', US Embassy Juba, South Sudan, 2013/0422, 17 Apr. 2013.
99. Even after the war, forced displacements due to oil production left local people in Upper Nile state 'reeling with bitterness against the Chinese' and the state governor. Moro, 'Local Relations of Oil Development in Southern Sudan', in Large and Patey, op. cit., p. 76.
100. Large, Daniel, 'Southern Sudan and China: 'Enemies into Friends'?', in Large and Patey, ibid., p. 168.
101. This was reported by, among others, *Bloomberg*, 'China to Loan South Sudan $8 Billion for Infrastructure Projects' http://www.bloomberg.com/news/2012–04–28/china-to-loan-south-sudan-8-billion-for-infrastructure-projects.html and *Sudan Tribune*, 'Kiir says China to Loan South Sudan $8 billion', http://www.sudantribune.com/Kiir-says-China-to-loan-South,42431 both accessed on 15 Mar. 2013.
102. 'China envoy says there was no $8 billion South Sudan aid offer', Reuters, http://www.reuters.com/article/2013/03/14/us-china-sudan-south-idUSBRE92D0JD20130314 accessed on 15 Mar. 2013.
103. These figures are from the Chinese Embassy in Juba.
104. This relationship will be the subject of the following chapter.
105. 'South Sudan Shrugs off Gloom to Celebrate Year of Freedom', AFP, available at http://www.alarabiya.net/articles/2012/07/09/225414.html accessed on 24 Feb. 2013.
106. LeRiche and Arnold, op. cit., p. 203.
107. LeRiche and Arnold, ibid., p. 203.
108. The LRA is no longer considered a great threat to Uganda or South Sudan. It has at most a few hundred troops, mainly concentrated in the DRC and CAR. There are some claims that the LRA's leader Joseph Kony is in Darfur. However, the leader of the Ugandan troops in Nzara, and the senior American officer working with them, both said in 2012 that they believed he was in the CAR.

109. LeRiche and Arnold, op.cit., p. 204.
110. See, for example, 'Tension Looms at Border Point', Daily Monitor (Uganda), http://www.monitor.co.ug/News/National/Tension-looms-at-border-point/-/688334/1627118/-/11tuw3gz/-/index.html accessed on 24 Feb. 2013.
111. In the most well-known case, a teacher at a school owned by John Garang's widow was shot dead. South Sudanese soldiers apparently were furious that the car she was travelling in did not stop as the South Sudan flag was ceremoniously lowered, and one opened fire. 'South Sudan: Teacher Shot Dead While Driving, Others Killed in Different Sites', *The Citizen*, http://allafrica.com/stories/201205151288.html accessed on 24 Feb. 2013.
112. 'South Sudan and DRC Vow to Enhance Bilateral Cooperation', *Sudan Tribune*, http://www.sudantribune.com/spip.php?article45719 accessed on 12 Mar. 2013.
113. 'Pres Peres and PM Netanyahu met with South Sudan President Kiir', Israel Ministry of Foreign Affairs, http://www.mfa.gov.il/MFA/Government/Communiques/2011/President_Peres_meets_South_Sudan_President_Kiir_20-Dec-2011.htm accessed on 25 Feb. 2013.
114. 'S Sudan Downplays Criticism Over Voting for Palestinian UN Status', *Sudan Tribune*, http://www.sudantribune.com/spip.php?article44717 accessed on 25 Feb. 2013.
115. 'South Sudan Seeks Big Investments from UAE', *The National*, http://www.thenational.ae/news/uae-news/politics/south-sudan-seeks-big-investments-from-uae accessed on 4 Apr. 2013.
116. Conversation with a Western diplomat in Sudan, who was on good terms with the Egyptian mission in Khartoum.
117. Prunier, op. cit., p. 154. Prunier points to Hosni Mubarak's visit to southern Sudan in 2008 as a turning point. However, even after this the Egyptians were privately sceptical about whether southern Sudan would really choose to secede.
118. 'Juba Rebuffs Cairo on Nile Water Agreements', *Africa Review*, http://www.africareview.com/News/Juba-rebuffs-Cairo-on-Nile-waters-agreements/-/979180/1725630/-/40dvaw/-/index.html accessed on 4 April 2013. This information was confirmed by Akec Khoc, South Sudan's ambassador to the US.
119. There have been some suggestions that the Jonglei canal project—which would divert some of the Sudd and Nile waters into a canal flowing up to Egypt—could be revived. Construction on this ambitious scheme began in 1978. However it was extremely unpopular in southern Sudan, because southerners believed they would see no benefits, and they were upset that 'their' water was being sent to Egypt. The SPLA targeted the canal in the early days of its rebellion, halting its construction. It seems unlikely that a newly-independent South Sudan would support relaunching the project.
120. 'Near-Verbatim Transcript of the Press Conference by SRSG Hilde Johnson', *UNMISS*, available at http://www.gurtong.net/ECM/Editorial/tabid/124/ctl/ArticleView/mid/519/articleId/5457/categoryId/120/Near-Verbatim-Transcript-Of-The-Press-Conference-By-SRSG-Hilde-Johnson.aspx accessed on 25 Feb. 2013.
121. Letter from Vice President Riek Machar to the UN Security Council, dated 12 June 2012, a copy of which is in the author's possession.
122. State governors who spoke to me about the so-called dependency culture included Rizik Hassan in Western Bahr el Ghazal and Paul Malong in Northern Bahr el Ghazal.
123. NGOs and UN agencies have been denied access to conflict areas, in particularly in Jonglei state. There has also been an attempt to regulate the work international organisations do. See, for example, 'Minister Tables Policy to Regulate NGOs Activities', Gurtong, http://www.gurtong.net/ECM/Editorial/tabid/124/ctl/ArticleView/mid/519/articleId/8235/Minister-Tables-Policy-to-Regulate-NGOs-Activities.aspx accessed on 25 Feb. 2013.

7. THE SUDANS

1. Garang's father, Thomas Dhel (sometimes written Dhol) was one of the leaders of the Anyanya rebels in the first north-south civil war in the Bahr el Ghazal region. He was integrated in SAF after the Addis Ababa peace agreement, eventually becoming a general.
2. Hiba's family come from the Jaaliyin and Shaigiyya, the two ethnic groups which dominate Sudanese political and economic life.
3. Garang, of course, has Sudanese as well as South Sudanese blood, or northern as well as southern origins, to use the pre-separation terms. However, in the eyes of society and, crucially, Hiba's family, he was a southerner, because of his southern father.
4. Marriages between northern Sudanese Muslim women and southern Sudanese men were almost unheard of.
5. The phrase is trotted out so often that its origins are difficult to ascertain, but it is sometimes ascribed to Guinea's President Sékou Touré, who ruled from independence from the French in 1958 until his death in 1984.
6. According to the disputed 2008 census, 12,925,167 people live in the border states. The statistics can be accessed at South Sudan's National Bureau of Statistics website, http:// ssnbs.org/, last visited on 4 April 2013.
7. Many South Sudanese in Juba and elsewhere prefer speaking Arabic too, particularly the local version, Juba Arabic. However the geographical proximity of Sudan, and the high concentration of returnees who grew up in Sudan, make Arabic speakers probably more prevalent in the northern part of South Sudan. Those who lived as refugees outside Sudan often prefer English.
8. The 1 Jan. 1956 boundary itself was largely based on the boundaries between different ethnic groups, as perceived by the often poorly informed colonialists. Irrespective of whether they had made mistakes, or whether the ethnic frontiers had subsequently shifted, the colonialists' 1956 line would become the border between the two Sudans.
9. Johnson, Douglas H., *When Boundaries Become Borders: The Impact of Boundary-Making in Southern Sudan's Frontier Zones*, London: Rift Valley Institute, 2010, p. 15.
10. Some do live in the region permanently, in the northern part of Abyei. However, they are outnumbered by those who pass through seasonally.
11. Deng Majok and the late Misseriya paramount chief Babo Nimr were friends, and were often able to resolve the differences between their people. See, for example, Deng, Francis Mading, *The Man Called Deng Majok: A Biography of Power, Polygyny, and Change*, New Haven and London: Yale University Press, 1986.
12. Young, John, *The Fate of Sudan*, London: Zed Books, 2012, p. 266.
13. 'South Sudan Annual Report 2012', *IOM*, available at https://www.iom.int/files/live/sites/iom/files/Country/docs/IOM_South_Sudan_Annual_%20Report_2012.pdf accessed on 16 Apr. 2013.
14. Confidential interview with a UN official who was aware of the case.
15. Confidential interview, 2012.
16. Daly, M. W., *Darfur's Sorrow: The Forgotten History of a Humanitarian Disaster*, New York: Cambridge University Press, 2010, p. 76.
17. Pa'gan was suspended as Secretary General of the SPLM in July 2013. He announced that he would contest this decision in court. He was also replaced as South Sudan's negotiator with Sudan.
18. Briefing by Finance Minister Kosti Manibe, 18 Sept. 2012, Juba.
19. At this point only one official accompanied each president to the meeting, and al Khatib was with Bashir.
20. This is according to several international and Sudanese sources.
21. Unlike most international observers, the US Special Envoy Princeton Lyman believes Kiir was right to refuse to sign. He says South Sudan obtained nothing new from the document. However, Lyman believes the South Sudanese should have threatened to shut the oil down, rather than actually doing it, because of the devastating effect it had on the economy.

22. The photo was taken by Dominic Nahr for *Time*. It can be seen at 'Tracing the Consequences of War in Divided Sudan', http://lightbox.time.com/2012/04/23/tracing-the-consequences-of-war-in-divided-sudan/#2 accessed on 1 March 2013.

23. For the sake of simplicity, I will refer to the area as Heglig, as many South Sudanese have continued to do. This does not imply anything about the relative merits of Sudan or South Sudan's claim.

24. See, for example, 'SPLA Recaptures Heglig from Sudan Armed Forces', Gurtong, http://www.gurtong.net/ECM/Editorial/tabid/124/ctl/ArticleView/mid/519/articleId/6695/SPLA-Recaptures-Heglig-From-Sudan-Armed-Forces.aspx accessed on 28 Mar. 2013.

25. On both occasions SAF denied that they had attacked first. However, interviews with Sudanese citizens from the area, South Sudanese officials, South Sudanese rebels and diplomats all point towards an initial Sudanese attack, followed by a successful South Sudanese riposte, on both occasions. It may well be possible that on 10 Apr. SAF was attempting to regain control of a border post at Teshwin that it had lost on 26 Mar.

26. Mac Paul said the SSLA camp at Kilo 23, 23 kilometres to the north of Heglig, was attacked and destroyed.

27. This was first described in the Insecurity chapter.

28. Mac Paul, the deputy head of military intelligence, told me this in a 2012 interview.

29. 'Press Statement', AU Peace and Security Council, 12 Apr. 2012, PSC/PR/BR/2.(CCCX-VII).

30. 'UN Chief Chides South Sudan Over 'Illegal' Occupation of Heglig', *Sudan Tribune*, http://www.sudantribune.com/spip.php?article42325 accessed on 29 Mar. 2013.

31. This was confirmed by Mac Paul, the deputy head of military intelligence.

32. 'Human Rights Groups Condemn SPLA's Harassment of Sudan Tribune Journalist', *Sudan Tribune*, http://www.sudantribune.com/spip.php?article42325 accessed on 29 Mar. 2013.

33. 'S. Sudan Government Orders JEM to Burn Heglig Oilfield, Destroy Infrastructure before Withdrawal', *Sudan Vision*, http://news.sudanvisiondaily.com/details.html?rsnpid=209286 accessed on 4 Apr. 2013. Taban Deng was sacked as governor of Unity in July 2013.

34. See, for example, Johnson, Douglas H., 'Note on Panthou/Heglig', published on the Gurtong website, http://www.gurtong.net/ECM/Editorial/tabid/124/ctl/ArticleView/mid/519/articleId/6915/categoryId/24/Dr-Douglas-H-Johnson-Note-on-PanthouHeglig.aspx accessed on 23 Apr. 2013.

35. 'Position Paper on the Delineation of the North-South Sudan Boundary Line', written on 10 June 2010 by southern Sudanese members of the Border Technical Committee Between Northern Sudan and its Southern Part, which was set up to delineate the 1 Jan. 1956 boundary, and thus the border between Sudan and South Sudan. The government of southern Sudan's representative on the committee, Riek Degoal Juer, was one of those who signed. The author has a copy of the position paper.

36. For more on the disputed border areas, see Johnson, op. cit.

37. The then US special envoy for the Sudans, Princeton Lyman, who was at the talks, says the South Sudanese military were particularly unhappy about 14 Miles, and Abyei. They went over the text word for word.

38. The nine agreements were: Banking; Borders; Certain Economic Matters; Post-Service Benefits; Security Arrangements; Trade; Nationals; Oil; Co-operation.

39. 'Northern Bahr el Ghazal Governor Objects to 'Demilitarization' of Mile 14 Area', *Sudan Tribune*, http://www.sudantribune.com/spip.php?article44055 accessed on 31 Mar. 2013.

40. 'Do Not Cede Our Land to Khartoum: Aweil Community Rejection to 14 Miles', Gurtong, available at http://www.gurtong.net/ECM/Editorial/tabid/124/ctl/ArticleView/mid/519/articleId/8029/Do-Not-Cede-Our-Land-to-Khartoum-Aweil-Community-Rejection-to-14-Miles.aspx accessed on 31 Mar. 2013.

41. In both cases South Sudan would pay $1/barrel for transit fees, and $1.60/barrel for processing fees. South Sudan agreed to pay $8.40/barrel for transportation fees in the GNPOC transportation facilities (i.e. from Unity state) and $6.50/barrel for the Petrodar transportation facilities (i.e. from Upper Nile).

42. South Sudanese leaders, including President Salva, had always welcomed Sudanese traders. It was the Sudanese authorities who threatened the South Sudanese. However the agreement should protect the rights of citizens of both countries even if the attitudes of leaders change.

43. The article, dated 17 Dec. 2012, is available on John Akec's website, http://johnakecsouthsudan.blogspot.co.uk/ accessed on 4 April 2013.

44. Meles Zenawi died on 20 Aug. 2012, and was succeeded by his protégé, Hailemariam Desalegn.

45. Confidential interview, Khartoum, July 2013.

46. Some have joined part of JEM which fights in South Kordofan rather than Darfur. Others even joined SPLM-North.

47. Several South Sudanese made this point, along with Princeton Lyman, the US envoy.

48. The dynamic has undoubtedly changed in Abyei. After separation, Khartoum's ability to advocate with Juba for the Misseriya's safe passage into South Sudan has diminished. The Misseriya may look to build up their relationship with the South Sudanese.

49. The old united Sudan was the result of 'lines drawn in Whitehall', the Sudanese businessman Osama Daoud says. No wonder then if its history, even after separation, is a disputed and bloody one.

CONCLUSION

1. Abdallah Deng Nhial was the presidential candidate for the PCP, Turabi's party, in 2010.

AFTERWORD

1. The full text of the press statement is available at 'Senior SPLM Leaders Give Kiir Ultimatum over Party Crisis', *Sudan Tribune*, http://www.sudantribune.com/spip.php?article49087 accessed on 8 Jan. 2014.

2. Confidential interview, January 2014.

3. 'From Dr. Adwok: Sorry, Sir, it was not a Coup', *SouthSudanNation.com*, available at http://www.southsudannation.com/from-dr-adwok-sorry-sir-it-was-not-a-coup/ accessed on 8 Jan. 2014.

4. On 9 Jan. See, for example, 'US Official Dismisses Alleged Failed 'Coup' in South Sudan', *Sudan Tribune*, available at http://www.sudantribune.com/spip.php?article49510 accessed on 25 Jan. 2014.

5. 'South Sudan: Ethnic Targeting, Widespread Killings', *Human Rights Watch*, available at http://www.hrw.org/news/2014/01/16/south-sudan-ethnic-targeting-widespread-killings accessed on 25 Jan. 2014.

6. 'S. Sudan Accuses Opposition of Hospital Deaths', *Voice of America*, available at http://www.voanews.com/content/south-sudans-government-accuses-opposition-of-hospital-deaths/1835583.html accessed on 25 Jan. 2014.

7. 'Despatches: Counting the Dead in South Sudan', *Human Rights Watch*, available at http://www.hrw.org/news/2014/01/30/dispatches-counting-dead-south-sudan accessed on 31 Jan. 2014.

8. 'Uganda Admits Combat Role in South Sudan', *Al Jazeera*, available at http://www.aljazeera.com/news/africa/2014/01/ugandan-troops-battling-south-sudan-rebels-201411683225414894.html accessed on 25 Jan. 2014.

9. By 31 Jan. 2014, the UN estimated 739,100 people had been displaced inside South Sudan, and a further 123,400 had fled the country. 3.2 million people were facing 'acute and emergency food insecurity.' UN document in the author's possession.

10. 'South Sudan Troops Recapture Town: Rebels', *Al Jazeera*, available at http://www.aljazeera.com/news/africa/2014/02/s-sudan-troops-recapture-rebel-held-town-20142211026300211.html accessed on 2 Feb. 2014.

INDEX

Abbas, Ahmad 90
Abboud, Ibrahim 30, 86 118
Abdelatif, Ali 217–18
al Abdin, Izmat Abdel Rahim Zain 144
Aboulela, Leila 19
Abraham, Isaiah 74
Abu Kershola 158–9
Abu Shouk camp 152
Abuk, Joseph 38–9
Abyei 48, 196, 221–3, 233, 236, 240–1 250
Abyei Boundary Commission (ABC) 222, 233
Acholi people 35
Adigo, Onyoti 62
Adwok Nyaba, Peter 58, 255
Afewerki, Isaias 195
African Development Bank 15, 91
African Union (AU) 67, 144, 161, 181, 194, 221, 225, 228, 231, 234, 240–1, 248, 257
  High Implementation Panel (AUHIP) 228, 234, 236–7, 240
  Peace and Security Council 242
  United Nations Hybrid Operation in Darfur (UNAMID) 198
Agar, Malik 66, 147, 150–1, 157–160, 196, 246

agriculture 87–90, 101–105
Ahfad University, Omdurman 22
Ahmadinejad, Mahmoud 192
Ahmed, Mohamed Abakr Idriss 122
Ajour, Yassir 110–1, 124, 146
Akec, John 239
Akol, Lam 61–4, 71, 167, 207, 211, 235, 257
Al Intibaha 50
Al Shifaa factory 182
Al Waha farm 87–9
Al Waha mall 181
Alafif Mukhtar, Albaqir 14, 19–20, 119, 191
alfalfa 88
Algeria 63, 83
Alier, Abel 30
Alim, Mohamed Hassan 51, 54, 85
Alin Akol, Manyang 132
Alor, Deng 72, 219, 222, 236, 254–6
Aluong, Gier Chuang 129
Alwan 190
Amnesty International 146, 174
Amum, Pa'gan 65, 71–2, 136, 225, 227, 229, 237, 243, 254–255, 258
Angessana people—see Ingessana
Anglo-Egyptian Condominium 2–3, 11, 15, 22, 26, 29, 78, 102, 116–18, 204, 220, 245

Angola 194
Ansar 52
Antonov transport planes 141, 145
Anyanya insurgency 63, 66, 207
Anyuak people 170
Arab League 181, 191, 193, 211
Arab Spring 42, 189, 247
Arab supremacism 153
Arabic 14–16, 39, 49, 110, 123, 132, 150, 211, 218
Arab-Israeli War 44, 190
Arensen, Jon 172
Arman, Yassir 160, 241–2
Arnold, Matthew 184, 207
Aswan Dam 120
Atabani, Ghazi Salaheddin 47–8, 50, 56, 117, 120, 123, 146, 183, 219, 254
Athor, George 61, 166–7 170
Atta, Mohamed 232
Atuot people 27–9
AUHIP 228, 234, 237
Australia 88, 216
Avongura 35
Aweil 67–9, 129–30, 133, 161, 216–8
    hospital 129, 216
    rice scheme 102–4, 129
Awuol, Diing Chan—see Abraham, Isaiah
Azande people 29, 35, 38, 104, 209
al Azhari, Ismail 1

Babikir Alamin, Mohamed 89
Badawi, Mahmoud 124
Badi III, king of Sennar 19
Badri, Gassim 22
Baggara people 20, 24
Bahr el Ghazal 33, 36, 38, 70
Ban Ki Moon 231
Bari people 35, 135

Bari-speakers 35
Bashar, Mohamed 155
al Bashir, Omar Hassan Ahmed 3, 30–31, 41–50, 53–7, 75, 78–80, 83–6, 91, 107, 114, 121, 143–4, 146–151, 154, 160, 180–1, 183–5, 189–97, 199, 207, 212–3, 219, 228, 230–3, 235–6, 238–40, 246–7, 249–50, 253–4, 259–60
Baw Elementary school 150
Beijing Olympics 188
Beja people 16, 20, 119
Beni Hussein people 156
Bentiu 161–2, 230–2, 255–6, 258–9
Bergid people 156
Berti people 156
Biar Ajak, Peter 102, 249
Bible 31
Biel 35
'Big Tent' strategy 67–8, 70, 138–9, 259
Bilal, Fatna Khamis 2
bin Laden, Osama 46, 120, 182, 184
Biong, Luka 59, 98, 222, 248
Black Book, The 15
Blue Nile 23, 88, 115, 190
Blue Nile state 4, 12, 16, 40, 53, 112, 121, 142–3, 147, 150–2
    2011 war 150–2, 160–2, 186, 196, 199, 241, 246, 253
    Damazin 121, 150–1
    Ingessana people 16, 20, 150–1
    Kurmuk 151
Bol Akol, Ayii 102–4, 129
Bol, Elizabeth 97
Bol, Kuol 168, 171
Bol, Simon 126
Bong, Ngungdeng 35
Bor 255–9
Borgo people 147
Boushi—see Alim, Mohamed Hassan

Boyoi, Mary 36–8, 173–4, 209, 249
Bromwich, Brendan 153
Buay, Gordon 164
Burkina Faso 194
Burtail, Al Nour 111
Bush, George Walker 91, 182

Canada 187, 204
Carson, Johnnie 201–2
Carter Centre 144
cattle 24, 27–8, 32–5, 37, 68, 88,
    101–2, 105, 127–8, 168–71, 222,
    233
Central African Republic (CAR)
    195, 197, 207, 209
Central Bank 65, 81, 86–87, 94
Central Equatoria state 35, 104,
    134, 166
Central Intelligence Agency (CIA)
    184
Chad 5, 147, 152–3, 190, 194–5, 250
Chatinga 22
China 83, 93, 154, 180–1, 187–9,
    198, 205–6, 214, 228
China National Petroleum Com-
    pany (CNPC) 83, 187–8, 205
Chop, Mayen 213
Christianity 12, 21–22, 29–31, 35,
    116, 204, 246
City of Dust, A 121–2
Claimed Areas 221, 241
Clinton, Hillary 202
Clinton, William Jefferson 91, 182
Clooney, George 145, 179, 182, 186
Coca Cola 91
Collier, Paul 82, 107
Communist party 52, 66
Comprehensive Peace Agreement
    (CPA) 3–4, 29–30, 34, 43, 53–4,
    61, 65–7, 77, 79, 94, 101, 103, 120,
    122, 127–8, 133, 139, 142, 144,

182–5, 195–7, 204–5, 208, 220,
    222, 226, 234, 246
Congo, Democratic Republic of
    (DRC) 5, 197, 206–7, 209
Congressional Black Caucus (CBC)
    181–2
Corruption Perception Index 113
Cymbeline 39

D'Agoot, Majak 60, 165–7, 170–1,
    174, 242, 255–6, 258
Dagne, Ted 203
DAL Group 87–9
Damazin 151
Danagla people 15, 47
Danis, Daniel 131
Daoud, Osama 78–9, 81–2, 87–8,
    97, 114
Dar Petroleum 97
Darfur 2, 4, 16–18, 20, 23, 40, 43,
    54–5, 89, 112, 116, 118–19, 123,
    152–9, 181–2, 189, 191, 195, 221,
    246
2003 War 17, 48, 91, 119, 146–7,
    153–9, 180–2, 184–5, 188, 195,
    198–9
2006 Darfur Peace Agreement
    (DPA) 154–6, 184, 246
2011 Doha Document for Peace
    in Darfur (DDPD) 154–5, 159,
    246
Abu Shouk camp 152
Beni Hussein people 156
Bergid people 156
Berti people 156
Darfur Regional Authority
    (DRA) 154
Fur people 16–19, 153–4
Jebel Amir 156
Jebel Marra highlands 17–18, 23,
    155

Justice and Equality Movement
(JEM) 55, 155–7, 159, 161,
190, 194–5, 197, 230, 232
Liberation and Justice Movement
(LJM) 154
Ma'aliah people 156
Masalit people 16, 153
Mima people 156
Rizeigat people 23, 69, 156, 220
Sudan Liberation Army–Abdul
Wahid faction (SLA-AW) 155,
157
Sudan Liberation Army-Minni
Minnawi (SLA-MM) 156, 157
Tunjur people 156
Zaghawa people 16–17, 153,
155–6, 156, 194
Zalingei 18, 118
de Ngong, John Penn 74, 173
Deby, Idriss 194–5
Democratic Unionist Party (DUP)
52–3, 189
Deng Nhial, Abdallah 250
Deng, Afath 223
Deng, Daniel 171
Deng, Francis 25–6, 212, 222
Deng, Lual 64, 84, 95, 139, 228
Deng, Mary Chong 130
Deng, Nhial 63, 138, 200, 203–4,
206–7, 210, 226, 235, 257–8
Deng, Oyai 258
Deng, Taban 61, 66, 72, 133, 163,
232, 255, 257–8
Deng, Telar Ring 72
Denmark 204
Desalegn, Hailemariam 196, 209,
239
Dhel, Garang Thomas 129–30,
215–17, 220, 224, 243
Diab, Rashid 25, 78, 184
Didinga people 35

Dinka people 24, 27, 29, 33, 37, 64,
69–72, 135, 165, 172, 215–8, 225,
234, 248, 255–6
Dinka Bor 170, 173, 257
Dinka Malual 220, 237
Dinka Ngok 222–3, 240–1
Dirdiry, Ahmed 236
discrimination 19–22
Disputed Areas 221, 234, 241
Djibouti 101, 208
Doha Document for Peace in
Darfur (DDPD) 154, 159, 246
Dubai 15, 91, 206
'Dutch disease' 82

East African Community 200
Eastern Equatoria state 29–30, 32,
35, 106, 176
Kauto Payam 176
Eastern Front (EF) 195
Eastern Sudan Peace Agreement
(ESPA) 119, 195–6
effendiya 117
Egypt 5, 12, 83, 189–91, 211
1952 revolution 3
'Elbow-Licking Friday' 85
Emma Secondary School 126
Eritrea 5, 106, 194–6, 200, 209, 242
Ethiopia 5, 106, 152, 174, 181–2,
190, 194, 196–7, 206–7, 209, 212,
228, 242
European Union (EU) 103, 205, 231

Fadl Hassan, Yusuf 14
Fangak 166
al Fateh, Awad 232
Fellata people 16–17
Four Freedoms 190 (Sudan with
Egypt) 238–9 (Sudan with South
Sudan)
Frazer, Jendayi 182–3, 185, 201–3

Fur people 16–19, 153–4

gaar 34
Gaddafi, Muammar 88, 189–90
Gadet, Peter 163–4, 166–7, 255, 257
Gadir, Idriss Abdel 226
Gai Yoach, James 164
Gai, Gatluak 167
Gai, Riek 250
Garang de Mabior, John 3–4, 43, 52–3, 63–4, 66–7, 69, 71, 74, 101, 116, 133–4, 207, 210, 227, 242, 248, 257
Garang de Mabior, Mabior 74–5, 257
Gatkuoth, Ezekiel 258
Gatluak, David 127–8
Gatwech, Stephen 162
Gedarif state 85, 122
geography 3, 22–3, 38, 218
Germany 88
Ghandour, Ibrahim 180, 188–9, 195, 254
Giugale, Marcelo 98
gold 2, 78, 86–7, 90, 106, 156, 188
Gordon, Charles 2
Gore, Alfred Ladu 166, 259
'Gosh', Salah Abdallah 55, 184, 234
Gramazzi, Claudio 156
Gration, Scott 184–5
Great Ethiopian Renaissance Dam 190
Greater Equatoria 70, 106
Greater Nile Petroleum Operating Company (GNPOC) 77, 80
Guardian 72
Guinea 217
gum belt 89
Gurtong Project, The 32

hafiz 115

hakurat 153
Hala'ib Triangle 190
Hamas 192–3
Hamza, Abu Zaid Mohamed 50
Haroun, Ahmed 143–4, 147–9, 180, 199, 241
Hassan, Rizik Zachariah 100
al Hassan, Sabir 82, 86–7, 113, 120, 238
Heglig region 4, 80, 221–2
Heglig Crisis 4, 80, 229–32, 234–5, 248
al Hilu, Abdel Aziz 143–4, 160
Holland 88
Hosh Bannaga 44
'Hosh Bannaga' in Khartoum North 114
Hoth Mai, James 70, 72, 256
Hudson, Cameron 183–5, 202–3
Human Rights Watch 174–5, 256
Humanitarian Affairs Commission (HAC) 199
Hussain, Abdelaziz 23–4, 123–4, 218, 225, 243
Hussein Mohamed, Mustafa 92
Hussein, Abdel Rahim 48, 158–9, 180, 199, 227, 230, 236–7, 254
al Hussein, Ahmed Abdul Rahman 92
Hussein, Lubna 18
Hussein, Saddam 192

Ibrahim, Gibril 155, 197
Ibrahim, Hawa 17–19, 118, 122, 156, 247
Ibrahim, Khalil 155
identity politics 9–25
al Imam, Sheikh Yagout Sheikh Mohamed Sheikh Malik Sheikh 12–13
In the City 15

India 187
Ingaz regime 45–47
Ingessana people 16, 20, 150–1
Intergovernmental Authority on
　Development (IGAD) 257
International Criminal Court (ICC)
　43, 48, 53–4, 57, 147, 149, 154,
　180–1, 185, 191–2, 194, 197, 213,
　227, 241, 247, 254
International Monetary Fund (IMF)
　78, 86, 91, 200
International Women's Day 36
Iran 83, 181, 192
Islam 12–14, 20, 29, 43, 45, 49, 111,
　116, 189, 192
Islamism 17–18, 22, 25, 30, 42,
　45–57, 110, 189–91, 246, 254
Israel 180, 192–3, 200, 207, 210–1
Italy 91

Jaaliyin people 15–16, 47
Jal, Emmanuel 67, 126, 136, 169
James, Wendy 12
Jamila 131
Jebel Amir 156
Jebel Barkal 12
Jebel Marra highlands 17–18, 23,
　155
Jemins International Co. Ltd 206
Jie people 176
Jiech, Gatgong 33–5, 36, 100, 105,
　125–7, 243, 259
jihad 46, 57
Johnson, Douglas 220
Johnson, Hilde 212
Joint Donor Team 204
Joint Integrated Units (JIUs) 144,
　223
Jok, Jok Madut 26–7, 60, 67, 174
Jonglei state 4, 28, 36–7, 57, 61, 95,
　162, 165–77, 203, 212, 235, 255,
　259

Bor 255–7, 259
　cattle raiding 169
　ethnic violence 168–77, 203, 212
　Fangak 166
　Pibor 36–7, 165–9, 172–4
　Pieri village 168, 171
　Likuangole 166, 172, 174, 213
Juba 1, 35, 38, 73–4, 96–7, 133–5,
　160, 169, 208, 247, 254–6
　'land-grabbing' 69–70
Juba Central Prison 131
Juba Declaration 67, 166
Juba Teaching Hospital 130–1
Juba University 59, 66, 249, 255
Juju Baba, Angelo Adam 109–10
Justice Africa Sudan 45, 246
Justice and Equality Movement
　(JEM) 55, 155–7, 159, 161, 190,
　194–5, 197, 230, 232

Kababish people 20
Kadugli 21, 144–5, 148–9
Kafia Kingi region 221, 241
Kakuma refugee camp 131
Kaman, Jok 96
Kampala 157–8, 161, 197
Karti, Ali 193–4
Katchipo people 176
Katire 32
Kauda 109–11, 124, 142, 145, 149,
　186
Kauto Payam 176
Kenya 5, 37, 43, 99, 106, 131, 182,
　194, 197, 200, 206–9, 212, 228,
　258
Kenyatta, Uhuru 197
Khalil, Abdallah 118
Khartoum 47, 54, 77, 115–16,
　121–3, 183, 253
Khartoum International Airport 9
Khartoum North 114–5, 122

al Khatib, Said 218–9, 226–8, 233, 236, 240
Khatmiyya 52
Khoc, Akec 201–2, 210–12
Khogali, Mustafa 15–17, 19, 57, 79, 91, 93, 115, 184, 233, 253
Kibaki, Mwai 228
Kiir, Salva—see Mayardit, Salva Kiir
Koang, James 255
Konda, Nagwa Musa 20–22, 49, 110–1, 124, 143, 145, 186
Kony, Joseph 197
Konyi, Ismail 166
Konyi, Joshua 168, 171
Kordofan 20, 24, 116, 123, 222
Kuajok 131–3
Kueth, Dak 171, 174
kujour 22, 66
Kuku people 35
Kuku, Musa Konda 21
Kuol, Kuol Deng 241
Kurmuk 151
Kuron Peace Village 176
Kuwait 211

Ladu, Alfred—see Gore, Alfred Ladu
Lakes state 27–9, 65, 95, 130, 134, 169
Leer 33–5, 61, 71, 100–1, 125–8, 133, 213, 259
LeRiche, Matthew 184, 207
Liberation and Justice Movement (LJM) 154
Libya 83–4, 153, 189–90, 199
Likuangole 166, 172, 174, 213
Lino, Edward 222
Lokuji, Alfred Sebit 59, 61, 64, 66, 126, 249
Lord's Resistance Army (LRA) 197, 207

Lotuko people 35
Lou Nuer 168–76, 212, 257
Lugala, Victor 26, 31, 59, 62, 70, 96, 137, 145, 206, 242, 248
Luo Xiaoguang 189
Lyman, Princeton 98, 100, 181, 183, 186–7, 202–3, 219, 236, 241

Ma'aliah people 156
Madi people 32, 35
Machar, Riek—see Teny, Riek Machar
Mading, Dol 127
al Mahdi, Abda Yahia 90–1, 112–3
al Mahdi, Mohamed Ahmed 2, 32, 52, 116
al Mahdi, Mubarak al Fadil 54
al Mahdi, Sadig 45, 52, 79, 233
Mahdiyya period 116, 245
Mahjoub, Jamal 10
Mahmoud, Ali 83
Majak, Garang 68–9
Majok, Deng 222
al Mak, Ali 121–2
al Makki, Hiba 215–17, 224, 243
Malakal 33, 96, 255, 257–9
Malawi 181
Malaysia 93, 187
Malek, Nyandeng 174
Mali 217
Malik, Nesrine 182
Malong, Paul 68–9, 129, 237
Manasir people 121
Manibe, Kosti 72, 100, 228
Marial, Barnaba 204–5, 256
marissa 109–10
Masalit people 16, 153
Matip, Paulino 67, 125, 166
Mayardit, Salva Kiir 3, 31, 36, 58, 62–8, 70–2, 75, 98, 125–6, 134, 137, 150, 164, 166–7, 171, 174,

196, 202–3, 205, 210, 212, 219, 228–9, 231, 233, 235–6, 238–40, 248–9, 250, 254–9
'Big Tent' strategy 67–8, 70, 138–9, 259
Mayay, Chol Tong 65–6
Mayendit 60
Mayom 163–4
Mayom, Paul 212
Mbeki, Thabo 144, 221, 225, 228, 235, 240
McCune, Emma 126
McDonough, Dennis 202
McPhail, Alistair 204
Médecins Sans Frontières (MSF) 125, 130, 172, 174, 213, 259
Mekki, Yusif Kuwa 21
Meroe 12
Merowe Dam 120–21, 187
Mima people 156
Ministry of Defence 47
Minnawi, Minni 154–6, 197
al Mirghani, Mohamed Osman 52–3
Misseriya people 23–4, 69, 111, 123–4, 143, 149, 220, 222–3, 225, 240
Mitchell, Andrew 186
Mohamed, Hafiz 45, 246
Mokhtar, Maryam Mohamed 152
Monytuil, Bapiny 163–5, 167, 175, 229, 256
Morocco 189
Morsi, Mohamed 190–1
Mozambique 194
Mubarak, Hosni 189–90
Mundari people 35
Murle people 36–7, 165–6, 168–76, 212–3, 257–8
Musa, Carlo 224
Museveni, Yoweri 207, 257

Mustafa, Tayyeb 43, 50, 147, 238–9
My African-ness 21

Nafie, Nafie Ali 51, 54–6, 85, 147, 183, 234, 246, 254
Napoleon, Robert 70, 130–1
National Congress Party (NCP) 4–5, 29, 43, 45, 49–57, 61–2, 79–80, 82–89, 93, 113–15, 118, 120, 123, 143, 147, 153, 158–9, 180–99, 219, 222, 226–7, 230, 233–6, 238, 242–3, 245–6, 250, 253–4
National Intelligence and Security Service (NISS) 41, 45, 50–1, 55, 74, 112, 144, 158, 184, 199, 232
National Salvation Revolutionary Command Council 47, 79
Natsios, Andrew 203
Ndjamena 195
Netanyahu, Benjamin 210
Netherlands 200, 204
New Dawn Charter 157–8, 197
Ngor, Mading 62
Nigeria 181
Nile Trading and Development Ltd 104
Nile waters 190, 211–12
Nilo-Hamitic peoples 32, 35
Nilotic peoples 27, 31–3, 36, 69–71
Nimeiri, Jafaar 5, 78–9, 86, 91
Nimr, Sadig Babo 222
Non-Governmental Organisations (NGOs) 37, 91, 124–6, 130–3, 180, 199, 213
North Kordofan state 155, 158
Um Ruwaba 158
Northern Bahr el Ghazal state 68–9, 102–4, 129, 133, 221, 237
Aweil 67–9, 129–30, 133, 161, 216–8

Norway 200, 204
Norwegian People's Aid 204
al Nour, Abdul Wahid 155, 159, 197
Nuba Mountains 12, 21–3, 49, 53,
    109–11, 124, 142, 145–9, 159,
    179, 186, 197
Nuba people 16, 20–22, 49, 109–11,
    124, 143–9, 157, 186
Nuba Relief, Rehabilitation and
    Development Organisation
    (NRRDO) 22, 186
Nubia 12, 14, 120, 189
Nuer people 27, 29, 33–7, 63–4,
    69–72, 135, 163–5, 172, 248,
    255–7
    Bul Nuer 163, 165, 175
    Gawaar Nuer 170, 257
    Lou Nuer 168–76, 212, 257
Nugud, Mohamed Ibrahim 66
Nyakulang 35
Nyandeng, Rebecca 71, 254, 257
Nyandit 168–9, 172–3
Nyangatom people 176
Nyier, Jacob 164–5, 230
Nyok, Peter 100–101, 127, 133

Obama, Barack 183, 202, 231, 257
Ocampo, Luis Moreno 57, 180
oil 4–6, 38, 77–84, 93–9, 101, 107,
    135, 187–8, 208, 214, 225–9,
    237–9, 250
Olony, Johnson 167, 175
Olympic Games 188
Omar, Amin Hassan 54, 155, 159,
    183, 191, 242
Omdurman 2, 15, 55, 81, 85, 115,
    121–2, 155, 165, 195, 224, 233,
    253
Osman 151–2

Padar, Mary 27–9, 134
Page, Susan 203

Pal, Nyang 96
Palestine 211
Paul, Mac 229, 232, 237
Payne, Donald 203
Pepsi 91
Peres, Shimon 210
Permanent Court of Arbitration
    (PCA) 222, 233
Pibor 36–7, 165–9, 172–4
Pieri village 168, 171
Popular Congress Party (PCP) 52
Popular Defence Forces (PDF) 41,
    46, 123, 143–6
Post-Traumatic Stress Disorder 130
Pouch, Simon Kun 96
Powell, Colin 182
Prendergast, John 203
press freedom 50–51, 62
Pujulu people 35
Pul Jang, Matthew 167

Qatar 54, 83, 100, 159, 191–2, 211

Ramciel 134–5
Rashaida people 14, 20, 119, 196
Reeves, Eric 203
'resource curse' 82
Rice, Susan 141, 198
Riefenstahl, Leni 22
Rizeigat people 23, 69, 156, 220
Roots 28
Roseiris Dam 121
Rowland, Tiny 78
Russia 145, 198
Rwanda 194, 212
Rwandan genocide 182
Ryle, John 10, 16

Said, Mohamed 88
Saihoon 50, 55
Salafism 13, 50, 193

Salaheddin Atabani, Ghazi—see
   Atabani, Ghazi Salaheddin
Salih, Bakri Hassan 41, 48, 254
Salih, Mahjoub Mohamed 56
Salih, Tayeb 46
Sammaniya tariqa 13
Sanhouri, Salah 253
Satti, Al Tahir 113–4
Satti, Hassan 14–15, 78, 81–3, 92
Saudi Arabia 13–14, 83, 192–3
Season of Migration to the North 46
secularists 25, 52
Seisi, Tigani 119, 154
September 11th attacks 184
Sergio Vieira de Mello Prize 176
Shaigiya people 15, 47
Shakespeare, William 39
sharia law 13, 18, 46, 49–50, 158
Shawki, M. K. 90
Shilluk people 33, 175, 227
'Single Ladies' 36
sitt al shai 18
slavery 2, 19–20, 24–6, 78, 116, 201,
   237
Small Arms Survey 166, 197
Smokin primary school 110, 146
South Africa 63, 88, 200, 231
South Kordofan 4, 12, 21, 23–4, 40,
   49, 53, 112, 123–4, 142–50
   2011 elections 143–4
   2011 war 144–50, 152, 157–8,
      161–2, 179, 186, 188, 199,
      240–2
   Abu Kershola 158–9
   humanitarian aid 186–7
   Kadugli 21, 144–5, 148–9
   Kauda 109, 124, 142, 145
   Talodi 148–9, 160
   Um Bartumbu 146
South Sudan
   1955–1972 Civil War 3, 26, 30,
      69, 207, 210

1972 Addis Ababa agreement 69,
   222
1983–2005 Civil War 3, 21, 26–7,
   28, 42, 59–60, 63, 69, 103, 142
1991 Bor massacre 64, 256
2006 Juba Declaration 67, 166
2010 elections 61, 162, 165–6
2011 ethnic violence 168–77, 203,
   212
2011 independence 1, 42–3
2012 Addis Ababa negotiations
   235–41, 245, 249
2012 Heglig crisis 4, 229–35, 248
2012 oil shutdown 94, 97–101,
   126, 129, 132, 174, 204–6,
   227–9, 238–9, 247–8
2013 civil war 254–60
Acholi people 35
agriculture 101–5
alcohol law 130
anti-Arab sentiment 25, 69, 200,
   211
Anyanya insurgency 63, 66, 207
Atuot people 27–9
Aweil 67–9, 129–30, 133, 161,
   216–8
Aweil hospital 129, 216
Aweil rice scheme 102–4, 129
Azande people 29, 35, 38, 104,
   209
Bahr el Ghazal 33, 36, 38
Bari people 35
Canada, relations with 204
cattle 34–5, 37, 68, 101–2, 105–6
Central African Republic (CAR),
   relations with 207, 209
Central Equatoria state 35, 104,
   134, 166
China, relations with 205–6, 214,
   228
Christianity 29–31, 35, 116
citizenship 224–5

Claimed Areas 221, 241
Congo, Democratic Republic of
(DRC), relations with 206–7,
209
corruption 135–8
debt 225
Denmark, relations with 204
Didinga people 35
Dinka people 24, 27, 29, 33, 37,
64, 69–72, 135, 165, 170, 172–3,
215–18, 220, 222–3, 225, 234,
237, 240–1, 248, 255–7
Disputed Areas 221, 234, 241
Djibouti, relations with 208
Eastern Equatoria state 29–30, 32,
35, 106, 176
economy 93–107
education 27, 29, 34, 126–7, 139
Egypt, relations with 211–12
Eritrea, relations with 209
Ethiopia, relations with 206–7,
209, 228
ethnic divisions 25–6, 32–3,
69–72, 168–76
Four Freedoms 238–9
geography 38
Greater Bahr el Ghazal 70
Greater Equatoria 70, 106
Greater Upper Nile 70
health service 129–31
human rights 60, 64, 74, 95,
174–5, 203
identity politics 25–40
Islam 29–30
Israel, relations with 200, 207,
210–1
Jie people 176
Jonglei state 4, 28, 36–8, 57, 61,
95, 162, 165–77, 203, 212, 235,
255, 259
Juba 1, 35, 38, 73–4, 96–7, 133–5,
160, 169, 208, 247, 254–6

Katchipo people 176
Katire 32
Kenya, relations with 200, 206–9,
212, 258
Kuajok 131–3
Kuku people 35
Kuwait, relations with 211
Lakes state 27–9, 65, 95, 130, 134,
169
Leer 33–5, 61, 71, 100–1, 125–8,
133, 213, 259
Lotuko people 35
Madi people 32, 35
Mayendit 60
military 58–61, 138–40
mining 106
Mundari people 35
Murle people 36–7, 165–6,
168–76, 212–3, 257–8
national anthem 38–9
National Assembly 58, 61, 65, 73,
95
National Convention 71–2, 254
National Security Council 231
Netherlands, relations with 200,
204
Northern Bahr el Ghazal state
68–9, 102–4, 129, 133, 221, 237
Norway, relations with 200, 204
Nuer people 27, 29, 33–7, 63–4,
69–72, 135, 163–5, 168–76,
212, 248, 255–7
Nyangatom people 176
oil 4, 6, 38, 77–84, 93–9, 101, 107,
135, 208, 214, 226, 237–9
Palestine, relations with 211
Paloich oilfields 93–6
Post-Traumatic Stress Disorder
130
poverty 99, 128–9, 169–70
Pujulu people 35

Ramciel 134–5
rice 102–4
Shilluk people 33, 175, 227
slavery 2, 20, 24–6, 78, 116, 201, 237
South Africa, relations with 200, 231
Sudan Revolutionary Front (SRF), relations with 161–2, 241, 260
Sudd swamps 38
Sweden, relations with 204
tamazuj 218
Toposa people 176, 209
tourism 106
Transitional Financial Assistance (TFA) 226, 228, 237
Uganda, relations with 200, 206–8, 212, 257–8
United Arab Emirates, relations with 211
United Kingdom, relations with 200, 204
United Nations, relations with 200
United States, relations with 200–5, 210, 228
Unity state 4, 33–5, 61, 66, 70–2, 95, 100, 125–8, 133, 141, 161–4, 167, 169, 174, 213, 230–7, 255–6, 259
Upper Nile state 4, 33, 36, 38, 93, 95, 151, 162, 167, 169, 221, 237, 255, 259
Warrap state 66, 131–2, 169, 174
Western Bahr el Ghazal state 100, 102, 106, 161, 169
Western Equatoria state 35, 38, 104, 207
White Nile 31, 33, 38, 212, 218
women's rights 36–8
xenophobia 106

Yida 141–2, 152, 160
Yusuf Batil 151–2, 160
Zande Scheme 104
South Sudan Defence Force (SSDF), 67, 70
South Sudan Democratic Army (SSDA) Cobra faction 165, 175
South Sudan Liberation Army (SSLA) 162–5, 169, 229–30, 256
South Sudan Television 62, 171
Southern Eye 70
Sudan
    1955–1972 Civil War 3, 69, 207, 210
    1956 independence 1–3, 15
    1972 Addis Ababa agreement 69, 222
    1983–2005 Civil War 3, 21, 26–7, 28, 42, 59–60, 63, 69, 103, 142
    1989 coup d'état 45–6, 79
    1998 Al Shifaa factory bombing 182
    2003 Darfur War 17, 48, 91, 119, 146–7, 153–9, 180–2, 184–5, 188, 195, 198–9
    2006 Darfur Peace Agreement (DPA) 154–6, 184, 246
    2006 Eastern Sudan Peace Agreement (ESPA) 119, 195–6
    2010 elections 45, 52, 150, 180
    2011 internal conflict 141–52, 186, 196, 199, 241–2
    2012 Addis Ababa negotiations 235–41, 245, 249
    2012 currency devaluation 81
    2012 financial crisis 81, 84–86
    2012 Heglig crisis 4, 229–35, 248
    2012 protests 85–6, 250
    2012 Yarmouk arms factory explosion 193
    2013 protests 253–4

agriculture 87–90
Al Waha farm 87–9
alcohol laws 109
Ali dynasty 26
Anglo-Egyptian Condominium
  2–3, 11, 15, 22, 26, 29, 78, 102,
  116–18, 204, 245
Angola, relations with 194
Ansar 52
Arab supremacism 153
Arabic-speakers 14–16
Baggara people 20, 24
Beja people 16, 20, 119
Blue Nile state 4, 12, 16, 40, 53,
  112, 121, 142–3, 147, 150–2,
  186, 196, 199, 241
Borgo people 147
Burkina Faso, relations with 194
Canada, relations with 187
cattle 88
Central African Republic (CAR),
  relations with 195, 197
Chad, relations with 190, 194–5,
  250
China, relations with 180–1,
  187–9, 198
Christianity 12, 21
citizenship 224–5
Claimed Areas 221, 241
Communist party 52, 66
Congo (DRC), relations with 197
corruption 112–15
Damazin 151
dam-building 120–21, 187
Danagla people 15, 47
Darfur 16–19, 20, 23, 40, 54–55,
  112, 116, 118–19, 123, 152–9,
  181–2, 184, 189, 195, 221, 246
debt 91–2, 184–5, 225
Democratic Unionist Party
  (DUP) 52–3, 189

discrimination 19–21
Disputed Areas 221, 234, 241
Eastern Front (EF) 195
economy 77–93
education 126
effendiya 117
Egypt, relations with 189–91
Eritrea, relations with 194–6
Ethiopia, relations with 181–2,
  190, 194, 196–7
Fellata people 16–17
Fiscal and Financial Allocation
  and Monitoring Commission
  122
Four Freedoms 190, 238–9
Fur people 16–19, 153–4
Gedarif state 85, 122
geography 22–3
Gezira Scheme 78, 89
gold 86–7
Gold Refinery 86
gum belt 89–91
Heglig basin 4, 80
Heglig crisis 4, 229–35, 248
human rights 18, 45, 49–51, 91,
  145, 253
Humanitarian Affairs Commis-
  sion (HAC) 199
India, relations with 187
Ingaz regime 45–47
Ingessana people 16, 20, 150–1
Iran, relations with 181, 192
Islamism 17–18, 22, 25, 30, 42,
  45–57, 110, 189–91, 246, 254
Israel, relations with 192–3
Jaaliyin people 15–16, 47
Jebel Barkal 12
jihad 46, 57
Kababish people 20
Kadugli 21, 144–5, 148–9
Kauda 109, 124, 142, 145

Kenya, relations with 182, 194, 197

Khartoum 47, 54, 77, 115–16, 121–3, 183, 253

Khartoum North 114–5, 122

Khatmiyya 52

Kordofan 20, 24, 116, 123, 222

Kurmuk 151

Libya, relations with 189–90

Mahdiyya period 116, 245

Malawi, relations with 181

Malaysia, relations with 187

Manasir people 121

Masalit people 16, 153

Meroe 12

military 47–8, 112–13

Misseriya people 23–4, 69, 111, 123–4, 143, 149, 220, 222–3, 225, 240

Mozambique, relations with 194

National Museum, Khartoum 12

National Salvation Revolutionary Command Council 47, 79

New Dawn Charter 157–8, 197

Nigeria, relations with 181

North Kordofan state 155, 158

Nuba Mountains 12, 21–3, 49, 53, 109–11, 124, 142, 145–9, 159, 179, 186, 197

Nuba people 16, 20–22, 49, 109–11, 124, 143–9, 157, 186

oil 77–84, 187, 226, 237–8

Omdurman 2, 15, 55, 81, 85, 115, 121–2, 155, 165, 195, 224, 233, 253

Popular Congress Party (PCP) 52

poverty 111–12, 119

press freedom 50–51

Qatar, relations with 191–2

Rashaida people 14, 20, 119, 196

'resource curse' 82

Rizeigat people 23, 69, 156, 220

Russia, relations with 198

Rwanda, relations with 194

Saihoon 50, 55

Salafism 13, 50, 193

sanctions 91, 107, 182, 184, 85

Saudi Arabia, relations with 192–3

secularists 25, 52

Shaigiya people 15, 47

slavery 19–20, 24–26, 78, 116

South Kordofan state 4, 12, 21, 23–4, 40, 49, 53, 112, 123–4, 142–50

Sudan Revolutionary Front (SRF) 157–9, 161–2, 241, 260

Sufism 12–13, 17

Talodi 148–9, 160

tamazuj 218

trade 92

Turkiyya period 2, 116, 245

Uduk people 16

Uganda, relations with 182, 190, 194, 197

Um Bartumbu 146

Umma (National Umma Party) 52–3, 85, 222

United Arab Emirates, relations with 193

United Kingdom, relations with 185–6, 198

United States, relations with 181–7, 192, 198, 250

White Nile state 41

Zaghawa people 16–17, 153, 155–6, 194

Zalingei 18, 118

Sudan Change Now 182

Sudan Liberation Army-Abdul Wahid faction (SLA-AW) 155, 157

Sudan Liberation Army-Minni Minnawi (SLA-MM) 156–7

Sudan People's Liberation Army
  (SPLA) 27–8, 30, 42, 44, 47,
  58–64, 66–7, 69–70, 72, 74, 93,
  110–1, 125, 128, 130, 134, 138,
  142, 144–6, 160, 163–7, 169–175,
  195, 197, 201, 204, 209, 221, 223,
  229–33, 237–8, 248, 255–9
Sudan People's Liberation Army/
  Movement (SPLA/M) 3–4, 21,
  43, 58, 61, 64, 69, 71, 74, 167, 197,
  209
Sudan People's Liberation Movement (SPLM) 3–6, 29, 36, 43,
  52–3, 58–59, 61–75, 100–1,
  109–11, 124, 131, 133, 138–9,
  143, 161, 163, 172, 184, 197,
  201–12, 219–20, 222–3, 226–36,
  238, 240, 242–3, 245, 248–9,
  254–5
Sudan People's Liberation Move-
  ment-Democratic Change
  (SPLM-DC) 61–2
Sudan People's Liberation Move-
  ment-North (SPLM-North)
  52–4, 66, 109–11, 124, 142–9,
  151, 157, 159,-61, 179, 187, 197,
  202, 230, 241–2, 246
Sudan Revolutionary Front (SRF)
  157–9, 161–2, 241, 260
Sudanese Armed Forces (SAF) 41,
  48, 55, 68, 94, 141–7, 149, 151,
  153, 157, 159–60, 164, 169, 190,
  198, 205, 207, 213, 221, 223,
  229–33, 239
Sudanic peoples 32, 35
Sudd swamps 38
Sudd Institute 134
Sufi brotherhood 13
Sufism 12–13, 17
Sumbeiywo, Lazarus 197
Swansea University, Wales 22

Sweden 204

Taban, Paride 29–32, 133, 176, 258
Taha, Ali Osman 47, 54–6, 83, 147,
  254
tajility 226–7
Talisman 187
Talodi 148–9, 160
Tayara, Kafi 148
Teny, Angelina 61
Teny, Kueh 34
Teny, Riek Machar 34, 61, 63–5,
  71–2, 75, 98–100, 160, 167, 170,
  172, 174, 207, 211, 231, 235, 248,
  254–60
Timsaha 161
Tir, Hamid 148
Toposa people 176, 209
Transparency International 113
Tubiana, Jerome 156
Tunisia 189
Tunjur people 156
al Turabi, Hassan 45–7, 52, 54, 155,
  182, 189, 250
Turkana people 209
Turkiyya period 2, 116, 245
Twitter 56, 85

Uduk people 16
Uganda 5, 38, 63, 99, 106, 160, 182,
  190, 194, 197, 200, 206–8, 212,
  257–8
Ukraine 164
Um Bartumbu 146
Um Ruwaba 158
Umma (National Umma Party)
  52–3, 85, 222
UNAMID (African Union/United
  Nations Hybrid Operation in
  Darfur) 198
United Arab Emirates 193, 211

United Kingdom 39, 185–6, 198, 200, 204, 242
United Nations (UN) 18, 37, 102, 105, 119, 121, 125, 131–2, 145, 148, 154, 161, 165–6, 168, 170–1, 188, 198, 200, 212, 221–3, 230–1, 234, 240, 248, 256
  General Assembly 202
  Mission in South Sudan (UN-MISS) 172, 212–13
  Mission in Sudan (UNMIS) 145, 198
  resolution 1591 155
  resolution 2046 235, 240
  Security Council 141, 154, 188, 194, 198, 200, 223, 231, 235, 237, 242
  Sergio Vieira de Mello Prize 176
United States of America (USA) 47, 51, 63, 74, 91–2, 154, 160, 179, 180–8, 192–3, 198, 200–5, 210, 214, 228, 231, 242, 250, 257, 259
Unity state 4, 33–5, 61, 66, 70–2, 95, 100, 125–8, 133, 141, 161–4, 167, 169, 174, 213, 230–7, 255–6, 259
  Bentiu 161–2, 230–2, 255–6, 258–9
  Mayom 163–4
  Yida 141–2, 152, 160
University of Khartoum 51, 85
Upper Nile state 4, 33, 36, 38, 93, 95, 151, 162, 167, 169, 221, 237, 255, 259
  Malakal 33, 96, 255, 257–9
  Yusuf Batil 151–2, 160
USAID 129

Vomiting Stolen Food 137
von Chief Parek, Manyang Parek 31

Waal, Alex de 97

Wahhabism 13
'Wake Up Juba' 62
Wang Jianchao 206
Wani Igga, James 65, 71–3
Wani, Clement 25–6, 166
Warrap state 66, 131–2, 169, 174
Western Bahr el Ghazal 100, 102, 106, 161, 169
  Timsaha 161
Western Equatoria 35, 38, 104, 207
White Army 168, 171–3, 212–3, 257
White Nile 12, 23, 31, 33, 38, 77–8, 89, 93, 212, 218
White Nile state 41
White Nile Sugar Factory 86, 91
Winter, Roger 203
Wondu, Steven 136, 139
Woodward, Peter 180
World Bank 90–1, 98–9, 106, 138
World Food Programme 98, 103
World Health Organisation 119, 172
World Trade Centre 184
World Wrestling Entertainment 184
Woyee Film and Theatre Industry 131

Yang Jiechi 205
Yarmouk arms factory 193
Yau Yau, David 163, 165–7, 175–6, 235, 258
Yida 141–2, 152, 160
Young, John 67, 164
Youssif, Haj 122
YouTube 49, 52, 54
Yussif, Mukhtar 86
Yusuf Batil 151–2, 160

Zaghawa people 16–17, 153, 155–6, 194
  Zaghawa Kobe 155
zakat 111

Zalingei 18, 118
Zande Scheme 104
*zariba*s 116

Zenawi, Meles 150, 196–7, 209,
228–9
Zhong Jianhua 205